A Calendar

OF BRITISH TASTE

1600 to 1800

by

E. F. CARRITT

A Calendar
OF BRITISH TASTE

From 1600 *To* 1800

being

A MUSEUM OF SPECIMENS & LANDMARKS

chronologically arranged

by

E. F. CARRITT

ἐπιφυλλίδες ταῦτ'ἐστὶ καὶ στωμύλματα
χελιδόνων μουσεῖα, λωβηταὶ τέχνης
Aristophanes, *Frogs*, 92.

A choir of chattering swallows, smallest fry,
Who make themselves at home in artistry.

London
ROUTLEDGE & KEGAN PAUL LTD.
BROADWAY HOUSE 68-74 CARTER LANE E.C.4

Pres Miss Baillie

165402   828

PRINTED IN GREAT BRITAIN BY THE CHISWICK PRESS
LONDON, N.II

CONTENTS

INTRODUCTION

THERE is an old and true saying that no book will be read with pleasure which was written without it; but the converse positive, that readers enjoy every book as much as its writer did, will not hold; for there is an older and equally true saying that we all take inordinate pleasure in our offspring. I flatter myself, however, that this book may give as much pleasure to its readers as it did to its compiler, since it contains nothing of his own.

To me the most attractive by-path of history is that which leads me to realise the likes and dislikes of those who, with myself, have found great part of their enjoyments in books and buildings and pictures and in the varieties of natural scenery under the change of weather and season. If one of the objects of historical study is to give us a lively sympathy with the past, it will be scarcely less important to comprehend our ancestors' tastes than their politics; as we know and love our friends less for the votes they cast than for the books and scenes which please them.

But just because these things are more deeply bedded in a man's temperament than his party or his views upon the currency, they are harder to retrieve adequately by any summary description. I have so often grown tired in chewing the husks of literary and artistic history—the Augustan Age, the Romantic Revival and such dusty labels—that, in order to hold some living picture of the seventeenth and eighteenth centuries before my mind, I took to keeping a common-place book of my reading in the actual sources; and I came to think that these gleanings might furnish others with amusement and even with material for revising such hasty classifications. Work of this kind must clearly precede either a history of taste or an æsthetic philosophy; but equally clearly it could only be completed by many hands. The most illuminating asides light up the least likely places, and the gossip of Pepys or Walpole is historically as important as Dryden's theory of tragedy. Nothing short of a study in all the surviving literature could be exhaustive, and the anthology here offered can hardly even claim to be systematic. I chose the period simply because it happened to interest me, but I think the choice turned out well.

No age perhaps has ever seen such fascinating changes in taste and creation as that which included Shakespeare, Milton, Donne, Browne, Bunyan, Dryden, Pope, Gray, "Ossian", Johnson, Blake, Burns, Lamb and Wordsworth; Perpendicular, Palladian, Jacobean, Wren, *Chinoiserie*, Queen Anne, the Adams and neo-Gothic; the Carracci, Salvator, the Poussins, Velasquez, Van Dyck and Rembrandt, with Rubens, Ruysdall, Gainsborough, Constable and Turner; Scarlatti, Purcell, Bach, Handel, Mozart and Beethoven. Certainly no country or period has ever been more copious or dominant in æsthetic theory than was, between 1600 and 1800, Great Britain, the home of Bacon, Hobbes, Dennis, Shaftesbury, Addison, Hutcheson, Hume, Hogarth, Burke, Home, Reynolds, Alison, Price, Gilpin, Wordsworth and Coleridge. And its vigorous opposition was more healthy than totalitarianism.

Nor are the variations only chronological; it would be as apt to think of them as social, rather vertical than horizontal. To seek a date for the meeting of the Augustan and Romantic periods is like trying to bridge the Symplegades: our bases fluctuate and the chasm becomes a collision. When books were scarce and travel hard, fashions filtered slowly down from the Universities, the Inns and the Court, to the hall of a Northumbrian justice, as the bronze and iron ages may have coincided in the Mediterranean and in Thule. Probably the "fairy way of writing", or at least of "fabling", survived among inglorious Shakespeares till it was unmuted in Coleridge. The truth, I suppose, is that at all times and in every station souls are born "classical" and "romantic" by nature, but that when genius is born in either camp, even the opposing ranks cannot forbear applause. Yet most men of genius and the more respectable mediocrities are recalcitrant to either tyranny. As Doctor Johnson said to Fanny Burney: "There are three distinct kinds of judges; the first are those who know no rules but pronounce entirely from their natural taste and feelings; the second are those who know and judge by rules; and the third are those who know but are above the rules. These last are those you should wish to satisfy. Next to them rate the natural judges; but ever despise those opinions that are formed by the rules." Or as Anatole France has written in *Pierre Nozière*: "Notre langue c'est notre mère et notre nourrice; il faut boire à même. Les grammaires sont des biberons. Et Vergile a dit que les enfants nourris au biberon ne sont dignes ni de la table des dieux ni du lit des déesses." And it is as despicable to be swayed in our taste and feeling by the abstractions of literary history as by rules and grammarians. Why not drink at the source?

There were always to be found people who preferred Shakespeare to Pope, moors to cornfields, "Longinus" to Aristotle, the Bible to Boileau and Gothic to Vitruvius; there were also, more conspicuous, their parasitical hangers-on, the devotees of Melancholy and the Noble Savage, who preferred Beattie and Shenstone to Milton and raved of Simplicity and Nature, but could not see the romance which begins at home without banditti and charnel. Just so, well on into the nineteenth century, there were writers of learning and discrimination who preferred the "smoothness" and "correctness" of Pope or Waller; and there was also the host of timid or conventional philistines who sheltered under their authority because almost insensitive to any beauty. If, as Sainte-Beuve said, "L'écueil particulier du genre romantique c'est le faux"; the sands on which classicism drifts are those of *ennui*. Almost the only development I can trace is that at one time the school of classical authority can command the Press or the Chairs in the Universities and coffee-houses, so that its opponents appear as disreputable innovators, and at another time it cannot, but itself plays the part of reactionary rebel. Yet it is noteworthy that, while the "romantic spirit" was producing critics like Addison who spoke with maturity, its poetic offspring was still but lisping in numbers. There were indeed new workings of the creative spirit about, but this blew as it listed and refused regimentation. It left its mark upon sensitive natures of every tendency; the romantics remained romantics and the classical were classical still, but with a difference. It is as

A*

hard as ever to draw a line between the two; only the
feather-weight of fashion shifts now to one scale and now to
the other. Men of different temperament and training can
get genuine æsthetic experience from very different objects.
Beauty lives in seeming. Feeling makes it so.

It may perhaps be said that, at the beginning of the seventeenth century, criticism had inherited a set of dogmas supposed
to be founded on classical theory but bearing no very close
relation to Greek practice and curiously little to contemporary
creation—the *Faerie Queen*, Shakespeare's plays and poems,
Milton's early work—or even to the natural taste of the critics.
They liked *Chevy Chase* while they talked of Seneca his style.
For some two hundred years, from Sidney to Johnson, this
critical doctrine was stiffened and elaborated against revolt—
here modified by a concession to the facts, there fortified by
more accurate scholarship—till its façade was indeed
formidable.

What was more remarkable was that much of the poetry
produced, unlike that of Sidney's own day, came to be a
colourable embodiment of the theory. Dryden, Pope, Johnson
are more amenable to the *Ars Poetica* than either Spenser or
Coleridge. This may have been because the original flood of
poetry in them was weaker and more easily diverted into
academic channels; at any rate, upon the whole, it is their
less inspired work, that in which they display less individual
genius, that most conforms to the canon. It is Addison's
Cato, or his Latin poems praised by Boileau, not the *Spectator*,
Johnson's *Irene*, not the talk in Boswell, that are in the technical
sense classical. But it is not these which live. And all along,
under the fashionable orthodoxy, under the correctness, the
smoothness, the reasonableness of the great writers, there
persisted an obstinate and often crude hankering after something very different, something at once simpler and more
mysterious, rougher and more touching. Pepys enjoyed the
Elizabethan and Restoration dramas with no thought of
Aristotle; others found ingenious casuistries for fitting them
to the rules. The girls and boys, not without respectable
authority, sang *The Nut Browne Mayde* and *Johnnie Armstrong*;

their grave elders and the simple children read *The Pilgrim's Progress*; Walton's Piscator was for Marlowe; all were ripe for "Ossian", Burns—and Shenstone.

It was the scarcity of any but second- or third-rate work daring to be heterodox that kept the strong undercurrent of "enthusiasm" so timid, for there was no lack of self-confidence when a stream of original poetry burst upon the first years of the nineteenth century. The most curious effect of this unnatural situation upon reflective minds was that, since they acknowledged the established boundaries but enjoyed trespass, they came to imagine there must be two distinct kinds of beauty, perhaps equal, perhaps one inferior to the other; the one, to which the name beauty strictly belonged, regular, polite, "nice"; the other—more properly named the picturesque, the sublime or the romantic—wild, melancholy, savage, "horrid". On this view Shakespeare was revered as a sort of inspired rustic or madman, and "Gothic" was at first a reproach and later a religion. Hence arose all that literature, replacing the older definitions of the "kinds", which seeks to distinguish two principles, of character and beauty, of beauty and sublimity, imagination and fancy, Dionysiac and Apolline art, and which leads nowhere though it has said many good things by the way.

My belief throughout has been that, if history can really make us understand our strange forefathers it is the most humane and pious activity of thought; and perhaps it thereby best fits us to provide for the strange future of our children, by deparochialising our imagination and enlarging our tolerance. And to understand the life of a period we must look first at its art. As Froude wrote of an earlier and less articulate age:

"And now it is all gone—like an unsubstantial pageant faded; and between us and the old English there lies a gulf of mystery which the prose of the historian can never adequately bridge. They cannot come to us, and our imagination can but feebly penetrate to them. Only among the aisles of our cathedrals, only as we gaze upon their silent figures sleeping on their tombs, some faint conceptions float before us of what these men were when they were alive."

To confine ourselves to such high sources is a counsel of perfection, which, for our more vocal period, would be the enemy of the good. If we look at a dismoded work of art—say a Roubillac in Westminster Abbey—with modern spectacles, we shall not see what moved contemporaries, gentle and simple, polite and rude, to tears. And the same is true of music and poetry; we must learn the idiom and acquire its associations. That is what I have tried to do and to help others in doing, though I am well aware how easily such a pursuit is diverted by the merely curious or obscure. Moreover, in a work whose composition has, with enforced intervals, been the leisure recreation of a longish lifetime, there are bound to be inconsistencies, due to shifting interest, in the choice of instances and in the method of arranging and indexing them. The only remedy would have been to re-make the medley, and that would have needed another lifetime as long. While not unmindful, then, of Froude's high ideal, I have ventured to epitomise my own humbler effort in treating this period by adapting an ironic verse of one of its own minor poets, Richard Cambridge (1751):

> Be mine the task, industrious, to disclose
> The short liv'd dogg'rel and the long shelv'd prose,
> Expound Heroic Poetry and instill
> Palladian *gusto*, *ton* for Strawberry Hill,
> Commend the charm of charnel gloom, explain
> What Britons wept at in great Anna's reign.

I can best summarise the paradoxical antithesis of the period as it appears to me, and perhaps of every period, by the two quotations following, just outside my limiting date:

In 1820 Mrs. Piozzi (Thrale) wrote: "How changed is the taste of verse, prose and painting from *le bon vieux temps*! Nothing attracts us but what terrifies and is within a hair's breadth of positive disgust; some of the strange things they write remind me of Squire Richard's visit to the Tower Menagerie, when he says, 'They are pure grim devils'—particularly a wild and hideous tale called Frankenstein."

But already in 1806 Payne Knight had complacently remarked in his *Principles of Taste*: "While the magnificent and beautiful objects of nature fill us with joy, we feel no distress in travelling among straight hedges and cornfields." No distress indeed! The whirligig of taste had come full circle.

If any readers desire fuller introduction to the more abstract and systematic cricitism of the times I make bold to refer them to the longer extracts in my *Philosophies of Beauty from Socrates to Robert Bridges*. Those with more special interests may find the present indices useful for following the development in some particular fashion or in the opinions of some critic or about some artist, or in the change of meaning given to words like Nature, Enthusiasm, Romantic. The mere distribution of references to some such words is significant of their changing vogue.

For my dates I have relied mainly on the *Dictionary of National Biography*, *Annals of English Literature* (Clarendon Press, ed. J. C. Ghosh) and *The Cambridge Bibliography of English Literature* (ed. F. W. Bateson). The date given for each quotation is that of its publication unless it refers to a past time or there is reason to think it was written earlier.

Oxford, 1948.

PART I
1600—1675

1600 r. Elizabeth

MANNERS AND TASTES

Franco-Chinese trading company founded.
Bruno, friend of Sidney, burned at Rome for supporting Copernicus.

> When some one peculiar quality
> Doth so possess a man, that it doth draw
> All his effects, his spirits, and his powers,
> In their confluctions, all to run one way,
> This may be truly said to be a Humour.
> > B. Jonson, Introduction to *Every Man Out of his Humour.*

Lord Say . . . bredd a scholar, and (though nobly born) a fellow of New College. . . . His parts were not quicke, but much above those of his own ranke.
> Clarendon, *History of the Rebellion* (1702-4).

MUSIC

I am never merry when I hear sweet music.
> Shakespeare, *Merchant of Venice.*

More, I prithee, more, I can suck melancholy out of a song, as a weasel sucks eggs. . . . I do love it better than laughing.
> Shakespeare, *As You Like It.*

POETRY

Let this duncified world esteeme of Spenser and Chaucer, I'll worship sweet Mr. Shakespeare and to honoure him I will lay his Venus and Adonis under my pillow. . . . Why here is one fellow Shakespeare puts them [Ovid and *Metamorphoses*] all downe, ay and Ben Johnson too.
> *Pilgrimage to Parnassus* and *Return from Parnassus* I and II (acted at Christmas at St. John's, Cambridge, 1597-1601).

Minime tacendus Poëtarum Anglorum princeps Galfredus Chaucer.
> Camden, *Britannia.*

3

The famous Chaucer yealds his Laurell crowne
Unto thy sugred penn for thy renowne.

> F. Thynne, *Emblems and Epigrams* (to
> Spenser).

E. Fairfax, *Godfrey of Bulloigne;* translation of *Jerusalem Delivered*
of Tasso, read by Charles I in prison (cf. Dryden, 1700).

🎔 1601 r. Elizabeth 🎔

ARCHITECTURE

Inigo Jones first visited Italy.

MANNERS AND TASTES

Bill to restrain superfluous and excessive use of coaches in
London thrown out by Lords.

> For what we want in wealth we have in flowers
> And what we lose in halls we find in bowers.
>
> T. Heywood (?), *Robert Earl of Huntingdon.*

MUSIC

There are some who, to appear the more deep and singular
in their judgment, will admit no music but that which is long,
intricate, bated with fugue, chained with syncopation, and
where the nature of every word is precisely exprest in the
Note, like the old exploded action in Comedies, when if they
did pronounce Memini, they would point to the hinder part
of their head, if Video put their finger to their eye.

> Rosseter, *Book of Ayres.*[1]

POETRY

I am sure you are become a good Chaucerist.

> R. Winwood to Sir T. Edwardes, 12.1.

Ben Jonson in the prologue to *Everyman in his Humour*, blamed
the neglect of the Unities.

---

[1] Cf. T. Morley, *Introduction to Practical Musicke* (1597). You must have a
care that when your matter signifieth ascending, high, heaven, and such like,
you make your musicke ascend: and by the contraries. (Composer of *It Was
a Lover and His Lass.*)

4

❧ 1602 r. Elizabeth ❧

MANNERS AND TASTES

Sir J. Beaumont, *The Metamorphosis of Tabacco.*

POETRY

That vulgar and easie kind of Poesie which . . . we abusively call Rime.

> T. Campion, *Observations in English Poesy.*

For (Chaucer's) verses, although in divers places they may seeme to vs to stand of vnequall measures: Yet a skilfull Reader, that can scan them in their nature, shall find it otherwise.

> Speght, *Works of Our Ancient & Learned English Poet Geffrey Chaucer* (2nd ed. First in 1598. cf. 1687, 1721).

❧ 1603 r. Elizabeth—James I ❧

MANNERS AND TASTES

Population of London estimated at 200,000-250,000 (see 1625).

POETRY

All our understandings are not to be built by the square o *Greece* and *Italie.* We are the children of nature as well as they; we are not so placed but that the Sunne of Discretion shineth uppon us; we have our portion of the same virtues as well as of the same vices. . . . Nor can it be but a touch of arrogant ignorance to hold this or that nation Barbarous, these or those times grosse. . . . Accent, the chiefe Lord and Grave Governour of Numbers. . . . To mine owne eare those continuall cadences of couplets used in long and continued Poemes are verie tyresome. . . . I thinke a Tragedie would indeede best comporte with a blank Verse and dispence with Ryme, saving in the *Chorus,* or where a sentence shall require a couplet.

> S. Daniel, *A Defence of Ryme* (in answer to Campion, 1602).

5

❧ 1604 r. James I ☙

MANNERS AND TASTES

Hampton Court Conference (see 1611).

> She that could think and ne'er disclose her mind,
> See suitors following and not look behind,
> She was a wight, if ever such wight were—
> To suckle fools and chronicle small beer.
>
> <div align="right">Shakespeare, <i>Othello</i>.</div>

POETRY

> Petrarche, in his thoughts divine,
> Tasso in his highest line,
> Ariosto's best invention,
> Dante's best obscured intention,
> Ovid in his sweetest vaine:
> Pastor Fido's purest strain.
>
> <div align="right">N. Breton, <i>The Passionate Shepherd</i>.</div>

❧ 1605 r. James I ☙

NATURE

If that great Workmaster had been of a human disposition, he would have cast the stars into some pleasant and beautiful works and orders, like the frets in the roofs of houses ... so differing an harmony there is between the Spirit of Man and the Spirit of Nature.

Bacon, Advancement of Learning (cf. 1689, T. Burnet).

POETRY

Ruggiero the Archbishop, who upon suspicion of Treason immured *Conte Hugolino* a Noble *Pisano*, and his foure Children, causing them to be starved: of whom *Dante* the Poet in his 33 Chapter *dell' inferno*, very elegantly discourseth, faining, that there for a Torment due to such a fact, the *Conte* liveth upon the Bishops-head with a never satisfied greedinesse.

R. Dallington, Survey of Tuscany.

6

Therefore it [poetry] was ever thought to have some partici-
pation of divinenesse, because it doth raise and erect the
Minde, by submitting the shewes of things to the desires of
the Mind, whereas reason doth buckle and bowe the Mind
unto the Nature of things. . . .
The whole inclination and bent of those (last) times was
rather towards copie than weight.

> Bacon, *Two Bookes of the Proficience and
> Advancement of Learning.*

Our English Languadge for all or the most is macheable, if
not preferable, before any other in vogue at this daye.

> R. Carew, *Epistle on the Excellency of the
> English Tongue.*

If it be objected that what I publish is no true Poëme in the
strict Lawes of *Time*, I confesse it, as also in the want of a
proper *Chorus.*

> B. Jonson, Preface to *Sejanus.*

Malherbe, aged 50, appeared as Parisian poet.

> (cf. Boileau, 1674, *enfin vint Malherbe.*)

STAGE

Movable scenery first mentioned in England.

B. Jonson, *The Queene's Masque of Blacknesse.* Staged by Inigo
Jones.

1606 r. James I

MUSIC

> Let chromatic tunes, harsh without ground,
> Be sullen music for a tuneless heart.
>> J. Daniel, *Songs.*

POETRY

Indeed Sir the best *Tales* in England are your Canterburie
tales.

> Anon. (G. Chapman?), *Sir Gyles
> Goosecappe.*

7

The best of these which first began to reduce the confused garden of our language into some proportion, were the two laureate knights of their times, *Gower* & his scholler *Chaucer*. . . . One *Lydgate* a monke of Edmondsburie succeeded them in that worke.

B. Barnes, *Foure Bookes of Offices*

❧ 1607 r. James I ❧

MANNERS AND TASTES

A hat which must sit close and firme upon your heade. About your neck you shall wear a falling band, and no ruffe. Your doublet shal be made close and hansome to your bodie. Your hose would be large, rounde and full, your bootes must be cleane, blacke, long and close to your legge. Your boothose must come some two inches higher than your bootes being hansomely tied up with points.

Markham, *Cavelarice*.

Let us to billiards.

Shakespeare, *Antony & Cleopatra* (cf. 1608).

NATURE

O sovereign mistress of true melancholy (the moon).

Shakespeare, *Antony & Cleopatra* (cf. 1608).

POETRY

Old *Chaucer*, reuerend for prioritie, blythe in cheare, buxsome in his speeches, and benigne in his haviour.

Dekker, *A Knight's Conjuring*.

Here's Pastor Fido, All our English writers,
I mean such as are happy in Italian,
Will deign to steal out of this author, mainly;
Almost as much as from Montagnié:

.   .   .   .

Dante is hard and few can understand him.

B. Jonson, *Volpone*.

8

The impossibility of any mans being the good *Poët*, without first being a good *Man*. . . . Doctrine, which is the principall end of Poesy, to informe men in the best reason of living . . . it being the office of a *Comick*-Poet to imitate justice and instruct to life, as well as puritie of language, or stirre up gentle affections.

B. Jonson, Dedicatory Epistle to Volpone.

The learned Greek, rich in fit epithets
Blest in the lovelymarriage of pure words,

. . . . .

The Roman eloquent, and Tuscan grave
The braving Spanish, and the smooth-tongued French.

. . . . .

(tragedy in buskins, (comedy) in pumps.

T. Tomkis, Lingua.

1608 r. James I

MANNERS AND TASTES

Virginia first colonized. See 1630.

5 gallons of sack bought for Eton College at 11d. per qt. with 8d. discount on the whole. On draught only and from The Christopher, till 1650.

I hold it for a most delicate and pleasing thing to have a fair Gallery, great Chamber or other lodging, that openeth fully upon the East or West Sun, to be inwardly garnished with sweet Hearbs and Flowers, yea and Fruit if it were possible.

H. Platt, Florae's Paradise.

Coryate walked across Europe.

1609 r. James I

MANNERS AND TASTES

(Mistress Otter) the rich China-woman that the courtiers visit so often.

B. Jonson, The Silent Woman.

Give me a look, give me a face,
That makes simplicity a grace;
Robes loosely flowing, hayre as free:
Such sweet neglect more taketh me,
Than all th'adulteries of Art;
They strike mine eyes, but not my heart.
                              B. Jonson, *The Silent Woman*.

A game of bowles now and then, or prickes when I have got
bow and arrows, for our Master loves shooting well, and we
must follow.
                              Life and Correspondence of Sir G. Radcliffe
                              (from University College, Oxford, to his
                              Mother), 28.5.

STAGE

The Structure and Ornament of (*The House of Fame*) was
entirely by Mr. Jones his invention and designe. . . . In which
he profest to follow that noble description made by Chaucer.
                              B. Jonson, *The Masque of Queenes*.

1610 r. James I

ARCHITECTURE

Carfax conduit erected at Oxford; removed to Nuneham
Park, 1787.

Nave of St. Peter's built at Rome.

MANNERS AND TASTES

East India Co. founded.

Honoré d'Urfé published *L'Astrée*, first French pastoral
romance (and a *Roman à clef*), imitating Tasso's *Aminta* and
Guarini's *Pastor Fido*. Admired by Rousseau, cited by Leibniz,
read by Corneille, Bossuet, Fénelon, La Fontaine, Racine,
Boileau, St. François de Sales.

The University (of Oxford) is much reformed about drinking, long hair and other vices, especially our house (University College), out of which I have lately gone to avoid expulsion for drunkenness.

Life and Correspondence of Sir G. Radcliffe (to his Mother), 14.12.

POETRY

Giles Fletcher (jnr.) in preface to *Christ's Victory and Triumph*, comments on scarceness of sacred poetry (see Watts, *Horæ Lyricæ* 1706, cf. Herbert).

> Fill me a pipe boy of that lusty smoke,
> That I may drink the god into my brain,
> And so enabled write a buskind strain;
> For nothing great or high can come from thence,
> Where that blest plant denies his influence.

R. Thorius, *Hymnus Tabaci.*

✤ 1611 r. James I ✤

ARCHITECTURE

One chimney-piece with fower dorrick columns upon 2 pedestals with 2 wide panels between, supporting a vase with a frieze and swelling panels under it with 4 great curbs bearing 4 Ionic columns with pedestals and wide panels between and compt swelling panel in the middle with small cartooses round about.

Hatfield House Accounts.

POETRY

Of all bookes extant in all kinds, *Homer* is the first and best. (Preface).
As when about the silver Moone, when aire is free from wind,
And stars shine cleare; to whose sweete beames, high
    prospects, and the brows
Of all steepe hills and pinnacles thrust up themselves for
    showes;

And even the lowly vallies joy, to glitter in their sight,
When the unmeasr'd firmament, bursts to disclose her light,
And all the signes in heaven are seene, that glad the
    shepheard's heart;
So many fires disclos'd their beames made by the Trojan
    part.

> G. Chapman, *Iliads* VIII, 490 (cf. 1614,
> 1674, 1720, 1726 and 1791).

Authorized Version of the Bible published (see 1604).

⚜ 1612 r. James I ⚜

MANNERS AND TASTES

About this date William Murray, later Earl of Dysart, "whipping boy" to Charles I.

15 women indicted and 12 condemned for witchcraft at Lancaster.

NATURE

For, in respect of Plaines, what pleasure can be found
In darke and sleepie shades where mists and rotton fogs
Hang in the gloomie thicks, and make unsteadfast bogs.

> M. Drayton, *Polyolbion* iii.

STAGE

Playes, wherein, now, the Concupiscence of Iigges and Daunces so raigneth, as to runne away from Nature, and be afraid of her, is the onely point of art that tickles the *Spectators*.

> B. Jonson, *Preface to the Alchemist*.

⚜ 1613 r. James I ⚜

ARCHITECTURE

Portico of Old Schools, Oxford, built.

Wadham College, Oxford. Gothic with orders superimposed.

Lord Arundel took Inigo Jones to Italy (Vicenza &c.).

POETRY

Beaumont and Fletcher in *Knight of the Burning Pestle*, quoted old ballads, e.g., *Fair Margaret and Sweet William*.

> Chaucer (of all admir'd) the Story gives;
> There constant to Eternity it lives.
> > J. Fletcher, Prologue to *Two Noble Kinsmen*.

STAGE

C: Nay, we must now have nothing brought on Stages
But puppetry, and pied ridiculous antics.
Men thither come to laugh and feed fool-fat;
Check at all goodness there as being profaned;
When, wheresoever Goodness comes, she makes
The place still sacred though with other feet
Never so much 'tis scandal'd and polluted.
Let me learn anything, that fits a man,
In any Stables shewn, as well as Stages.

B: Why is not all the world esteemed a Stage?
. . . . .

C: To make the proudest outside, that most swells
With things without him, and above his worth,
See how small cause he has to be so blown up;
And the most poor man, to be grieved with poorness;
Both being so easily borne by expert Actors;
The Stage and Actors are not so contemptful,
As every innovating Puritan,
And ignorant Swearer out of jealous envy,
Would have the world imagine.
> George Chapman, *Revenge of Bussy d'Ambois.*

✤ 1614 r. James I ✤

ANTIQUARIANISM

The holy Druides composing songs
Of everlasting life to victory.
> Beaumont & Fletcher, *Bonduca.*

MANNERS AND TASTES

A sweet melancholie my sences keeps.
> Drummond of Hawthornden, *When'as She Smiles.*

POETRY

The servants then (commanded) soone obaid
Fetcht Coach, and Mules joyn'd in it. Then the Maid
Brought from the Chamber her rich weeds, and laid
All up in Coach: in which, her mother plac't
A maund of victles, varied well in taste
And other junkets.
> G. Chapman, *Oddysey* (cf. 1611, 1674,
> 1720, 1726 and 1791).

1615 r. James I

ARCHITECTURE

Inigo Jones returned from Italy a Palladian.

PAINTING

The Earl of Somerset (R. Carr) imported pictures by Tintoretto, Veronese, Bassano, Titian, Schiavone. These passed to the Earl of Arundell.

1616 r. James I

MANNERS AND TASTES

Accademia degli Umoristi (i.e., writers and critics of comedy), founded in Naples.

Galileo abandoned the Copernican system.

Ben Jonson in his *Masque of Christmas*, which included Misrule, Gambol and Father Christmas with his sons and daughters "good dancing boys all", embodied the spirit of the old popular sword-dances and mumming.

POETRY

Divinest Spenser heav'n-bred, happy Muse! . . .
    Sidney began . . . the Past'rall. . . .
        The learned Shepherd (Chapman).
           Our second Ovid . . . all-loved Drayton. . . .
Jonson whose full of merit to reherse
Too copious is to be confinde in verse.
                W. Browne, *Britannia's Pastorals.*

Donne, the delight of Phoebus, and each Muse
Who, to thy one, all other braines refuse.
                B. Jonson, *Epigrammes*, 23.

1617 r. James I

ARCHITECTURE

Inigo Jones built a Gothic Chapel in Lincoln's Inn.

MANNERS AND TASTES

Sack and Claret bought for Winchester College at 3/4 per gall.

The English husbandmen eat barley and rye brown bread, and
prefer it to white bread as abiding longer in the stomach and
not so soon digested with their labour, but citizens and
gentlemen eat most pure white bread. . . . England, yea
perhaps one County thereof, hath more fallow deer than all
Europe that I have seen. No kingdom in the world hath so
many dove houses. Likewise brawn is a proper meat to the
English, not known to others. English cooks, in comparison
to other nations, are most commended for roasted meats. . . .
The world affords not such inns as England hath, either for
food and cheap entertainment after the guests' own pleasure,
or for humble attendance. . . . While he eats, if he have company especially, he shall be offered music, which he may freely
take or refuse. And if he be solitary, the musicians will give
him good-day in the morning.
                Fynes Moryson, *Travels.*

PAINTING

A very diligent gatherer of all I can get of Holbein's, or any other excellent master's hand.

Lucy, Countess of Bedford.

POETRY

The Citty and state of Florence both yealded most famous men, as Dante, Petrarcha, Boccacio, for Poets. . . . Michael Angelo Bonaritio, most famous for the Arts of Paynting, Sculpture and Architecture.

Fynes Moryson.

🎔 1618 r. James I 🎔

MANNERS AND TASTES

Ben Jonson walked to Scotland and visited Drummond.

GARDENS

About this time John Tradescant, later gardener to Charles I, introduced scarlet runners and Algerian apricots. He established the first "physic garden".

🎔 1619 r. James I 🎔

ANTIQUARIANISM

The Druides imbrew'd
With Gore, on Altars rude
With Sacrifices crown'd
In hollow Woods bedew'd
Ador'd the Trembling sound.

M. Drayton, *To Himselfe and the Harpe.*

ARCHITECTURE

Inigo Jones began Whitehall banqueting-hall.

Trinity College (Oxford) hall built.

MANNERS AND TASTES

Blackfriars petition against the crowd of hackney and other coaches at the theatre.

Savilian professorship of Astronomy at Oxford founded; but a fear of being "smutted with the black art".

The Fellows of University College, Oxford, warned a bachelor, S. Wilson, that he should not enter any house in the town to drink or to take tobacco and that he should neither drink nor smoke in his room.

POETRY

Ben Jonson appointed laureate by letters patent. (Spenser had held the place without them till 1599, when he was succeeded by S. Daniel.) Also created M.A. at Oxford.

That couplets . . . be the bravest sort of verse, especially when they are broken. . . . That Sidney did not keep a decorum, in making everyone speak as well as himself. [Sidney blamed rustic language in pastorals]. . . . Spenser's stanzaes pleased him not, nor his matter. . . . He told Mr. Done that if (*The Anniversarie*) had been written of the Virgin Marie it had been something; to which he answered that he had described the Idea of a Woman, and not as she was. That Done, for not keeping of accent, deserved hanging. That Shakespeare wanted art. . . . That the best pieces of Ronsard were his Odes. (*All this was to no purpose for he neither doeth understand French nor Italiannes*). . . . Esteemeth John Done the first poet in the world in some things: His verses of *The Lost Chaine* he heth by heart, and that passage of *The Calme, That dust and Feathers doe not stirr, all so was quiet.* . . . Sir Edward [=Henry] Wotton's verses of a happie lyfe he hath by heart; and a piece of Chapman's translation of the 13 of the Iliads. . . . For a Heroik Poeme, he said, there was no such ground as King Arthur's fiction; and that S. P. Sidney had ane intention to have transform'd all his *Arcadia* to the stories of King Arthure. . . . He scorned such verses as could be transposed:—

> Wher is the man that never yett did hear
> Of faire Penelope, Ulisses queen?

> B. Jonson in Drummond of Hawthornden
> (published 1711).

❧ 1620 r. James I ❧

PAINTING

Vandyck came to England and was employed by the king.

(To paint landscapes as in Kepler's Camera Obscure) were illiberal; though surely no painter can do them so precisely.
Sir. H. Wotton to Bacon.

There liv'd in this latter Age six famous Painters in *Italy* who were excellent and emulous of the ancients: Raphael di Urbino, Michel Angelo Buonarota, Titian, Antonie of Correggio, Sebastian of Venice, Julio Romano, and Andrea Sartorio.
B. Jonson, *Timber or Discoveries* (published 1641).

POETRY

The Players have often mentioned it as an honour to *Shakespeare*, that in his writing, whatsoever he penn'd, hee never blotted[1] out a line. My answer hath beene, would he had blotted a thousand. . . . I lov'd the man, and doe honour his memory, on this side Idolatry, as much as any. He was indeed honest, and of an open and free nature, had an excellent *Phantasie*, brave notions, and gentle expressions, wherein hee flow'd with that facility that sometime it was necessary he should be stop'd. *Sufflaminandus erat.* . . . His wit was in his owne power; would the rule of it had beene so too. Many times hee fell into those things, could not escape laughter; As when hee said in the person of *Caesar*, one speaking to him: *Caesar, thou dost me wrong.* Hee replyed: *Caesar did never wrong but with just cause*; . . . . But hee redeemed his vices with his vertues. There was ever more in him to be praysed than to be pardoned. . . . Now because they speake all they can, however unfitly, they are thought to have the greater copy. . . . The true Artificer will not run away from nature as hee were afraid of her; but speake to the capacity of his hearers. And though his language differ from the vulgar somewhat, it shall not fly from all humanity, with the Tamerlanes and Tamer-Chams of the late Age, which had nothing in them but the *scenicall* strutting and

[1] Cf. Pope, 1737.

furious vociferation to warrant them to the ignorant gapers. Hee knows it is his onely Art, so to carry it as none but Artificers perceive it. In the meanetime, perhaps, he is called barren, dull, leane. . . .

(Of Bacon) No man ever spake more neatly, more presly, more weightily, or suffer'd less emptinesse less idlenesse, in what hee uttered . . . hee may be nam'd and stand as the *marke* and ἀκμή of our language. . . . *Language* most shewes a man: speake, that I may see thee. . . . Let *Aristotle* and others have their dues: but if we can make farther Discoveries of truth and fitnesse than they, why are we envied? . . . To judge of Poets is only the facultie of Poets; and not of all Poets but the best.

B. Jonson, Timber or Discoveries.

[N.B. "Language most shewes a man", "Would he (Shakespeare) had blotted a thousand", "No man ever spoke more presly" (than Bacon). Cf. 1605 Bacon.]

Juliet: 'Tis almost morning, I would have thee gone:
    And yet no further than a wanton's bird;
    Who lets it hop a little from her hand,
    Like a poor prisoner in his twisted gyves,
    And with a silk thread plucks it back again,
    So loving jealous of his liberty.

Shakespeare, Romeo & Juliet II.

N. Richardson, Fellow of Magdalen College, Oxford, inserted these lines into a sermon twice preached (this year and next), at the University church, "applying them to God's love to his saints either hurt with sin or adversity, never forsaking them." (Cf. 1772).

🙦 1621 r. James I 🙤

MANNERS AND TASTES

To see a strange outlandish fowl,
A quaint baboon, an ape, an owl,
A dancing bear, a giant's bone,
A foolish engine move alone,

A morris-dance, a puppet-play,
Mad Tom to sing a roundelay,
A woman dancing on a rope,
Bull-baiting also at the *Hope*,
A rhymer's jests, a juggler's cheats,
A tumbler showing cunning feats,
Or players acting on the stage—
There goes the bounty of our age:
    But unto any pious motion
    There's little coin and less devotion.
H. Farley, St. Pauls Church.

A Romancy, that relates of Knights, and distressed Damosells
the sad Aduentures.
Lady M. Wroth, Urania.

The Archbishop of Canterbury (Abbot), shooting buck, killed
a gamekeeper with a crossbow. Received the King's pardon.

❧ 1622 r. James I ❧

MANNERS AND TASTES

A *Weekly News* and *London Weekly Courant* appeared.

POETRY

Poetrie was the first Philosophie that ever was taught. . . . Of
English Poets of our owne Nation, esteeme Sir *Geoffrey Chaucer*
the father; although the stile for the antiquitie may distast you,
yet as under a bitter and rough rinde there lyeth a delicate
kernell of conceit and sweete invention.
H. Peacham (?), Of Poetrie.

When I go musing all alone,
Thinking of divers things foreknown,
When I build castles in the air,
Void of sorrow, void of fear,
Pleasing myself with phantoms sweet,
Methinks the time runs very fleet.
    All my joys to this are folly;
    Nought so sweet as melancholy.

20

When to myself I act and smile,
With pleasing thoughts the time beguile,
By a brook-side or wood so green,
Unheard, unsought for, or unseen,
A thousand pleasures do me bless
And crown my soul with happiness.
    All my joys besides are folly;
    None so sweet as melancholy.

Methinks I hear, methinks I see
Sweet Music, wondrous melody,
Towns, palaces and cities fine;
Here now, then there the world is mine,
Rare beauties, gallant ladies shine,
Whate'er is lovely, is divine.
    All other joys to this are folly;
    None so sweet as melancholy.

R. Burton, *Anatomy of Melancholy.*

1623 r. James I

POETRY

Drummond of Hawthornden, who owned a *Divina Commedia*, wrote *An Hymn of the Passion*, 79 lines in *terza rima*.

So have I seen when Caesar would appear,
And on the stage at half-sword parley were
Brutus and Cassius: oh how the audience
Were ravish'd, with what wonder they went hence,
When some new day they would not brook a line
Of tedious though well labour'd Catiline;
Sejanus too was irksome, they prized more
Honest Iago or the jealous Moor;
And though the Fox and subtle Alchemist,
Long intermitted, could not quite be miss'd,
Though these have shamed all th'ancients and might raise
Their author's merit with a crown of bays,

Yet these sometimes, even at a friend's desire
Acted, have scarce defray'd the sea-coal fire
And doorkeepers: when let but Falstaff come,
Hal, Poins the rest, you scarce shall have a room,
And Benedick be seen, lo in a trice
The cockpit, galleries, boxes, all are full,
To hear Malvolio, that cross-garter'd gull.

L. Digges, Pref. to Shakespeares Poems.

The applause! Delight! The wonder of our Stage!

.   .   .   .   .

He was not of an age but for all time!

B. Jonson, On Shakespeare (1st folio).

STYLE

These modern languages will at one time or other play the bankrupt with books.

Bacon to Sir Tobie Matthew.

1624 r. James I

ARCHITECTURE

Vitruvius our principall Master ... Leon Battista Alberti the first learned architect beyond the Alpes. .... Birds do build their nests spherically. ... As semicircular arches or Hemispherical vaults being raised upon the totall diameter, bee of all others the roundest and consequently the securest ... so those are the gracefullest which, keeping precisely the same hight, shall yet bee distended one fourteenth part longer than the sayd entire diameter, which addition of distent will conferre much to their Beauty, & detract but little from their strength. .... As for those arches which our artizans call of the third and fourth point: and the Tuscan writers di terzo & di quarto acuto, because they do always concurre in an acute angle and doe springe from the division of the Diameter into three, foure, or more parts at pleasure; I say such as these: both from the natural imbecillity of the sharpe angle it selfe, & likewise for their very Uncomelinesse, ought to be exiled from judicious eyes, & left to their first inventors, the *Gothes* or Lumbards, amongst other reliques of that barbarous age. ....

... that agreeable harmony between the length, breadth & height of all the rooms of the fabric, which suddenly, where it is, taketh every beholder by the secret power of proportion. ... S. Carita (Accademia at Venice) and Riccio's S. Giustina (at Padua) do ravish the beholder & he knows not how by a secret harmony in the proportions. ...

How an artificer whose end is the imitation of nature can be too natural ... is the fault or (to speak more gently) the too great perfection of Albert Durer and perhaps also of Michael Angelo ... the German did too much express that which was and the Italian that which should be. Which severe observation of Nature, by the one in her commonest and by the other in her absolutest forms, must needs produce in both a kind of rigidity, & consequently more naturalness than gracefulness. ...

There is a Lordship likewise of the Eye which being a raunging, and imperious, and (I might say) an usurping Sence, can indure no narrow circumspection; but must be fed both with extent and varietie.

H. Wotton, *Elements of Architecture.*

NATURE

The sumptuousness of the Building (Warwick Castle), the strength of the brave, ancient, high towers. ... (In the Lake District) nothing but hideous hanging hills and great Pooles, that in what respect of the murmuring noyse of those great waters, and those high mountainous, tumbling, rocky Hills, a man would think he were in another world.

A Relation of a Short Survey of 26 Counties by a Captain, a Lieutenant and an Ancient.

PAINTING

A most beautiful piece of Tintoret, another head of Titian, a St. Francis from the hand of Cavalier Bellion, a picture of Our Lady by Raphael.

Balthazar Gerbier to Duke of Buckingham (his employer).

23

🦋 1625 r. James I and Charles I 🦋

ARCHITECTURE

Houses are built to live in, and not to look on; therefore let use be preferred before uniformity, except where both may be had. . . . You shall have sometimes fair houses so full of glass, that one cannot tell where to become to be out of the sun or cold.

Bacon, *Essay of Building.*

MANNERS AND TASTES

Fountain-heads, and pathless groves,
Places which pale passion loves;
Moonlight walks, when all the fowls
Are warmly housed, save bats and owls;
    A midnight bell, a parting groan,
    These are the sounds we feed upon;
Then stretch our bones in a still gloomy valley
Nothing's so dainty sweet as lovely melancholy.

J. Fletcher (?), *The Nice Valour* (*circa*, published 1647).

By which we note the fairies
    Were of the old profession,
The songs were Ave Maries,
    Their dances were procession;
But now alas! they all are dead
    Or gone beyond the seas,
Or further from religion fled,
    Or else they take their ease.

R. Corbet, *Certain Elegant Poems* (*circa*, published 1647).

French manners and tastes introduced at Court by Henrietta Maria.

Population of London estimated at 250,000-300,000.

PAINTING

"In Beauty, that of Favour [=feature] is more than that of
Colour. And that of Decent and Gracious Motion, more than
that of Favour. That is the best Part of *Beauty* which a Picture
cannot expresse; No, nor the first Sight of the Life. There is
no excellent *Beauty*, that hath not some Strangeness in the
Proportion. A Man cannot tell whether *Apelles*, or *Albert Durer*,
were the more Trifler; Whereof the one would make a Person-
age by Geometricall Proportions; The other, by taking the
best Parts out of divers Faces to make one Excellent. . . . Not
but I think a Painter may make a better Face, than ever was;
But he must doe it by a kind of Felicity, (as a Musician that
maketh an excellent Ayre in Musicke) and not by Rule. A
Man shall see Faces, that if you examine them, Part by Part,
you shall finde never a good;And yet all together doe well. . . .
No *Youth* can be comely, but by Pardon, and considering
the *Youth* to make up the comelinesse.

Bacon, *Essay of Beauty*.

POETRY

La vera regola è saper rompere le regole à tempo e luogo,
accomodandosi al costume corrente e al gusto del secolo.

G. Marini to G. Preli (*circa*).

❧ 1626 r. Charles I ❧

GARDENS

Garden laid out by Countess of Bedford (see 1654).

MUSIC

Professorship founded at Oxford. The holder also Choragus.

PAINTING

Orazio Gentileschi (pupil of Caravaggio) appointed court
painter to Charles I.

🏵 1627 r. Charles I 🏵

POETRY

That noble *Chaucer*, in those former times,
The first inrich'd our *English* with his rimes.

. . . .

Graue morall *Spenser* after these came on,
Than whom I am perswaded there was none
Since the blind *Bard* his *Iliads* vp did make,
Fitter a taske like that to undertake.

. . . .

Next *Marlow* bathèd in the *Thespian* springs
Had in him those braue translunary things,
That the first Poets had, his raptures were
All ayre, and fire, which made his verses cleere;
For that fine madnes still he did retaine,
Which rightly should possesse a Poets braine.

. . . .

Shakespeare, thou hadst as smooth a Comicke vaine,
Fitting the socke, and in thy naturall braine,
As strong conception and as Cleere a rage,
As any one that trafiqu'd with the stage.

Next these, learn'd *Iohnson*, in this List I bring,
Who had drunk deepe of the *Pierian* spring,
Whose knowledge did him worthily prefer,
And long was Lord here of the Theater.

M. Drayton, Of Poets (Epistle to Reynolds).

🏵 1628 r. Charles I 🏵

ANTIQUARIANISM

(The antiquary) will go you forty miles to see a saint's well or
a ruin'd abbey. . . . He is one that hath that unnatural disease
to bee enamour'd of old age and wrinckles and loves all things
(as Dutchmen doe Cheese) the better for being mouldy and
worme-eaten. . . . Beggars coozen him with musty things which
they have rak't from dunghills.

Earle, Micro-Cosmographie.

POETRY

When I began to read, and to take some pleasure in it, there was wont to lie in my mother's parlour (I know not by what accident, for she herself never read any book but of devotion— but there was wont to lie) Spenser's works. This I happened to fall upon, and was infinitely delighted with the stories of the knights and giants and monsters and brave houses which I found everywhere there (though my understanding had little to do with all this), and, by degrees, with the tinkling of the rime and dance of the numbers; so that I think I had read him all over before I was twelve years old, and was thus made a poet as irremediably as a child is made an eunuch.

> Cowley (b. 1618), *Essay on Myself.*

Doe not his Arcadian romantics live after him?

> Fulke Greville Lord Brooke, *Life of Sidney* (written some time before this date, published 1652).

Not those new-fangled toys, and trimming slight
Which take our late fantasticks with delight.

> Milton, *Vacation Exercise.*

STAGE

Fulke Greville (Lord Brooke) assassinated. His page, Davenant, passed on the Shakespearian tradition to Betterton, etc. of "the Duke's players" whom he controlled after the restoration.

1629 r. Charles I

ARCHITECTURE

Foundation stone laid of Gothic parish church at Hammersmith.

POETRY

The relish of the Muse consists in rime;
One verse must meete another like a chime.
Our Saxon shortnesse hath peculiar grace
In choice of words, fit for the ending place,

Which leave impression in the mind as well
As closing sounds of some delightful bell.

. . . . .

Similitudes contracted, smooth and round;
Not vexed by learning, but with Nature crown'd,
Strong figures drawn from deep Invention's springs,
Consisting less in words and more in things.

> Sir J. Beaumont, *"Concerning the true Forme of English poetry"*, dedicated to his "Late Majesty James I" (published this year. He died 1627).

STAGE

A French company first brought women on the English stage (see 1656).

❦ 1630 r. Charles I ❦

POETRY

Early American poem (anon) on hardships of Pilgrim Fathers. "If it were not for the pumpkins we had surely been undone."

> Higginson, *New England's Plantation.*

Then thou, our fancy of itself bereaving,
Dost make us marble with too much conceiving."

> Milton, *Sonnet to Shakespeare* (folio 1632).
> cf. Donne, *Elegie on Ld. C.* (about 1597?).

His children are his pictures, Oh they bee
Pictures of him dead, senselesse, cold as he.
Here needs no marble Tombe, since hee is gone,
He, and about him, his, are turn'd to stone.

B. Jonson's pension increased from 100 marks to £100, and a yearly tierce of Canary added. The last was withdrawn by James II, but restored and finally commuted for £27 to Pye.

❧ 1631 r. Charles I ❧

ARCHITECTURE

The Salute at Venice built.

POETRY

What gentle ghost, besprent with April deaw
Hayles me so solemnly to yonder Yewgh
B. Jonson, Elegy on Lady Jane Pawlett
(cf. Pope 1717 and T. Warton 1747).

But *Spenser* is grown hoarse, he that of late
Sung *Gloriana* in her *Elfin* state:
And so is *Sydney*, whom we yet admire
Lighting our little Torches at his fire. . . .
A. Cokayne, Elegy on Mr. M. Drayton.

❧ 1632 r. Charles I ❧

ARCHITECTURE

St. Mary's porch at Oxford, designed probably by Inigo Jones.

MANNERS AND TASTES

Hail, divinest Melancholy.
Milton, Il Penseroso (published 1645).

PAINTING

Vandyck returned to England; knighted and made court-painter; began to fix an ideal type of English aristocracy (see National Portrait Gallery).

POETRY

C: Adjectives! they're the flower, the grace of all our
language.
A well chosen Epithet doth give new soul
To fainting poesy, and makes every verse
A Bride! With Adjectives we bait our lines,
When we do fish for Gentlewomen's loves,

29

And with their sweetness catch the nibbling ear
Of amorous ladies; with the music of
These ravishing nouns we charm the silken tribe,
And make the Gallant melt with apprehension
Of the rare Word. I will maintain 't against
A bundle of Grammarians, in Poetry
The Substantive itself cannot *subsist*
Without its adjective.

F: But, for all that,
Those words would sound more full, methinks, that are
      not
So larded; and if I might counsel you,
You should compose a Sonnet clean without 'em,
A row of stately Substantives would march
Like Switzers and bear all the fields before 'em;
Carry their weight; shew fair, like Deeds Enrolled;
Not Writs, that are first made and after fill'd.

    .   .   .   .   .

Thence first came up the title of Blank Verse:—
You know, Sir, what Blank signifies?—when the sense
First framed, is tied with Adjectives like points,
And could not hold together without wedges;
Hang 't, 'tis pedantic, vulgar Poetry.
Let children, when they versify, stick here
And there these piddling words for want of matter.
Poets write Masculine Numbers.

> J. Shirley, *The Changes*. (Cf. R. L.
> Stevenson: 'War to the adjective'. To
> H. James.)

Nowadays the philosophers are the true poets.

> H. Reynolds, *Mythomystes*.

❧ 1633 r. Charles I ❧

ARCHITECTURE

Inigo Jones restored St. Paul's classically.

Ben Jonson in *A Tale of a Tub* satirised Inigo Jones as Vitruvius
Hoop.

GARDENS

T. Johnson edited J. Gerards *Herbal* (1596). Gerard probably introduced lilac, laburnum and Judas tree.

MANNERS AND TASTES

The King proclaimed that country landowners should reside for part of the year. Suckling informed against but excused.

The first hackney coach-stand in London opposed by watermen.

A "Passage of Arms" held at the Hague by the Prince of Orange. Prince Rupert "carried away the Palme". See 1645, 1768 and cf. the Eglinton Tournament of 1833.

POETRY

The Muses garden with Pedantique weedes
O'erspread, was purg'd by thee; The lazie seeds
Of servile imitation, throwne away,
And fresh invention planted . . .
                              Open'd Us a Mine
Of rich and pregnant phansie, drawne a line
Of masculine expression. . . .
But thou art gone, and thy strict lawes will be
Too hard for Libertines in Poetrie,

They will repeale the goodly exil'd train
Of gods and goddesses, which in thy just raigne
Were banish'd nobler Poems, now, with these,
The silenc'd tales o' th' Metamorphoses.
                              T. Carew, *Donne's Poems.*

1634 r. Charles I

ARCHITECTURE

University College, Oxford, buildings begun (W. quad.)

MANNERS AND TASTES

Sedan chairs put on the London streets.

31

POETRY

Before the starry threshold of Jove's court
My mansion is, where those immortal shapes
Of bright aerial spirits live inspher'd
In regions mild of calm and serene air
[Amidst th' Hesperian gardens, in whose banks
Bedew'd with nectar and celestial songs,
Eternal roses grow and hyacinth
And fruits of golden rind, on whose fair trees
The scaly-harnessed dragon ever keeps
His unenchanted eyes; around the verge
And sacred limits of this blissful isle
The jealous ocean, that old river, winds
His far extended arms, till with steep fall
Half his waste flood the wild Atlantic fills
And half the slow, unfathom'd Stygian pool.
I doubt me, gentle mortals, these may seem
Strange distances to hear, and unknown climes.
But soft! I was not sent to court your wonder
With distant words and strange removed climes.
Yet thence I come, and oft from thence behold]
(Above) the smoke and stir of this dim [narrow] spot
Which men call earth.

Milton *Comus.* First draft. The parts in square brackets were
deleted on revision and the word (above) added.

STYLE

Every Author has his own Genius, directing him by a secret
Inspiration to that wherein he may most excell.

> Sir William Alexander, Earl of Stirling,
> *Anacrisis.*

(This is a transitional use of the word "genius" from the classical
to the modern; see 1662).

❊ 1635 r. Charles I ❊

MANNERS AND TASTES

English depot at Canton.

Sir W. Brereton carried off "many branches and leaves" from
the Glastonbury thorn. *Travels.*

A light and sprightly Mademoiselle who, being well mounted,
... fear'd not to ride in the darke, whether it were up hill or
downe dale. (In a Canterbury inn) this pretty she rider at
that time held it no nicety, nor point of incivility, to disrobe
and bed her little, tender, weary'd corps in our presence,
which I understood afterwards, is common and familiar
amongst them of that nation.

> Hammond, *Short Survey of the Western
> Counties.*

MUSIC
As a church-window, thick with paint,
Lets in a light but dim and faint;
So others with division hide
The light of sense, the poet's pride;
But you alone may truly boast
That not a syllable is lost.

> Waller, *To Mr. H. Lawes* (cf. 1648
> Milton and 1668 Pepys).

POETRY
The *Académie Française* founded by Richelieu. Boisrobert read
to it, violently attacking Homer; Gombauld *Sur le je ne sçay
quoi.*

The Hierarchie of the Blessed Angels (contains 27 lines from the
Italian of the *Divina Commedia*).

> T. Heywood.

1636 r. Charles I

POETRY
Longinus, *On the Sublime*, edited G. Langbaine.

1637 r. Charles I

MANNERS AND TASTES
Wrapt in a pleasing fit of melancholy
To meditate my rural minstrelsy.

> Milton, *Comus.*

Your change of gaudy furniture, and pictures
Of this Italian master and that Dutchman.

J. Shirley, *The Lady of Pleasure.*

There came in my time to the Coll; [Balliol] one Nathaniel
Conopios out of Greece, from Cyrill the Patriarch of Constantinople, who returning many years after, was made (as
I understand) Bishop of Smyrna. He was the first I ever saw
drink coffe, wch custom came not into England till 30 years
after.

Evelyn, 10.5.

Royal proclamation "to settle a running post or two, to run
night and day between Edinburgh and London, to go thither
and come back again in six days and to take with them all
such letters as shall be directed to any post-town in or near
that road". Two years later made a monopoly of the Post-
master-General. In 1640 the rates were: 80 miles 2d, 140
miles 4d, further in England 6d, to Scotland 8d.

PAINTING

An Artificer, therefore, is to take good heed that he does not
by a malapert wantonneese of his vainly conceived wit devise
all kinds of monstrous and prodigious Images of things not
known in nature. . . . Grace of comelinesse and beauty which
as it cannot be found in any particular bodie, so it may be
gathered out of many bodies.

Francois du Jon (Junius), *De Pictura
Veterum,* translated into English 1638.

❧ 1638 r. Charles I ❧

ANTIQUARIANISM

Where your old Bards, the famous Druids ly.

.   .   .   .   .

Beyond the stormy Hebrides.

Milton, *Lycidas.*

POETRY

Wherein [*Comus*] I should much commend the tragical part if
the lyrical did not ravish me with a certain Dorique delicacy
in your songs and odes; whereunto I must plainly confess to
have seen yet nothing parallel in our language, *ipsa mollities*.

Sir H. Wotton to J. Milton, 13.4.

> I am no Poet here; my pen's the spout,
> Where the rain-water of my eyes run out.
> In pity of that name, whose fate we see
> Thus copied out in griefs Hydrography.

J. Cleveland, *Juxta Edouardo King*.

A Paraphrase upon the Divine Poems (Grotius), by G. Sandys.
Waller, Sidney Godolphin, Falkland, H. King, T. Carew,
Digges contributed "in the new style". (published 1640).

> None hath a larger heart, a fuller head,
> For he hath seen as much as you have read:
> The nearer countries past, his steps have prest
> The new found world, and trod the sacred East;
> Where, his browes due, the lofty palmes doe rise,
> Where the proud Pyramids invade the skies;
> And, as all think who his rare friendship own,
> Deserves no lesse a journey to be known.
> Ullyses, if we trust the Grecian song,
> Travell'd not farre, but was a prisoner long;
> To that by tempest forc'd; nor did his voice
> Relate his fate; his travels were his choice,
> And all those numerous realmes, returned agen,
> Anew he travell'd over with his pen.

Falkland, preface to Sandys' translation
of Grotius' "*Christ's Passion*".

Davenant succeeded Jonson as laureate, but not confirmed
till 1660.

> Who first reform'd our *Stage* with justest *Laws*
> And was the first best *Judge* in his own *Cause*,
> Who (when his *Actors* trembled for *Applause*)

35

Could (with a *noble confidence*) prefer
His *own*, by right, to a noble *Theater*;
From *Principles*, which *he* knew could not *err*.
J. Cleveland, Jonsonius Virbius.

STAGE

A calme River, that tooke the Shadowes of the Trees by the
light of the Moone.
Davenant, Luminalia (stage direction).

❧ 1639 r. Charles I ❧

MANNERS AND TASTES

The obedience of our nobles to (Lesley's) advice was as great
as their forbears wont to be to their King's commands: yet
that was the man's understanding of our Scots humours, that
gave out, not only to the nobles, but to very mean gentlemen,
his directions in a very homely and simple form, as if they
had been but the advices of their neighbour and companion;
for, as he rightly observed, a difference would be used in
commanding soldiers of fortune and of soldier volunteers, of
which kind the most part of our camp did stand. He kept
daily in the Castle of Duns an honourable table for the nobles
and strangers with himself, for gentlemen waiters thereafter,
at a long side table. I had the honour, by accident, one day,
to be his chaplain at table on his left hand; the fare was as
became a General in time of war: not so curious by far as
Arundel's to our nobles; but you know that the English
sumptuosity, both in war and peace, is despised by all their
neighbours. . . . Had you lent your ear in the morning, or
especially at even, and heard in the tents the sound of some
singing psalms, some praying and some reading scripture,
you would have been refreshed; true, there was swearing,
and cursing, and brawling in some quarters.
Principal Robert Baillie, Letters and Journals.

POETRY

The melancholy and pleasant humour were in him so con-
tempered, that each gave advantage to the other, and made
his company one of the delights of Mankind. His fancy was
inimitably high, equalled only by his great wit; both being
made useful by a commanding judgement. His aspect was
chearful and such as gave a silent testimony of a clear knowing
soul, and of a conscience at peace with itself. . . . He was by
nature highly passionate, but more apt to reluct at the excesses
of it. A great lover of the offices of humanity, and of so merciful
a spirit, that he never beheld the miseries of Mankind without
pity and relief.

> I. Walton, *Life of John Donne* (pubd. 1640.
> An early biography).

🙚 1640 r. Charles I 🙚

ANTIQUARIANISM

. . . Delphos ruins . . . Athens. . . .
For Antiquity,
I do not store up any under Grecian:
Your Roman antiques are but modern toys
Compared to them. Besides they are so counterfeit
With mouldings, 'tis scarce possible to find
Any but copies.

> T. Nabbes, *The Bride.*

ARCHITECTURE

The hall staircase at Christ Church, Oxford, built.

MUSIC

Select Church Music, J. Barnard.

PAINTING

Nicholas Poussin called to Paris by Richelieu.

POETRY

Dante in his 19th Canto of Inferno, hath thus, as I will render it to you in English blank verse.

Milton, *Of Reformation.*

Suckling, *Ballad upon a Wedding* ("His *opus magnum;* indeed for grace and simplicity it stands unrivalled in the whole compass of ancient or modern poetry." Wordsworth. Yet it is "courtly" and the "language of a gentleman". Dryden 1668).

🏵 1641 r. Charles I 🏵

ARCHITECTURE

Haerlem is a very delicate town, and hath one of the fairest Churches, of the Gotiq designe, I had ever seene.

Evelyn, *Diary,* 19.8 (first "Gothic"? But see 1624).

GARDENS

The Parke (at Bruxelles) . . . so naturally is it furnish'd with whatever may render it agreeable, melancholy, and country-like. Here is a stately heronry, divers springs of water, artificial cascades, rocks, grotts.

Evelyn, 8.9.

PAINTING

Lely came to England till 1680. Van Dyck died (b. 1599).

🏵 1642 r. Charles I (Civil War begins) 🏵

MANNERS AND TASTES

Hire of two sedan-chairs from Bedford House to St. Clement Danes 5/-. The Earl of Bedford borrowed the cash from Rose the housemaid.

Regular newspapers began with the *Mercuries.* But see 1622.

NATURE

While the steepe horrid Roughness of the Wood
Strives with the gentle Calmness of the Flood.
Such huge Extremes, when Nature doth unite,
Wonder from thence results, from thence Delight.

But his proud head the ayery Mountain hides
Among the clouds; his Shoulders, and his Sides
A shady Mantle cloathes . . .
Low at his Foot a spacious Plaine is plac'd
Betweene the Mountain and the Streame embrac't.

Denham, *Cooper's Hill.*

POETRY

(Waller) The best of Poets.

Denham, *Cooper's Hill.*

—whether the rules of *Aristotle* herein are strictly to be kept, or nature to be follow'd, which in them that know art and use judgement, is no transgression but an inriching of art.

Milton, *Reason of Church Government.*

1643 r. Charles I

POETRY

(Thames)
O, could I flow like thee; and make thy stream
My great example, as it is my theme;
Though deep, yet clear; though gentle, yet not dull;
Strong without rage, without o'erflowing full.

Denham, *Cooper's Hill* (added this year).

1644 r. Charles I

ARCHITECTURE

We found the (Jesuit) Fathers in their church at the Rue St. Anthoine, where one of them shew'd us that noble fabriq, which for its cupola, pavings, incrustations of marble, the pulpit, altars (especially the high altar) organ, *lavatorium*, etc., but, above all, the richly carv'd and incomparable front, I esteeme to be one of the most perfect pieces of architecture in Europ.

4.1.

Francis I (that true virtuoso) made it (St. Germains) compleate, speaking as to the style of magnificence then in fashion, which was with too greate a mixture of ye Gotic.

27.2.

Fontaine Bleau . . . is nothing so stately and uniforme as Hampton Court. 7.3.

7.5.

(Sienna) The Domo or Cathedral . . . of inexpressible beauty, . . . but what exceeds all description is the pavement.

25.10.

Palace Farnezi . . . built by Michael Angelo, of the 3 orders of columns after the antient manner, and when architecture was but newly recovered from the Gotic barbarity.

6.11.

(St. Peter's at Rome) That most stupendious and incomparable Basilicum far surpassing any now extant in the world, and perhaps, Solomon's temple excepted, any that was ever built. . . . Mosaiq of the famous Giotto.

Evelyn, 19.11.

GARDENS

A little garden, which, though very narrow, by the addition of a well painted perspective is to appearance greatly enlarged; . . . a stream of water, rising in the aviary, out of a statue, and seeming to flow for some miles by being artifically continued in the painting when it sinks under the wall.

1.3.

One of the greatest Virtuosos in France for his collection of pictures, agates, medals and flowers, especially tulips and anemones.

Evelyn, 1.3.

PAINTING

(At Paris)   P. Veronese, M. Angelo, Corregio, Raphael, Bassano, Brill, Mantegna, Titian, L. van Leyden, Leonardo, Palma, Sniders.

1.3.

(At Florence) Da Vinci, Pontorno, Titian, Bronzini.

(At Florence) Andrea del Sarto in ye Annunciata (Madonna del Sacco) a piece infinitely valued—Bartolomeo, Pordenone, P. Veronese, Guerchino.

(At Florence)   The cabinet . . . called the Tribuna . . . Over the door is a round of M. Angelo; in the cabinet Leo the Tenth, with other paintings of Raphael, del Sarto, Perugino and Coreggio, viz., a St. John, a Virgin, a Boy, 2 Apostles, 2 heads of Durer rarely carved.

(At Siena)   Raphael (=Pinturicchio?).

(At Rome)   Agostino Caracci—so deepe and well-studied are all the figures (in the Farnezi Palace) that it would require more judgement than I confesse I had, to determine whether they were flat or emboss'd—Annibal Carracci (*sic*) Sposaliccio of St. Sebastian (in Barberini) . . . a table in my judgement superior to anything I had seene in Rome—Guido Rheno, Caravaggio, Perugino, Cortona, Bassano, Coreggio, Durer, Badassare, Michael Angelo (last judgement) Julio Romana (the Paynters' Academy), Raphael (a Cupid playing with a Dolphin) . . . certainly one of the most wonderful pieces of worke in the world, Salviati, Vasari.

(At Caprarola) Hannibal Caracci.

(At Milan) Breughel.

(At Poggio Imperiale) Adam and Eve by Durer, very excellent.

(At Venice)   Giorgione, Tintoret, Final Judgement . . . esteem'd among the best pieces in Europe.

1644-5 (various unprecise dates).

(Palazzo Ghisi in Trastevere) The Amours of Cupid and Psych, by the hand of the celebrated Raphael d'Urbin. Here you always see painters designing and copying after it, being esteemed one of the rarest pieces of ye art in the world and with great reason.

Evelyn, 29.11.

POETRY

(Poetry contrasted with Rhetorick) as being "lesse suttle and fine", but more "simple, sensuous and passionate".

Milton, *Of Education* (cf. 1711, Dennis.)

SCULPTURE

(At Florence) What is most admirable is the Rape of a Sabine with another man underfoot, the confusion and turning of whose limbs is most admirable. It is of one entire marble, the work of John di Bologna and is most stupendous . . . here is also the famous statue of David by M. Angelo; Hercules and Cacus by Baccio Bandinelli; the Perseus in copper by Benvenuti, and the Judith of Donatelli.

25.10.

David of Cavaliero Bernini—the arte of the statuary plainely stupendious.

17.11.

Bernini, a Florentine sculptor, architect, painter, and poet, who, a little before my coming to the citty, gave a publiq opera (for so they call shews of that kind) wherein he painted the scenes, cut the statues, invented the engines, compos'd the musiq, writ the comedy and built the theatre.

19.11.

(In Medici Palace) Happly preferable to any in the world are the Two Wrestlers; for the inextricable mixture wth each others armes and legges is stupendious. In the great chamber is the Gladiator whetting a knife; but the Venus is without parallel, being the masterpiece of whose name you see graven under it in old Greeke characters. Nothing in sculpture ever approached this miracle of art.

29.11.

(At Rome) Torso of Amphion and Dirces, represented in
5 figures ... to be valued beyond all the marbles of the world
for its antiquity and workmanship. Statues of Niobe and her
family ... among the best pieces of worke in the world for the
passions they expresse, and all other perfections of that
stupendous art; ... the gladiator ... the thorn-extractor (much
admired by artists) ... the horses of Praxiteles.

Evelyn, 6.11

🌸 1645 r. Charles I 🌸

ARCHITECTURE

The Pantheon ... of all the Roman antiquities the most
worthy of notice.

21.2.

(The front of the Library at Sienna) tho' Gotic is very fine.

21.4.

(St. Marc's, Venice) The church is also Gotic; yet for the
preciousnesse of the materials, being of severall marbles,
aboundance of porphyrie, Serpentine, etc., far exceeding any
in Rome, St. Peter's hardly excepted. ... The roofe is of most
excellent Mosaic; but what most persons admire is the new
work of the emblematic tree at the other passage out of the
Church. ... After all that is said, this church is in my opinion
much too dark and dismal, and of heavy work.

Evelyn, May

MANNERS AND TASTES

Wearing red cloaks, as the mode then was.

8.2.

There was little more to be seene in the rest of the civil world,
after Italy, France, Flanders, and the Low Countrys but plaine
and prodigious barbarisme.

8.2.

Academia degli Umoristi ... I was invited by a Dominican Frier, whom we usually heard preach to a number of Jewes, to be godfather to a converted Turk and Jew. The ceremony was performed in the church of Santa Maria sopra la Minerva.

25.2.

There had been in the morning a joust and tournament of severall young gentlemen on a formal defy ... the prizes being distributed by the ladies after the knight errantry way. The launcers and swordsmen running at tilt against the barriers, with a greate deale of clatter, but without any bloodshed, giving much diversion to the spectators, and was new to us travellers.

6.5 (Easter Monday).

The hall of the Academia della Crusca is hung about with impresses and devices painted, all of them relating to corne sifted from the brann; the seates are made like bread baskets and other rustic instruments us'd about wheate, and the cushions of satin, like sacks.

Evelyn, 21.4 (nearest date).

NATURE

And as in prospects we are there pleas'd most,
Where something keeps the eye from being lost,
And leaves us room to guess—
Sir J. Suckling, *Against Fruition*, cf. 1687
Norris and 1799 Campbell.

PAINTING

For sculptors and architects, we found Bernini and Algardi were in the greatest esteeme; Fiamingo as a statuary, who made the Andrea in St. Peter's and is said to have died madd because it was placed in an ill light. Among the painters, Antonio della Cornea, who has such an addresse in counterfeiting the hands of the ancient masters, so well as to make his copies pass for originals; Pietro de Cortone, Monsieur Poussine a Frenchman, and innumerable more.

Evelyn, 8.5.

POETRY

Hylas, O Hylas, why sit we mute
   Now that each bird saluteth the Spring;
Wind up the slackenèd string of thy lute,
   Never canst thou want matter to sing.
> Waller, *Chloris and Hylas* (with *Go Lovely Rose* and *On a Girdle*).

SCIENCE

Dr. Wilkins (later Bishop of Chester), Foster (Professor of Astronomy at Gresham College), Wallis (mathematician) and "divers worthy persons inquisitive into natural philosophy, and other parts of human learning, did by agreement meet weekly in London on a certain day, to treat and discuss", among other subjects, the circulation of the blood, the Copernican hypothesis, the weight of air, Nature's abhorrence of vacuities, the Torricellian experiment, the descent of heavy bodies. This was the germ of the Royal Society (q.v.).

SCULPTURE

(Laocoon) Pliny says this statue is to be esteem'd before all pictures and statues in the world; and I am of his opinion, for I never beheld anything of art approach it.

> 18.1.

The statue of Christ at the Columna is esteem'd one of the master-pieces of M. Angelo.

> Evelyn, 25.2.

⚘ 1646 r. Charles I ⚘

MANNERS AND TASTES

Evelyn and Waller sailed down Loire to Orleans.

⚘ 1647 r. Charles I ⚘

MANNERS AND TASTES

Nature herself doth Scotch-men beasts confess,
Making their Country such a wildernesse.

    .   .   .   .   .

Had *Cain* been *Scot*, God would have chang'd his doom,
Not forc't him wander, but confin'd him home.

They're Citizens o' th' world; they're all in all,
Scotland's a Nation Epidemicall.

J. Cleveland, The Rebell Scot.

Ah, yet, e'er I descend to th' Grave,
May I a *small House*, and *large Garden* have!
And a *few Friends*, and *many Books*, both true
Both wise, and both delightful too!
And since *Love* ne'er will from me flee,
A *Mistress* moderately fair,
And good as *Guardian-Angels* are,
Only belov'd, and loving me.

A. Cowley, The Mistress.

POETRY

Mystical grammar of amorous glances,
Feeling of pulses, the physic of love,
Rhetorical courtings, and musical dances,
Numb'ring of kisses arithmetic prove.

J. Cleveland, Mark Anthony.

She, she is my mistress, her suitors are many,
But she'll have a square-cap[1] if e'er she have any

J. Cleveland, The Square Cap.

1648 r. Charles I

MANNERS AND TASTES

First meeting of Friends under Fox? (or 1647).

If ye will with *Mab* find grace,
Set each Platter in his place:
Rake the Fire up, and get
Water in, ere Sun be set.

---

[1] i.e., marry a University man.

Wash your Pailes and clense your Dairies;
Sluts are loathsome to the Fairies:
Sweep your House: Who doth not so
Mab will pinch her by the toe.

> Herrick (End of natural fairies in
> English?)

MUSIC

Harry, whose tuneful and well-measured song
First taught our English musick how to span
Words with just note and accent, not to scan,
With Midas ears, committing short and long.

> Milton, *To Mr. H. Lawes* (cf. 1635
> Waller, and 1668 Pepys).

PAINTING

Royal Academy of Painting and Sculpture, Paris.

❧ 1649 Charles I beheaded ❧

POETRY

Was there no milder way but the small-pox
The very filthiness of Pandora's box?
So many spots, like nœves on Venus' soil,
One jewel set off with so many a foil;
Blisters with pride swell'd, which through's flesh did sprout
Like rose-buds, stuck i' the lily-skin about.
Each little pimple had a tear in it,
To wail the fault its rising did commit;
Which, rebel-like, with its own lord at strife,
Thus made an insurrection 'gainst his life.
Or were these gems sent to adorn his skin,
The cabinet of a richer soul within?

> Dryden, *On the Death of Lord Hastings.*

❧ 1650 Commonwealth ❧

MANNERS AND TASTES

About this year coffee and chocolate began to be frequently drunk in Oxon.

A. Wood, *Life and Times.*

POETRY

Poets, whose business should represent the Worlds true image often to our view, are not less prudent than Painters, who when they draw Landschaps entertain not the Eye wholly with even Prospect and a continued Flat, but for variety terminate the sight with lofty Hills, whose obscure heads are sometimes in the clouds. . . . Wise Poets think it more worthy to seek out truth in the Passions than to record the truth of Actions. . . . Truth narrative and past is the Idol of Historians, who worship a dead thing, and truth operative, and by effects continually alive, is the Mistris of Poets, who hath not her existence in matter but in reason. . . . Wit is a Webb consisting of the subt'lest threads; and like that of the *Spider* is considerately woven out of ourselves; for a *Spider* may be said to consider, not only respecting his solemnesse and tacit posture. . . . Nor have I refrain'd to be oblig'd to men of any Science, as well mechanicall as liberall.

Wit is not only the luck and labour, but also the dexterity of thought, rounding the world, like the Sun, with unimaginable motion, and bringing swiftly home to the memory universall surveys. . . .

My endeavour was, in bringing Truth, too often absent, home to mens bosoms, to lead her through unfrequented and new ways, and from the most remote Shades, by representing Nature, though not in an affected, yet in an unusual dress.

Tasso . . . both in time and merit, the first of the Moderns; . . . for I will yield to their opinion, who permit not *Ariosto*, no nor *Du Bartas* in this eminent rank of the Heroicks: rather than to make way by their admission for *Dante*, *Marino* and others. . . . (Inspiration) a dangerous word which many have of late successfully us'd.

Davenant to Hobbes, *Preface to Gondibert.*

48

Man, enabled to speak wisely from the principles of nature and his own meditation, loves rather to be thought to speak by inspiration, like a Bagpipe.

... Great persons that have their mindes employed on great designes have not leasure enough to laugh.

... Dialect of the Inferior sort of people. ... Such Metaphors and Comparisons as cannot come into men's thoughts but by mean conversation and experience of humble or evil Arts.

> (or 1651?) Hobbes, *Answer to Davenant* (cf. Congreve 1694 and Chesterfield 1748).

Songs of shepherds and rustical roundelays
  Formed of fancies and whistled on reeds,
Songs to solace young nymphs upon holidays,
  Are too unworthy for wonderful deeds.
Phoebus ingenious, or wingëd Cyllenius,
  His lofty genius may seem to declare
In verse better coinëd and voice more refinëd
  How stars divinëd the hunting the hare.

> *Westminster Drolley*, II (published 1671).

1651 Commonwealth

POETRY

Johnson hath writ things lasting, and divine,
Yet his Love-Scenes, *Fletcher*, compar'd to thine,
Are cold and frosty, and exprest love so
As heat with Ice, or warm fires mix'd with Snow.

. . . . .

Shakespeare to thee was dull, whose best Jest lies
I' th' Ladies questions, and the Fools replies,

. . . . .

Whose wit our nice times would obsceneness call,
And which makes Bawdry pass for Comicall:
Nature was all his Art, thy vein was free
As his, but without his scurrility.

> W. Cartwright (died 1643), *Mr. J. Fletcher*.

STYLE

Those that observe their similitudes (of things), in case they be such as are but rarely observed by others, are sayd to have a *Good Wit*; by which, in this occasion, is meant a *Good Fancy*. . . . He that hath this Vertue, will be easily fitted with similitudes, that will please, not only by illustration of his discourse, and adorning it with new and apt metaphors; but also by the rarity of their invention. But without Steddinesse, and Direction to some End, a great Fancy is one kind of Madnesse. . . . In a good Poem, whether it be Epique, or Dramatique, as also in Sonnets, Epigrams and other Pieces, both Judgement and Fancy are required; But the Fancy must be more eminent; because they please for the Extravagancy; but ought not to displease by Indiscretion. . . . "Natural wit" consisteth principally in two things, "celerity of imagining" that is swift succession of one thought to another, and steady direction to some approved end. . . . The light of human minds is Perspicuous Words, but by exact definitions first snuffed and purged of ambiguity. . . . Metaphors, and senseless and ambiguous words, are like *ignes fatui*.

Hobbes, *Leviathan* (cf. 1653 Flecknoe).

1652 Commonwealth

ANTIQUARIANISM

Henry Jacob (Merton College) *De Origine Druidum*, in *Delphi Phoenicizantes*.

ARCHITECTURE

Inigo Jones died (b. 1573).

MANNERS AND TASTES

Groomsbridge, a pretty melancholy seat, well wooded and water'd.

Evelyn, 4.7.

PAINTING

Pictures painted for Sir Daniel Fleming (of Rydal) of the views from his house.

POETRY

As Nature's prime confectioner, the bee
  By her flower-nibbling chemistry
Turns *vert* to *or*: so, verse gross prose does rarify.
Benlowes, Theophila.

To Thee, meek Majesty, soft King
    Of simple graces and sweet loves!
Each of us his lamb will bring,
    Each his pair of silver doves!
(1651) At last, in fire of Thy bright eyes, (*or*)
(1652) Till burnt at last in fire of Thy fair eyes
  Ourselves become our own best sacrifice!
Crashaw, Carmen Deo Nostro.

(The later version also adds some stanzas and the choric refrain)

❄ 1653 Commonwealth ❄

MANNERS AND TASTES

Consignment of "claret wine" to Woburn Abbey.

Seals are much in fashion . . . such as are oldest and oddest are most prized . . . a Nepture riding upon a dolphin . . . any old Roman head is a present for a prince. (January). . . .

Have you read *Cleopatra*? (La Calprenède 1646). I have six times. (February). . . .

About 6 or 7 (p.m.) I walk into a common . . . where a great many young wenches keep sheep and cows, and sit in the shade singing of ballads. I go to them and compare their voices and beauties to some ancient shepherdesses that I have read of, and find a vast difference there; but, trust me, I think these are as innocent as those could be. I talk to them and find they want nothing to make them the happiest people in the world but the knowledge that they are so[1]. (May).

---

[1] Evidently a Virgilian allusion.

Cyrus (Scudery). . . . Battledore and shuttlecock. (June). . . .

Last night I was in the garden till 11 o'clock. It was the sweetest night that e'er I saw. The garden looked so well and the jasmine smelt beyond all perfume. And yet I was not pleas'd . . . had you been there I should have liked it much more than ever I did; but that not being, it was no more to me than the next field. (July). . . .

D. Osborne to W. Temple.

POETRY

Marlowe's *"Come, live with me and be my love"* at least fifty years ago and Raleigh's *"If all the world and love were young"*—old-fashioned poetry but choicely good; I think much better than the strong lines that are now in fashion in this critical age. (Also, *Come Shepherds, deck your herds, As at noon Dulcinea rested, Phillida flouts me, Chevy Chase, Johnny Armstrong* and *Troy Town*.

Izaak Walton, *Compleat Angler*, 3rd day.

STYLE

The Perfecting of our language towards which it was (earlier in the century) advancing amain. . . .
Where have you for that which we call Rhetoricke, Eloquence, and high expression, a Language excelling ours? or that speakes more by Figure and Metaphor (the mayne ornaments of speech).

Flecknoe, *Miscellania* (see 1651 Hobbes).

🙾 1654 Commonwealth 🙾

ARCHITECTURE

(York Minster) A most entire and magnificent piece of Gothic architecture.

Evelyn, 17.8.

MANNERS AND TASTES

Were Sir Guy's grot improved as it might be t'were capable of being made a most *romantiq* and pleasant place. . . .

Salisbury Plain reminded me of the pleasant lives of the shepherds we read of in romances.

3.8.

I now observed how the women began to paint themselves, formerly a most ignominious thing and us'd only by prostitutes.

Evelyn, 11.5 (see 1667).

❧ 1655 Commonwealth ❧

GARDENS

"Because I take the garden (Moor Park, near Rickmansworth, laid out by the Countess of Bedford before 1626, where he was on honeymoon with Dorothy Osborne) to have been in all kinds the most beautiful and perfect—at least in the figure and disposition that I have ever seen, I will describe it for a model to those that meet with such a situation and are above the regards of common expense. It lies on the side of a hill, (upon which the house stands) but not very steep. The length of the house, where the best rooms and of most use or pleasure are, lies upon the breadth of the garden; the great parlour opens into the middle of a terras gravel walk that lies even with it, and which may be, as I remember, about 300 paces long and broad in proportion, the border set with standard laurels, and at large distances, which have the beauty of orange trees out of flower and fruit. From this walk are 3 descents by many stone steps, in the middle and at each end, into a very large parterre. This is divided into quarters by gravel walks and adorned with 2 fountains and 8 statues in the several quarters; at the end of the terras walk are 2 summer houses, and the sides of the parterre are ranged with 2 large cloisters open to the garden upon arches of stone and ending with 2 other summer houses even with the cloisters, which are paved with stone and designed for walks of shade, there being none other in the whole parterre. Over these 2 cloisters are 2 terrasses covered with lead and fenced with balusters, and the passage into these airy walks is out of the 2 summer houses at the end of the first terrass walk. The cloister facing S. is covered with vines and would have been proper for an orange-house, and the other for myrtles or other more common greens ... if this piece of gardening had been then in as much vogue as it is now (1690?). From the middle of the parterre is a descent by many steps flying on each side of a grotto that lies between them (covered with lead and flat) into the lower garden, which is all fruit trees, ranged about the several quarters of a wilderness, which is very shady, the walks here are all green, the grottos embellished with figures of shell-rock work, fountains and water-works. .... They might have added a third quarter of all greens; but this want is supplied by a garden the other side the house, which is all of that sort, very wild, shady and adorned with rough rock work and fountains."

> Sir W. Temple, *On Gardens* (published 1690).

PAINTING

Académie des Beaux Arts founded by Mazarin.

POETRY

Chaucer was a great *Refiner* and *Illuminer* of our English tongue (and if he left it so bad, how much worse did he find it?) witness *Leland* thus praising him,

> Praedicat Algerum merito Florentia Dantem,
> Italia et numeros tota Petrarche tuos.
> Anglia Chaucerum veneratur nostra Poetam,
> Cui veneres debet patria lingua suas (1589).
> T. Fuller, *Church History of Britain.*

RELIGION

R. Overton (? or C. Wrighter), *Man's Mortality*, published in London (1643 and 1644 in Amsterdam). Probably influenced Milton's cosmology.

🍃 1656 Commonwealth 🍃

ARCHITECTURE

In the (Osney) windows were the effigies of saints, kings, bishops and abbots most artificially (according to that age) depicted. .... The light was diminished, did impose a more aufull reverence upon the adorer or[1] religious apprehensions, resembling therein the antient Romanes who for the most part made choise of shady places for their devotion.

> Anthony Wood, *Antiquities of the City of Oxford* (published 1674, cf. Knox 1778).

MANNERS AND TASTES

J. Harrington, *Oceana*, ascribed revolutions more to changes in property-balance than to persons.

PAINTING

That price for things in colours oft we give,
Which we'd not take to have them while they live,
Such is the power of painting that it makes
A loving sympathy twixt men and snakes.

> (A. Wright?) *Parnassus Biceps* (Church Windows). (Allusion to Aristotle's *Poetics*).

POETRY

I conceive it to be a vulgar error, in translating poets, to affect being a *fidus interpres* ... if Virgil must needs speak English, it were fit he should speak not only as a man of this Nation, but as a man of this Age. .... Poesie is of so subtle a spirit, that in pouring out of one language into another, it will all evaporate; and if a new spirit be not added in the transfusion, there will remain nothing but a *caput mortuum*.

> Denham, *Essay on Translated Verse* (on *Aen* II, 2nd ed. First in 1636).

Tell me, O tell, what kind of thing is Wit?

.   .   .   .   .

'Tis not such *Lines* as almost crack the *Stage*
    When Bajazet[2] begins to rage,
Nor a tall *Met'phor* in the *Bombast way*,
Nor the dry chips of short lung'd Seneca,
    Nor upon all things to obtrude,
    And force some odd Similitude.

> A. Cowley, *Of Wit*.

---

[1] The MS. is defaced, *v.l.*, "of"?
[2] Racine.

So that the unlearned lost their money, and
Scholars saved onely, that could understand.

.   .   .   .   .

Thy Scene was free from monsters, no hard plot
Call'd down a God t' untie the unlikely knot,
The stage was still a stage, two entrances
Were not two parts of the world disjoyn'd by Seas.
> (J. Mayne?) *Parnassus Biceps, to Memory
> of B. Jonson.*

Evelyn translated Lucretius I in verse with an Essay.

STAGE

Davenant—*The Siege of Rhodes*, opera with elaborate scenery
and a woman (Mrs. Colman) in heroine's part (first English?
see 1629). Recitative in heroic couplets.

🌸 1657 Commonwealth 🌸

MANNERS AND TASTES

A melancholy delight in taking a prospect of the ruin of
(Einsham Abbey) . . . to instruct the pensive beholder with an
exemplary frailty.
> Anthony Wood, *Life and Times.*

Caves, Grots, Mounts, and irregular ornaments of gardens
do contribute to contemplative and philosophical enthusiasm.
> Evelyn to Sir T. Browne, 28.1.

James Fair, barber, by Inner Temple Gate, presented by the
Inquest of St. Dunstan's in the West, for making a sort of
liquor called coffee, to the great nuisance and prejudice of
the neighbourhood.
> *New View of London* (1708).

🌸 1658 Commonwealth 🌸

MANNERS AND TASTES

Woburn Abbey laid in 8 doz. Rhenish at £1 the doz., 65 galls.
Canary at 8/- the gall., 1 puncheon Burgundy £16, 1 puncheon
Paris wine £14.

Stage Coaches. London to Salisbury, 2 days 20/-; to Exeter or Wakefield, 4 days 40/-; Plymouth 50/-; Durham 55/-; to Oxford 2 days, to Dover 2½ days.

PAINTING

I went to see the Earl of Northumberland's pictures (at Suffolk House) whereof that of ye Venetian Senators [The Cornaro Family?] was one of the best of Titian's, and another of Andrea del Sarto, viz., a Madona, Christ, St. John, and an Old Woman; a St. Catherine of Da Vinci with divers portraits of Van Dyke; a nativity of Giorgioni: the last of our blessed Kings (Charles I) and ye Duke of York by Lely.

Evelyn, 9.6.

POETRY

Love's Victory (in West Country dialect), W. Chamberlayne.

Gracian introduced the term "good taste".

> Come, follow follow me,
> You, fairy elves that be;
> Which circle on the green,
> Come, follow Mab your queen,
> Hand in hand let's dance around,
> For this place is fairy ground.

Anon. *Mysteries of Love & Eloquence.*

🕸 1659 Commonwealth 🕸

MANNERS AND TASTES

A private and lone house in or neare to Bagley Wood, between Oxon and Abendon (called Bayworth) is an old house situated in a romancey place, and a man that is given to devotion and learning cannot find out a better place . . . to refresh his mind with a melancholy walke, and with the retiredness of the place as well as with the shady box arbours in the garden.

A. Wood, *Life & Times.* February.

That imagination which is most free, such as we use in romantic inventions.

H. More, *Immortality of the Soul*.

POETRY

W. Chamberlayne published *Pharonida*, written some years earlier, in Keatsian couplets.

Davenant, *The Playhouse to Let*, i.e., a suppressed theatre. First called *History of Sir Francis Drake*. Uses Molières *Sganarelle*.

RELIGION

R. Fludd, *Mosaic Philosophy*, an adaptation of the Kabbalah, published in English in London (1638 in Latin at Gouda). Probably influenced Milton, or possibly he collaborated in it.

❧ 1660 Restoration Charles II ❧

MANNERS AND TASTES

I did send for a cup of tee (a China drink) of which I never had drunk before.

25.9.

The first day that ever I saw my wife wear black patches.

Pepys, 30.8.

Hair powder and shaving gradually became fashionable.

The Countess of Bedford bought a sedan-chair.

Sir G. Mackenzie, *Apologie for Romances*.

Polixandre and *Le Grand Cyrus* (Scudéry), read by Mrs. Pepys.

Mlle de Scudéry *Clélie*.

Fuller, *History of Abbeys*, read by Pepys.

To the Hague, playing crambo in the waggon.

Pepys, 19.5.

The Fruitless Precaution . . . the best writ tale that ever I read in my life.

15.10.

A certain thing called Good Nature; . . . England is the only Indies where this bottomless mine of pure gold is to be found. . . . No man is more remote than an Englishman from the doggedness of long-lasting and indelible revenge.

Sir Tobie Matthew (d. 1655), *Introduction to Letters.*

Colonel Norton said "Freedom of Parliament is the just right and interest of the nation, and if they thought it right to bring in the Turk, they ought not to be imposed on the contrary."

Verney Memoirs.

MUSIC

After dinner we had pretty good singing, and one, Hazard, sung alone after the old fashion, which was very much cried up, but I did not like it. Thence we went to the Green Dragon, on Lambeth Hill, both the Mr. Pinknys', Smith, Harrison, Morrice that sang the bass, Shepley and I, and there we sang of all sorts of things at first sight, and after that I played on my flageolette.

16.1.

A variety of brave Italian and Spanish songs, and a canon for eight voices.

Pepys, 21.2.

PAINTING

The King's closet, where I saw most incomparable pictures. Among the rest a book open upon a desk, which I durst have sworn was a reall book.

Pepys, 3.10.

Sheldonian roof and Hampton Ct. (R. Streater, sergeant painter to Ch. II.)

c*

59

POETRY

Davenant confirmed in laureateship (see 1638).

Dined at the Bullhead upon the best venison pasty that ever I eat of in my life, and with one dish more, it was the best dinner I ever was at. Here rose in discourse at table a dispute between Mr. Moore and Dr. Clerke, the former affirming that it was essential to a tragedy to have the argument of it true, which the Doctor denied, and left it to me to be the judge, and the cause to be determined next Tuesday morning at the same place, upon the eating of the remains of the pasty, and the loser to pay 10s.

31.9.

To the Bullhead, where we had the remains of our pasty, where I did give my verdict against Mr. Moore upon last Saturday's wager, where Dr. Fuller coming in do confirm me in my verdict.

Pepys, 4.10.

Il faut nous accomoder avec (les règles) mais notre malheur est qu'Aristote et Horace après lui en ont écrit assez obscurement.

Corneille, *Du Poème Dramatique.*

(O an otiose passage in *Le Cid* 1636) Je l'avais fait pour montrer que la pièce était dans les vingt quatre heures.

Corneille, *Discours de la Tragédie.*

STAGE

Plays seen by Pepys:—
Merry Wives of Windsor (Shakespeare). *The Scornful Lady* (Beaumont and Fletcher). *Henry IV* (Shakespeare). *The Loyall Subject* (B. and F.). One Kinaston made the loveliest lady that ever I saw. *The Moor of Venice* (Shakespeare). A very pretty lady that sat by me cried out to see Desdemona smothered. *The Woman's Prize* or *Tamer Tam'd* (J. Fletcher). *Beggars' Bush* (B. and F.). *The Traitor* (Shirley). A very good tragedy.

1661 r. Charles II

ARCHITECTURE

Cl. I love no such triumphant Churches—
They scatter my devotion; whilst my sight
Is courted to observe their sumptuous cost,
I find my heart lost in my eyes;
Whilst that a holy horror seems to dwell
Within a dark obscure and humble cell.

Cr. But I love Churches mount up to the skies,
For my devotion rises with their roof;
Therein my soul doth heav'n anticipate.

> "Philonax Lovekin" (J. Wilson?),
> *Andronicus* (published 1664).

GARDENS

For future shade, young trees upon the banks
Of the new stream appear in even ranks;
The voice of Orpheus or Amphion's hand,
In better order could not make them stand.

> Waller, *On St. James' Park as lately
> improved by His Majesty* (the designer
> André Mollet).

MANNERS AND TASTES

(At St. Gregory's) . . . Dr. Buck started a difficulty, which he left to another time to answer, about why God should give means of grace to those people which he knew would not receive them, and deny to others which he himself confesses . . . would have received them, and they would have been effectual too. I would I could hear him explain this when he do come to it.

> Pepys, 11.10.

Royal proclamation against excessive gilding of coaches (disregarded).

St. Evremond introduced port to England.

MUSIC

Drums, which are much cried up, though I think it dull, vulgar music.

Pepys, 3.2.

STAGE

I saw *Hamlet, Prince of Denmark* played, but now the old plays begin to disgust this refined age since His Majestie's being so long abroad.

Evelyn, November 26.

Plays seen by Pepys:—

The Beggars' Bush (B. and F.). The first time that ever I saw women come upon the stage. *The Scornful Lady* (B. and F.) (2 visits). *The Silent Woman* (Ben Jonson), an excellent play. *The Widdow* (Jonson, Fletcher and Middleton). *The Lost Lady* (Sir W. Barclay), which do not please me much (2 visits). *The Mayd in ye Mill* (B. and F.). *Argalus and Parthenia* (adapted from Sidney's *Arcadia*). *The Virgin Martyr* (Massinger). *The Changeling* (T. Middleton). *The Bondman* (Massinger), an excellent play . . . Betterton (3 visits). *The Queen's Maske,* or *Love's Mistress* (T. Heywood) (3 visits). *King and No King* (B. and F.). *All's lost by Lust* (W. Rowley). *Rollo* (J. Fletcher). *The Spanish Curate* (Fletcher and Massinger?). *Rule a Wife and Have a Wife* (Fletcher) . . . do not like it. *The Little Thiefe* (Fletcher) . . . a very merry and pretty play. *Love's Quarrell* (Anon), I do not like the design or words. *The Humersome Lieutenant* (Fletcher). *The Chances* (B. and F.) (2 visits). *The Mayd's Tragedy* (B. and F.) . . . methinks it is too sad and melancholy. *The Silent Woman* (B. Jonson) . . . which pleased me. *Harry the Fourth* (Shakespeare) . . . a good play. *Bartholomew Fair* (B. Jonson) . . . the first time it was acted nowadays (8.6) a most admirable play . . . but too much prophane and abusive (4 visits). *The Alchymist* (B. Jonson) . . . a most incomparable play (2 visits). *The Siege of Rhodes* (Sir W. Davenant). *Claracilla* (T. Killigrew) . . . but strange to see this house, that used to be so thronged, now empty since the Opera began. *Brenoralt* (Sir J. Suckling) . . . seemed a good play. *The Jovial Crew* (R. Brome) . . . as merry and the most innocent play that ever I saw (3 visits). *The Merry Devill of Edmunton* (Anon. 1608 Drayton?). *The Witts* (Sir W.

Davenant) . . . I liked exceddingly (3 visits). *Hamlett* (Shakespeare) (2 visits). *The Antipodes* (R. Brome) . . . much mirth but no great matter else. *The Elder Brother* (J. Fletcher). *'Tis Pity she's a Whore* (Ford). *Twelfth Night* (Shakespeare). *The Merry Wives of Windsor* (Shakespeare). *Father's Owne Son* (Anon). *Victoria Corombona* (Webster) . . . a very poor play. *The Traytor* (Shirley) . . . a most excellent play. *Love and Honour* (Sir W. Davenant) . . . a very good play (three visits on consecutive nights!). *Argalus and Parthenia* (Sidney's *Arcadia*) . . . where a woman acted Parthenia, and came afterwards on the stage in men's clothes, and had the best legs that ever I saw, and I was very well pleased. *Wit without Money* (B. and F.) which I do not much like. *The Country Captain* (W. Cavendish, D. of Newcastle) . . . so silly a play as in all my life I never saw and the first that ever I was weary of (2 visits). *Philaster* (B. and F.) . . . far short of my expectations. *Love at First Sight* (T. Killigrew) . . . a poor thing. *The Mad Lover* (B. and F.), not much pleased. *Cutter of Colman Street* (Cowley) . . . very good. *Siege of Rhodes*, Part II (Davenant).

✺ 1662 r. Charles II ✺

ARCHITECTURE

Hampton Court is as noble and uniforme a pile and as capacious as any Gotic architecture can have made it . . . hangings designed by Raphael, very rich with gold . . . Caesarian Triumphs of Andr. Mantegna.

Evelyn, 9.6.

MANNERS AND TASTES

Mr. Mills preached such a sermon (. . . that God might have made all of us and the whole world from the beginning to have been in hell, arguing from the power the potter has over his clay), that I could have wished he had let it alone.

Pepys, 19.1.

The Earle of Oxford's Misse (as at this time they began to call lewd women).

Evelyn, 9.1.

Censorship of newspapers (see 1695).

PAINTING

Lilly (Lely) . . . Wright the painter: but, Lord! the difference that is between these two works.

Pepys *Diary*, 18.6.

Evelyn (*Sculptura*) speaks of Hugen's "universal mathematical *genius*" in the modern sense.

POETRY

Falling into discourse of a new book of drollery in verse called *Hudebras*, I would need go find it out, and met with it at the Temple: cost me 2s. 6d. But when I came to read it, it is so silly an abuse of the Presbyter Knight going to the warrs, that I am ashamed of it and by and by meeting at Mr. Townsend's at dinner [sic] I sold it him for 18d.

Pepys, 26.12.

SCIENCE

Royal Society founded by Charter.

STAGE

Davenant adapted Shakespeare's *Measure for Measure* as *Law against Lovers*. Shakespeare not restored till 1740.

Plays seen by Pepys:—

Spanish Curate (Fletcher and Massinger?), a good play. *Rule a Wife and Have a Wife* (Fletcher). *The Law against Lovers* (Sir W. Davenant's version of *Measure for Measure*), a good play. At the Opera saw *Romeo and Juliet* (Shakespeare) the first time it was ever acted, a play the worst that ever I heard in my life.
The Little Thief (Fletcher), a pretty play. *The Mayde in the Mill* (B. and F.), a pretty good play. To the Opera and there saw *The Bondman* (Massinger). *The Knight of the Burning Pestle* (B. and F.) which pleased me not at all. An Italian puppet play, which is very pretty. To the Opera and there saw the 2nd part of *The Siege of Rhodes* (Davenant). *The French Dancing Master* (W. Cavendish, D. of Newcastle) pleased us very well. *Love in a Maze* (*The Changes*, Shirley), the play hath

little in it. *Witt in a Constable* (H. Glapthorne), the first time it is acted, but so silly a play I never saw. *Doctor Faustus* (Marlowe). *Midsummer Night's Dream* (Shakespeare), which I had never seen before, nor shall ever again, for it is the most insipid, ridiculous play that ever I saw in my life. *The Duchess of Malfy* (Webster). *The Cardinall* (Shirley). *The Scornfull Lady* (B. and F.). *The Valiant Cidd* (from Corneille). *The Villaine* (T. Porter). *The Tamer Tamed* (J. Fletcher).

1663 r. Charles II

ARCHITECTURE

The Sheldonian Theatre, Oxford, designed by Wren (one of his first buildings, "infinitely superior to anything in the world of its kind" Defoe, *Tour* 1726).) Brasenose Chapel finished.

MANNERS AND TASTES

(The preacher) said that if a minister of the word and an angell should meet him together, he would salute the minister first; which methought was a little too high.

9.8.

Bought my wife a chint, that is, a painted Indian callico, for to line her new study.

Pepys, 5.9.

Mr. Edwd. Phillips came to be my Sonne's preceptor; this gentleman was nephew to Milton, who wrote against Salmasius's *Defensio*, but was not at all infected with his principles.

Evelyn, 24.10.

POETRY

Shakespeare Third Folio.

Sir J. Minnes brought many fine expressions of Chaucer, which he doats on mightily, and without doubt he is a very fine poet.

Pepys, 14.6.

(Chaucer) may be esteemed our English *Homer*. He is our best English Poet, and *Spenser* the next.

E. Leigh, *Treatise of Religion and Learning*.

STAGE

Plays seen by Pepys:—

The Villane (T. Porter) again; and the more I see it, the more I am offended by my first undervaluing the play, it being very good and pleasant, and yet a true and allowable tragedy. *Claracilla* (T. Killigrew), a poor play. *Twelfth Night* (Shakespeare), a silly play, and not related at all to the name or day. *Adventures of Five Hours* (transl. from Calderon by S. Tuke), the best for the variety and the most excellent continuance of the plot to the very end, that ever I saw, or think ever shall, and all possible, not only to be done in the time, but in most other respects very admittable, and without one word of ribaldry; and the house, by its frequent plaudits did show their sufficient approbation. *The Slighted Mayde* (Sir R. Stapylton). *The Wild Gallant* (Dryden), so poor a thing, as I never saw in my life almost. *Scarronides* or *Virgil's Travestie* (C. Cotton). *Witt without money* (B. & F.), which I do not like much. *The Humerous Lieutenant* (B. and F.), a play that hath very little good in it. *Hamlett* (Shakespeare). *The Slighted Mayde* (Sir R. Stapylton). *Love in a Maze* (Shirley), pretty good, but the life of the play is the Clowne. *The Committee* (Sir R. Howard), a merry but indifferent play. *The Faithfull Sheepheardesse* (J. Fletcher) a most simple thing and yet much thronged after.

1664 r. Charles II

ANTIQUITIES

Thomas Smith, *Syntagma de Druidum Moribus et Institutis*.

GARDENS

Is there under heaven a more glorious and refreshing object of the kind, than an impregnable hedge of about four hundred feet in length, nine feet high and five in diameter which I can show in my now ruined gardens at Say's Court?

Evelyn, *Sylva*.

MANNERS AND TASTES

Woburn Abbey laid in 1 tierce barrel of claret £5, 39 gallons £5, £4 worth of Rhenish, 157 galls. Canary at 7/- & 6/- a gall. 2 doz. white Gk. wine from Syracuse, 62 bottles of Shably for £4-12-6, 3 pieces of Sillery (still champagne) at £12-8-4 the piece.

For God's sake, whereabouts does the pleasure of walking lie? I swear I have often sought it till I was weary. (Allusion to Charles II?)

T. Killigrew, The Parsons Wedding.

Sir Matthew Hale at Bury condemned two women for witchcraft, Sir Thomas Browne being present and giving opinion against them.

Compagnie des Indes founded. (See 1600).

MUSIC

To hear some instrument musique; . . . I must confess, whether it be that I hear it but seldom, or that really voice is better, but so it is that I found no pleasure at all in it, and methought two voyces were worth twenty of it.

Pepys, 10.9.

PAINTING

The Earl of Bedford bought from Royal Tapestry Factory, Mortlake, 5 pieces after Raphael's cartoons for £309.

POETRY

(Sir W. Petty) saying that in all his life these three books were the most esteemed and generally cried up for wit in the world— *Religio Medici*, Osborne's *Advice to a Son* [1656-8] and *Hudibras*.

Pepys, 27.1.

(English) must needs be very Copious and Adapt, for she openly declares it to be her Business to grow Rich with the Spoils of all dead Languages, and every Day impunedly to appropriate all that is good and proper for her from the living ones.

Sorbières, A Voyage to England (translated 1709).

Shakespeare (who, with some errors not to be avoided in that Age, had, undoubtedly, a larger Soul of Poesy than ever any of our nation) was the First, who, to shun the pains of continual rhyming, invented that kind of writing which we call blank verse, [N.B., really Surrey first used it in Aen. IV, about 1548] but the French more properly *prose mesurée*; into which the English tongue so naturally slides, that, in writing prose, it is hardly to be avoided. . . . But the excellence and dignity of (rime) were never fully known till Mr. Waller taught it: he first made writing easily an art; first showed us how to conclude the sense most commonly in disticks, which, in the verse of those before him, runs on for so many lines together, that, the reader is out of breath to overtake it. This sweetness of Mr. Waller's lyric poesy was afterwards followed in the Epic, by Sir John Denham, in his *Cooper's Hill* . . . the exact standard of good writing. . . . But that benefit, which I consider most in it, because I have not seldom found it, is, that it bounds and circumscribes the fancy. For imagination in a poet is a faculty so wild and lawless, that like an high-ranging spaniel, it must have clogs tied to it, lest it outrun the judgement. The great easiness of blank verse renders the poet too luxuriant.

> (cf. Howard 1665). Dryden, *The Rival Ladies*, Preface, (first play in heroic couplets for 60 years).

Cataline, Ben Johnson, a very excellent piece (read).
> Pepys, 18.12.

STAGE

Plays seen by Pepys:—

Henry VIII (Shakespeare), which though I went with resolution to like it, is so simple a thing, made up of a great many patches, that besides the shows and processions in it, there is nothing in the world good or well done. *The Usurper* (Ed. Howard), no good play, though better than *Henry VIII*. *The Indian Queen* (R. Howard and Dryden) a most pleasant show, and beyond my expectation; the play good, but spoiled with the rhyme, which breaks the sense. *The Unfortunate Lovers* (Sir W. Davenant) I was not much pleased. *Heraclius* (transl. from Corneille). *The German Princess* (Anon.), very simple. *The Labryinth* (from Corneille), the poorest play that ever I saw.

The Silent Woman (B. Jonson). *Worse and Worse* (G. Digby, Lord Bristol). *The Bondman* (Massinger), nothing more taking in the world with me. *Bartholomew Fayre* (B. Jonson), the best comedy in the world, I believe. *The Rivall Ladys* (Dryden), a very innocent and most pretty witty play. *Henry the Fifth*, writ by my Lord Orrery (Roger Boyle) . . . the whole play most full of height and raptures of wit and sense, that ever I heard. *The Court Secret* (J. Shirley). *The General* (R. Boyle, Lord Orrery). *Macbeth* (Davenant's Version). *The Rivals* (Davenant), the play not good (2 visits).

1665 r. Charles II (Great Plague)

ARCHITECTURE

Fontainbleau has a stately Wildness and Vastness suitable to the Desert it stands in . . . The Palace, or if you please, the Cabinet of *Versailles* (Mansard) call'd me twice to view it, the Mixtures of Brick, Stone, blue Tile and Gold make it look like a rich Livery: Not an Inch within but is crowded with little curiosities of Ornaments; the Women as they make here the Language and Fashions, and meddle with Politics and Philosophy, so they sway also in Architecture; works of Filigrand, and little Knacks are in great Vogue; but Building certainly ought to have the Attribute of eternal, and therefore the only thing uncapable of new Fashions. The masculine Furniture of *Palais Mazarine* pleased me much better . . . *Bernini's* Design of the *Louvre* I could have given my skin for.

> Chr. Wren, Letter from Paris (*Parentalia*, pd. 1750).

MANNERS AND TASTES

(1665 *circa*) Portrait of *Highland Chieftain* in kilt (the first known in painting) by J. M. Wright (in Scottish National Portrait Gallery).

. . . My wife, very fine in a new yellow birds-eye hood as the fashion is now. Masks have gone out of fashion.

> Pepys, October 1.

I found Dr. Wilkins, Sir W. Petty, and Mr. Hooke contriving
. . . a wheele for one to run races in.

4.8.

Supped at my Lady Mordaunt's at Ashted, where was a roome
hung with pintado [printed East Indian cotton] full of figures
great and small, prettily representing sundry trades and
occupations of the Indians with their habits.

Evelyn, Diary, 30.11.

I thought when I went first to dwell in the country, that
without doubt I should have met there with the simplicity of
the old poetical age; I thought to have found no inhabitants
there but such as the shepherds of Sir Philip Sidney in Arcadia,
or of M. d'Urfé.

Cowley.

POETRY

I do really prefer our Plays . . . before any other Nations. . . .
Our best Poets have differ'd from other Nations (though not
so happily) in usually mingling and interweaving Mirth and
Sadness. . . . Whether Verse in Rhime or Verse without the
sound, which may be call'd Blank Verse (though a hard
Expression) is to be preferr'd? . . . they are both proper, that
is the one for a Play, the other for a Poem or Copy of Verses,
a Blank Verse being as much too low for one as Rhime is
unnatural for the other. . . . There is yet another thing which
makes Verse upon the Stage appear more unnatural; when a
Piece of Verse is made up by one that knew not what the other
meant to say. . . . It may be said that Rhime is such a confinement to a quick and luxuriant Phansie, that it gives a stop
to its speed till slow Judgement comes in to assist it; but he
that wants Judgement in the liberty of his Phancy may as
well shew the defect of it in its confinement.

(Cf. Dryden, 1664). Howard, Preface to
Four New Plays.

The Siege of Rhodes (Davenant), which is certainly (the more I
read it the more I think so) the best poem that ever was wrote.

Pepys, 1.10.

SCIENCE

Royal Society Transactions begun.

STAGE

Plays seen by Pepys:—

Love in a Tubb (Etherege), very merry but only so by gesture, not wit at all, which methinks is beneath the house. *The Traytor* (Shirley), *Vulpone* (B. Jonson), a most excellent play, the best, I think, I ever saw. *Mustapha* (Roger Boyle, Lord Orrery), not good. *Loves Maistresse* (T. Heywood). Some pretty things and good variety in it, but no or little fancy.

STYLE

An Academie for the Art & Improvement of speaking & writing well ... as that of the *Beaux Esprits* in Paris ... for the polishing & in-riching of the language. ... In order to it three or fowre meetings were begun at Gray's Inn, by Mr. Cowley, Dr. Sprat, Mr. Waller, the D. of Buckingham, Matt. Clifford, Mr. Dryden, & some other; ... it crumbled away & came to nothing.

Evelyn to Pepys, 12.8.1689.

I would humbly propose (to the Gray's Inn Academy) 1) a Gram'ar ... 2) a more certaine Orthography as by leaving out superfluous letters &c, such as *o* in woomen, people, *u* in honour, *a* in reproach, *ugh* in though. ... 3) New periods and accents. ... 4) A Lexicon ... of all the pure English words ... 5) To collect all the technical words. ... 6) That things difficult to be translated ... were better interpreted. ... 7) A full catalogue of exotic words. ... 8) Particular dialects, idiomes, and proverbs in use in every several county of England. ... 9) A collection of ye most quaint and courtly expressions. ... 10) The reduction of some of the old layd-aside words and expressions. ... We have hardly any words that do so fully expresse the French *clinquant, naïveté, ennuy, bizarre, concert, façonière, chicaneries, consummé, èmotion, defer, effort, chocq, entours, débouche*, or the Italian *vaghezze, garbato, svelto*. Let us therefore ... make as many of these do homage as are like to prove good citizens.

Evelyn to Sir P. Wyche (Pres. Royal Society), 20.6.

🥨 1666 r. Charles II (Fire of London) 🥨

ARCHITECTURE

(Commission for repairing or rebuilding of the decayed steeple of old St. Paul's. Wren) had a mind to built it with a noble cupola, a form of church-building not as yet known in England, but of wonderful grace.

Evelyn, *Diary*, 27.8.

It will be as easy to perform (St. Paul's) after a good *Roman* manner, as to follow the *Gothick* Rudeness of the old Design. ... A Rotundo bearing a Cupola, and then ending in a Lantern: and this with incomparable more Grace in the remoter aspect, than it is possible for the lean Shaft of a steeple to afford. . . .

Chr. Wren, *Survey* (before the Fire), (*Parentalia*, published 1750).

GARDENS

Discoursing of the present fashion of gardens to make them plain, that we have the best walks of gravell in the world, France having none, nor Italy; and our green of our bowling allies is better than any they have. So our business here being ayre, this is the best way, only with a little mixture of statues or pots, which may be handsome, and so filled with another pot of such or such a flower or greene as the season of the year will bear. And then for flowers, they are best seen in a little plat by themselves; besides their borders spoil the walks of another garden; and then for fruit, the best way is to have walls built circularly one within another, to the South on purpose for fruit, and leave the walking garden only for that.

Pepys, 22.7.

MANNERS AND TASTES

(Windsor:—) The most romantique castle that is in the world.

26.2.

A romantique case (that of a crew who asked leave to revenge the death of their captain, Sir Christopher Ming).

Pepys, 13.6.

Académie des Sciences founded by Colbert.

This day the King begins to put on his vest . . . being a long cassocke close to the body, of black cloth, and pinked with white silk under it and a coat over it, and the legs ruffled with black ribband like a pigeon's leg . . . a very fine and handsome garment. . . . The King of France hath, in defiance to the King of England, caused all his footmen to be put into vests.

Pepys, 22.11.

POETRY

Reading 'Othello, Moore of Venice (Shakespeare), which I ever heretofore esteemed a mighty good play, but having so lately read *The Adventures of Five Houres* (from Calderon by S. Tuke) it seems a mean thing.

Pepys, 20.8.

STAGE

Plays seen by Pepys:—
(The first play I have seen since before the great plague) *Love in a Tub* (or *The Comical Revenge* by Sir J. Etherege). *The Mayd's Tragedy* (B. & F.), a good play. *The English Mounsieur* (J. Howard), *The Scornfull Lady* (B. & F.). *Macbeth* (Shakespeare), a most excellent play for variety. *Henry the Fifth* (Roger Boyle, Lord Orrery) [these two seen the same day].

🎔 1667 r. Charles II 🎔

MANNERS AND TASTES

On what new happy Climate are we thrown!

.   .   .   .   .

Methinks we walk in Dreams on Fairy Land,
Where golden Ore lies mixt with common Sand,
Each downfal of a Flood the Mountains pour
From their rich Bowels, rolls a Silver Show'r.
Dryden, *The Indian Emperor or Conquest of Mexico*.

73

By the rich scent we found our perfum'd Prey

.   .   .   .   .

Some preciously by shatter'd Porc'lain fall,
And some by Aromatick Splinters die;

.   .   .   .

The Ghosts of Traitors from the *Bridge* descend,
With bold Fanatick Spectres to rejoice:
About the fire into a Dance they bend,
And sing their Sabbath Notes with feeble voice
> Dryden, *Annus Mirabilis* (cf. 1779,
> Johnson).

I find her painted which makes me loathe her.
> Pepys, 16.9 (see 1654, Evelyn).

MUSIC

T. Killigrew . . . hath gone several times, eight or ten times,
he tells me, hence to Rome to hear good musique; . . . That
he hath even endeavoured in the late King's time, and in this,
to introduce good musique, but he never could do it, there
never having been any musique here better than ballads.
Nay, says "Hermit poore" and "Chevy Chase" [Ferrabosco,
Ayres 1609] was all the musique we had; and yet no ordinary
fiddlers get so much money as ours do here, which speaks our
rudenesse still. That he hath gathered out Italians from several
Courts in Christendome, to come to make a concert for the
King, which he do give £200 a year a piece to; but badly paid.
> Pepys, 12.2.

Singing with many voices is not singing, but a sort of instrumental musique, the sense of the words being lost by not being
heard, and especially as they set them with Fuges of words,
one after another, whereas singing properly, I think, should
be with but one or two voices at most and the counterpoint.
> Pepys, 15.9.

NATURE

High objects, it is true, attract the sight; but it looks up with
pain on craggy rocks and barren mountains, and continues
not long on any object, which is wanting in shades of green
to entertain it.
> Dryden, Dedication to *The Indian Emperor.*

PAINTING

Lely painted Lady Diana Russell (framed) for £29-10-0 and Robert Russell for £25.

A great many pictures, and not one good one in the house (Audley End) but one of Henry the Eighth done by Holben.
Pepys, 8.10.

POETRY

> Old *Chaucer*, like the morning Star,
> To us discovers day from far.
>
>   .   .   .   .   .
>
> Next (like *Aurora*) *Spenser* rose,
> Whose purple blush the day foreshows;
>
>   .   .   .   .   .
>
> By *Shakespeare's*, *Johnson's*, *Fletcher's* lines
> Our Stage's lustre Rome's outshines.
>
>   .   .   .   .   .
>
> Time, which made them their Fame outlive.
> To *Cowley* scarce did ripeness give.
> Old Mother-Wit and Nature gave,
> *Shakespeare* and *Fletcher* all they have;
> In *Spenser* and in *Johnson*, Art
> Of slower Nature got the start;
> But both in him so equal are
> None knows which bears the happy'st share.
>
> Sir J. Denham on *Mr. A. Cowley*.

As those who, in a logical dispute, keep in general terms, would hide a fallacy; so those who do it in any poetical description, would veil ignorance. . . .
'Tis not the jerk or sting of an epigram, nor the seeming contradiction of a poor antithesis (the delight of an ill judging audience in a play of rhyme) . . . neither the morality of a grave sentence . . . but some lively and apt description dressed in such colours of speech that sets before your eyes the absent object as perfectly and more delightfully than nature. . . .
So then the first happiness of the poet's imagination is properly invention, or finding of the thought; the second is fancy, or the variation, deriving, or moulding, of that thought, as the

75

judgement represents it proper to the subject; the third is elocution, or the art of clothing and adorning that thought so found and varied in apt, significant and sounding words. . . . For the two first of these, Ovid is famous among the poets; for the latter Virgil.
(Foreshadows Coleridge's distinction).

Dryden, *Annus Mirabilis*, Preface.

Read a piece of a play, *Every Man in his Humour* (B. Jonson), wherein is the greatest propriety of speech that ever I read in my life.

9.2.

Dr. Clarke did say that Sir W. Davenant is no good judge of a dramatick poem, finding fault with his choice of Henry V [Lord Orrery?] and others for the stage, when I do think, and he confesses, the *Siege of Rhodes* (Davenant) as good as ever was writ.

Pepys, 13.2.

Paradise Lost published. Sold for £5 down and £15 promised. 1300 sold in 20 months. Three editions (say 4500) by 1688 (see 1711 and 1763).

PROSE

The first masters of knowledge ... were as well Poets as Philosophers; for Orpheus, Linus, Musaeus and Homer, first softened man's natural rudeness, and by the charms of their Numbers, allur'd them to be instructed by the severe doctrines of Solon, Thales and Pythagoras. This was a course that was useful at first, when men were to be delightfully deceiv'd to their own good. But perhaps it left some ill influence on the whole Philosophy of their Successors; and gave the Grecians occasion ever after of exercising their wit, and their imagination, about the works of Nature, more than was consistent with a sincere Inquiry into them. . . .
When the fabulous Age was past, Philosophy took a little more courage; and ventured more to relye upon its own strength, without the Assistance of Poets. . . . (English) has been hitherto a little too carelessly handled, and, I think, has had less labour spent about its polishing than it deserves. . . . Who can behold,

76

without Indignation how many mists and uncertainties these specious Tropes and Figures have brought on our knowledge? ... To reject all amplifications, digressions and swellings of style; to return back to the primitive purity, and shortness, when men deliver'd so many things, almost in an equal number of words. ... A close, naked, natural way of speaking, positive expressions, clear senses; a native easiness; bringing all things as near the Mathematical plainness, as they can: and prefering the language of Artizans, Countrymen, and Merchants before that, of Wits or Scholars. ... From the time in which the Real Philosophy has appear'd ... every man is unshaken at those Tales at which his Ancestors trembled. The course of things goes quietly along, in its own true channel of Natural Causes and Effects. ... These two subjects, God and the Soul, being forborne, in all the rest they (the Fellows of the Royal Society) wander at their pleasure.

> T. Sprat, Bishop of Rochester, *History of the Royal Society* (cf. 1666, 1675 and J. B. Rousseau, 1715).

STAGE

Plays seen by Pepys:—

The Custom of the Country (B. & F.), of all the plays that ever I did see, the worst—having neither plot, language nor anything in the earth that is acceptable. *Mustapha* (R. Boyle, Lord Orrery), a most excellent play for words and design ever I did see. *The Humerous Lieutenant* (Fletcher), a silly play. *The Goblins* (Suckling). *Heraclius* (from Corneille by Carlell), an excellent play. *The Chances* (B. & F.), a good play. *The Mayd's Tragedy* (B. & F.). *The Mayden Queen*, a new play of Dryden's' mightily commended for the regularity of it and the strain and wit. *The English Princess or Richard III* (J. Caryl), a most sad, melancholy play, and pretty good, but nothing eminent in it, as some tragedys are. *The Mayden Queen* (Dryden), again, which indeed the more I see the more I like, and is an excellent play. The silly play of my Lady Newcastle's (really by W. Cavendish, Duke of N.) called *The Humourous Lovers*, the most silly thing that ever came upon a stage. I was sick to see it. *The Surprisall* (Sir R. Howard), wherein was no great matter I thought. *The Taming of a Shrew* (or *Sawney the Scott*, adapted from Shakespeare by Lacy), which hath some very good pieces in it, but generally is but a mean play. *The Custome of the Country* (B. & F.), an ill play. *Love Trickes* (J. Shirley), a silly play which I do find but little in. *Brenoralt* (Sir J. Suckling), which I do find but little in. *The Committee* (Sir R. Howard), not liking it before, I do now find it a very good play. *The Country Captain* (W. Cavendish, D. of N.), a very ordinary play. Methinks I had no pleasure in it at all. *The Merry Wives of Windsor* (Shakespeare), which did not please me at all, in no part of it. *The Feign'd Innocence or Sir Martin Mar-all*, a play made by my Lord Duke of Newcastle (W. Cavendish), but as everybody says, corrected by Dryden. It is the most entire piece of mirth, a complete farce, from one end to the other that certainly was ever writ. I never laughed so in all my life and at very good wit therein; not fooling. *Queen Elizabeth's Troubles and the History of 88* (=*If you know not me you know nobody*, by T. Heywood 1605), the most ridiculous that sure ever came upon the stage; and indeed is merely a show . . . a puppet play acted by living puppets. Neither the design nor the language better. *Sir Martin Mar-all* again . . . the most comical play that ever I saw in my life. *Sir Martin Mar-all* again . . . and still find it a very ingenious play and full of variety. *The Indian Emperour* (Dryden), pretty good. *The Mayden Queen* (Dryden), which pleases me mightily. *The Cardinal* (J. Shirley), wherewith I am mighty pleased. *The Surprizall* (Sir R. Howard), a very mean play. *Mustapha* (Roger Boyle), which the more I see the more I like; and is a most admirable poem. *Heraclius* (from Corneille by Carlell), which is a good play. *Ungrateful Lovers* (=*Unfortunate Lovers* by Davenant). *Tu Quoque* (John Cooke), a very silly play . . . but it will please the citizens. *The Northerne Castle* (Anon.), a mean sorry play . . . It seems it hath not been acted a good while. *The Scornfull Lady* (B. & F.). *The Mad Couple* (=*All Mistaken* by J. Howard), a pretty pleasant play. *The Storme*, a play of Fletchers (adapted from Shakespeare's *Tempest*), which is but so-so, methinks; only there is a most admirable dance at the end, of the ladies, in a military manner, which did please me mightily. *Sir Martin Mar-all* (D. of Newcastle) (again). *The Change of Crownes*, a play of Ned Howard's, the best that ever I saw at that house, being a great play and serious [forbidden by King as satirising court]. *The Silent Woman* (B. Jonson), I never was more taken with a play than I am with this, as old as it is, and as

78

often as I have seen it. There is more wit in it than goes to ten new plays. *Rollo* (J. Fletcher), a play I like not much. *Macbeth*, alter'd by Sir William Davenant; being drest in all it's finery, as new cloathes, new scenes, machines as flyings for the Witches; with all the singing and dancing in it; . . . it being . . . in the nature of an opera, it recompenc'd double the expence; it proves still a lasting play, which though I have seen it often, yet it is one of the best plays for a stage, and variety of dancing and musique that ever I saw. *The Wits* (Davenant), a play I formerly loved, and is now corrected and enlarged: . . . yet I like not much in the play now. *Love in a Maze* (= *The Changes*, Shirley), a sorry play. *The Goblins* (Suckling). *The Mayden Queen* (Dryden), which though I have often seen yet pleases me, infinitely . . . the Queen's part is very good and passionate, and Florimel's part the most comicall that ever was made. *The Traytour* (Shirley), which still I like as a very good play. *The Coffee House* (T. St. Serfe). *Flora's Figary's* (= *Vagaries*, R. Rhodes). *Sir Martin Mar-All* (W. Cavendish, D. of N.). *The Coffee-House*, the most ridiculous insipid play that ever I saw in my life. *Macbeth* (Shakespeare). *Brenoralt* (Sir J. Suckling), a good tragedy that I like well. *The Black Prince* (2), mightily bettered by that long letter being printed, and so delivered to everybody at their going in and some short reference made to it in the heart of the play, which do mighty well; but when all is done, I think it the worst play of my Lord Orrery's. *The Committee* (Sir R. Howard), a play I like well. *Taming of a Shrew* (Shakespeare), a silly play and an old one, *Henry IV* (Shakespeare). *The Tempest* (6 times this month), an old play of Shakespeare's—the most innocent play that ever I saw; and a curious piece of music [by Banister] in an echo of half sentences, the echo repeating the former half, while the man goes on to the latter; which is mighty pretty. The play no great wit, but yet good above ordinary plays. *The Indian Emperour* (Dryden), a good play, but not so good as people cry it up. *Macbeth* (Shakespeare), which we still like mightily. *The Tempest* (Shakespeare), again which is very pleasant, and full of so good variety that I cannot be more pleased almost in a comedy, only the seamen's part a little too tedious. *The Mistaken Beauty* (Corneille, *Le Menteur*), much in it that I like. *The Tempest* which as often as I have seen it I do like very well, and the house very full. *The Surprizall*

(Sir R. Howard). *The Mad Couple* (B. & F.). *Love's Cruelty*
(J. Shirley), a very silly play. *The Mayden Queen* (Dryden),
which the more I see the more I love, and think of as the best
play I ever saw.
(Apparently about 70 visits to the theatre).

🦢 1668 r. Charles II 🦢

ARCHITECTURE

(Salisbury) Minster most admirable; as big I think, and
handsomer than Westminster . . . to Stonage, over the Plain
and some great hills, even to fright us.

Pepys, 11.6.

MANNERS AND TASTES

I confess, I love Littleness almost in all things, a little convenient
Estate, a little Cheerful House, A little Company, and a very
little Feast, and if I were ever to fall in Love again (which is a
great Passion, and therefore I hope I have done with it) it
would be, I think, with Prettiness rather than with Majestical
Beauty.

Cowley, *Of Greatness.*

Spanish tobacco 10/- a pound, Virginia 3/4. (Earl of Bedford
averaged 25 pounds weight purchase a year).

MUSIC

Though they sang fine things, yet I must confess that I did
take no pleasure in it, or very little, because I understood
not the words, and with the rests that the words are set, there
is no sense nor understanding in them though they be English,
which makes me weary of singing in that manner, it being but
a worse sort of instrumental music.

9.2 (cf. 1635 Waller and 1648 Milton).

That which did please me beyond any thing in the whole
world was the wind-musique when the angel comes down
(at the *Virgin Martyr*, Massinger 1622), which is so sweet that
it ravished me, and indeed in a word, did wrap up my soul so

that it made me really sick. Just as I have formerly been
when in love with my wife; that neither then nor all the
evening going home, and at home I was able to think of
anything, but remain all night transported.

27.2 (cf. Dryden, 1669).

Did buy a recorder which I do intend to learn to play on,
the sound of it being, of all sounds in the world, most pleasing
to me [a reed instrument with a hole on the mouth-piece
covered by a piece of bladder].

Pepys, 8.4.

PAINTING

An idea of the Perfection of Painting; demonstrated from the
Principles of Art, and by Examples conformable to the
observations which Pliny and Quintilian have made upon the
most celebrated pieces of the Antient Painters, written in
French by Roland Freart and rendered English by J. E. Esq.

Evelyn

(In historical painting)
>   Ut pictura poesis erit; similisque poesi
>   Sit pictura; refert pars aemula quaeque sororem,
>   Alternatque vices et nomina.

Du Fresnoy, *De Arte Graphica* (posthumous; translated by Dryden, 1695, and
by Mason, 1783).

To Chyrugeons'-hall ... to see ... their great picture of
Holben's [at Barber Surgeons' Hall] ... I did think to give
£200 for it, it being said to be worth £1000; but ... it is not
a pleasant though a good picture.

Pepys, 28.8.

POETRY

Rime being no necessary adjunct or true ornament of poem
or good verse, in longer works, especially, but the invention of a
barbarous age, to set off wretched matter and lame meeter;
grac'd indeed since by the use of some famous modern poets,
carried away by custom, but much to their own vexation,
hindrance, and constraint to express many things otherwise
and for the most part worse than else they would have exprest

them. Not without cause therefore some both Italian and Spanish poets of prime note have rejected rime both in longer and shorter works, as have also long since our best English tragedies, as a thing of itself, to all judicious ears, trivial and of no true musical delight; which consists only in apt numbers, fit quantity of syllables, and the sense variously drawn out from one verse into another, not in the jingling sound of like endings.

Milton, Paradise Lost (Preface 5th issue).

Dryden succeeded Davenant as laureate, confirmed 1670.

Milton, the old blind schoolmaster, has lately written a poem on the Fall of Man remarkable for nothing but its extreme length.

Waller to Duke of Buckingham.

Native tenderness and Innocent gayety of his Mind . . . but nothing of this Nature should be published.

Sprat, Life of Cowley (12 folio editions of Cowley before 1700. Most popular poet of century).

He who writ this not without pains and thought
From *French* and *English* theatres has brought
The' exactest rules, by which a play is wrought.

Dryden, Secret Love, Prologue.

Poets that lasting Marble seek,
Must carve in *Latine* or in *Greek*,
We write in Sand; our language grows,
And, like the Tide, our work o'erflows.

Chaucer his sense can only boast,
The glory of his numbers lost,
Years have defac'd his matchless strain,
And yet he did not sing in vain.

E. Waller, Of English Verse.

Why is not Jeptha's Daughter as *good a woman* as Iphigenia, and the friendship of *David* and *Jonathan* more worthy celebration than that of *Theseus* and *Pirithous*? Does not the passage of *Moses* and the *Israelites* into the *Holy Land* yield incomparably more Poetical variety than the voyages of *Ulysses* or *Aeneas*?

Cowley, *Works*.

The Court is the best and surest judge of writing (Dedication)....
Eug. The last age ... can produce nothing so courtly writ, or which expresses so much the conversation of a gentleman, as Sir John Suckling[1]; nothing so even, sweet, and flowing, as Mr. Waller; nothing so majestic, so correct, as Sir John Denham; nothing so elevated, so copious, and full of spirit as Mr. Cowley ... The sweetness of English Verse was never understood or practised by our fathers. . . .
Lis. A play ought to be a just and lively image of human nature, representing its passions and humours, and the changes of fortune to which it is subject, for the delight and instruction of mankind. . . .
Crit. We have added nothing of our own (to the Greeks) except we have the confidence to say "our wit is better", of which none boast in our age, but such as understand not theirs. . . . The time of the feigned action, or fable of the play, should be proportioned as near as can be to the duration of that time in which it is represented; . . . that the intervals or inequalities of time be supposed to fall out between the acts . . . The stage . . . is never empty all the time; . . . this Corneille calls *la liaison des scènes*. . . . The greatest man of the last age, Ben Johnson, was willing to give place to (the ancients) in all things. . . .
Eug. (Donne) gives us deep thoughts in common language. . . . (Seneca's *Troades*) bears the nearest resemblance of any thing in (ancient) tragedies to the excellent scenes of passion in Shakespeare or in Fletcher. . . .
Lis. Corneille and some other Frenchman, reformed their theatre, which before was as much below ours as it now surpasses it . . . in the Unity of Time and . . . the Unity of Place; . . . the Unity of Action in all (French) plays is yet more conspicuous, for they do not burden them with underplots. . . . There is no theatre in the world that has any thing so absurd as the English tragi-comedy. . . . (French plays) are always grounded in some known history. . . . The French avoid the tumult which we are subject to in England by representing

[1] Cf. 1640. Walton.

duels, battles and the like; . . . I have observed that in all our tragedies, the audience cannot forbear laughing when its actors are to die; . . . you never see any (French) play end with a conversion or simple change of will. . . .

Nean. He that will look upon (French plays) which have been written till these last ten years or thereabouts, will find it a hard matter to pick out two or three passable humours amongst them. . . . But of late years Moliere, the younger (T.) Corneille, Quinault and, some others, have been imitating afar off the quick turns and fences of the English stage. They have mixed their serious plays with mirth. . . . By their servile observations of the Unities . . . (the French) have brought on themselves . . . narrowness of imagination. . . . Shakespeare was the man who of all modern, and perhaps of ancient poets, had the largest and most comprehensive soul. All the images of Nature were still present to him, and he drew them, not laboriously but luckily; when he describes anything you more than see it, you feel it too. Those who accuse him to have wanted learning, give him the greater commendation: he was naturally learned; he needed not the spectacles of books to read Nature; he looked inwards and found her there. I cannot say he is everywhere alike; were he so, I should do him injury to compare him with the greatest of mankind. He is many times flat, insipid; his comic wit degenerates into clenches, his serious swelling into bombast. But he is always great, when some great occasion is presented to him. . . . I must acknowledge (Jonson) the more correct poet, but Shakespeare the greater wit; . . . I admire him but I love Shakespeare. . . . Tò γτλοῖον of the Old Comedy, of which Aristophanes was Chief, was not so much to imitate a man, as to make the people laugh at some odd conceit, which had commonly somewhat of unnatural or obscene in it. . . . Tragedy is wont to image to us the minds and fortunes of noble persons, and to portray these exactly; heroic rhyme is nearest Nature, as being the noblest kind of modern verse. . . . A play to be like Nature, is to be set above it.

Dryden, *Essay of Dramatick Poesy.*

(*Eugenius*=C. Sackville, Lord Buckhurst, Earl of Dorset. *Lisideius*=Sir C. Sedley. *Crites*=Sir R. Howard. *Neander*=Dryden.) ("the noise of the cannon from both navies [in the Thames] reached our ears".)

I rather blame the unnecessary understanding of some that have labour'd to give strict rules to things that are not Mathematical. . . . In the difference of *Tragedy* and *Comedy*, and of *Fars* it self, there can be no determination but by Taste; nor in the manner of their Composure. . . . 'Tis as impossible for one stage to present two Hours or two Roomes truely as two Countreys. Sir Robert Howard, Preface to *The Duke of Lerma*.

Delight is the chief, if not the only, end of Poesy; instruction can be admitted but in the second place, for poesy only instructs as it delights. . . . Prose is not to be used in serious plays because it is too near the nature of converse.
Dryden, *Defence of an Essay of Dramatic Poesy* (A reply to Howard's criticism of it in his preface to the *Duke of Lerma*).

STAGE

They strein Love and Honour to that Ridiculous height that it becomes Burlesque. . . . I never saw one except that of *Falstaffe* . . . comparable to any of Johnson's considered Humours.
T. Shadwell, *The Sullen Lovers*, Preface.

I went to see ye old play of *Cataline* (Ben Jonson) acted, having been now forgotten almost 40 years.
Evelyn, 19.12.

Plays seen by Pepys:—
Sir Martin-all (W. Cavendish, D. of Newcastle), which I have seen so often and yet am mightily pleased with and think it mighty witty, and the fullest of proper matter for mirth that ever was writ . . . pit at 2s. 6d. . . . 12d. and 18d. places. *The Tempest* (Shakespeare). *The Schoole of Compliments* (*Loves Tricks*, J. Shirley) and *Henry IV* (Shakespeare) not liking either of the plays. *Aglaura* (Sir J. Suckling) mightily cried up, but do find nothing extraordinary in it at all, and but hardly good in any degree. *Wild Goose Chase* (B. and F.'s first play), a famous play . . . but very dull inventions and designs. *The Tempest* (Shakespeare), I was pleased again, and shall be again to see it, it is so full of variety. *She Would if she Could* (Etherege) 1000 people turned back that could not have room. How silly the play, there being nothing in the world good in it and but

few people pleased . . . though something very rogueish and witty; but the design of the play and the end mighty insipid. *Love in a Maze* (Shirley), a dull, silly play. *Mustapha* (Lord Orrery). *Flora's Vagaries* (R. Rhodes), a very silly play. *The Duke of Lerma*, of Sir Robert Howard's a well-writ and good play. *Albumazar* (T. Tomkiss 1615). *Jeronimo is Mad Again* (*Spanish Tragedy*, T. Kyd). *The Faythful Shepherd* (from Guarini). *The Virgin Martyr* (Massinger and Dekker) (2) not that the play is worth much. *The Discontented Colonel* (*Brenoralt*, Sir J. Suckling). *The Spanish Gipsys* (T. Middleton & W. Rowley), a very silly play. *The Storme* (Fletcher), a mean play compared with *The Tempest*. *The Man is the Master* (Sir W. Davenant), nothing extraordinary at all. *Indian Emperour* (Dryden), a very good play indeed. *The Black Prince* (Lord Orrery), a very good play. *The Master and the Man*, (Sir W. Davenant). *The English Monsieur* (Hon. J. Howard), much mirth in it. *The Unfortunate Lovers* (Sir W. Davenant), no extraordinary play. *Loves' Cruelty* (J. Shirley). *The Maids' Tragedy* (B. & F.), a good play. *The Surprizall* (Sir R. Howard). *Duke of Lerma* (R. Howard). *The Indian Emperor* (Dryden). *Beggars Bush* (B. and F.). *Sir Martin Mar-All* (W. Cavendish, D. of N.), which the more I see the more I like. *The Cardinall* (Shirley), a good play. *Love in a Maze* (Shirley). *Love in a Tubb* (Etherege). *The Tempest* (Shakespeare or Dryden), which still pleases me mightily. *The Surprizall* (Sir R. Howard). *The Sullen Lovers or Impertinents* (T. Shadwell), having many good humours in it, but the play tedious and no design at all (2) a very contemptable play, though there are many little witty expressions. *The Virgin Martyr* (Massinger and Dekker). *The Man's the Master* (Davenant), a very good play. *The Mayd's Tragedy* (B. and F.), a good play. *The Tempest* (Shakespeare). *The Country Captain* (W. Cavendish, Duke of Newcastle), a very dull play. *The Committee* (Sir R. Howard). *The Sea Voyage* (Fletcher). *The Mulberry Guarden* (Sir C. Sedley), here and there a pretty saying, and that not very much neither, yet the whole of the play had nothing extraordinary in it at all, neither of language nor design. *Sir Martin Mar-all* (W. Cavendish, D. of N.), undoubtedly the best comedy that ever was wrote. *Philaster* (B. and F.). *The Scornfull Lady* (B. & F.). (Mrs. Pepys saw) the new play *Evening's Love* of Dryden's which, though the world commends, she likes not. . . . Very smutty and nothing

so good as *The Maiden Queen* (Dryden), or *The Indian Emperor* (Dryden). *The Impertinents* (T. Shadwell), a pretty good play. *The Indian Queen* (Dryden). *The Mulberry Garden* (Sir C. Sedley). *Henry V* (Shakespeare or R. Boyle). *Hide Parke* (Shirley). *The Slighted Maid* (Stapylton), a mean play. *The Mad Couple* (J. Howard), a mean play altogether. *Monsieur Ragou* (or the *Old Troop* by Lacy), a farce. *The Guardian* (Cowley), formerly called *The Cutter of Coleman Street*, a silly play. *Macbeth* (Shakespeare), to our great content. *Love's Mistresse* (T. Heywood), pretty good. *Cupid's Revenge* (*Love Despised*, B. and F.), something very good in it though I like not the whole body. *The Impertinents* (T. Shadwell). *Marry Andry*, a ridiculous, obscene little play. *Hamlet* (Shakespeare), which we have not seen this year before, or more; and mightily pleased with it. *Polichinelle*. *Bartholomew Fayre* (B. Jonson), an excellent play, the more I see it, the more I love the wit of it. *The Maid in the Mill* (B. and F.), a pretty, harmless old play. *The Ladys à la Mode* (Flecknoe?), a mean thing. *Rollo, Duke of Normandy* (J. Fletcher), which for old acquaintance, pleased me pretty well. *Henry the Fourth* (Shakespeare or Hayward). *The Silent Woman* (B. Jonson), the best comedy, I think, that ever was wrote; and sitting by Shadwell, the poet, he was big with admiration of it. *Puppet-show of Whittington*, pretty to see, and how that idle thing do work upon people that see it, and even myself too! *The City Match* (J. Maine), but a silly play. *The Faythful Shepherdess* (J. Fletcher). *The Queene of Arragon* (W. Habington), an admirable one. *The Duchesse of Malfy* (Webster), a sorry play. *The Usurper* (E. Howard), a pretty good play in all but what is designed to represent Cromwell . . . which is mighty silly. *The Unfortunate Lovers* (Davenant), a mean play, I think, but some parts very good. *Tryphon* (R. Boyle, Lord Orrery), admirable, yet . . . just the very same design, and words, and plot as every one of his plays have. *Catiline's Conspiracy* (B. Johnson), a play of much good sense and words to read, but that do appear the worst upon the stage, I mean the least diverting, that ever I saw any. *Macbeth* (Shakespeare). *Women Pleased* (Fletcher), indifferent, yet there is a good design for a good play. *King Harry th' Eighth* (Shakespeare), mightily pleased, better than ever I expected, with the history and shows.
(Apparently about 80 visits to the theatre).

🥀 1669 r. Charles II 🥀

ARCHITECTURE

Gothic an unstable Construction . . . (Salisbury Cathedral), one of the best patterns of Architecture of the age wherein it was built. . . . The Breadth to the Height of the *Navis*, and both to the shape of the Ailes bear a good Proportion. The Pillars and the Intercolumniations are well suited to the Height of the Arches, the Mouldings are decently mixed with large Planes without an affectation of filling every Corner with Ornaments, which, unless they are admirably good, glut the Eye as much as, in Musik, too much Division the Ears. The Windows are not made too great, nor yet the Light obstructed with many Mullions and Transomes of Tracery-work; which was the ill Fashion of the next following Age: our artist knew better, that nothing could add Beauty to Light, he trusted to a stately and rich Plainness, that his Marble Shafts gave to his work.

> Chr. Wren, *Survey* (*Parentalia*, published 1750).

NATURE

Nothing in the world so magnificent (as Chamonix).

> René le Pays (cf. 1789).

POETRY

When smiling, to the Ax she bow'd her Head
.   .   .   .
Aetherial Musick did her Death prepare,
Like joyful sounds of Spousals in the Air.
A radiant Light did her crown'd Temples gild
And all the Place with Scents was fill'd.
The balmy Mist came thickning to the Ground
And sacred Silence cover'd all around
But when (its Work perform'd) the Cloud withdrew,
     . . . . from afar our Sight
Discover'd in the Air long Tracks of Light;
Of Charming Notes we hear the last Rebounds
And Musick dying in remoter Sounds.

> Dryden, *The Royal Martyr* or *Tyrannic Love* (cf. Pepys, 1668).

The treatise (*De Sublimitate*) is in everybody's hands, especially since it has been translated into French by Boileau.

> Le Clerc, *Parrhasiana* (Translated to English 1700).

(Ben Johnson was) the best judge of, and fittest to prescribe rules to Poetry and Poets, of any man who had lived with, or before him, or since; if Mr. Cowley had not made a flight beyond all men.   Lord Clarendon, *Life* (published 1759).

STAGE

Plays seen by Pepys:—

The Mayden Queen (Dryden). *The Island Princess* (B. & F.), a pretty good play, many good things being in it. *The Jovial Crew* (R. Brome). *The Maiden Queen* (Dryden). *Macbeth* (Shakespeare). *The Witts* (W. Davenant), a medley of things but some similes mighty good, though ill mixed, *Horace* (P. Corneille transl. Kath. Philips), a silly tragedy. *Twelfth Night* (Shakespeare), as it is now revived, I think one of the weakest plays that ever I saw on the stage. *The Tempest* (Shakespeare). *The Five Hours Adventure* (from Calderon by S. Tuke), a most excellent play. *The Heyresse* (Anon.). *She Would if she Could* (Etherege). *The Moor of Venice* (Shakespeare). *The Island Princesse* (J. Fletcher), which I like mighty well, as an excellent play. *The Five Hours Adventure* (from Calderon by S. Tuke). *The Mad Lover* (B. & F.). *The Gratefull Servant* (J. Shirley), a pretty good play. *Bartholomew Fayre* (B. Jonson). *The Royal Shepherdesse* (J. Fountain, vamped by Shadwell), the silliest for words and design and everything that ever I saw in my whole life. *The Lady's Tryall* (J. Ford), but a sorry play. *The Mocke Astrologer* (*An Evening's Love*, Dryden), an ordinary play. *Claricilla* (T. Killigrew), which do not please me almost at all, though there are some good things in it. *The Coxcombe* (B. and F.), the first time acted, but an old play and a silly one. *The Impertinents* (T. Shadwell), a play which pleases me well still. *Guzman* (R. Boyle, Lord Orrery), very ordinary. *The Alchemist* (B. Jonson), still a good play. *The Generous Portugalls* (*Island Princess*, Fletcher), a play that pleases me better and better every time. *The General* (R. Boyle, Lord Orrery), a good play, that pleases me well. *The Roman Virgin* (Betterton's adaptation of Webster's *Appius and Virginia*) but ordinary. *The Spanish Curate* (B. and F.), a pretty good play.

❧ 1670 r. Charles II ❧

GARDENS

Herbs . . . fit to set knots with . . . Dutch or French box.

> Meager, *English Gardner* (11 editions by 1710).

MANNERS AND TASTES

Those that anciently danced the hobby-horse in country mumming.

> Lassels, *Voyage of Italy* (died. 1668).

Whether it be unavoidably necessary to keep lads to 16 or 17 years of age in pure slavery to a few Latin or Greek words? . . . As suppose some part of time was allotted them, for the reading of some innocent English authors! When they need not go, every line, so unwillingly to a tormenting dictionary.

> J. Eachard, *Grounds of Contempt of the Clergy.*

(About this date an apparition appeared at Cirencester, which, on being challenged, vanished with a strange perfume and a most melodious twang).

> Aubrey, *Miscellanies* (1696).

POETRY

Laureateship confirmed to Dryden and officially regularised.

STAGE

Dryden's and Davenant's adaptation of Shakespeare's *Tempest* (Davenant d. 1668).

❧ 1671 r. Charles II ❧

MANNERS AND TASTES

(About this date Sir Christopher Wren, being ill in Paris, dreamed of palm trees and a woman who gave him dates. On eating some dates, which he procured, he was relieved).

> Aubrey. *Miscellanies* (1696).

PAINTING

I. Lanskip is that which appeareth in lines the *perfect* vision of the earth, and all things thereupon, placed above the Horizon, as Towns, Villages, Castles, Promontories, Mountains, Rocks, Valleys, Ruins, Woods, Forests, Chases, Trees, Houses, and all other Buildings, both beautiful and ruinous.

VII. Make your Landskip to shoot (as it were) away, one part lower than another, that the Landskip may appear to be taken from the top of an hill.

VIII. Let everything have its proper motion, as in *Trees*, when they are shaken by the wind, making the smaller boughs yielding; the stiffer less bending: in *Clouds* that they follow the Winds: in Rivers the general current.

XII. Lastly let every site have its proper *parerga*, adjuncts or additional graces, as the Farmhouse, Wind-mill, Water-mill, Woods, Flocks of Sheep, Herds of Cattle, Pilgrims, Ruines of Temples, Castles and Monuments; with a thousand such other only proper to particular subjects.

> W. Salmon (?), *Polygraphice; or, the Arts of Drawing, etc.* (Eight editions before 1701).

POETRY

Sur le Je ne Scais Quoi, Bouhours (A phrase invented by Mdlle de Gournay, 1590).

I must take leave to Dissent from those who seem to insinuate that the ultimate end of a Poet is to delight without correction or instruction.

> T. Shadwell, Preface to *The Humourists*.

Mr. Cowley (who had a greater portion of it than any man I know) tells us in his *Character of Wit* (1656), rather than all wit, let there be none. I think there is no folly so great in any poet of our age, as the superfluity and waste of wit was in some of our predecessors; particularly we may say of Fletcher and Shakespeare what was said of Ovid:—*facilius quod rejici, quam quod adjici potest, invenies.* The contrary of which was

D*

true in Virgil, and our incomparable Johnson. . . . Comedy is not so much obliged to the punishment of faults which it represents, as Tragedy.

> Dryden, Preface to *An Evening's Love, or, The Mock Astrologer.*

Bayes (=Dryden). Ever make similes when you are surprised; 'tis the new way of writing.

> G. Villiers Duke of Buckingham, *The Rehearsal.*

By raising pity and fear or terror, to purge the mind of those and such like passions, that is to temper and reduce them to just measure with a kind of delight, stirr'd up by reading or seeing those passions well imitated.

> Milton, *Preface to Samson Agonistes.*

Sion's songs, to all true tasts excelling.

> Milton, *Paradise Regained* (early æsthetic 'taste').

✿ 1672 r. Charles II ✿

ARCHITECTURE

Gothic church built at Welland.

MANNERS AND TASTES

> Obeyed as sovereign by thy subjects be,
> But know that I alone am king of me.
> I am as free as nature first made man,
> Ere the base laws of servitude began
> When wild in woods the noble savage ran.
>
> Dryden, *Conquest of Granada*, I, i.1

POETRY

Very few tragedies in this age shall be received without (Heroic Verse). . . . Mr. Cowley's authority is almost sacred to me.

> Dryden, *Of Heroic Plays.*

The language, wit, and conversation of our age are improved and refined above the last. . . . Let any man, who understands English, read diligently the works of Shakespeare and Fletcher, and I dare undertake that he will find in every page either some solecism of speech, or some notorious flaw of sense. . . . Well-placing of words, for the sweetness of pronunciation was not known till Mr. Waller introduced it . . . Ben Johnson has many such lines as . . .

"brought up in 's sister's prostitution"

Shakespeare, who many times has written better than any poet in any language, . . . writes, in many places, below the dullest writer of ours or any precedent age. For Ben Johnson, the most judicious of poets, he always writ properly, and as the character required.

Dryden, *On the Dramatic Poetry of the Last Age.*

🏵 1673 r. Charles II 🏵

MANNERS AND TASTES

These Coaches and Caravans are one of the greatest mischiefs that hath hapened of later years to the Kingdom. . . . They have left off keeping of Horses, and travel without Servants. And York, Chester and Exeter Stage Coaches, each of them with forty Horses a piece, carry eighteen passengers a week from London to either of these places.

The Grand Concern of England.

She does want a gown indeed! She is in her "Dishabiliee" . . . a great mode in England.

Wycherley, *The Dancing-Master.*

Evelyn visited Sir T. Browne.

POETRY

So Poetry, which is in Oxford made,
An Art, in London onely is a Trade.

. . . . .

Kings make their Poets whom themselves think fit,
But 'tis your suffrage makes Authentique wit.

> Dryden, *Prologue to Silent Woman* (at Oxford).

I can fear nothing but the gods,
And, for this glory, often I have seen
The canopy of state spread wide above
In the abyss of heaven, the court of stars,
The blushing morning and the rising sun,
What greater can I see?

> Dryden, *Marriage à la Mode.*

You are one of those that applaud our country plays, where drums, and trumpets, and blood, and wounds, are wit. . . . You are an admirer of the dull French poetry, which is so thin that it is the very leaf-gold of wit, the very wafers and whip't cream of sense, for which a man opens his mouth and gapes, to swallow nothing.

> Dryden, *Marriage à la Mode.*

1674 r. Charles II

ANTIQUARIANISM

Carrey sketched Parthenon.

Wood's *History of Antiquities of Oxford* translated into Latin.

ARCHITECTURE

Gothic Church built at Hanley.

University College, Oxford, east quadrangle finished.

Reason must never bend to fancy. (Tortuous old streets compared with modern town-planning). Malebranche, *Recherche de la Vérité.*

94

MUSIC

I saw an Italian opera in musiq, the first that had been in England of this kind.

Evelyn, 5.1.

POETRY

O Goddess, sing what woe the discontent
   Of Thetis' son brought to the Greeks, what souls
Of heroes down to Erebus it sent,
   Leaving their bodies unto dogs and fowls.

Hobbes, *Odyssey* (cf. 1611, 1614, 1720, 1726 and 1791).

The *language* (of Poetry) must be *clear*, that it may be intelligible, for one of the greatest faults in discourse is *obscurity*; and the thoughts of Dante are so *profound* that much art is requir'd to dive into them . . . (Rapin blames French ladies for the intrusion of love interest in French tragedy and) confesses that we have a *Genius* for Tragedy above all other people. . . . *Chaucer* in whose time our language, I presume, was not capable of any Heroick character. . . . Spenser, I think, may be reckon'd the first of our Heroick Poets; he had a large spirit, a sharp judgment, and a Genius for *Heroic Poesie*, perhaps above any that ever writ since Virgil. But . . . all is fanciful and chimerical, without any uniformity, without any foundation in truth; his Poem is perfect *Fairy-land*. . . . A Poet is oblig'd to know all Arts and Sciences . . . some Poets dote on the very terms and jargon.

Rymer, Preface to Rapin, *Reflection sur la Poétique d'Aristote.*

Quelque sujet qu'on traite, ou plaisant, ou sublime,
Que toujours le bon sens s'accorde avec la rime.

. . . . .

Aimez donc la raison: que toujours vos écrits
Empruntent d'elle seule et leur lustre et leur prix.

. . . . .

Qui ne sait se borner ne sut jamais écrire.

. . . . .

Voulez-vous du public mériter les amours?
Sans cesse en écrivant variez vos discours.

. . . . .

Heureux qui, dans ses vers, sait d'une voix legère
Passer du grave au doux, du plaisant au sevère!

. . . .

Quoi que vous écriviez, évitez la bassesse:
Le style le moins noble a pourtant sa noblesse.

. . . .

Que toujours dans vos vers le sens coupant les mots
Suspende l'hémistiche, en marque le repos.

. . . .

Enfin Malherbe vint, et, le premier en France,
Fit sentir dans les vers une juste cadence,
D'un mot mis en sa place enseigna le pouvoir,
Et réduisit la muse aux règles du devoir.

. . . .

J'aime mieux un ruisseau qui, sur la molle arène,
Dans un pré plein de fleurs lentement se promène,
Q'un torrent débordé.

. . . .

      Cet autre, abject en son langage
Fait parler ses bergers comme on parle au village.

. . . .

Il n'est point de serpent, ni de monstre odieux,
Qui, par l'art imité, ne puisse plaire aux yeux.

. . . .

Qu'en un lieu, qu'en un jour, un seul fait accompli
Tienne jusqu'à la fin le théâtre rempli.

. . . .

Bientôt ils défendront de peindre la Prudence,
De donner à Thémis ni bandeau ni balance,
Et partout des discours, comme une idolâtrie,
Dans leur faux zèle iront chasser l'allégorie.

. . . .

Quelquefois dans sa course un esprit vigoureux
Trop resserré par l'art sort des règles prescrites
Et de l'art même apprend à franchir leurs limites.

. . . .

Partout joigne au plaisant le solide et l'utile.

Boileau, *L'Art Poétique, Traité du Sublime de Longin.* (Several translations to English, one by Pulteney, 1680).

STAGE

Davenant's adaptation of Shakespeare's *Macbeth* as opera. (D. died 1668).

STYLE

To shun the Latinisms of immensity, eternity, penetrability, etc., useth these, all-placeness, all-timeness, thorowfareness, etc.

> J. Glanvill, *Essay Concerning Preaching* (1678), quoting N. Fairfax, *A Treatise of the Bulk and Selvedge of the World.*

1675 r. Charles II

ARCHITECTURE

The *Roman* Stile (of Sir C. Wren's design for St. Paul's) was not so well understood and relish'd by others, who thought it deviated too much from the old *Gothick* Form of cathedral Churches, which they had been used to see and admire in this country.

> Chr. Wren, (jnr.), *Parentalia.*

POETRY

I. Ce serait une injustice de prétendre que les Règles nouvelles détruisent celles de nos premiers maîtres.

II. Notre manière de parler est simple, propre, et sans détour, et celle des Anciens était pleine de mystères et d'allégories. 3. L'Epopée est un discours inventé avec art pour former les moeurs par des instructions déguisés sous les allégories d'une action importante qui est racontée en vers d'une manière vraisemblable divertissante et merveilleuse. 5. Le fin de la Poesie est de plaire. . . . Les véritables poëmes sont L'Epopée, la Tragédie et la Comédie, parce qu'elles sont toutes allégoriques et fabuleuses.

(III. 7. Seneca blames Virgil for shutting winds in a cave; contrary to their nature. Vossius replies that it is a true account of their physical genesis. Virgil excusable for putting stags in Africa. Scaliger blames Homer for saying Jupiter thundered and snowed at once; but quite lately a church spire of Chalons struck by lightning in snow-storm. IV. 1. Character caused by God, stars, birthplace).

Le Bossu, Poème Epique.

The first Indiscretion is, The use of such words as to the Readers of Poesie (which are commonly Persons of the best Quality) are not sufficiently known. Forein words, till by long use they become vulgar, are unintelligible to them. Also the names of Instruments and Tools of Artificers, and works of Art, though of use in the Schools, are far from being fit to be spoken of by a Heroe.

Hobbes, Vertues of an Heroique Poem.

Let us look back as far as about 30 or 40 years, and we shall find a profound silence of the Poets beyond that time except of some few Dramatics. . .

Spenser's Stanza . . . is above the way either of Couplet or Alternation of four verses . . . The Dissylable . . . is in our language very applicable to Rime, and hath been very much used formerly, I was going to say with as much grace sometimes, if not more, than the Monosylable, but that I am loath to appear too singularly addicted to that which is now so utterly exploded.

History painting is the highest perfection in the Art of Picture . . . *Linsie-woolsie* intermixture of *Comic* mirth with Tragic seriousness. . . . Wit, Ingenuity and Learning in Verse, even Elegance itself, though that comes nearest, are one thing, true Native *Poetry* is another; in which there is a certain Air and Spirit which perhaps the most learned and judicious in other Arts do not perfectly apprehend, much less is it attainable by any Study or Industry; nay, though all the Laws of *Heroic Poem;* all the Laws of *Tragedy* were exactly observed, yet still this *tour entrejéant*, this Poetic *Energie*, if I may so call it, would be required to give life to all the rest. . . . Spenser, with all his Rustic, obsolete words, with all his rough-hewn clouterly Verses, yet take him throughout, and we shall find in him a gracefull and Poetic Majesty: in like manner Shakespeare, in spight of all his unfiled expressions, his rambling and indigested Fancies, the laughter of the *Critical,* yet must be confesst a *Poet*, above many that go beyond him in Literature some degrees.

Edward Phillips, Preface to Theatrum
Poetarum Anglicanorum.

PART II
1676—1714

❧ 1676 r. Charles II ❧

PAINTING

The Earl of Bedford bought "a landscape of Plymouth and the citadel there and parts adjacent" for £10.

Lely painted Earl of Bedford for £60 (see 1682 and 1694).

POETRY

> Our Author by experience finds it true,
> 'Tis much more hard to please himself than you,
>   .   .   .   .
> And, to confess a Truth (though out of Time)
> Grows weary of his long-loved Mistris Rhyme,
> Passion's too fierce to be in Fetters bound,
> And Nature flies him like Enchanted Ground.
> What Verse can do, he has perform'd in this,
> Which he presumes the most correct of his.
>   .   .   .   .
> But spite of all his pride, a secret Shame
> Intrudes his Breast at Shakespeare's sacred name.
> > Dryden, Prologue to *Aurungzebe.*

> Oxford to him a dearer Name shall be,
> Than his own Mother University.
> *Thebes* did his green, unknowing youth ingage,
> He chuses *Athens* in his riper Age.
> > Dryden, *Prologue* (3) *to University of Oxford.*

❧ 1677 r. Charles II ❧

MANNERS AND TASTES

> In a melancholy fancy
>   Out of myself,
> In the vulcan dancy,
> All the world surveying,
> Nowhere staying,
>   Just like a fairy elf;

Out o'er the tops of highest mountains skipping,
Out o'er the hills, the trees and valleys tripping,
Out o'er the ocean seas, without an oar or shipping.
Hallo my fancy, whither wilt thou go?

W. Cleland, *Hallo my Fancy!*

POETRY

"*The State of Innocence* an opera in Heroique Verse" (adapted from *Paradise Lost* with leave of Milton by Dryden).

They wholly mistake the nature of criticism who think its business is principally to find fault. . . . Longinus, who was undoubtedly, after Aristotle, the greatest critic among the Greeks. . . . Heroic Poetry . . . has ever been esteemed, and ever will be, the greatest work of human nature. The greatest (critics) of this age, Boileau and Rapin; the latter of which is alone sufficient, were all other critics lost, to teach anew the rules of writing. . . .
The Plain Dealer (Wycherley) . . . a most useful satire. . . . Are all the flights of Heroic Poetry to be concluded bombast, unnatural and mere madness, because (men) are not affected with their excellencies? . . . Ought they not rather, in modesty, to doubt of their own judgements, when they think this or that expression in Homer, Virgil, Tasso or Milton's *Paradise* to be too far strained, than positively to conclude that 'tis all fustian and mere nonsense? . . . The boldest strokes of poetry when they are managed artfully are those which most delight the reader. . . . The knowledge of Nature was the original rule; and all poets ought to study her, as well as Aristotle and Horace, her interpreters. But this also undeniably follows, that those things which delight all ages, must have been an imitation of Nature. (Paradise Lost) one of the greatest, most noble and most sublime poems which either this age or nation has produced.

Dryden, *Apology for Heroique Poetry.*

⁘ 1678 r. Charles II ⁘

ARCHITECTURE

The porch leading into (Malmburie abbey) is the most statlie and costlie carved piece of work that my eyes ever beheld,

carrying with it also a verie venerable face of antiquity; . . .
well carved little scripture stories in every little part of each
column. . . . When I entered into the Church I had a strange
veneration came upon me to see the ruins of such a majestick
and gigantick pile, with windowes over windowes and walkes
over walkes in the walls, statlie pillars, curious carved work
every where.

A. Wood, Life & Times, 28.6.

GARDENS

Walk'd to Ham . . . which is indeed inferior to few of the best
villas in Italy itself; . . . parterres, flower gardens, orangeries,
groves, avenues, courts, statues, perspectives, fountaines,
aviaries, and all this at the banks of the sweetest river in the
world.

Evelyn, Diary, 27.8.

MANNERS AND TASTES

After evening prayer visited Mr. Sheldon (nephew to the late
Abp. of Canterbury) and his pretty melancholy garden (near
Weybridge).

Evelyn, 25.8.

Cornish ceased to be used for divine service (see 1778).

Christian "roundeth up" Demas (=answers roundly) Bunyan
Pilgrims' Progress I (eleven editions, 100,000 copies, besides
translations, before his death 1688).

This Theology of Epicurus was but Romantical.

Cudworth, Intellectual System. (Cf Butler,
1728.)

La Princesse de Clèves (a late Romance).

Mme. de la Fayette.

POETRY

Dryden, *All for Love* in blank verse.   Preface criticising the
Phèdre of Racine.

When all their worst miscarriages delight
And please more than the best that Pedants write.

Butler, Hudibras, Part III.

The choicest and most applauded *English Tragedies* of this last age, as *Rollo* (J. Fletcher), *A King and no King* (B. & F.), the *Maid's Tragedy* by *Beaumont* and *Fletcher* and *Julius Caesar* by *Shakespeare*, and *Cataline* by Worthy *Ben*. . . . A kind of *Stagequacks* and *Empiricks* in Poetry, who have got a *Receipt* to *please*. . . . A *Poet* must of necessity see *justice* exactly administered if he intend to please, [perhaps first "poetic justice"; cf. Dryden 1679]. . . . Tragedy cannot represent a woman without modesty as natural and essential to her. . . . I question whether in Poetry a King can be an accessory to a crime. . . . I believe the end of all Poetry is to *please*. Some sorts of Poetry please without profiting. I am confident whoever writes a Tragedy cannot please but he must also profit. . . . That *Paradise Lost* of *Milton's* which some are pleased to call a Poem.

Rymer, Tragedies of the Last Age.

✿ 1679 r. Charles II ✿

GARDENS

The grotts in the chalky rock are pretty; 'tis a romantic object (Duke of Buckingham's house at Clifden) and the place altogether answers the most poetical descriptions that can be made of solitude, precipice, prospect or whatever can contribute to a thing so very like their imagination.

Evelyn, 23.7.

POETRY

(Shakespeare's) whole style is so pestered with figurative expressions that it is as affected as it is obscure. . . . I undertook to remove that heap of rubbish under which many excellent thoughts lay wholly buried. . . . Rapin, a judicious critic, has observed from Aristotle that pride and want of commisersation are the two most predominant vices of mankind; therefore to cure us of these two, the inventors of Tragedy have chosen to work upon two other passions, which are fear and pity. . . . It

is absolutely necessary to make a man virtuous, if we desire
he should be pitied: we lament not, but detest a wicked man;
we are glad when we behold his crimes are punished, and that
poetical justice [cf. Rymer 1678] is done upon him. . . .
Manners must be suitable, . . . when a poet has given the
dignity of a king to one of his persons, in all his actions and
speeches that person must discover majesty, magnanimity
and jealousy of power, because these are suitable to the
general manners of a king. . . . Racine's Bajazet is bred at
Constantinople; but his civilities are conveyed to him, by some
secret passage, from Versailles into the Seraglio. . . . The
Greek Emperor . . . was noted of extreme covetousness, a vice
which is contrary to the character of a hero or prince . . . no
fit person to be presented in a tragedy. . . . Shakespeare seems
(in Caliban) to have created a person which was not in Nature,
a boldness which at first sight would appear intolerable. . . .
Our reverence for Shakespeare is much more just than that
of the Grecians for Aeschylus. . . . I imagine it to be false read
where (Aristotle) says of Poetry that it is Εὐφυοὺξ ἢ μαν.κοῦ
that it had always somewhat in it either of a genius or of a
madman. 'Tis more probable that the original ran thus, that
Poetry was Εὐφυοῦζ οὐ μανικοῦ that it belongs to a witty man,
but not to a madman. . . . No man is at leisure to make
sentences and similes, when his soul is in agony.

> Dryden, *Troilus and Cressida* adapted,
> with *Grounds of Criticism in Tragedy.*

❦ 1680 r. Charles II ❦

MANNERS AND TASTES

(To a monkey)
>   Kiss me, thou curious miniature of man,
>   How odd thou art, how pretty, how japan!

>   (Date uncertain). J. Wilmot, Earl of
>   Rochester, *Artemizia to Chloë* (by a
>   Person of Honour).

Audley End . . . the greatest house in England . . . a vast
building or rather town walled in (750 rooms).

> Thoresby, *Diary.*

POETRY

Well, Sir, 'tis granted, I said D(ryden's) Rhimes,
Were stol'n, unequal, nay dull many times;
What foolish Patron, is there found of his,
So blindly partial to deny me this?
But that his Plays, embroider'd up and down
With Wit and Learning, justly pleas'd the Town
In the same Paper, I as freely own.

    .   .   .   .   .

Which blund'ring S(ettle), never could attain
And puzzling O(tway), labours at in vain.

    .   .   .   .   .

The Style may rise, yet in its rise forbear,
With useless Words, t'oppress the weary'd Ear,
Here be your Language lofty, there more light,
Your Rhetorick with your Poetry unite:
For Elegance sake, sometimes allay the Force,
Of *Epithets*, 'twill soften the discourse;
A jest in scorn points out, and hits the thing
More home, than the *Morosest* Satires sting,
Shake-spear and *Johnson* did herein excell,
And might in this be imitated well;
Whom refin'd E(therege), copies not at all,
But is himself, a sheer Original.
Nor that slow Drudge, in swift *Pindarick* strains,
F(latman), who C(owley) imitates with pains.

Of all our Modern Wits none seem to me,
Once to have touched upon true Comedy,
But hasty S(hadwell) and slow *Wicherley*,

    .   .   .   .   .

Waller, by Nature, for the *Bays* design'd,
With Force and Fire, and fancy unconfin'd,
In Panegyricks does excell Mankind.

    .   .   .   .   .

For pointed Satyrs I would B(uckhurst) choose,
The best good Man with the worst natur'd Muse,
For Songs and Verses, mannerly, obscene,
That can stir Nature up by spring unseen,

And without forcing blushes please the Queen,
S(edley) has that prevailing, gentle Art,
That can with a resistless charm impart
The loosest Wishes to the chastest Heart.

. . . . .

D(ryden), in vain try'd this nice way of Wit,
For he to be a tearing *Blade* thought fit,
To give the Ladies a dry Bawdy bob,
And thus he got the name of Poet *Squab*,
But to be just, 'twill to his praise be found,
His Excellencies more than faults abound.

. . . . .

But does not D(ryden) find even Jonson dull?
Fletcher and *Beaumont,* incorrect and full
Of lewd lines as he calls 'em? Shakespeare's stile
Stiff and affected? to his own the while
Allowing all the justness that his Pride
So arrogantly had to them deny'd?

> J. Wilmot, Earl of Rochester, *Allusion to Horace.*

Horace will our superfluous Branches prune,
Give us new rules and set our Harp in tune,
Direct us how to back the winged Horse,
Favour his flight and moderate his force.

> Waller, *To Lord Roscommon* on his *Horace's Art of Poetry.*

1681 r. Charles II

MANNERS AND TASTES

'Twas never good days but when great tables were kept in large halls, the buttery-hatch always open; black jacks, and a good smell of meat and March beer; with dogs' t-ds and marrow bones as ornaments in the hall. These were signs of good housekeeping. I hate to see Italian fine buildings with no meat or drink in 'em.

> Shadwell, *The Lancashire Witches.*

(At Chatsworth)

> The primitive casements modell'd were no doubt
> By that through which the pigeon was thrust out,
> Where now whole shashes are but one great eye,
> T'examine, and admire thy beauties by.
>
> <div align="right">C. Cotton, <i>The Wonders of the Peake.</i></div>

Oxford's a place where Wit can never starve.

Dryden, Prologue to the University.

NATURE

Oculos meos et animum nihil magis delectare solet, quam Oceanum intueri et magnos montes terrae. Nescio quid grande habent et augustum uterque horum, quo mens excitatur ad ingentes affectus et cogitationes; ... mentemque nostram, quae cum voluptate res magnas contemplatur, non esse rem parvam cum gaudio recognoscimus. Et quaecumque umbram infiniti habent ... gratum quendam stuporem animo affundunt ... Nihil hic elegans aut venustum sed ingens et magnificum.

T. Burnet, Sacra Telluris Theoria (see 1685, 1689).

> Montagnes de qui l'audace
> Va porter jusqu'aux cieux
> Un front d'éternelle glace,
> Soutien du séjour des dieux;
> Dessus vos têtes chenues
> Je cueille au-dessus des nues
> Toutes les fleurs du printemps.
> A mes pieds, contre la terre,
> J'entends gronder la tonnerre,
> Et tomber mille torrents.
>
> .   .   .   .   .
>
> Mais dans ce rude paysage,
> Où tout est capricieux
> Et d'une beauté sauvage,
> Rien ne rappelle à mes yeux
> Les bords que mon fleuve arrose;

Fleuve où jamais le vent n'ose
Les moidres flots soulever,
Où le ciel serein nous donne
Le printemps après l'automne,
Sans laisser place à l'hiver.

Fénelon, *Ode à l'Abbé de Langeron,
Description du prieuré de Carenac.*

The *Groves*, whose curléd *Brows* shade ev'ry *Lake*
Do everywhere such waving *Landskips* make,
As *Painters* baffled *Art* is far above,
Who *Waves* and *Leaves* could never yet make move. . . .
To view from hence the glitt'ring Pile above . . . .
Environ'd round with Nature's Shames and Ills,
Black Heath, Wild Rock, bleak Crags and naked hills,
Who is it but must presently conclude
That this is *Paradise* which seated stands
In midst of Deserts, and of Barren *Sands?*

Ch. Cotton, *The Wonders of the Peak.*

POETRY

When I was a boy (b. 1631) I thought inimitable Spenser a
mean poet, in comparison of Sylvester's *Dubartas* (*The Divine
Weekes*, 1598), and was rapt into an ecstasy when I read these
lines:

Now, when the Winter's keener breath began
To chrystallize the Baltick Ocean;
To glaze the Lakes, to bridle up the Floods,
And periwig with Snow[1] the bald-pate Woods.

I am much deceived if this be not abominable fustian, that is,
thoughts and words ill-sorted, and without the least relation
to each other.

Dryden, Dedication to *Spanish Friar.*

Annihilating all that's made
To a green Thought in a green Shade

Marvell, *The Garden.*

[1] In the original, "Wool".

❦ 1682 r. Charles II ❦

ARCHITECTURE

Tom Tower, Christ Church, Oxford built from Wren's design.

MANNERS AND TASTES

(Mr. Bohun's house) a cabinet of all elegancies, especially Indian; in the hall are contrivances of Japanese skreens instead of wainscot . . . the landskips of the skreens represent the manner of living and country of the Chinese.

Evelyn, Diary, 30.7.

PAINTING

Lely's collection of picturs sold in London (April 18) Among the prices were:—
Veronese £200
Van Dyck, *Family of Endymion Porter* £155 (see 1687).

Kneller painted Earl of Bedford for £8 (see 1676 and 1694).

POETRY

Away with these fellows' contriving,
    They've spoilt all our pleasant design,
We were once in a way to true living
    Improving discourse with good wine.

Alex. Radcliffe, The Ramble ("with some
terrestrial Hymns and Carnal Ejacula-
tions").

And this unpolish'd, rugged Verse I chose;
As fittest for Discourse, and nearest prose.

Dryden, Religio Laici.

As all is dullness when the Fancy's bad,
So without Judgment, Fancy is but mad.

Reason is that substantial, useful part
Which gains the Head, while t'other wins the Heart.

But Falstaff seems unimitable yet.

Heroick Poems have a just pretence
To be the chief effort of human sence.

Read Homer once, and you can read no more,
For all things else will seem so dull and poor. . . .
Must above *Cowley*, nay, and *Milton* too prevail,
Succeed where great *Torquato*, and our greater *Spenser* fail.

> J. Sheffield, Earl of Mulgrave, Duke of
> Buckingham, *Essay upon Poetry.*

In later editions, when Milton's fame established, (1691)
last two lines changed to
> Must above Tasso's lofty flights prevail,
> Succeed where Spenser and ev'n Milton fail.

"If anything of mine is good 'tis Mac-Flecnoe."
> Dryden as reported by Lockier in
> Spence's *Anecdotes.*

❦ 1683 r. Charles II ❧

ANTIQUARIANISM
History and Antiquities of Winchester Cathedral. Clarendon.

ARCHITECTURE
Verrio's invention is admirable, his ord'nance full and flowing,
antiq and heroical; his figures move.
> Evelyn, 16.6.

Claude Perrault, *Ordonnance des Cinq Espèces de Colonnes selon la
Méthode des Anciens* (translated 1708). He built the Louvre
colonnade.

POETRY
Dryden revised Sir William Soame's translation of Boileau's
Art Poétique, and substituted English equivalents for French
names. Marot is replaced by Fairfax as first reformer of
barbaric verse; Ronsard by Davenant—"changed all, spoiled
all"; Malherbe by Waller—"came at last" (=enfin vint).
Spenser is added.

✦ 1684 r. Charles II ✦

MANNERS AND TASTES

That Heav'n would bless me with a small Estate,
Where I might find a close obscure retreat;
There, free from Noise, and all ambitious ends,
Enjoying a few choice books and fewer friends,

. . . . .

There live unthought of, and unheard of die,
And grudge Mankind my very Memory.

J. Oldham, Works (see below).

Scheme for lighting London streets on dark nights by lamps at every tenth house.

Woburn Abbey laid in two hogsheads of port for £10-0-0.

Dr. Tenison communicated to me his intention of erecting a library in St. Martin's Parish for the public use and desired my assistance with Sir Christopher Wren; . . . and indeed a great reproach it is that so great a city as London should not have a public library.

Evelyn, Diary.

The skeletons and stuffed human skins in the Anatomy School (at Oxford) suited my melancholy temper.

Thoresby, Diary.

POETRY

But who did ever in *French Authors* see
The comprehensive *English Energy*?
The weighty *Bullion* of *one Sterling Line*
Drawn to *French Wire* would through whole *Pages* shine

. . . . .

Of many faults Rhyme is perhaps the Cause;
Too *strict* to *Rhyme*, We slight more useful *Laws*.

W. Dillon, Earl of Roscommon, Essay on
Translated Verse (contains an Essay on
(and in) Blank Verse imitating Paradise
Lost, B. VI).

But Italy, reviving from the trance
Of Vandal, Goth, and Monkish ignorance,
With pauses, cadence, and well-vowell'd words,
And all the graces a good ear affords,
Made rhyme an art, and Dante's polish'd page
Restor'd a Silver, not a Golden Age.

Dryden, *To Roscommon.*

[Age] might (what Nature never gives the Young)
Have taught the Numbers of thy Native tongue.
But Satire needs not these and Wit will shine
Through the harsh Cadence of a rugged Line.

Dryden, *To the Memory of Mr. Oldham*
(see above).

Dryden, *Miscellany Poems* including *Johnnie Armstrong, Chevy Chase,* &c.

1685 r. Charles II, James II

GARDENS

Among us, the Beauty of Building and Planting is placed chiefly in some certain Proportions, Symmetries, or Uniformities; our Walks and our Trees ranged so as to answer one another, and at exact Distances. The Chinese scorn this way of Planting . . . their Imagination is employed in contriving Figures where the Beauty shall be great, and strike the eye, without any Order or Disposition of parts, that shall be commonly or easily observed. . . . We have hardly any Notion of this sort of Beauty. . . . The best Indian gowns. . . . Tho' there may be more Honour if they succeed well, yet there is more dishonour if they fail, and 'tis 20 to 1 they will; whereas in regular figures, 'tis hard to make any great and remarkable Faults. . . . The romantic palace of Alcinous in Homer. . . . The Chinese have a particular word to express (the studied beauty of irregularity)—*Sharawadgi.*

Sir W. Temple, *The Gardens of Epicurus*
(published 1690).

MANNERS AND TASTES

I should grow an extreme dull creature to be confined to such a smooth uniform habitation and should desire to be transplanted into this misshapen irregular world he (T. Burnet) finds us in, where we have the variety of delightful motions and prospects both by sea and land.

> H. Croft, *Animadversions upon the Theory of the Earth* (cf. 1681, 1689).

Woburn Abbey bought brandy from the oilman.

At the entrance off each room (at Wilton) is a line of pipes that appear not till, by a sluice moved, it washes the spectators, designed for diversion.

> Celia Fiennes *Diary* (*circa*).

MUSIC

An imitation of a song sung by some natives of India before the late King.

> Crowne, *Sir Courtley Nice*.

J. S. Bach, Händel, Scarlatti born.

NATURE

The Arcadia is about Vernditch and Wilton, and these romancy plaines and boscages did no doubt conduce to the heightening of Sir Philip Sydney's phancie.

> Aubrey, *Natural History of Wiltshire*.

POETRY

Fourth Folio of Shakespeare. Since 1623 there had been three editions of the plays, say 3,000 copies.

Our tongue ... approaches nearest to the Roman in its majesty; nearest indeed, but with a vast interval.

> *Preface to Sylvae.*

Our original Teutonic consisting most in monosyllables. ... The rest of our words, which are derived from the Latin chiefly ... are some relief in Poetry, and help us to soften our uncouth numbers; which together with our English genius, incomparably beyond the trifling of the French, in all the nobler parts of verse, will justly give us the pre-eminence.

Preface.

> In France the oldest man is always young,
> Sees operas daily, learns the tunes so long,
> Till foot, hand, head, keep time with every song,
> Each sings his part, echoing from pit to box,
> With his hoarse voice, half harmony, half pox.

Dryden, *Prologue to Albion and Albanius* (opera).

My Lord's (of Rochester) constant living at Court, and the Conversation of Persons of Quality . . . gave him . . . a nicer knowledge both of Men and Manners, an Air of good Breeding, and a Gentleman-like easiness in all he writ, to which *Fletcher's* obscure Education and the mean Company he kept had made him wholly a Stranger. . . . Every Ass that's Romantick believes he's inspired. . . . Poetical Wit . . . nothing else but *a true and lively expression of Nature.* By *Nature* I do not only mean all sorts of material Objects . . . but also general Notions and abstracted Truths, such as exist only in the Minds of men.

R. Wolseley, *Preface to Fletcher's Valentinian as alter'd by the Earl of Rochester.*

🎛 1686 r. James II 🎛

MANNERS AND TASTES

New Judges also here, among wch. was Milton [Sir Christopher] (brother to that Milton who wrote for ye Regicides) who presum'd to take his place without passing ye Test.

Evelyn, 2.6.

PAINTING

> The *Sylvan* Scenes of Herds and Flocks,
> And fruitful Plains, and barren Rocks,

. . . . .

Of lofty Trees with sacred Shades
And Perspectives of Pleasant Glades
. . . . .
The Ruins, too, of some Majestick Piece,
Boasting the Pow'r of ancient *Rome* or *Greece*.

> Dryden, *Death of Mistress Anne Killigrew*.

If *Cimabue* had not been followed so close, and so much
Outdone by his Schollar *Ghiotto*, his fame would have been
much greater; as appears by these Verses of Dante. . . .

> W. Aglionby, *Painting Illustrated* (selec-
> tions from Vasari).

🌸 1687 r. James II 🌸

ARCHITECTURE

Morosini bombarded the Acropolis. In 1684 Carrey had
sketched the Parthenon and in 1682 Wheeler published his
Tour in Greece.

MANNERS AND TASTES

The Earl of Bedford bought an umbrella for 16/6.

PAINTING

Sometimes you curious *Landskips* represent,
And arch 'em o'er with gilded *Firmament*:
Then in *Japan* some *rural Cottage* paint.

> Dryden, *Poetical Recreations*, to Clarinda.

It was wonderful to see with what earnestness people attended
this sale (Sir Peter Lely's prints and drawings). One would
have thought bread was exposed in a famine.

> R. North, *Autobiography* (see 1682).

POETRY

(Milton's) Fame is gone out like a Candle in a Snuff, and his
Memory will always stink.

> W. Winstanley, *Lives of the most Famous
> English Poets*.

Bayes. I hate such a rough unhewen Fellow as Milton, that a Man must sweat to read him.

> Prior and Montagu (Halifax), *Hind and Panther Travers'd.*

By this the northern waggoner had set
His sevenfold team behind the steadfast star
That was in ocean waves yet never wet,
Now had Bootes' team far passed behind
The northern star when hours of night declined.

Spenser Redivivus, the First Book of the Fairy Queen. His Essential Design preserved, but his Obsolete Language and Manner of Verse totally laid aside. Delivered in Heroic Numbers. By a Person of Quality.

Barefoot and ragged, with neglected Hair,
She whom the Heavens at once made poor and fair,
With humble voice and moving words did stay,
To beg an Alms of all who passed that way.

> P. Ayres, *Lyric Poems in Imitation of the Italian* (including sonnets).

La docte Antiquité dans toute sa durée
A l'égal de nos jours ne fut point éclairée.

· · · · ·

La belle Antiquité fut toujours vénérable,
Mais je ne crus jamais qu'elle fust adorable,
Je voy les Anciens, sans plier les genoux,
Ils sont grands, il est vray, mais hommes commes nous
Et l'on peut comparer sans craindre d'estre injuste,
Le Siècle de Louis au beau Siècle d'Auguste.

> Ch. Perrault, *Siècle de Louis le Grand.* (He defended Moderns in the Académie this year. Also wrote *Contes des Fées,* including *Cinderella*).

L'Écriture Sainte, qui avec sa simplicité a tant du sublime. . . . L'Esprit et le Coeur sont bien a la mode ("Eudoxe" defends classical taste and "le bon sens" and "Philareté" prefers Italy and Spain, "tout ce qui est fleuri, tout ce que brille".)

La fiction imite et perfectionne en quelque façon la nature; la fausseté la gaste et la détruit entièrement. (One good taste for all nations. But) il y falloit ajouter quelque chose d'extraordinaire qui frappât l'esprit . . . grandeur, agrément, délicatesse . . . la délicatesse consistoit en partie dans je ne sçay quoi de mystérieux . . . mais le rafinement est le pire de toutes les affectations.

> Bouhours—*Dialogues sur la manière de bien penser dans les Ouvrages d'Esprit.* (2nd ed. by 1700, 13 by 1800, translated 1705 as *The Art of Criticism.* Anti-Italian and pro-classical).

Chaucer reprinted, cf. 1602, 1721.

> Distance presents the object fair,
> With Charming Features and a graceful Air,
> But when we come to seize th'inviting prey,
> Like a Shy Ghost, it vanishes away.
>
> > J. Norris of Bemerton, *The Infidel,* (cf. 1645, Suckling and 1799, Campbell).

❧ 1688 r. James II and William and Mary ❧

MANNERS AND TASTES

Il y a dans l'art un point de perfection. . . Celui qui le sent et qui l'aime a *le goût* parfait.

> La Bruyère: *Les Caractères; ou les moeurs du siècle,* translated 1699.

The glory of one country, Japan alone, has exceeded in beauty and magnificence all the pride of the Vatican at this time and Pantheon before.

.   .   .   .   .

(Japan) Natures Darling and the Favourite of the Gods.

> Stalker, *Treatise of Japanning and Varnishing.*

NATURE

(Alps) a delightful Horrour, a terrible Joy, and at the same time that I was infinitely pleas'd I trembled. . . . I am delighted, 'tis true, at the prospect of Hills and Valleys, of flowry Meads, and murmuring Streams, yet 'tis a delight that is consistent with Reason, a delight that creates and improves Meditation. But transporting Pleasures followed the sight of the Alps, and what unusual Transports think you are those, that are mingled with Horrours, and sometimes almost with Dispair? . . . Ruins upon Ruins, in monstrous Heaps, and Heaven and Earth confounded. The uncouth Rocks that were above us, Rocks that were void of all form, but what they had received from Ruine: the frightful View of the Precipices, and the foaming Waters that threw themselves headlong down them, made all such a Consort to the eye, as that sort of Music does for the Ear, in which Horrour can be joyn'd with Harmony.

J. Dennis, *Letter*.

POETRY

Three poets in three distant ages born,
Greece,Italy and *England* did adorn.
The first in Loftiness of thought surpass'd,
The next in Majesty; in both the last;
The Force of Nature could no farther go;
To make a third she join'd the former two.

Dryden, *On Milton*.

Waller the God of Verse we will proclaim,
Not Phoebus now but Waller be his name.

(Date?) Lord Lansdowne ("Granville the Polite").

✵ 1689 r. William and Mary ✵

MANNERS AND TASTES

If the sea had been drawn round the earth in regular figures and borders, it might have been a great beauty to our globe. . . . What a beautiful Hemisphere (the stars) would have made if they had been placed in Rank and Order; if they had been disposed into regular Figures . . . according to the rules of Art and Symmetry.

T. Burnet, *Sacred Theory of the Earth*.
(English version. See 1681, 1685 and Bacon 1605. Coleridge

couples him with Plato and Jeremy Taylor to prove that "poetry of the highest kind may exist without metre". Biographia Literaria XIV).

Dutch taste introduced by the Queen, especially china.

PAINTING

I am in perfect indignation at this folly as often as I consider what extravagant summes are given for a dry scalp of some, forsooth, Italian painter, let it be of Raphael or Titian himself.

To Pepys, 26.8.

(Holbein) really painted to the life beyond any man this day living.

Evelyn to Pepys, 12.8 (see 1665).

POETRY

Racine introduced chorus in *Esther*.

Shadwell succeeded the disgraced Dryden as laureate and historiographer,=(Og who) "in clumsy verseun lick'd, un-pointed, Hast shamefully defied the Lords annointed."

(Dryden, *Absalom & Achitophel*, 1681.)

✿ 1690 r. William and Mary ✿

GARDENS

Leaden figure factory started in England.

Levens gardens laid out by Beaumont in its present Dutch style about this time.

PAINTING

The Arts of Painting and Statuary began to revive with learning in Europe, and made a great but short flight so as for these last Hundred Years we have not had One Master in either of them who deserved a Rank with those that flourished in that short Period after they began among us. . . . Plutarch whose Greek is much more estimable than the Latin of Tacitus, his contemporary.

> Sir W. Temple, *Ancient and Modern Learning.*

POETRY

The parent of English verse and the first that shew'd us our tongue had beauty and numbers in it . . . first in the list of refiners, and for aught I know, last too; for I question whether in Charles II's reign English did not come to its full perfection; and whether it has not had its Augustan Age, as well as the Latin . . . 'tis a surprising reflection that between what Spenser (d. 1599) wrote last and Waller (b. 1606) first there should not be much above twenty years distance . . . the other's words are like old coins. New turn of verse . . . more polysyllables, and smoother measures; bound up his thoughts better, and in a cadence more agreeable to the nature of the verse he wrote in; so that wherever the natural stops of that were, he contriv'd the little breakings of his sense so as to fall in with 'em. And for that reason, since the stress of our Verse lies commonly on the last syllable, you'll hardly ever find him using a word of no force there! . . . English Richelieu . . . everything that is either great or graceful in poetry.

> Anon (Atterbury?), *Preface to Waller's Posthumous Poems,* d.1687.

Rapin tells us that Dantes Aligerus wants fire, and that he has not heat enough.

> Sir T. Pope Blount, *Censura.*

Accademia degli Arcadi founded by Gravina and Crescimbeni to foster arcadian simplicity in literature.

Wit lying most in the assemblage of ideas, and putting those together with quickness and variety wherein can be found any resemblance or congruity, thereby to make up pleasant pictures and agreeable visions in the fancy; judgement, on the contrary, lies quite on the other side, in separating carefully one from another ideas wherein can be found the least difference.

> Locke, *Essay on Human Understanding,* II, xi, §2.

The fame of the poem (Paradise Lost) is spread through the whole of England, but being written in English, it is as yet unknown in foreign lands.

W. Hog (with Latin paraphrase)

All the educated Englishmen I have known extol to the skies a poem written in English by Milton and called Adam; they speak of it as the *non plus ultra* of the human spirit.

Minatoli to Bayle.

The Song or Epicedium of *Regnor Ladbrog*, one of their famous Kings, which he composed in the *Runick* Language, . . . is very well worth reading, by any that love Poetry. . . . Such an Alacrity or Pleasure in dying was never express'd in any other Writing. . . . The two Stanza's are thus Translated into Latin by Olaus:

XXV

Pugnavimus Ensibus;
Hoc ridere me facit semper
Quod Balderi Patris Scamna
Parata scio in aula.
Bibemus cerevisiam
Ex concavis crateribus craniorum,
Non gemit vir fortis contra mortem,
Magnifici in Odini domibus,
Non venio desperabundus
Verbis ad Othini aulam.

XXIX

Fert animus finire,
Invitant me Dysae
Quas ex Odini aula
Othinus mihi misit.
Laetus cerevisiam cum Asis
In summa sede bibam;
Vitae elapsæ sunt horae,
Ridens Moriar.

I am deceived, if in this Sonnet, . . . there be not a vein truly Poetical, and in its kind Pindaric.

(Cf. Downman 1781), Sir W. Temple,
Of Heroic Virtue.

So many should cry, and with down-right tears, at some Tragedies of Shake-speare ... Homer vastest, sublimest and most wonderful genius (compared with Virgil) ... Yet I am deceived if our English has not in some kind excelled both the Modern and the Antient, which has been by force of a Vein Natural, perhaps, to our Country, and which with us is Called Humour, a Word peculiar to our Language too ... nor is it, that I know of, to be found in any foreign writers, unless it be Molière, and yet his itself has too much of the Farce ... Shakespeare was the first. ... The Truth is, there is something in the Genius of Poetry, too Libertine to be confined to so many Rules; ... 'tis as if to make excellent Honey you shall cut off the wings of your Bees. ... Spenser's Execution was excellent, and his Flights of Fancy very noble and high, but his Design was poor, and his Moral lay so bare, that it lost the Effect; 'tis true, the Pill was gilded, but so thin, that the Colour and the Taste were too easily discovered.

Sir W. Temple, Of Poetry.

1691 r. William and Mary

NATURE

A flat and open Country not overgrown with wild and un-wholesome Forests, nor dreadful high Mountains. What *Hills* it has are generally very gentle and pleasant. ... (Westmorland) one of the worst counties in England; ...

G. Miège, New State of England

(Mountains) are very Ornamental to the Earth, affording pleasant and delightful Prospects, both (1) To them that look downwards from them ... as they must needs acknowledge, who have been but on the Downs of Sussex. ... And (2) To those that look upward ... which what a refreshing and pleasure it is to the Eye, they are best able to judge, who have lived in the Isle of Ely.

J. Ray, Wisdom of God (written about 1648?).

Dryden's *King Arthur or the British Worthy*, set to music by Purcell. (Revived 1735 "The second scene is a British temple enough to make one go back a thousand years, and really be in ancient Britain: the songs are all church-musick." Gray to Walpole, 3.1.1736).

Edmund Gibson edited *Crists Kirk on the Green* (James I?).

L'Écriture Sainte, qui avec sa simplicité a tant du sublime.
> Bouhours, *La Manière de bien Penser* (translated 1705).

La mer n'est jamais si belle que dans sa colère; lorsqu'elle s'enfle, qu'elle s'agite, qu'elle mugit d'une manière effroyable et qu'il se fait une espèce de guerre entre les vents et les flots.
> Bouhours, *Entretiens d'Ariste et d'Eugène*, I. (IV is *Le Bel Esprit*, V *Le Je ne scay Quoi*).

As (Apollo) was going to make an oration
He threw by one lock, with a delicate fashion,
Upon the left foot most genteely did stand,
Had drawn back the other, and waved his white hand.
> (Date?) Lady Winchilsea.

Had (Milton's) Principles been as good as his Parts he had been an excellent Person.
> Langbaine, *Account of the English Dramatic Poets*.

🕸 1692 r. William and Mary 🕸

Largamente ancora spiegò le piume del suo ingegno Dante, il quale felicemente ardì di sollevar le forze del suo spirito all' alto disegno di "descriver fondo a tutto l'Universo"; sicchè in un' opera, non solamente le comune e le civili cose, ma le divine e le spirituali mirabilmente comprese ... Non

so se (l'*Endimione* di Guidi) sia tragedia o commedia; . . .
ella è una rappresentazione dell' amore d'Endimione e di
Diana; . . . se non s'incontra vocabolo alcuno non vogliamo
noi per macanza di nome, privarci di cosa si bella. . . . Novità
. . . maraviglia.

> Gravina, *Discorso su l'Endimione.*

Dr. Donne, the greatest wit, though not the best poet of our
nation.

> Dryden, *Dedication to Eleonora.*

Shadwell, laureate, died (see 1689). Succeeded by Tate, who
wrote *The History of Richard II, The History of King Lear* and other
plays, *Syphilis* and other poems, an *Essay for Promoting of
Psalmody,* and in 1696, with Brady, *A New Version of the Psalms.*

Le goût est une harmonie, un accord de l'esprit et de la raison.

> Mme Dacier, *Comédies Grecques d'Aristophane.*

W. Walsh published perhaps the only sonnet (irregular)
between Milton and Gray, but see 1687 (Ayres).

STAGE

A transparent prospect of a Chinese garden . . . Six pedestals
of China-work rise from under the stage; they support six
large vessels of porcelain, in which are six China-orange trees.

> Settle, *The Fairy Queen* (operatic *Mid-
> summer-Night's Dream*).

1693 r. William and Mary

PAINTING

I saw a great auction of Pictures in the Banqueting House,
Whitehall. They had ben my Lord Melford's . . . There were
some very excellent of Vandyke, Rubens and Bassan. Lord
Godolphin bought the picture of the Boys by Morillio the
Spaniard for 80 guineas, deare enough; my nephew Glanville,
the old Earl of Arundell's Head by Rubens for £20.

> Evelyn, 21.6.

Saw and admir'd the Venus of Coreggio, wch. Lord Mulgrave had newly bought of Mr. Daun for £250, one of the best paintings I ever saw.

Evelyn, 18.7.

POETRY

Poetry admits no odd numbers above nine.

Dennis, Miscellanies (cf. "bashful fifteen",
Sheridan; "long-expected one and
twenty", Johnson; "fifteen men on the
dead man's chest", Stevenson).

Shakespeare, who created the stage among us, had rather written happily than knowingly and justly. . . . Donne . . . affects the metaphysics, not only in his satires, but in his amorous verses, where nature only should reign. . . . Some admirable piece of Holbein or Vandyck. . . . Neither will I justify Milton for his blank verse, though I may excuse him by the example of Hannibal Caro (1507-1566, translated Aeneid). . . . . In his *Juvenilia* . . . his rhyme is always constrained and forced . . . Sir G. Mackenzie asked me why I did not imitate in my verse the turns of Mr. Waller and Sir J. Denham. . . . I looked over the darling of my youth, the famous Cowley; there I found instead of them, the points of wit, and quirks of epigram. . . . An extraordinary turn upon the words is that in Ovid's *Epistolae Heroidum*, of Sappho to Phaon:

> Si, nisi qua forma poterit te digna videri,
> Nulla futura tua est, nulla futura tua est.

Dryden, Progress of Satire.

There is a vast difference betwixt arguing like Perrault[1] in behalf of the French poets, against Homer and Virgil, and betwixt giving the English poets their undoubted due, of excelling Aeschylus, Euripides and Sophocles . . . The Earl of Mulgrave and Mr. Waller, two of the best judges of our age, have assured me that they could never read over the translation of Chapman without incredible pleasure and extreme transport. This admiration of theirs must needs proceed from the author himself, for the translator has thrown him down as low as harsh numbers, improper English, and a monstrous length of

[1] See 1687.

verse could carry him. What then would he appear in the harmonious verse of one of the best writers, living in a much better age than was the last? I mean for versification, and the art of numbers; for in the drama we have not arrived to the pitch of Shakespeare, and Ben Johnson.

Dryden, Dedication to *Examen Poeticum.*

> The fearful infant turn'd his Head away,
> And on his Nurse's neck reclining lay,
> His unknown Father shunning with affright
> And looking back on so uncouth a sight,
> Daunted to see a Face with Steel o'erspread,
> And his high Plume that nodded o're his Head.

Dryden, *Examen Poeticum, translation of the Parting of Hector and Andromache in Homer's Iliad* (VI. 467).

Gorboduc (Norton and Sackville, 1561) ... might have been a better guide to *Shakespeare* and Ben Johnson than any guide they have had the luck to follow. ... *Shakespear* ... would pass upon us (Iago) a close, dissembling, false, insinuating rascal instead of an open-hearted, frank, plain-dealing Souldier, a character constantly worn by them for some thousands of years in the World. *Philosophy* tells us it is a principle in the Nature of Man *to be grateful.* History may tell us that *John an Oaks, John a Stiles,* or *Jago* were ungrateful. *Poetry* is to follow Nature; Philosophy must be its guide. ...

(*Shakespear*) in tragedy is quite out of his element, his brains are turned; he raves and rambles without any coherence, any spark of reason, or any rule to control him.

Rymer, *Short View of Tragedy.*

1694 r. William and Mary and William III

MANNERS AND TASTES

Strong paper hangings, with fine Indian figures in pieces about 12 yds. long and about half ell broad at 2s. and 2s. 6d. a piece. Also fine screens and fine figures for sash windows.

Gazette, No. 2697.

There is nothing more unbecoming a man of quality than to laugh.

> Congreve, *Double Dealer* (cf. 1650, 1748, Hobbes and Chesterfield).

PAINTING

Kneller painted Earl of Bedford in length for £40 (see 1682).

> *Raphael's*, like *Homer's*, was the Nobler part.
> But *Titian's* Painting looked like *Virgil's* Art.
>
> . . . . .
>
> More cannot be by Mortal art exprest;
> But venerable Age shall add the rest,
>
> . . . . .
>
> Mellow your colours and imbrown the Teint,
> Add every Grace, which Time alone can grant.
> > Dryden *To Kneller*.

POETRY

Strong were our Syres, and as they fought they Writ,
Conqu'ring with Force of Arms and Dint of Wit:
Their's was the Giant Race before the Flood;
And thus when *Charles* returned our Empire stood,
Like *Janus*, he the stubborn Soil manur'd,
With Rules of Husbandry the rankness cur'd,
Turn'd us to Manners when the Stage was rude,
And boistrous *English* Wit with Art indu'd,
Our Age was cultivated thus at length,
But what we gain'd in Skill we lost in Strength,
Our builders were with want of Genius curs'd,
The second Temple was not like the first.

. . . . .

In easie Dialogue is *Fletcher's* Praise:
He mov'd the Mind, but had no Pow'r to raise,
Great *Johnson* did by Strength of Judgement please,
Yet, doubling *Fletcher's* Force, he wants his Ease,
In diff'ring Talents both adorn their Age,
One for the Study, t'other for the Stage,
But both to *Congreve* justly shall submit,
One match'd in Judgement, both o'er matched in Wit,

In him all Beauties of this Age we see,
Etherege his courtship *Southern's* Purity,

. . . . .

Time, place, and action may with Pains be wrought,
But genius must be born and never can be taught,
This is Your Portion, this Your Native Store:
Heav'n, that but once was Prodigal before
To Shakespeare gave as much; she cou'd not give him more.

> Dryden, *To Mr. Congreve* on *The Double Dealer.*

After I have confess'd this much of our modern heroick poetry, I cannot but conclude with Mr. Rymer, that our English comedy is far beyond anything of the Ancients: and notwithstanding our irregularities, so is our tragedy. Shakespeare had a genius for it; and we know, in spite of Mr. Rymer, that genius alone is a greater virtue (if I may so call it) than all other qualifications put together. Almost all the faults which he has discovered, are truly there; yet who will read Mr.— or not read Shakespeare? . . . There is another part of poetry in which the English stand almost upon an equal foot with the Ancients; and 'tis that we call Pindaric, introduced, but not perfected, by our famous Mr. Cowley.

> Dryden to Dennis (March).

Whether Milton and Waller were not the best English poets; and which the better of the two? . . . They were both excellent in their kind, and exceeded each other and all besides. Milton was the fullest and loftiest, Waller the neatest and most correct poet we ever had.

> Athenian Mercury.

Old Spenser next, warm'd with poetic rage,
In ancient tales amus'd a barbarous age.

. . . . .

But now the mystic tale, that pleas'd of yore,
Can charm an understanding age no more;
The long spun allegories fulsome grow,
While the dull moral lies too plain below.

> Addison, *Account of the Greatest English Poets.*
> (He told Spence that when he wrote this he had not read Spenser.)

Un auteur classique (est) un auteur ancien fort approuvé, et qui fait autorité dans la matière qu'il traite.

Dictionnaire de l'Académie (1st ed.).

🎕 1695 r. William III 🎕

MANNERS AND TASTES

Newspaper censorship abolished (see 1662).

PAINTING

("Gothic" is) All that has nothing of the ancient Gust. . . . Holbein, Rubens, Vandyck, Raphael, Titian, Coreggio, Michael Angelo (can be seen in England). . . . For colouring Titian and Coreggio. . . . Correcting Nature from what she actually is in individuals to what she ought to be and what she was created. Now, as this Idea of perfection is of little use in portraits . . . so neither is it in the characters of Comedy and Tragedy . . . (but only) in Epic poetry. The heroes of the poets are to be drawn according to this rule. There is scarce a frailty to be left in the best of them. . . . All perfections are not suitable to all subjects. . . . The moral, as Bossu[1] observes, is the first business of the poet. . . . The Gothic manner, and the barbarous ornaments, which are to be avoided in a picture, are just the same with those in an ill-ordered play. For example, our English tragi-comedy must be confessed to be wholly Gothic, notwithstanding the success which it has found upon our Theatre, and in the *Pastor Fido* of Guarini; . . . Neither can I defend my *Spanish Friar*, as fond as otherwise I am of it, from this imputation: for though the comical parts are diverting, and the serious moving, yet they are of an unnatural mingle: for mirth and gravity destroy each other, and are no more to be allowed for decent than a gay widow laughing in a mourning habit. . . .

Dryden, *A Parallel of Poetry and Painting*.

(prefixed to translation of Bellori and Du Fresnoy).

[1] Translated into English this year.

The artful painter and the sculptor, imitating the Divine Maker, form to themselves, as well as they are able, a model of the superior beauties; and reflecting on them, endeavour to correct and amend the common nature and to represent it as it was at first created, without fault, either in colour or lineament.

> Bellori, translated by Dryden.

The principal part of painting is to know what is most beautiful in nature and most proper in that art.

> Du Fresnoy, *De Arte Graphica* (1693),
> translated by Dryden.

1696 r. William III

MANNERS AND TASTES

Average incomes at this time given by Gregory King, *State and Condition of England:*—Nobleman £3,200, Bishop £1,300, Baronet £880, Knight £650, Esquire £450, Country Gentleman £280, Merchant £400, Lawyer £154, Dignified clergyman £72, Inferior clergyman £50, Freeholder £90-55, Farmer £42-10s., Shopkeeper £45, Artisan £38.

(Cf. Thorold Rogers, *Work and Wages*). Purchasing power was perhaps four times that of 1900.

POETRY

Rules are nothing but an observation of Nature.

> J. Dennis, *To W. Moyle.*

Il buon gusto nei componimenti rettorici, . . . usare le specie più che i generi (perocchè questi, coll' essere più universali di quelle, sono meno sensibili) gli' individui più che le specie, gli effetti più che le cagioni, il numero di più anzi che quel del meno.

> Camillo Ettori.

(Sentimental Comedy *Love's Last Shift*), Cibber.

PROSE

1696. The Gospel affords the most illustrious Example of close and perspicuous Ratiocination conceivable.

Toland, *Christianity not Mysterious*.

1697 r. William III

ARCHITECTURE

New St. Paul's first used (see 1710).

MANNERS AND TASTES

(At Chatsworth) you went down two steps into the bath big enough for two people; at the upper end are two cocks to let in one hott the other cold water.

Celia Fiennes, *Diary*.

It is no derogation to a man in England to be a merchant, yet it is very rare for Peers to put their younger sons out apprentices, as 'tis said they used to do.

Misson, *Observations in Travel over England* (translated 1719).

MUSIC

At last divine *Cecilia* came,
Inventress of the Vocal Frame;
The sweet Enthusiast, from her Sacred Store,
Enlarg'd the former narrow Bounds,
And added Length to solemn Sounds,
With Nature's Mother-wit, and Arts unknown before.

Dryden, *The Power of Musique*.

PAINTING

(In Lord Exeter's house at Burleigh) Very fine paint in pictures, but they were all without garments, or very little, that was the only fault, the immodesty of the pictures, especially in my Lord's appartment.

Celia Fiennes, *Diary*.

POETRY

(Milton) Fameux apologiste du supplice de Charles I . . . Il se mêloit de poesie, et plusieurs de ses poëmes, tant en Latin qu'en Anglois, ont vu le jour, soit pendant sa vie, soit après sa mort.

> Bayle, *Dictionnaire historique et critique* (translated 1710).

A heroic poem, truly such, is undoubtedly the greatest work which the soul of man is capable to perform. The design of it is to form the mind to heroic virtue by example; 'tis conveyed in verse, that it may delight while it instructs . . . Better a mechanic rule were stretched or broken than a great beauty were omitted. . . . Spenser wanted only to have read the rules of Bossu; for no man was ever born with a greater genius or had more knowledge to support it. . . . Rhyme is certainly a constraint even to the best poets. . . . *Mollis amaracus* on which Venus lays Cupid in the First Aeneid. If I should translate it *sweet marjoram,* as the word signifies, . . these village words, as I may call them, give us a mean idea of the thing. . . . It raises our fancies, to conceive somewhat more noble than a common herb, and to spread roses under him, and strew lilies over him; a bed not unworthy the grandson of the goddess. . . . I writ not always in the proper terms of navigation . . . Virgil has avoided those proprieties because he writ not to mariners, but to all in general, and in particular to men and ladies of the first quality who have been better bred than to be too nicely knowing in the terms.

> Dryden, *Dedication to Translation of Aeneis.*

the bleating lambs
Securely swig the dug beside their dams.
> Dryden, *Aeneis,* IX, 72-3.

There are a sort of Men, who having little other merit than a happy chime, would fain fix the Excellence of Poetry in the smoothness of the Versification, allowing but little to the more Essential Qualities of a Poet, great Images, good Sense, etc. . . . They allow none but Iambics.

> *Poems on Affairs of State* (Pref.).

STAGE

A Prospect of Terras Walkes on Eight several Stages mounted one above another, each Stage contains a Range of Stonework extending from side to side, decorated from Paintings in Fresco of Heroick History; over each Piece of Painting are carved Rails and Banisters with Pedestals: On Thirty Two Pedestals are plainted Sixteen Golden Flower-Pots, and Sixteen Statues of Gods and Goddesses... Through the center, and advancing Twenty Four Foot high, is an Ascent of Marble Steps. This Sett of Scenes is encompass'd round with Arboragework, circled round with double Festoons of Flowers tyed up in Ribbons of Gold, terminating at Fifty Foot deep, being the Extent of the House, with a prospect of a Garden above the highest Terras.

> Settle, *The World in the Moon* (opera: directions).

✂ 1698 r. William III ✂

MANNERS AND TASTES

Sash windows, a novelty in France, introduced from England.

'Tis most evident and plain that simple Nature is the most harmless, inoffensive and vertuous Mistress.

> Aphra Behn (d. 1689) *Oroonoko*, collected novels.

Then each tuck'd his Napkin up under his Chin.
That his Holiday-Band might be kept very clean;
And Pin'd up his Sleeves to his Elbows, because
They should not hang down and be Greas'd in the Sauce.
Then all went to work, with such rending and tearing,
Like a Kennel of Hounds on a Quarter of Carri'n.
When done with the Flesh, they claw'd off the Fish,
With one hand at Mouth and th' other in th' Dish.
When their Stomachs were Cloy'd, what their Bellies Denied,
Each clap'd in his Pocket to give to his Bride;
With a *Cheese-cake* and *Custard* for my little Johnny,
And a Handful of *Sweetmeats* for poor Daughter *Nanny*.

> E. Ward, *O Raree-Show or The City Feast.*

(In Cornwall) a universal smoaking, both men, women and children, have all their pipes of tobacco.

(In Windsor Castle) a half-bedstead, as the new make.
Celia Fiennes, Diary.

STYLE

An Essay on Sublime . . . compared with the French of Sieur Despréaux Boileau (the first translation of ὕψος as *sublime?* Earlier translations used "Height of Eloquence" (Hall 1652) and "Loftiness or Elegancy" (Pultney 1680).).

✨ 1699 r. William III ✨

ANTIQUARIANISM

I have fifteen young students (in Anglo-Saxon).
E. Thwaites, Fellow of Queen's College,
Oxford (Nichols' Literary Anecdotes).

ARCHITECTURE

(Henry VII's Chapel, Westminster can) justly claim the admiration of the whole universe, such inimitable perfections are apparent in every part of the whole composure, which looks so far exceeding human excellence that a man would think it was knit together by the fingers of angels, pursuant to the directions of omnipotence.
E. Ward, London Spy VIII (cf. 1706).

The Goths and Vandals, having demolished the Greek and Roman architecture, introduced in its stead a certain fantastical and licentious manner of building which we have since called modern or Gothic—of the greatest industry and expressive carving, full of fret and lamentable imagery, sparing neither pains nor cost. . . . (Henry VII's Chapel) nice embroidered work . . . flutter of arch buttresses. . . . To deviate from the old would be to run into a disagreeable Mixture, which no form of good taste could relish.
Wren, Report on Westminster Abbey (cf. 1706).

Wren's spire at St. Dunstan's-in-the-East finished.

GARDENING

I am however so singular as to prefer Fontainebleau. It is situated among rocks and woods, that give you a fine variety of savage prospects. . . . I think there is something more charming in these rude heaps of stone than in so many statues, and would as soon see a river winding through woods and meadows as when it is tossed up in such a variety of frying at Versailles.

Addison to Congreve, December.

The Compleat Gard'ner, London and Wise. (London was a pupil of Rose, gardener to the king, who had studied Versailles. Wise became Gardner to Queen Anne).

MANNERS AND TASTES

The Duke of Bolton who died this year asserted that the eccentricity of his later life was feigned in imitation of Junius Brutus.

(Burnett, *History of my own Times*).

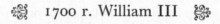 1700 r. William III

MANNERS AND TASTES

Dull romantic Honour!

N. Rowe, *Ambitious Stepmother*.

Ah Rustick! ruder than Gothick.

Congreve, *Way of the World*.

> All, all of a piece throughout;
> Thy Chase had a Beast in View;
> Thy Wars brought nothing about;
> Thy Lovers were all untrue.
> 'Tis well an Old Age is out,
> And time to begin a New.

Dryden, *Secular Masque* (to the past century).

Near some fair Town, I'd have a private Seat,
Built Uniform, not little nor too Great,
.   .   .   .   .
It should within no other things contain
But what are useful, necessary, plain.
.   .   .   .   .
To this Fair Creature I'd sometimes Retire;
Her conversation wou'd new joys inspire;
.   .   .   .   .
But so Divine, so Noble a Repast,
I'd seldom and with Moderation Taste,
For Highest Cordials all their Virtue lose
By a too frequent and too bold an Use;
And what wou'd cheer the Spirits in Distress
Ruines our Health, when taken to Excess.
>   Rev. J. Pomfret, *The Choice* (see 1779,
>   Johnson).

(He was refused a rich benefice by the Bishop of London for
this allusion to the "obliging Fair").

Happy the man, whose wish and care,
A few paternal acres bound,
Content to breathe his native air,
    In his own ground,
.   .   .   .   .
There let me live, unseen, unknown,
Thus unlamented, let me die,
Steal from the world, and not a stone,
    Tell where I lie.
>   Pope, *Solitude* (about 12 years old).

NATURE

(Wookey Hole) the most admirable piece of Nature's workmanship, . . . both horrour and astonishment.
>   Rev. J. Brome, *Travels over England*, etc.

POETRY

One of our late great poets [Cowley] is sunk in his reputation,
because he could never forgive any conceit that came in his
way; but swept like a drag-net, great and small; . . . for ten
impressions, which his works have had in so many successive

years, yet at present a hundred books are scarcely purchased
once a twelve month; for as my last Lord Rochester said,
though somewhat profanely, *Not being of God, he could not stand.* . . .
Homer is more according to my genius than Virgil. . . . Would
any man who is ready to die for love describe his passion like
(Ovid's) Narcissus? Would he think of *Inopem me copia fecit?* . . . .
Spenser more than once insinuates, that the soul of Chaucer
was transfused into his body . . . Milton has acknowledged to
me that Spenser was his original, and many besides myself
have heard our famous Waller own that he derived the
harmony of his numbers from *Godfrey of Bulloign* which was
turned into English by Mr. Fairfax. . . . The other harmony
of prose [= ἦς λεκτικῆς ἁρμονίας Ar. Poet. iv.]. . . . (Of Chaucer's
Canterbury Tales) *Here is God's plenty.*

Dryden, Preface to the Fables (see 1601).

Waller, Spenser and Dryden were Mr. Pope's great favourites,
in the order they are named, in his first reading till he was
about 12 years old (b. 1688).

Spence, Anecdotes.

❁ 1701 r. William III ❁

ARCHITECTURE

The Domo, or principal Church (at Florence) is one of the
most magestick in Europe.

E. Veryard, Divers Choice Remarks.

Upon my arrival at Rome, I took a view of St. Peter's and the
Rotunda. . . . St. Peter's seldom answers expectation at first
entering it, but enlarges itself on all sides insensibly, and
mends upon the eye every moment. The proportions are so
very well observed, that nothing appears to an advantage,
or distinguishes itself above the rest. It seems neither extremely
high, nor long, nor broad, because it is all of them in a just
equality. As on the contrary in our Gothic cathedrals, the
narrowness of the arch makes it rise in height, or run out in

length; the lowness often opens it in breadth, or the defective-
ness of some other particular makes any single part appear in
great perfection. . . . After having seen these two masterpieces
of modern and ancient architecture, I have often considered
with myself whether the ordinary figure of the heathen, or
that of the Christian temples be the most beautiful, and the
most capable of magnificence; and cannot forbear thinking
the cross figure more proper for such spacious buildings than
the Rotund. I must confess the eye is better filled at first
entering the Rotund, and takes in the whole beauty and
magnificence of the temple at one view. But such as are built
in the form of a cross, give us a greater variety of noble prospects.
. . . . I think there is something more astonishing in this
cascade (Terni) than in all the waterworks of Versailles. . . .
Augustus's bridge (at Narni) one of the stateliest ruins in
Italy. . . .
I saw between Pavia and Milan the convent of Carthusians,
which is very spacious and beautiful. Their church is extremely
fine, and curiously adorned but of a Gothic structure.

Addison, Remarks on Italy.

MANNERS AND TASTES

I wou'd not give a farthing for a Monkey that wou'd not
break me three or four pounds worth of China.

Burnaby, The Ladies Visiting Day.

NATURE

You can't imagine how glad I am with the sight of a plain
(after the Alps).

Addison, Remarks on Italy.

POETRY

Poetry is an imitation of nature by a pathetic and numerous
speech. . . . It would be no hard matter to prove that most
of our thoughts are naturally attended with some sort and
some degree of passion. And 'tis the expression of this passion
which gives so much pleasure both in conversation and in
human authors. . . . Our Gothick and Barbarous manner, . . .
Homer . . . the father of poetical diction. Virgil is to be
preferr'd to Homer (Psalm XVIII preferred to Aeneid X).

Milton in the seventh Book of the Paradise Lost, has described creation better than either Ovid or Virgil himself has done. . . . He writ in a language that was not capable of so much Beauty.

> J. Dennis, *Advancement and Reform of Modern Poetry* (perhaps influenced Addison).

Cadwalader and Arthur, ancient kings,
Full famous in Romantic tale.

> J. Philips, *Splendid Shilling* (burlesque on Milton).

1702 r. William III and Anne

MANNERS AND TASTES

I do give and bequeath . . . a Black person; commonly called Brown, whom I take to be in the nature of my goods and Chattles.

> T. Papillon, Will.

May fat geese gaggle[1] with melodious voice,
And ne'er want gooseberries or apple sauce!
. . . . .
Thy white-wine, sugar, milk, together club
To make that gentle viand syllabub.

> W. King, *Mully of Maintown*.

The capture of Spanish Cargos at Vigo Bay made snuff fashionable.

Daily Courant, first daily with long run.

NATURE

The view (of Naples from Capri) must have been more pleasant when the whole bay was encompassed with so long a range of buildings, that it appeared to those who looked on it at a distance, but as one continued city.

> Addison, *Remarks on Italy*.

---

[1] Cf. the collective noun "a gaggle of geese".

POETRY

Beauty of Colouring in which consists chiefly the Poet's Art.
... (Shakespeare invented blank verse) to escape the tiresome
constraint of rhyme.

E. Bysshe, *Art of English Poetry.*

Le goût est exquis, quand il est reglé par la raison; et ceux
qui ne suivent que leur inclination pour guide, ont d'ordinaire
le goût mauvais.

Abbé de Bellegarde, *Lettres curieuses de
Littérature et de Morale.*

(Shakespeare's) genius was jocular, but when disposed he
could be very serious.

J. Collier, *Historical Dictionary* (1701-21).

SCULPTURE

The four finest figures perhaps that are now extant; the
Hercules Farnese, the Venus of Medicis, the Apollo in the
Belvedere, and the famous Marcus Aurelius on horseback.

Addison, *Remarks on Italy.*

🎔 1703 r. Anne 🎔

ANTIQUARIANISM

*Linguarum Veterum Septentrionalium Thesaurus Grammaticocriticus
et Archaeologicus.*

G. Hickes.

ARCHITECTURE

The cathedral (of Siena) a man may view with pleasure after
he has seen St. Peter's, though it is quite of another make
and can only be looked upon as one of the masterpieces of
Gothic architecture. The windows are formed like so many
scenes of perspective, with a multitude of little pillars retiring
one behind another ... the front covered with so many little
mazes and labyrinths of sculpture, that nothing in the world

can make a prettier show to those who prefer false beauties, and affected ornaments, to a nobler and majestic simplicity.

. . . . .

One sees in (the *Hofkirche* at Innsbruck) a kind of offer at modern architecture; . . . the architect has shown his dislike of the Gothic manner but . . . they were not arrived at the knowledge to the true way . . . The portal consists of a composite order unknown to the ancients; the ornaments, indeed, are taken from them, but so put together, that you see the volutas of the Ionic, the foliage of the Corinthian, and the Uovali of the Doric mixed without any regularity.

Addison, *Remarks on Italy*.

My ancient manor-house, that's noted for good eating, demolished to build up a modern kickshaw like my Lord Courtair's seat about a mile off, with sashes, pictures and china, but never any victuals dressed in the house for fear the smoke of the chimney should sully the nice furniture.

T. Baker, *Tunbridge Walks*.

MANNERS AND TASTES

(At Windsor) a little place with a seate of easement of marble with sluces of water to wash all down. . . .
Epsom shall be clutter'd with Company from Satturday to Tuesday and then they many times goe, being so neare London, so come againe on more Satturdays.

Celia Fiennes, *Diary*.

NATURE

It lies in the prettiest solitude imaginable, among woods and rocks which at first sight, dispose a man to be serious. . . . The Alps, which are broken into so many steeps and precipices, that they fill the mind with an agreeable kind of horror, and form one of the most irregular mis-shapen scenes in the world.

Addison, *Remarks on Italy*.

Description of the Western Isles of Scotland, M. Martin (read by Johnson).

POETRY

About fifteen I got acquainted with Mr. Walsh. He used to encourage me much, and used to tell me, that there was one way left of excelling: for though we had several great poets, we never had any one great poet that was correct; and he desired me to make that my study and aim.

Pope in Spence, *Anecdotes* (b. 1688).

1704 r. Anne

ANTIQUARIANISM

Rymer *Foedera*, Vol. I.

MANNERS AND TASTES

Last French sumptuary law on women's dress.

POETRY

Vulgar Passion . . . moved by the objects themselves, or by the Ideas in the ordinary Course of Life . . . Enthusiastic Passion (moved by) Ideas in Contemplation or the Meditation of things that belong not to Common Life [cf. Wordsworth 1800]. . . . What can produce a greater Terror, than the Ideas of an angry God? . . . (Milton) justly and reasonably excites great passions.

J. Dennis, *Grounds of Criticism*.

True wit, I believe, may be defined a justness of thought and a facility of expression.

Pope to Wycherley, 26.12.

"Bluish hills".
Pope *Windsor Forest*, first 290 lines now written. When published in 1713 "*blushing* violets", "vintage" and "wolves" omitted and "laurels" changed to "willows". "Bluish" or "blewish" is found in 1389 and 1586.

1705 r. Anne

ARCHITECTURE

(Blenheim) house is like one mass of stone, without taste or relish.

Memoirs of the Earl of Ailesbury.

MANNERS AND TASTES

Marlborough on his campaigns carried a screen of Chinese work with figures in European clothes of the period.

(See Trevelyan, *Ramillies*, p. 62).

NATURE

The Deserts (between Marseilles and Genoa) which have been rendered famous by the penance of Mary Magdalene . . . It is so romantic a scene, that it has always probably given occasion to such chimerical relations. . . . Irregular misshapen scenes (Alps).

Addison, *Remarks on Italy*.

PAINTING

Niece: I would be drawn like the Amazon Thalestris, with a Spear in my hand, and an Helmet on a Table before me . . .

Clerimont: Madam . . . there shall be a Cupid setting away your Helmet, to shew that Love should have a part in all gallant Actions.

Niece: That Circumstance may be very Picturesque.[1]

Steele, *The Tender Husband*.

POETRY

(Marlborough)
Inspir'd repuls'd battalions to engage
And taught the doubtful battle where to rage.
So when an Angel, by divine Command,
With rising tempests shakes a guilty land,
Such as of late o'er pale Britannia past,
Calm and serene he drives the furious blast,
And, pleas'd the Almighty's orders to perform
Rides in the whirlwind and directs the storm.

Addison, *The Campaign*.

("One of the noblest thoughts that ever entered into the heart of man" *The Tatler*).

[1] A very early use in this sense (cf. Goldsmith, 1766.).

144

T'enjoy the World's Conveniences,
Be famed in War yet live in Ease
Without great Vices, is a vain
EUTOPIA seated in the Brain.

> Mandeville, *Fable of the Bees, Private Vices Public Benefits.*

(Published first this year as *The Grumbling Hive or Knaves turn'd Honest.* "Pirated and cry'd about the Streets in a Half-Penny Sheet". Six editions by 1732).

THE STAGE

Theatre opened at Bath with stock company.

❈ 1706 r. Anne ❈

ARCHITECTURE

After the Irruption, and Swarmes of those Truculent People from the North (Goths and Vandals); the Moors and Arabs from the South and East. . . . I dare Report myself to any Man of Judgment and that has the least Taste of Order and Magnificance; If after he has look'd a while upon *King Henry the VIIth's Chappel* at *Westminster;* Gazed on its sharp *Angles, Jetties,* Narrow Lights, lame *Statues, Lace* and other *Cut-work* and *Crinkle-Crankle;* and shall then turn his Eyes on the *Banqueting-House* built at *White-hall* by *Inego Jones* after the Antient manner, or on what his *Majesties* present *Surveyor* Sir *Christopher Wren* has lately advance'd at St. *Paul's;* and consider what a Glorious Object the design'd *Cupola, Portico, Colonads* and other (yet unfinish'd) Parts, will then present the Beholder: Or compare the *Schools* and *Library* at *Oxford* with the *Theatre* there, . . . Not, as we said, that there is not something of solid and Odly Artificial too, after a sort. But then the Universal and unreasonable Thickness of the Walls, Clumsy Buttresses, Towers, sharp pointed Arches, . . . Turrets, and Pinacles thick set with *Munkies* and *Chimaeras* . . . that one cannot consider it with any Steadiness where to begin or end; taking off from that Noble *Aier* and *Grandure,* Bold and Graceful manner, which the Antients had so well and judiciously establish'd ... Witness ... Westminster, Canterbury, Salisbury, Peterborow, Ely, Wells, Beverly, Lincoln, Gloucester, York, Durham, ... and compare them (almost numberless as they are) with *One* St. *Peter's* at *Rome* only.

> Evelyn, *Account of Architects & Architecture* (2nd ed. cf. 1699).

To be Let, a New Brick House, Built after the Newest Fashion, the Rooms wainscotted and Painted, Lofty Stories, Marble Foot paces to the Chimneys, Sash Windows glaised with fine Crown Glass, large half Pace Stairs, that 2 people may go up on a Breast, in a new pleasant Court planted with Vines, Jesamin and other Greens, next door to the Crown near the Sarazen's Head Inn in Carter Lane, near St. Paul's Church Yard.

> Quoted Richardson, *Georgian England* (about this date).

GARDENS

Here a Chimaera opens wide her Jaws,
And from her gaping Mouth a Torrent throws;

. . . . .

There from a Dragon whirling round in Haste,
On the Spectators gushing Streams are cast;
There with his Arms, and watching of his Game,
A brazen Huntsman stands and takes his Aim,
To kill the Prey, but shoots a harmless Stream;
A pleasing Cheat, at which the wondring Rout
At once with Laughter and Applauses shout.

. . . . .

If more extended Walks run round the Plain,
Light Chairs should bear in State the Female Train;
Yet trusting to their Feet, the youthful Fair,
Walk the long Circuit, and despise the Chair.

> J. Gardiner, translated from Rapin, *On Gardens* (Latin).

146

MANNERS AND TASTES

Aetate hac opiniosissima, fide intemeratus Camelus Sudburiensis (because, though rich, he entered the kingdom of Heaven).

Epitaph in St. Gregory's, Sudbury.

MUSIC

Those Arts that make the Senses instrumental to the Pleasure of the Mind, as Painting and Musick, do it by a great deal of Rule and Order.

J. Dennis, *Essay on the Operas after the Italian Manner which are about to be establish'd on the English Stage.*

PAINTING

We cannot find in *Rembrant* either *Raphael's Gout*, or that of the *Antique;* or any Poetical Thoughts or Elegance of Design.

De Piles *Abridgement*, translated.

POETRY

First part of *A choice Collection of Comic and Serious Scots Poems both Ancient and Modern* "this being the first of its nature which has been published in our own native Scots dialect".

J. Watson.

My two great examples, Horace and Spenser, in many things resemble each other; both have a height of imagination, and a majesty of expressions in describing the sublime; and both know how to temper those talents, and sweeten the description so as to make it lovely as well as pompous; both have equally that agreeable manner of mixing morality with their story, and that *curiosa felicitas* in the choice of their diction, which every writer aims at and so few have reached; both are particularly fine in their images, and knowing in their numbers.

Prior, Preface to *Ode to the Queen in imitation of Spencer's Stile* (ten lines to stanza, alternate rhymes except last two. Apologises for *behest, band, prowess, weet, ween, whilom*).

F

I have not attempted anything of a pastoral comedy, because I think the taste of our age will not relish a poem of that sort. People seek for what they call wit, on all subjects and in all places; not considering that nature loves truth so well that it hardly ever admits of flourishing. Conceit is to nature what paint is to beauty.

Pope to Walsh.

The best of the modern poets in all languages are those that have the nearest copied the ancients..

Walsh to Pope.

This profanation and debasement of so divine an art has tempted some weaker Christians to imagine that poetry and vice are naturally akin. . . . Boileau:—

> De la foi d'un Chrétien les mystères terribles
> D'ornements egayés ne sont pas susceptibles.

(He quotes *contra* Corneille, Racine, Cowley, Blackmore, the Bible, Longinus "Let there be light". See Giles Fletcher, 1610) . . . It degrades the excellency of the best versification when lines run on by couplets. . . . tedious uniformity.

Watts, *Horae Lyricae* (preface).

[Cf. Pope, 1710. It is surprising how little critical notice Vaughan attracted in this connection (or for his return to a polished simplicity ascribed to Waller). The same is true of Herbert, Crashaw, Traherne and, to a less extent, Donne's *Holy Poems*. They were hardly reprinted or noticed till the nineteenth century except Herbert by J. Wesley.]

❦ 1707 r. Anne ❦

ANTIQUARIANISM

Society of Antiquaries revived (organised 1717).

GARDENS

Were the inclosure (at Blenheim) fill'd with trees, principally Fine Yews and Hollies, Promiscuously set to grow up in a wild Thicket so that all the Building left (Woodstock Manor), which

is only the Habitable part, and the Chapel might appear in two Risings amongst 'em, it wou'd make one of the most agreeable Objects that the best of Lanskip Painters can invent.
                                    Vanbrugh to Duchess of Marlborough.

MANNERS AND TASTES

Dr. Bull the High Church Bishop of St. David's smoked his pipe in the House of Lords lobby while the Bill for the Security of the Church of England was debating. He wrote *Defensio Fidei Nicœnœ*.

POETRY

The Nut-Brown Maid a black-letter reprint in *The Muses' Mercury*.

On voit que son unique fin est de plaire.
                                    H. de la Motte, *Discours sur la Poèsie*.

❧ 1708 r. Anne ❧

MANNERS AND TASTES

(At a sale) Mrs. *Trapes* in *Leadenhall* Street is hawling away the Umbrellas for the walking Gentry, Mrs. *Kanister* in *Hatton Garden* buys up all the course Bohee-Tea for the *Holborn* Ladies Breakfasts, and Mrs. *Furnish* at St. *James's* has order'd lots of Fans, and China, and India Pictures. . . . But Madam I ha' brought you a couple of the prettiest Parrokeets, and the charming'st Monkey for my Lady that ever was seen; a Coster-monger's Wife kiss't it, burst into Tears, and said, 'Twas so like an only child she had just buried.
                                    T. Baker, *The Fine Lady's Airs*.

Though I was only nine years old when my father died (1708), I still remember his lamenting that my grandfather had taken down the Gothic windows on the first floor (at Long Leat), in one of the fronts and put up sashes . . . As soon as the present Lord Weymouth married (1726) and came to live here he ordered the sashes to be pulled down.
                                    Lady Hartford to Lady Pomfret (1740).

An eminent, learned, and truly Christian prelate you once knew (E. Fowler, Bp. of Gloucester, d.1714) who could have given you a full account of his belief in fairies.

Shaftesbury, *Enthusiasm.*

POETRY

(Chair of Poetry at Oxford founded.) Poetry "institutionem et admittere et mereri".

J. Trapp, *Inaugural Lecture* (see 1715, 1741).

(Caxton's) *Destruction of Troy* in 3 books. 13th. Edition.

(The true "ratio" of poetry behind the ephemeral fashions and rules. Disguised truth. Homer the chief example. Aeschylus best dramatist. Virgil's *Georgics* his best. Dante best Italian, then Ariosto). La poesia é una maga, ma salutare, ed un delirio che sgombra le pazzie.

Gravina, *Ragion Poetica.*

> Nor are the hills unaimiable, whose tops
> To heaven aspire, affording prospect sweet
> To human ken.

J. Philips, *Cyder.*

("Shrubby browze", "sky-dyed plumbs", "pippins burnish'd o'er with gold", "perfummy, flowery Bean", etc. Thomson in *Autumn* called Philips "the first to use blank verse after Milton").

SCULPTURE

Grinling Gibbons given £253-13-4 for monument of Sir Clowdisley Shovell. (*sic.*)

❧ 1709 r. Anne ❧

ANTIQUARIANISM

Discoveries at Herculaneum (see 1738).

MANNERS AND TASTES

(At Box Hill) it is very easy for Gentlemen and Ladies insensibly to lose their company in these pretty labyrinths of Box-wood and divert themselves unperceived, . . . it may justly be called the Palace of Venus. . . .

(Hampstead's) neareness to London brings so many loose women in Vampt-up clothes to catch the City apprentices, that modest company are ashamed to appear here. . . . It seems to me to be overstock'd with Jews and sharpers.

Macky, A Journey through England (published 1714).

This rallying humour . . . has passed from the men of pleasure to the men of business. Politicians have been infected with it. . . . A false sort of wit which so delighted our ancestors, that their poems and plays, as well as sermons were full of it. All humour had something of the quibble. The very language of the Court was punning. . . . We should find, perhaps, that what we most admired, even in the turn of outward features, was only a mysterious expression, and a kind of shadow of something inward in the temper.

Shaftesbury, Freedom of Wit and Humour.

MUSIC

Percussion pianos invented (or 1714? but see 1767).
Anniversary of St. Cecilia . . . performing Purcel's [*sic*] Cecilia Song and much other music (at Wells).

Dr. Claver Morris, Diary, 22.10.

NATURE

O glorious Nature! supremely fair and sovereignly good! all-loving and all-lovely, all-divine! . . . whose every single work affords an ampler scene and is a nobler spectacle than all which art ever presented! . . .
Deep shades of a vast Wood. . . . Here Space astonishes, Sense itself seems pregnant; whilst an unknown Force works on the Mind, and dubious Objects move in the wakeful sense. Mysterious voices are either heard or fancy'd; and various Forms of Deity seem to present them selves and appear more manifest in these sylvan Scenes.

151

(In mountains) thoughtless Men, seized with the Newness of such objects, become thoughful, and willingly contemplate the incessant Changes of this Earth's Surface. They see, as in one instant, the Revolutions of past Ages, the fleeting forms of Things, and the Decay even of this our Globe.

I shall no longer resist the Passion growing in me for Things of a *natural* kind; where neither *Art,* nor the *Conceit* or *Caprice* of Man has spoil'd that genuine Order, by breaking in upon that *primitive State.* Even the rude *Rocks,* the mossy *Caverns,* the irregular unwrought *Grottos* and the broken *Falls* of Waters, with all the horrid Graces of the *Wilderness* it-self, as representing *Nature* more, will be the more engaging and appear with a Magnificence beyond the Mockery of princely Gardens. . . . What is beautiful is harmonious and proportionable; what is harmonious and proportionable is true; and what is at once both beautiful and true is of consequence agreeable and good. . . . Beauty and Good are still the same.

Shaftesbury, *Characteristics.* (*The Moralists*).

POETRY

Some account of the Life of Mr. William Shakespeare.
(First critical edition), Rowe.

An unspeakable sort of satisfaction (at) a little country-dwelling, advantageously situated amidst a beautiful variety of hills, meadows, fields, woods and rivulets. (*Preface*) . . . "lambkins" . . . "bloomy". (Blamed as neologisms, but really sixteenth century words).

Ambrose Philips ("Namby Pamby Philips", Carey), *Pastorals* (Influence of Spenser), published with Pope's *Pastorals.*

(Di regole vere e perpetue) ve ne son così poche da contarsi sul naso. . . . Che per leggere i gran poeti . . . non sia nulla meno necessario quell' ardore di fantasia, e quel commovimento, e quell'ebrietà di spirito agitatore di quel ch'ei si veda necessario al trovator del poema. . . . Quell'empito sovrumano, che, senza riconoscere i nostri giudizi, rapisce la nostra ammirazione.

> Montani di Pesaro (accademico della Crusca), *Lettera intorno alle Considerazioni* (dell' Orsi) *sopra Bouhours* (cf. Pope, *Essay on Criticism*, 1711).

(In genuine religious poetry) The Song would end where the Inspiration ceases; the whole Composure would be of a Piece, all meridian Light and meridian Fervour.

> Isaac Watts, preface to *Horae Lyricae* (2nd ed.).

SCULPTURE

The greatest of the ancient as well as modern artists . . . when they erred in their designs, or draughts, it was on the side of greatness, by running into the unsizable and gigantic, rather than into the minute and delicate. Of this Mich. Angelo.

> Shaftesbury, *Freedom of Wit and Humour*.

1710 r. Anne

ARCHITECTURE

St. Paul's finished (see 1697).

Magdalen College chapel, (Oxford), which is very elegant but small and rather dark . . .
Queens College, when the new building is finished this will be a truly regal edifice. . . .
Trinity College chapel is incomparably beautiful and is built in the Italian style without a ceiling. . . . The altar is especially beautiful and graceful with carved foliage and fine ornamentation. . . . In the Ashmolean . . . Andromeda with Perseus, incomparably carved in alabaster on a black wooden panel. . . .
Ch. Ch. Hall . . . fearfully large and high but otherwise poor and ugly. . . . All Saints Church a beautiful edifice of uniform style.

> Z. C. von Uffenbach, *Travels in England*.

MANNERS AND TASTES

Many gentlemen whom we hear censured as atheists.

Shaftesbury, *Advice to an Author.*

The tuck'd up sempstress walks with hasty strides
While streams run down her oil'd umbrella's sides.

Swift, *City Shower.*

MUSIC

Händel came to London.

Academy of Ancient Music founded.

There must of necessity be the foundation of a right and wrong taste. . . . For harmony is harmony by nature, let men judge ever so ridiculously of music.

Shaftesbury, *Advice to an Author.*

PAINTING

Effeminacy pleases me. The Indian figures, the Japan work, the enamel strikes my eye. The luscious colours and glossy paint gain upon my fancy. A French or Flemish style is highly liked by me at first sight, and I pursue my liking. . . . How is it possible I should thus come to taste the beauties of an Italian master?

Shaftesbury, *Advice to an Author.*

POETRY

(Homer) describes no qualities or virtues; censures no manners; makes no encomiums, nor gives characters himself; but brings his actors still in view. 'Tis they who show themselves, . . . give more instruction than all the comments or glosses in the world. . . . Our dramatic Shakespeare, our Fletcher, Jonson, and our epic Milton preserve this style. . . . To their eternal honour, they have withal been the first of Europeans, who, since the Gothic Model of Poetry, attempted to throw off the horrid discord of jingling Rhyme. . . . The genius of (dramatic) poetry consists in the lively representation of the disorders and misery of the great; to the end that the people and those

154

of a lower condition may be taught the better to content them-, selves with privacy, enjoy their safer state, and prize the equality and justice of their guardian laws. ... Amidst the several styles and manners of discourse or writing, the easiest attained and earliest practised was the miraculous, the pompous, or what we generally call the sublime; ... the fine sights of Indians are enormous figures, odd and glaring colours, and whatever of that sort is amazingly beheld with a kind of horror and consternation. ... The baiting and slaughter of so many sorts of creatures, tame as well as wild for diversion merely, may witness the extraordinary inclination we have for amphitheatrical spectacles; ... our dramatic poets stand violently affected this way. ... (Shakespeare) may witness for our good ear and manly relish ... (Hamlet) which has perhaps been oftenest acted of any which have come upon our stage is almost one continued moral; ... no flattery of the sex; no ranting of the gods; no blustering heroism; nor anything of that curious mixture of the fierce and tender which makes the hinge of modern tragedy. ... Our relish or taste must of necessity grow barbarous, whilst barbarian customs, savage manners, Indian wars, and monsters of the terra incognita employ our leisure hours. ... These are, in our present days, what books of chivalry were in those of our forefathers. ... (Shakespeare) hit our taste in giving us a Moorish hero, full-fraught with prodigy, a wondrous story teller. ... Monsters and monsterlands were never more in request. ... They should search for that simplicity of manners and innocence of behaviour, which has been often known among mere savages, ere they were corrupted by our commerce. ... The wit of the best poet is not sufficient to reconcile us to the campaign of a Joshua, or the retreat of a Moses, by the assistance of an Egyptian loan. Nor will it be possible, by the Muses art, to make that royal hero appear aimiable in human eyes who found such favour in the Eye of Heaven.

Shaftesbury, *Advice to an Author*.

Addison in *Tatler* (31.9) prefers daisies and violets to the best ordered parterres.

Tatler, 31.9.

(On Crashaw). All that regards design, form, fable (which is the soul of poetry) all that concerns exactness or consent of parts (which is the body) will probably be wanting, only pretty conceptions, fine metaphors, glittering expressions, and something of a neat cast of verse (which are properly the dress, gems, or loose ornaments of poetry) may be found in these verses. . . . These authors should be consider'd as versifiers and witty men, rather than as poets.

Pope to Cromwell.

✤ 1711 r. Anne ✤

ARCHITECTURE

Many spires arising in our great city, with such hasty and sudden growth, may be the occasion that our immediate relish shall be hereafter censured, as retaining much of what artists call the Gothic kind.

Shaftesbury, Letter on Design.

MANNERS AND TASTES

Humour should always lie under the Check of Reason, and it requires the Direction of the nicest Judgement, by so much the more as it indulges itself in the most boundless Freedoms. . . . The deceased Mr. *Shadwell*, who had himself a great deal of the Talent which I am treating of, represents an empty Rake, in one of his Plays, as very much surprized to hear one say that breaking of Windows was not Humour.

Addison, Spectator, No. 35.

(Sir Roger de Coverly's "humour" is eccentricity. See Voltaire 1761).

The hoop-petticoat (i.e., a fardingale gathered at waist) introduced.

Her country-seat, which is situated in a kind of wilderness . . . looks like a little enchanted palace. The rocks about her are shaped with artificial grottoes covered with woodbine and jessamines. The woods are cut into shady walks, twisted into bowers, and filled with cages of turtles. The springs are made to run among pebbles, and by that means taught to murmur very agreeably. They are likewise collected into a beautiful lake, that is inhabited by a couple of swans, and empties itself by a little rivulet, which runs through a green meadow, and is known in the family by the name of "the Purling stream".

Addison, *Spectator*, 37.

MUSIC

Music ... changes and transports, ruffles and becalms, and almost governs with an arbitrary authority.

A. Bedford, *Great Abuse of Music*.

Musick is not designed to please only Chromatic Ears but, all that are capable of distinguishing harsh from disagreeable Notes.

Addison, *Spectator*, 29.

NATURE

So pleas'd at first the tow'ring Alps we try,
Mount o'er the vales, and seem to tread the sky,
Th' eternal snows appear already past,
And the first clouds and mountains seem the last:
But, those attain'd, we tremble to survey
The growing labours of the lengthen'd way,
Th' increasing prospect tires our wand'ring eyes,
Hills peep o'er hills, and Alps on Alps arise!

A. Pope, *Essay on Criticism*.

PAINTING

(Of colour) the pleasure is plainly foreign and separate; ... the subject, in respect of pleasure as well as science is absolutely completed when the design is executed and the proposed imitation once accomplished. And thus it always is the best when the colours are most subdued and made subservient. (e.g., Carlo Maratti).

Shaftesbury, *Notion of the Historical Draught*.

Kneller (as Governour) with Gibbs, Vertue and others, started an Academy of drawing and painting from the life.

POETRY

The finest Writers among the Modern *Italians* express themselves in such a florid Form of Words, and such tedious Circumlocutions as are used by none but Pedants in our own country. . . . I must entirely agree with Monsieur *Boileau*, that one verse in *Virgil* is worth all the *Clincant* or Tinsel of *Tasso*.

Addison, *Spectator*, 5.

The tragi-comedy, which is the product of the English theater, is one of the most monstrous inventions that ever entered into a poet's thought.

Addison, *Spectator*, 40.

Every Resemblance of Ideas is not that which we call Wit, unless it be such an one that gives *Delight* and *Surprize* to the Reader. . . . It is necessary that the Ideas should not lie too near one another. . . . When a Poet tell us, the Bosom of his Mistress is as white as Snow, there is no Wit in the Comparison; but when he adds, with a Sigh, that it is as cold too, it then grows into Wit. . . .
As *true Wit* consists in the Resemblance of Ideas, and *false Wit* in the Resemblance of Words, . . . there is another kind of Wit which consists partly in the Resemblance of Ideas, and partly in the Resemblance of Words, which for Distinction sake I shall call *Mixt Wit*. This kind of Wit is that which abounds in *Cowley*, more than in any Author that ever wrote. Mr. Waller has likewise a great deal of it. Mr. *Dryden* is very sparing of it. *Milton* had a Genius much above it. Spencer (*sic*) is in the Same Class with Milton. . . . The Passion of Love in its Nature has been thought to resemble Fire; for which Reason the Words Fire and Flame are made use of to signifie Love. The witty Poets therefore have taken an Advantage from the doubtful Meaning of the Word Fire, to make an infinite Number of Witticisms. . . . Wit as (Dryden) defines it is a "Propriety of Words and Thoughts adapted to the Subject". If this be a true Definition of Wit, I am apt to think that *Euclid* was the greatest Wit that ever sent Pen to Paper . . .
Bouhours whom I look upon to be the most penetrating of all the *French* Critics. . . .
I look upon these Writers as *Goths* in Poetry, who, like those in Architecture, not being able to come up to the beautiful

Simplicity of the old *Greeks* and *Romans*, have endeavored to supply its Place with all the Extravagancies of an irregular Fancy. . . . The Taste of most of our *English* Poets, as well as Readers, is extremely *Gothick*.

> Addison, *Spectator*, 62.

Chevy Chase is the favorite Ballad of the common people of *England;* and *Ben. Johnson* used to say he had rather have been the Author of it than of all his Works.

> Addison, *Spectator*, 70.

Cf. Sidney *Apologie for Poetrie* (1581?) "my heart more moved than with a trumpet".

Poetry therefore is Poetry because it is more passionate and sensual than Prose. A Poet has two ways of exciting Passion. The one by Figurativeness the other by the Harmony of his Expression, but the Figures contribute more to the exciting of Passion . . . What one of these great Qualities has the old Ballad of Chevy Chase?

> J. Dennis on 70*th Spectator* (cf. 1644, Milton).

The *Two Children in the Wood* is one of the darling Songs of the common People, and has been the Delight of most *Englishmen* in some Part of their Age.

> Addison, *Spectator*, 85.

An Imitation of the best Authors is not to compare with a good Original; and I believe we may observe that very few Writers make an extraordinary Figure in the World, who have not something in their Way of thinking or expressing themselves that is peculiar to them.

> Addison, *Spectator*, 160.

Unless Poetry is taken in at the first glance, it immediately loses its force and point.

> Tickell, *De Poesi Didactica*.

Beauty and truth are plainly joined with the notion of utility and convenience (iii). At this hour romances and gallantries of like sort, together with works as monstrous of other kinds, are current and in vogue. . . . In our tragedy nothing is so common as wheels, racks and gibbets properly adorned. . . . An English author would be all genius. He would reap the fruits of art, but without study. . . . A hero without passion is in poetry as absurd as a hero without life or action. . . . A complete and perfect character is the greatest monster, and of all poetic fictions not only the least engaging but the least moral and improving (v).

Shaftesbury, *Miscellaneous Reflections.*

First follow Nature, and your judgment frame
By her just standard, which is still the same:
Unerring Nature, still divinely bright,
One clear, unchang'd, and universal light,
Life, form, and beauty, must to all impart
At once the source, and end, and test of art.

. . . . .

'Tis more to guide than spur the Muses' steed,
Restrain his fury, than provoke his speed.

. . . . .

Nature and Homer were, he found, the same.

. . . . .

From vulgar bounds with brave disorder part
And Snatch a grace beyond the reach of art.

. . . . .

A perfect judge will read each work of Wit
With the same spirit that his author writ

. . . . .

True Wit is Nature to advantage dress'd,
What oft was thought, but n'eer so well express'd.
But in such lays as neither ebb nor flow,
Correctly cold and regularly low,
That shunning faults, one quiet tenour keep,
We cannot blame indeed—but we may sleep.

. . . . .

While expletives their feeble aid do join
And ten low words oft creep in one dull line.

. . . . .

Where-e'er you find "the cooling western breeze"
In the next line it "whispers through the trees".
If crystal streams "with pleasing murmurs creep",
The reader's threatened (not in vain) with "sleep".

    ·   ·   ·   ·

A needless Alexandrine ends the song,
That like a wounded snake, drags its slow length along.

    ·   ·   ·   ·

'Tis not enough no harshness gives offence,
The sound must seem an echo to the sense:
Soft is the strain where Zephyr gently blows,
And the smooth stream in smoother numbers flows;
But when loud surges lash the sounding shore
The hoarse, rough verse should like the torrent roar.
When Ajax strives some rock's vast weight to throw,
The line too labours, and the words move slow.

    ·   ·   ·   ·   ·

The rhyming clowns that gladded Shakespear's age
No more with crambo entertain the stage
                          (omitted in later editions).

    ·   ·   ·   ·

Our sons their fathers' failing language see,
And such as Chaucer is, shall Dryden be.

    ·   ·   ·   ·

Thee, bold Longinus! all the Nine inspire,
And bless their critic with a poet's fire.

    ·   ·   ·   ·

A Raphael painted and a Vida sung.

    ·   ·   ·   ·

And Boileau still in right of Horace sways.

                     Pope, *Essay on Criticism.*

J. Tonson's edition of Milton, completed 1713, being the ninth
of Paradise Lost, the eighth of Paradise Regained, the seventh
of Samson Agonistes, and the sixth of the minor poems (see
1667 and 1763).

Tickell appointed to Chair of Poetry at Oxford. He wrote
Hunting and other poems (and see 1713).

STYLE

Fashion is indeed a powerful mistress. . . . The elegant court divine exhorts in miscellany, and is ashamed to bring his twos and threes before a fashionable assembly (ii). Till very late days the fashion of speaking (in Parliament) and the turn of art was after the figurative and florid manner. Nothing was so acceptable as the high-sounding phrase, the far-fetched comparison, the capricious point and play of words; and nothing so despicable as what was merely of the plain or natural kind (iii).

Shaftesbury, *Miscellaneous Reflections*.

1712 r. Anne

ARCHITECTURE

Let anyone reflect on the Disposition of Mind he finds in himself at his first Entrance into the *Pantheon* at *Rome*, and how his Imagination is filled with something Great and Amazing; and, at the same time, consider how little, in proportion, he is affected with the Inside of a *Gothick* Cathedral, tho' it be five times larger than the other; which can arise from nothing else, but the Greatness of the Manner in the one, and the Meanness in the other.

Addison, *Spectator*, 415.

GARDENS

Thorough-Views, call'd Ah, Ah, . . . are Openings . . . to the very Level of the Walks, with a large and deep Ditch at the Foot, . . . which surprizes.

J. James (translation of Le Blond), *Gardening*.

Why may not a whole Estate be thrown into a kind of Garden by frequent Plantations? . . . A Man might make a pretty Landskip of his own Possessions. . . . Our Trees rise in Cones, Globes, and Pyramids. We see the Marks of the Scissars upon every Plant.

Addison, *Spectator*, 414.

MANNERS AND TASTES

Chief Justice Parker at Essex Assizes said that he would have anybody who threw "witches" to sink or swim indicted for murder.

A witch convicted at Hereford but not executed.   The last English trial.

> One speaks the glory of the British Queen,
> And one describes a charming Indian screen
>
> .   .   .   .   .   .
>
> On shining altars of Japan they raise
> The silver lamp; the fiery spirits blaze:
> From silver spouts the grateful liquors glide,
> While China's earth receives the smoking tide.
>
> Pope, *The Rape of the Lock.*

John Bull in the main was an honest plain-dealing fellow, choleric, bold, and of a very inconstant temper.   He dreaded not old Lewis, either at back-sword, single falchion, or cudgel-play; but then he was very apt to quarrel with his best friends, especially if they pretended to govern him.   If you flattered him you might lead him as a child (His mother=Church of England; his sister Peg=Scotland, in love with Jack=Calvin).

Arbuthnot, *History of John Bull.*

NATURE

A Man of a Polite Imagination . . . makes the most rude uncultivated Parts of Nature administer to his Pleasures (411). The Mind of Man naturally hates every thing that looks like a Restraint upon it.   Wide and undetermined Prospects . . . pleasing to the Fancy; . . . a troubled Ocean, a Heaven adorned with Stars and Meteors.   (412).

There is something more bold and masterly in the rough careless strokes of Nature, than in the nice Touches and Embellishments of Art. . . . We always find the Poets in love with a Country Life.   (414).

(Addison), *Spectator, The Pleasures of Imagination.*

Cf. Kant's account of Sublimity (*Critique of Judgment*).

POETRY

The Poet seems to get the better of Nature; . . . raises in us such Ideas as are most apt to affect the Imagination. (416). If he would go beyond Pastoral and the lower kinds of Poetry, he ought to acquaint himself with the Pomp and Magnificence of Courts. . . . Homer—great, Virgil—beautiful, Ovid—strange. The *Iliad* is like . . . vast Desarts, huge Forests, . . . the *Aeneid* is like a well-ordered Garden, . . . in the *Metamorphoses* we are walking on Enchanted Ground. . . .

μέγαυ δ' ἐλέλιξευ Ὀλυμπου. . .
Et vera incessu patuit Dea . . .

If I were to name a Poet that is a perfect Master in all these Arts, I think *Milton* may pass for one. . . . So Divine a Poem in *English*, is like a stately Palace built of Brick. (417). . . . The Poet . . . is not obliged to observe Nature's conduct in the successive Production of Plants and Flowers. He may draw into his Description all the Beauties of the Spring and Autumn. . . . His Rose-trees, Wood-bines, and Jessamines may all flower together, and his Beds be cover'd at the same time with Lillies, Violets, and Amaranths. (419). . . .

Another Circumstance recommends a Description more than all the rest, that is if it represents to us such Objects as are apt to raise a secret Ferment in the Mind of the Reader, and to work, with Violence upon his Passions. (418) Fairies, Witches, Magicians, Demons and departed Spirits. This *Mr. Dryden* calls *the Fairy Way of Writing*. . . . I do not say with Mr. *Bays* in the *Rehearsal* that Spirits must not be confined to speak Sense, but it is certain their Sense ought to be a little discoloured. . . The *English* are naturally Fanciful, and very often disposed by that Gloominess and Melancholy of temper, which is so frequent in our Nation, to many wild Notions and Visions, to which others are not so liable. . . . We have no means by which to judge of them, and must confess, if there are such beings in the world, it looks highly probable they should talk and act as (Shakespeare) has represented them. (419) This talent of affecting the Imagination . . . has something in it like Creation. (421). (For *Creation* cf. 1751).

Addison, *Spectator*, *Pleasures of the Imagination*.

Cedite Romani Scriptores, cedite Graeci.

Whether *Milton's Paradise Lost* may be called an Heroick Poem. Those who will not give it that Title ... advance no more to the Diminution of it, than if they should say *Adam* is not *Aeneas* (267).

Notwithstanding the Fineness of this Allegory (of *Sin* and *Death*) may attone for it in some measure, I cannot think that Persons of such a Chymerical Existence are proper Actors in an Epic Poem; because there is not that measure of Probability. ... *Aristotle's* Rules for Epic Poetry ... cannot be supposed to quadrate exactly with the Heroick Poems which have been made since his Time (273). It shews a greater Genius in *Shakespear* to have drawn his *Caliban,* than his *Hotspur* or *Julius Caesar.* ... Milton's ... distinguishing excellence lies in the Sublimity of his Thoughts ... an Epic Poet should not only avoid such Sentiments as are unnatural or affected, but also such as are mean and vulgar (279).

The Language of an Heroick Poem should be both Perspicuous and Sublime. ... A Poet should take particular care to guard himself against Idiomatick Ways of Speaking. ... The Idiomatick Style may be avoided, and the Sublime formed by ... the Use of Metaphors: Such are those in Milton:

> Imparadised *in one another's Arms.*
> .... *And in his Hand a Reed*
> *Stood waving* tipt *with Fire,* ...
> *The grassie Clods now* calv'd. ...
> Spangled *with Eyes.* .... (285).

A true Critick ought to dwell rather upon Excellencies than Imperfections. ... A Man, who cannot write with Wit on a proper Subject, is dull and stupid, but one who shews it in an improper Place, is as impertinent and absurd (291). The Heroe in the *Paradise Lost* is unsuccessful, and by no Means a Match for his Enemies. This gave Occasion to Mr. *Dryden's* Reflection, that the Devil was in reality *Milton's* Hero. ... Our Language sunk under him. ... Terms of Art; ... I have often wondered how Mr. Dryden could translate a passage out of Virgil—

> *Tack to the Larboard and stand off to Sea*
> *Veer Star-board Sea and Land.* ...
> *Eccliptic* ... *Zenith* ... *Equator.* ... (297).

For Sublimity:—*He above the rest*
        In shape and gesture proudly eminent
        Stood like a tower
and . . .
        Better to reign in Hell than serve in Heaven . . .

The Account of Thammuz is finely Romantick;—

        Whose annual Wound in Lebanon *allured*
        The Syrian *Damsels to lament his fate,*
        In am'rous Ditties all a Summer's day,
        While smooth Adonis *from his native Rock*
        Ran purple to the Sea, supposed with Blood
        Of Thammuz *yearly wounded: the Love tale*
        Infected Sion's *Daughters with like Heat,*
        Whose wanton Passions in the sacred Porch
        Ezekiel *saw, when by the Vision led* (303).

The noblest Work of Genius in our Language (321)

        (Addison), Spectator, *On Milton*, (these
        articles were omitted in the French
        translation, as *Paradise Lost* was unlikely
        ever to be rendered into that tongue).

Spenser's . . . old Words are all true *English*, and numbers
exquisite.

                                  Steele, *Spectator*, 540.

    But Shakespeare's self transgress'd; and shall each elf
    Each Pygmy genius, quote Great Shakespeare's Self?
    What Critick dares prescribe what's just and fit
    Or mark out limits for such boundless Wit?
                R. Steele, Preface to A. Philip's *Distrest*
                Mother (2nd ed. adapted from Racine's
                Andromaque).

        He no longer writes of mammy,
        Andromache and her lammy,
        Hanging panging at the breast,
        Of a matron most distrerst.
                H. Carey, *Namby Pamby* (1725 Parody of
                A. Philip's *Distrest Mother*).

The Style of the (Distrest Mother) is such as becomes those of the first Education, and the Sentiments worthy those of the highest Figure. It was a most exquisite Pleasure to me to observe Tears drop from the Eyes of those who have long made it their Profession to dissemble Affliction.

Steele, *Spectator*, 290.

Mr. Phillips has two lines, which seem to me what the French call Picturesque:
O'erlaid with snow, in bright confusion lie,
And with one dazzling waste fatigue the eye.

Pope to Caryll, 21.12.

From individuals of distinguished Kind,
By her abstracting Faculty, the Mind
Precisely general Natures can conceive
And Birth to Notions Universal give.

.   .   .   .   .

Blue gulph of interposing sky.

Blackmore, *Creation*.

(Blackmore's Creation) deserves to be looked upon as one of the most useful and noble Productions of our *English* Verse. The Reader cannot but be pleased to find the Depths of Philosophy enlivened with all the Charms of Poetry, and to see so great a Strength of Reason, amidst so beautiful a Redundancy of the Imagination.

Addison, *Spectator*, 339.

(Johnson in *Lives of the Poets* (1779) cites the last passage and quotes Dennis: "a philosophical poem which has equalled that of Lucretius in the beauty of its versification and infinitely surpassed it in the solidity and strength of its reasoning". He adds "This poem, if he had written nothing else, would have transmitted him to posterity among the first favourites of the English Muse").

❁ 1713 r. Anne ❁
ANTIQUARIANISM

With sacred miselto the Druids crown'd
Sung with the Nymphs, and danced the pleasing Round.

W. Draper, *Dryades*.

ARCHITECTURE

Wren designed towers of Westminster Abbey.

GARDENS

Adam and Eve in Yew; Adam a little shattered by the fall of the Tree of Knowledge in the great storm. Eve and the Serpent very flourishing ... A Quickset Hog shot up into a Porcupine, by being forgot a week in rainy weather. ... A Lavender Pigg with Sage growing in his belly.

> Pope, *Guardian*, 173 (On Gardening), 29.9.

MANNERS AND TASTES

What a charming Idea does (Tillotson) give of the Deity. ... It is alone sufficient to make the Atheist wish these were a Deity.

> A. Collins, *Discourse of Freethinking*.

I could distinctly see ... a Lap-dog, who was succeeded by a *Guiney* Pig, a Squirril and a Monkey.

> Pope (Guardian, 106), *A Window in his Misstress's Breast*.

NATURE

Is there not something in the woods and groves, in the rivers and clear springs, that soothes and delights, that transports the soul? At the prospect of the wide and deep ocean, or some huge mountain whose top is lost in the clouds, or of an old gloomy forest, are not our minds filled with a pleasing horror? Even in rocks and deserts is there not an agreeable wildness?

> Berkeley, *Dialogue* II.

Persons of Genius are always most fond of Nature.

> Guardian, 29.9.

PAINTING

I was today at an auction of pictures with Pratt, and laid out two pounds five shillings for a picture of Titian; and if it were a Titian it would be worth twice as many pounds.

> Swift, *Journal to Stella*, 1.3.

POETRY

'Tis not in mortals to command success,
But we'll do more, Sempronius, we'll deserve it.

> Addison, *Cato* (Ran a month. Translated
> into Italian. "La seule tragédie bien
> écrite d'un bout à l'autre chez votre
> nation". Voltaire, *Epistle Dedicatory* to
> Bolingbroke. 1731).

Give me, O indulgent Fate!
Give me, yet, before I Dye
A sweet, but absolute Retreat,
'Mongst Paths so lost, and Trees so high,
That the World may ne'er invade,
Through such Windings and such Shade,
My unshaken Liberty.

.   .   .   .   .

Be no Tidings thither brought,
But Silent, as a Midnight Thought,
Where the World may ne'er invade,
Be those Windings, and that Shade.

.   .   .   .

Let th' Ambitious rule the Earth;
Let the giddy Fool have Mirth;
Give the Epicure his Dish,
Ev'ry one their sev'ral wish;
Whilst my Transports I employ
On that more extensive Joy,
When all Heaven shall be survey'd
From those Windings and that Shade.

> Countess of Winchilsea, *The Petition.*

(*Miscellany Poems*. Also praises Nightingales.)

No trifling scenes at Oxford shall appear;
Well what we blush to act, may you to hear.
To you our fam'd our standard plays we bring
The work of poets whom you taught to sing.

> Tickell to *Oxford.*

⚜ 1714 r. Anne and George I ⚜

NATURE

Nothing could have more of that melancholy which once used to please me than my last day's journey. . . . I rid over hanging hills, whose tops were edged with groves, and whose feet water'd with winding rivers, listening to the falls of cataracts below [in the Chilterns!] and the murmuring of the winds above: The gloomy verdure of Stonor succeeded to these. . . . About a mile before I reached Oxford, all the bells toll'd in different notes.

(About this date), Pope, *Letters to Several Ladies.*

POETRY

The Shepherd's Week, J. Gay (a series of eclogues in mock classical strain of country life).

(Les anciens) quoi que nous fassions, ils seront toujours nos mâitres.

De La Motte à Fénelon, 15.2.

Il faut observer le vrai, et peindre d'après nature. Les fables mêmes qui ressemblent aux contes des fées ont je ne sais quoi qui plâit aux hommes les plus sérieux: on redevient volontiers enfant, pour lire les aventures de Baucis et de Philémon, d'Orphée et d'Eurydice. J'avoue qu'Agamemnon a une arrogance grossière, et Achille un naturel féroce; mais ces caractères ne sont que trop vrais et que trop fréquents. Il faut les peindre pour corriger les moeurs. On prend plaisir à les voir peintes fortement par des traits hardis. Mais pour les héros des romans, ils n'ont rien de naturel; ils sont faux, doucereux et fades.

Fénelon, 22.11.

Let no nice Sir despise our hapless Dame
Because recording ballads chaunt her name;
Those venerable, ancient song-enditers
Soar'd many a pitch above our modern writers;
They caterwaul'd in no romantick ditty
Sighing for Phillis's or Chloe's pity.

· · · · ·

In such an Age, Immortal Shakespeare wrote
By no quaint Rules, nor hampering Criticks taught,
With rough majestic force he moved the Heart
And Strength and Nature make amends for Art.

N. Rowe, Prologue to Jane Shore.

Chaque nation a ses signes fixes pour représenter tous les objets que son intelligence embrasse. Qu'on ne dise donc plus que les beautés qu'on a senties en lisant Homère ne peuvent être parfaitement rendues en français. Ce qu'on a senti ou pensé, on peut l'exprimer avec une élégance égale dans toutes les langues.

Abbé de Pons.

PART III
1715—1750

1715 r. George I

MANNERS AND TASTES

Mr. Whatley knocked at my chamber door and called me up when I was in bed. He came to go with me to the cold bath. Went with him not fully designed to go in. When came there there was company. He undressed and went in first. It appeared a very small matter as he performed it. When he came out and was dressed I resolved to go in too and went to the brink of the bath and jumped in head forward with a great deal of resolution and swam about and went out and went in again. It is indeed a very small matter, the cold does not affect one at all and is scarce perceptible while in the water. I applauded myself mightily when I came out for my resolution and courage.

Dudley Ryder (b. 1691?), Diary, 18.8.

The King to Oxford sent a troop of horse; for why?
That learned body wanted loyalty,
To Cambridge he sent books, as well discerning
How much that loyal body wanted learning.

Dr. Trapp.

MUSIC

This kind of Church music (anthem) might be improved to very good purpose to raise the mind into a higher pitch of devotion and spiritualise it. It is a very unhappy thing though that they make so ill a use of singing in the cathedral (St. Paul's) by using it even in their prayers and recitations of the Psalms that are no better than the Italian recitativo's.

D. Ryder, Diary, 14.6.

NATURE

(The neighbouring mountains are) black, craigie, and of a melancholy aspect, with deep and horrid precipices, a wearisome and comfortless piece of way for travellers.

Pennecuik, Description of Tweeddale.

PAINTING

Portrait of Lord Duffus in kilt and full-bottomed wig by R. Waitt (in Scottish National Portrait Gallery).

A painter of (the historical) class must possess all the good qualities requisite to a historian. He must moreover know the forms of the arms, the habits, customs, buildings, etc., of the age and country in which the thing was transacted more exactly than the other needs to know. . . . He must . . . have the talents requisite to a good poet; the rules for the conduct of a picture being much the same as those to be observed in writing a poem. He should understood anatomy, osteology, geometry, perspective and many other sciences. A painter should read the best writers such as Homer, etc., but chiefly the Holy Scripture. . . . To be sublime the thought must be great; what is mean and trifling is incapable of it. There must be something that fills the mind, and that with dignity.

> J. Richardson, *Theory of Painting*.

POETRY

Rowe succeeded Tate as laureate (see 1709 and Index I).

Spenser has always been a favourite with me; he is like a mistress, whose faults we see, but love her with them all.

> Pope to Hughes (editor of Spenser).

The whole frame of (The Faery Queen) would appear monstrous if it were to be examined by the rules of epick poetry, as they had been drawn from the practice of Homer and Virgil; but as it is plain the Author never designed it by those rules, I think it ought rather to be considered as a poem of a particular kind. . . . To compare it, therefore, with the models of antiquity would be like drawing a parallel between the *Roman* and the *Gothic* Architecture. The former is more majestic on the whole, the latter may be very surprising and agreeable in its parts. . . . Dryden himself owned he learned these graces of verse chiefly from our author, and does not scruple to say, that, "in this particular, only Virgil surpassed him among the Romans, and only Mr. Waller among the English". (Glossary explains aghast, baleful, behest, bootless, carol, craven, dreary, forlorn, foray, guerdon, plight, welkin, yore.)

> J. Hughes' preface to his Edition of Spenser.

Chaucer the Parent of Britannic Lays
His Brow begirt with everlasting Bays,
All in a Kirtle of green silk array'd
With gleeful smile his merry Lesson play'd.
His fellow Bard beside him Spenser sate
And twitch'd the sounding Chords in solemn State.

J'ai souvent oui dire à Despréaux, que la philosophie de Descartes avait coupé la gorge à la poésie, et il est certain que ce qu'elle emprunte des mathématiques dessèche l'esprit et l'accoutume à une justesse matérielle qui n'a aucune rapport avec la justesse metaphysique, si cela se peut dire, des poètes et des orateurs.

> (Cf. Sprat, 1667), J. B. Rousseau to Brossette, 24.7.

More and more pleased with (Boileau) the more I read him, . . . very much in the style and manner of Juvenal and Horace. . . . Now he has once done it for you, you are apt to think you could have done it easily too. Boileau may very well be called witty, but then it is a humourous kind of wit that pleases me immeasurably more than all the lofty, far-fetched turns and high expressions.

> D. Ryder, *Diary*, 29.9.

(Of the Psalms.) The very next line that the Clerk parcels out to us, hath something so *Jewish* and cloudy, that darkens our Sight of God the Saviour.

> Isaac Watts, *Preface to Hymns & Spiritual Songs* (4th ed.).

SUBLIME

"Bring me no more vain oblations, your new moons and your feasts are all abominations to me." I thought it extremely sublime. 12.6.

My Lord Roscommon's translation (*Ars Poetica*) and the sublimity of David's psalms and the book of Job.

> D. Ryder, *Diary*, 9.9

❧ 1716 r. George I ❧

ARCHITECTURE

Gateway of Radcliffe quadrangle, University College, Oxford, vaulted with fan-tracery.

GARDENS

Kensington Gardens. I was mightily pleased with the disposition of these Gardens, especially the wilderness part of it, where the wildness of nature appears.

Dudley Ryder, Diary, 7.6.

MANNERS AND TASTES

The more I examine my own mind, the more romantic I find myself. . . . Let them say I am romantic; so is everyone said to be that either admires a fine thing or praises one.

To Lady M. W. Montagu.

The Epistle to Eloisa grows warm, and begins to have some breathings of the heart in it, which may make posterity think I was in love.

Pope to Mrs. M. Blount.

Most of the young physicians were Deists.

2.2.

Young Mr. Powell treats his parents in a very familiar way and talks to them as his equals and upon a level.

4.9.

The sun was set, but the evening continued extremely pleasant, it came into my head to talk of gallantry and knight-errantry and enchanted castles and cruel giants who barbarously treated the Fair. The houses that we saw in the distance I suspected to be enchanted castles. . . . I carried on this fancy as well as I could but I must confess did it but indifferently that I was glad to drop it.

31.3.

I think (Voiture's) is the best turn of raillery and the best manner in the world of writing letters of gallantry and politeness that have nothing of business or matters of importance.

178

They are writ in a very free negligent way with ease and without anything of stiffness, but a certain agreeable familiarity runs through the whole, which are full of wit and humour.

D. Ryder, Diary, 19.1.

MUSIC

Dioclesian (Purcell, 1691). A great many very good dances in it and singing, but as for the drama I think that is but very indifferent. The decorations are some of them very fine, but I think the Paris Opera is much finer.

17.1.

The French music has a very different air and manner from ours; it is extremely simple and easy, but there is a peculiar kind of harmony which touches me very sensibly.

D. Ryder, Diary, 27.3.

PAINTING

Each heav'nly piece unweary'd we compare,
Match Raphael's grace, with thy lov'd Guido's air,
Carracci's strength, Correggio's softer line,
Paulo's fine stroke, and Titian's warmth divine.

Pope to Jervas (fashionable portrait painter) with Du Fresnoy's Art of Painting (2nd ed.).

POETRY

Read some of Spenser's Fairy Queen. I was mightily pleased with it and intend to read it over.

26.1.

The Rape of the Lock, which is a very witty poem, I think one of the best we have had come out these many years.

D. Ryder, Diary, 22.8.

Dryden's Miscellany (new issue) this year gave an Icelandic poem with translation.

STAGE

The manner of speaking in our theatres in tragedy is not natural. There is something that would be very shocking and disagreeable and very unnatural in real life. Persons would call it theatrical.

D. Ryder, *Diary*, 6.11.

Pantomime introduced to England at Lincoln's Inn Fields. G. J. Rich played Harlequin, a part he played annually for many years.

❀ 1717 r. George I ❀

NATURE

The Sight of a Mountain is to me more agreeable than that of the most pompous Edifice; and Meadows and natural winding Streams please me before the most beautiful Gardens. The Prospects that in Italy pleas'd me most, were that of the *Valdarno* from the *Apennines,* that of Rome and the *Mediterranean* from the Mountain of *Viterbo.* . . . But from a Hill which I pass'd in my late Journey into Sussex, I had a prospect more extensive than any of these, and which surpass'd them at once in Rural Charms, in Pomp and in Magnificence . . . call'd *Lethe Hill.*

Dennis, Letter to Sergeant.

POETRY

Lady Mary Wortley Montagu sent Pope some Turkish verses first literally translated in "what they call the *sublime,* that is a style proper for poetry, and which is the exact Scripture style" and then rendered "into the style of English poetry".

"The nightingale now wanders in the vines,
Her passion is to seek roses."

becomes

"Now Philomel renews her tender strain
Indulging all the night her pleasing pain"

"nor do I think our English proper to express such violence of passion, which is very seldom felt among us".
She thinks that Pope's Iliad loses nothing of the original beauty, but "the hot-headed son of Peleus" is "extremely absurd" as compared with Ulysses "observer of men and manners".

I no longer look upon Theocritus as a romantic writer; he has only given a plain image of the way of life among the peasants of his country.

Lady Mary Wortley Montagu to Pope.

> The darksome pines that o'er yon rocks reclin'd,
> Wave high, and murmur to the hollow wind,
> The wand'ring streams that shine between the hills,
> The grots that echo to the tinkling rills,
> The dying gales that pant upon the trees,
> The lakes that quiver to the curling breeze.

Pope, Eloisa to Abelard.

> What beck'ning ghost along the moonlight shade
> Invites my step, and points to yonder glade?

Pope, In Memory of an Unfortunate Lady.
(Cf. Jonson, 1631, T. Warton, 1747).

Le génie merveilleux de M. Milton.

Journal Littéraire.

(The French translation of the *Spectator* omitted the essays on *Paradise Lost* since it was unlikely to be translated.)

> Green was her robe, and green her wreath,
> Whate'er she trod 'twas green beneath.

Parnell, Health.

STAGE

Drury Lane pantomime *The Loves of Mars and Venus.*

❧ 1718 r. George I ❧

ARCHITECTURE

One vast arch'd window beautifully darken'd with divers scutcheons of painted glass.

Pope to Duke of Buckingham (from Stanton Harcourt?).

GARDENS

Pope bought five acres at Twickenham and made a garden which contained a shell temple, a large mount, two small mounts, a bowling green, a vineyard, a quincunx and an obelisk as well as hot-houses and sheds. This was a protest against formalism. His grotto or geological museum is said to have contained a stalactite which he had broken off from Wokey Hole (see 1745).

The eye should not be bounded by high walls, woods misplaced, and several obstructions that are seen in too many places, by which the eye is as it were imprisoned and the feet fettered in the midst of the extensive charms of nature and the voluminous tracts of a pleasant country. . . . That inexpressible somewhat to be found in the Beauty of Nature.

Switzer, *Ichnographia Rustica*.

PAINTING

The Perfection of a Master Painter is, to be able to perform the same Wonders by Colours which the poet commands by Language.

The Free Thinker, No. 63.

POETRY

T. Warton (the elder) succeeded Trapp in Chair of Poetry, Oxford (see 1748 and Index).
Eusden succeeded Rowe as laureate. He fulfilled his official duties.
Bodmer at Geneva bought the *Spectator* in French.

Heroic with continued rhyme, as Donne and his contemporaries used it, carrying the sense of one verse most commonly into another, was found too dissolute and wild, and came very often too near prose. As Davenant and Waller directed and Dryden perfected it, it is too confined. It cuts off the sense . . . produces too frequent severity in the sound. . . . It is too broken and weak. . . . It looses the writer when he composes, (and) must do the same to the reader. . . . Dare not determine . . . only enquiring (if blank verse and stanza) be a proper remedy for . . . this poetical complaint.

Prior, preface to *Solomon*.

[O Lord what is this worldis blisse
That changeth as the mone!
The somer's day in lusty May
Is derked before the none.

.   .   .   .   .

For in my minde, of all mankynde
I love but you alone.] (before 1500).

What is our bliss that changeth with the moon,
And day of life that darkens ere 'tis noon,
What is true passion if unblest it dies?
And where is Emma's joy if Henry flies?

.   .   .   .

For I attest fair Venus and her son
That I, of all mankind, will love but thee alone.

Prior, *Henry & Emma* (*Nut-BrowneMayde* "versified").

❧ 1719 r. George I ❧

MANNERS AND TASTES

Ev'ry jilt of the town
Gets a callico gown;
Our own manufacks out of fashion
No country of wool was ever so dull:
'Tis a test of the brains of the nation
To neglect their own works,
Employ pagans and Turks,
And let foreign trumpery o'er spread 'em.

The Weavers' Complaint against the Callico Madams.

PAINTING

The Painters of the Roman school were the best designers and had more of the antique taste than any of the others . . . those of Florence were good designers, and had a kind of Greatness, but it was not antique. The Venetian and Lombard schools had . . . a certain Grace, but entirely modern. . . . The works of those of the German school have a dryness and ungraceful stiffness . . . odious, and as remote from the Antique as Gothicism could carry it. The Flemings have been good colourists and imitated nature as they conceived it.

J. Richardson, *Argument on Behalf of the Science of a Connoisseur.*

Watteau, in London, painted *A Pastoral Conversation* and *Two Comedians* for Dr. Mead (see 1754).

POETRY

The *Fairy Queen*, for great invention and Poetick Height, is judg'd little inferior, if not equal, to the Chief of the Ancient Greeks and Latins.

G. Jacob, *Lives of the Poets.*

(Citing Shaftesbury on Milton): Il est vrai que le Dieu des Juifs et des Chrétiens peut fournir d'infiniment plus belles et plus grandes Images que les Idoles du Paganisme, et que la Poésie Orientale est infiniment plus noble que la Latine et la Grecque. . . . Si je puis instruire et plaire en même tems, pourquoi m'amuserai-je à plaire seulement?

A. Conti to Mme. Ferront, 13.7.

Se livrer aux impressions que les objets étrangers font sur nous; Men will always prefer the poetry which moves to that made on the rules. (anti-rationalist). . . .

Du Bos, *Réflexions Critiques sur la Poésie et sur la Peinture* (translated 1748).

Traité du Poème Epique, Du Bos, translated into English.

Lady Wardlaw forged old ballad *Hardyknut*; reprinted in Ramsay's *Evergreen* (1724), deceived H. Walpole.

🏵 1720 r. George I (South Sea Bubble Burst) 🏵

ARCHITECTURE

St. Martins-in-Fields begun (Gibbs).

POETRY

The most obvious defect in our Poetry, and I think the greatest it is liable to, is, that we study Form and neglect Matter.

A. Hill, *The Creation (Preface to Mr. Pope)*.

Homer is universally allow'd to have had the greatest *Invention* of any writer whatever. The praise of Judgment *Virgil* has justly contested with him. . . . That unequall'd Fire and Rapture, which is so forcible in *Homer*, that no Man of a true Poetical Spirit, is Master of himself while he reads him. . . . Tho' attended with Absurdities, it brightens all the Rubbish about it, till we see nothing but its own Splendor. This *Fire* is discern'd in Virgil, but discern'd as thro' a Glass, reflected from Homer, and more shining than fierce, but every where equal and constant. In *Lucan* and *Statius*, it bursts out in sudden, short, and interrupted Flashes; in *Milton*, it glows like a Furnace, kept up to an uncommon Ardor by the Force of Art: In *Shakespeare*, it strikes before we are aware, like an accidental Fire from Heaven: But in *Homer*, and in him only, it burns everywhere clearly and everywhere irresistibly. . . . *Homer* makes us hearers and Virgil leaves us readers. . . . We acknowledge him the Father of Poetical Diction, the first who taught that *language of the Gods* to men, . . . found out *living words*. There are in him more daring Figures and Metaphors than in any good author whatever. . . . in the same degree that a Thought is warmer an Expression will be brighter. . . . To throw his language more out of Prose, *Homer* seems to have affected the *compound Epithets* . . . *Homer* was the greater Genius, *Virgil* the better Artist. . . . Simplicity is the mean between Ostentation and Rusticity, . . . nowhere in such perfection as in the *Scripture* and our author.

Pope, *Preface to Iliad*.

Achilles' wrath, to Greece the direful spring
Of woes unnumber'd, heavenly goddess, sing!
That wrath which hurl'd to Pluto's gloomy reign
The souls of mighty chiefs untimely slain;

185

Whose limbs unburied on the naked shore,
Devouring dogs and hungry vultures tore
> Pope, *Iliad* I. i. (cf. 1611, 1614, 1674,
> 1726 and 1791).

PROSE

I have been better entertained, and more informed, by a few
pages in the *Pilgrim's Progress* than by a long discourse upon
the will and the intellect.
> Swift, *Letter to a young Clergyman* (cf.
> Berkeley, 1732).

❧ 1721 r. George I ❧

MANNERS AND TASTES

Oft let me range the gloomy Iles [aisles] alone
(Sad luxury! to vulgar minds unknown.)
> T. Tickell to Earl of Warwick *on Death
> of Mr. Addison.*

NATURE

Brown shades, and flowering meadows, the winding stream,
and the old ruins, the distant woods gilded with sunshine, and
beyond all the bluish mountains.
> J. W. M. D., *Secret History of Pythagoras,*
> "translated from the original copy lately
> found at Otranto in Italy."

There being more valuable and agreeable things and places
to be seen (in Northumberland) than in the tame South of
England.
> Sir J. Vanbrugh, Letters.

POETRY

There is not perhaps any harder task than to tame the natural
wildness of wit, and to civilize the Fancy. The generality of
our old English Poets abound in forced conceits and affected
phrases;—our country owes it to him that the famous Monsieur
Boileau first conceived an opinion of the English Genius for
Poetry, by perusing the present he made him of the *Musae
Anglicanae* (in Latin). . . .

Can I forget the dismal night that gave
My soul's best part for ever to the grave!
How silent did his old companions tread,
By midnight lamps, the mansions of the dead.

> T. Tickell, *Life of Addison* (praised by
> Johnson, 1779).

I have found time [in the Tower?] to read some parts of
Shakespeare, which I was least acquainted with. I protest to
you, in a hundred places I cannot construe him. I do not
understand him. The hardest part of Chaucer is more intel-
lible to me than some of those scenes, not merely through the
faults of the edition, but the obscurity of the writer, for obscure
he is, and a little (not a little) inclined now and then to bombast, whatever apology you may have contrived on that head
for him. There are allusions in him to an hundred things of
which I know nothing and can guess nothing. . . . Aeschylus
does not want a comment to me more than he does.

> Atterbury to Pope.

Chaucer reprinted, cf. 1602, 1687.

Bodmer and Breitinger. *Die Discourse der Mahlern* (imitation
of *Spectator*).

✤ 1722 r. George I ✤

GARDENS

Stourhead grounds designed by Kent[1] for H. Hoare with
Temple of Flora, Pantheon, Temple of the Sun, Bridge,
Grottos, a Convent and lakes. The temples decorated with
antiques and works by Rysbrack who competed with Roubillac
and Scheemaker. (A Hercules: "the head he borrowed from
a Farnesian God, the arms from Broughton, a celebrated
pugilist, the breast from a noted bruising coachman, and the
legs from Ellis, a painter".)

> J. Britton, *Beauties of Wiltshire*, 1801, see
> Wesley, 1776).

[1] These grounds are still practically as laid out.

There Hercules with sinewy arms is seen,

. . . . .

Cecilia bring from yon baronial hall
The old bard's harp and sweep its magic chords;
The enthusiast's ear shall catch each dying fall,
And echo shall reverberate the sound.

F. Skurray, *Bidcombe Hall.*

(At Lord Digby's, Sherborne) Behind these old trees, which
makes this whole part inexpressibly awful and solemn, runs
a little, old, low wall, beside a trench covered with elder
trees and ivies; which being crossed by another bridge, brings
you to the ruins, to complete the solemnity of the scene.

Pope to Martha Blount.

MANNERS AND TASTES

Even now 'tis said the Hinds o'er-hear their strain;
And strive to view their airy forms in vain:
They to their cells at Man's approach repair,
Like the shy Leveret, or the mother Hare,
The whilst poor mortals startle at the sound,
Of unseen footsteps in the haunted ground.

T. Tickell, *Kensington Gardens.*

I . . . wish you may love the town . . . these many years. It
is time enough to like, or affect to like, the country, when one
is out of love with all but oneself.

Pope to Mrs. J. Cowper.

POETRY

I wish you would review and polish that piece (Samson
Agonistes) . . . it is written in the very spirit of the ancients,
it deserves your care, and is capable of being improved, with
little trouble.

Atterbury to Pope.

STAGE

" . . . present taste of theatrical representation; where nothing
that is not violent, and, as I may say, grossly delightful, can
come on, without hazard of being slighted."

Steele, Dedication to Congreve of
Addison's *Drummer* (Reply to Tickell).

✤ 1723 r. George I ✤

ARCHITECTURE

Wren died (b. 1632).

NATURE

The decay of the year . . . the best time . . . for a painter;
there is more variety of colours in the leaves, the prospects
begin to open thro' the thinner woods, over the valleys, and
thro' the high canopies of trees to the higher arch of heaven:
the dews of the morning impearl every thorn, and scatter
diamonds in the verdant mantle of the earth; the frosts are
fresh and wholesome: what would you have? the Moon shines
too.

> Pope to Digby, October 10.

The whole situation (of Durham) somewhat romantic, but to
me not unpleasant . . . but others of better judgement condemn
this site. . . .
This (plantation at Kinnoul) is the finest sight I have yet seen,
or expect to see, in the whole of the kingdom of Scotland.

> Edward Harley (2nd) Earl of Oxford,
> *Diary.*

POETRY

Old Homer . . . was nothing more than a blind Ballad-singer.

> A. (Namby Pamby) Philips, *Collection of
> Old Ballads.*

Pieces of the old Provencal poets, which abound with fancy,
and are the most amusing scenes in nature. . . . I have long
had an inclination to tell a fairy tale, the more wild and exotic
the better; therefore a *vision*, which is confined to no rules of
probability, will take in all the variety and luxuriancy of
description you will; provided there be an apparent moral to it.

> Pope to Mrs. J. Cowper.

STAGE

Drury Lane pantomime with harlequin Dr. Faustus.

✣ 1724 r. George I ✣

ARCHITECTURE

Wells, where is one of the neatest, and, in some respects the most beautiful, cathedrals in England, particularly the west front of it, is one complete draught of imagery, very fine, and yet very antient.

Defoe, *Tour.*

MANNERS AND TASTES

(At Martock, Som.) The lesson was in the Cant. 5, 3 of which the words are these, " I have put off my coat, how shall I put it on, I have washed my feet, how shall I defile them?" The boy read thus, with his eyes full on the text. "Chav a doffed my cooat, how shall I don't, Chav a washed my Veet, how shall I moil 'em?"

. . . . .

(Hampstead) is so near Heaven that it is not a proper situation for any but a race of mountaineers whose lungs have been used to a rarify'd air.

Defoe, *Tour Through England.*

MUSIC

Three choirs festival inaugurated at Gloucester.

POETRY

Poetry in this respect resembles Painting; no Performance in it can be valuable, which is not an Original. . . . The most beautiful Polish is at length given to our Tongue.

Welsted, *A Dissertation.*

We are not (in older English) carried to *Greece* or *Italy* for a Shade, a Stream or a Breeze . . . I find not Fault with those Things as they are in Greece or Italy, but with a *Northern Poet* for fetching his Materials from these Places, in a poem, of which his own Country is the Scene. Readers of the best and most exquisite Discernment frequently complain of our *modern Writings*, as filled with affected Delicacies and studied Refinements, which they would gladly exchange for that natural Strength of Thought and Simplicity of Stile our Forefathers practised.

Allan Ramsay, *The Evergreen.*

Busk ye, busk ye, my bony, bony bride,
Busk ye, busk ye, my winsome marrow,
. . . . . .
Sweet smells the birk, green grows, green grows the grass,
Yellow on Yarrow bank the gowan:
Fair hangs the apple frae the rock,
Sweet the wave of Yarrow flowin'.

> W. Hamilton of Bangour, *Braes o' Yarrow*.

❦ 1725 r. George I ❦

MANNERS AND TASTES

If any *Colour* or *Fashion* be commonly us'd by Rusticks, or by
men of any disagreeable Profession, Employment, or Temper;
these additional Ideas may recur constantly with that of the
Colour or *Fashion*, and cause a constant Dislike to them. . . .
The *Deformity* of old Age in a Picture, the *rudest Rocks* or
Mountains in a *Landskip*, if well represented, shall have abundant
Beauty, tho' perhaps not so great as if the Original were
absolutely beautiful. . . .
The unattentive Goth . . . mistaken, when from Education, he
imagines the *Architecture* of his Country to be the most perfect:
. . . and yet it is still real Beauty which pleases the Goth,
founded upon *Uniformity amidst Variety*. . . . We know how
agreeable a very *wild Country* may be to any Person who has
spent the chearful Days of his Youth in it, and how disagreeable very *beautiful Places* may be, if they were the Scenes
of his Misery. . . .
The greatest happiness of the greatest numbers.

> Hutcheson, *Enquiry into the Original of our Ideas of Beauty and Virtue*.

MUSIC

(Händel given management of Italian Opera, 1720).

> Some say, compar'd to *Bononcini*
> That Mynheer *Handel's* but a *Ninny*,
> Others aver that he to *Handel*
> Is scarcely fit to hold a *Candle*,

Strange all this Difference should be
'Twixt Tweedle-dum and Tweedle-dee!

J. Byrom.

The Money which is drawn out of England by Italian Musicians.

Hutcheson, *Inquiry into the Original of our Ideas of Beauty and Virtue.*

POETRY

I will conclude by saying of Shakespeare that with all his faults and with all the irregularity of his *drama*, one may look upon his works, in comparison with those that are more finished and regular, as upon an ancient and majestick piece of Gothick architecture compared with a neat modern building. The latter is more elegant and glaring, but the former is more strong and solemn. . . . Nor does the whole fail to strike us with greater reverence, though many of the parts are childish, ill placed and unequal to its grandeur.

Pope, *Preface to Shakespeare.*

A shady Wood must have its *solemn venerable Genius* and proper *rural Gods;* every clear Fountain its *sacred chaste Nymph;* and River, its *bountiful God*, with his *Urn*, and perhaps a *Corncopia.* . . . Every one perceives a greater Beauty in this. . . .

Hutcheson, *Inquiry into the Original of our Ideas of Beauty and Virtue*, II, vi. 7.

My Peggy is a young thing,
And I'm not very auld,
Yet well I like to meet her at
The wawking of the fauld.

Allan Ramsay, *The Gentle Shepherd.*

❧ 1726 r. George I ❧

ANTIQUARIANISM

History of the Druids. Toland (posthumous).

MANNERS AND TASTES

To make pleasure, and mirth, and jollity, our business, and be constantly hurrying about after some gay amusement, some new gratification of sense or appetite, to those who will consider the nature of man and our condition in this world, will appear the most romantic scheme of life that ever entered into thought.

> Bishop Butler, *Sermons in Rolls Chapel VI*, published with preface, 1729. (Cf. Cudworth, 1678.)

POETRY

Version (1) [The quick'ning Sun a Show'ry Radiance sheds
And lights up all the Mountain's russet Heads.
Gilds the fair Fleeces of the distant Flocks,
And, glittering, plays betwixt the broken Rocks.]

Version (2) Half his beams Apollo sheds
On the yellow mountain-heads!
Gilds the fleeces of the flocks
And glitters on the broken rocks!

. . . . .

And ancient towers crown his brow,
That cast an awful look below;
Whose ragged walls the ivy creeps,
And with her arms from falling keeps;
So both a safety from the wind
In mutual dependence find.

'Tis now the raven's bleak abode;
'Tis now th' appartment of the toad . . .
While ever and anon there falls
Huge heaps of hoary moulder'd walls . . .
The town and village, dome and farm,
Each gives each a double charm,
Like pearls upon an Ethiop's arm . . .
How close and small the hedges lie!
What streaks of meadows cross the eye! . . .

And often, by the murm'ring rill,
Hears the thrush, while all is still,
Within the groves of Grongar Hill.

> Dyer, *Grongar Hill*, two versions (cf.
> Wordsworth, *Sonnet on Dyer* and his own
> two versions of *Dear Native Regions*, 1786
> and *Prelude* VIII, 468, ed. De Selincourt).

Welcome, kindred Glooms!
Congenial Horrors, hail! . . .

(The Robin) half-afraid he first
Against the window beats; then brisk alights
On the warm hearth; then hopping o'er the floor,
Eyes all the smiling family askance,
And pecks, and starts, and wonders where he is;
Till, more familiar grown, the table-crumbs
Attract his slender feet.

> J. Thomson, *Winter*.

1726. I know no subject more elevating, more amusing; more ready to awake the poetical enthusiasm, the philosophical reflection and the moral sentiment, than the works of Nature. . . . Poets have been passionately fond of retirement and solitude. The wild romantic county was their delight.

> Thomson, *Winter* (preface).

Still shall each kind returning season
Sufficient for our Wishes give:
For we will live a Life of Reason,
And that's the only Life to live.

. . . . .

And, when with Envy Time transported,
Shall think to rob us of our Joys.
You'll in your Girls again be courted,
And I'll go wooing in my Boys.

> Anon. *Translation from the Ancient British*,
> D. Lewis, *Miscellaneous Poems*.

Epithets are of vast service and the right use of them is often the only expedient to render the narrative poetical.

> Pope, *Postcript to Odyssey*. (See following.)

The Man for wisdom's *various* arts renown'd,
Long exercis'd in woes, O muse! resound;
Who, when his arms had wrought the *destin'd* fall
Of *sacred* Troy, and raz'd her *heaven-built* wall,
Wandering from clime to clime, *observant* stray'd,
Their manners noted, and their states survey'd.

> Pope *Odyssey* I. i. (cf. 1611, 1614, 1674,
> 1726 and 1791), italics by the present
> editor.

On ne lit plus Dante dans l'Europe.

> Voltaire, *Lettres sur les Anglais* (translated
> 1733).

Mr. Pope, the best poet of England, and at present of all the
world. . . . *Essay on Criticism* superior to the *Art of Poetry* of
Horace; and his *Rape of the Lock* is, in my opinion, above the
Lutrin of Despreaux.

> Voltaire, *Letters*, 22 (15.10).

❧ 1727 r. George II acceded ❧

PAINTING

The four pieces of Canal(etto) come to 88 *sequeens* and the
Rosalba *etc.* (i.e., "a fine gold frame and Chrystal") to 24,
which comes to about *Fifty Six Guineas sterling*.

> O. McSwiney (at Venice) to Duke of
> Richmond, 28.11.

POETRY

To coin new words, or to restore the old,
In southern bards is dangerous and bold,
But scarcely, very rarely, will succeed,
When minted on the other side of Tweed.
Let perspicuity o'er all preside.

> W. Somerville, *Epistle to Mr. Thomson*.

(Cornfields) A gaily chequered, heart-expanding view.

. . . . .

Young Day pours in a-pace,
And opens all the lawny Prospect wide;
The dripping Rock, the Mountain's misty Top
Swell in the Eye, and brighten with the Dawn.

Thomson, *Seasons, Summer.*

Milton is the last in Europe who wrote an Epick Poem. . . .
In all other Poems, Love is represented as a Vice, in Milton
only 'tis a Virtue . . . *Paradise Lost* had been so long neglected,
(nay, almost unknown) in England, (till the Lord Sommers,
in some measure, taught Mankind to admire it) . . . The
Fiction of Death and Sin seems to have in it some great Beauties
and many gross Defects . . . such shadowy Beings as Death, Sin,
Chaos, are intolerable when they are not allegorical. For
Fiction is nothing but Truth in Disguise. . . . There are
Perfections enough in Milton, to attone for all his Defects. . . .
A very good Poem may end unfortunately, in spite of all their
pretended rules. . . . The noblest work which human imagina-
tion hath ever attempted.

Voltaire, *Essay on Epic Poetry* (in English).

🎗 1728 r. George II 🎗

ARCHITECTURE

All the rules of architecture would be reducible to three or
four heads. The justness of the openings, bearings upon
bearings, and the regularity of the pillars. That which is not
just in building is disagreeable to the eye.

Pope in Spence's *Anecdotes.*

GARDENS

No three trees to range together in a straight line. . . . Nothing
. . . more *Shocking* than a *stiff, regular* Garden . . . *Ruins of
Buildings*, after the old Roman manner to terminate such walks
that end in *disagreeable objects;* which Ruins may be either
painted upon canvas, or actually built in that Manner with brick
and covered with plastering. . . . Haystacks and Wood-Piles.

B. Langley, *New Principles of Gardening.*

I have sometimes had an idea of planting an old Gothic cathedral in trees.

Pope in Spence.

MANNERS AND TASTES

That Idea of the Picturesque, from the swan just gilded with the sun amidst the shade of a tree over the water. A tree is a nobler object than a prince in his coronation robes. . . . A thorough-bred lady might admire the stars *because* they twinkle like so many candles at a birthnight.

Pope in Spence.

The Beggars Opera, Gay.

A Serious Call, Law (Influenced Wesley and Johnson).

> A violated decency now reigns,
> And nymphs for failings take peculiar pains,
> With Chinese painters modern toasts agree,
> The point they aim at is deformity.
> They throw their persons with a hoyden air,
> Across the room and toss into the chair.
> So far their commerce with mankind is gone,
> They for our manners have exchanged their own.
> The modest look, the castigated grace,
> The gentle movement and slow-measured pace,
> For which her lovers dy'd, her parents pray'd,
> Are indecorous with the modern maid.
> Stiff forms are bad; but let not worse intrude.
> Nor conquer Art and Nature to be rude.
>   E. Young, *The Universal Passion*.

POETRY

Je demandais un jour à *Pope* pourquoi *Milton* n'avait pas rime son poème, dans le temps que les autres poètes rimaient leurs poèmes à l'imitation des Italiens; il me repondit: *Because he could not.*

Voltaire (in England 1726-9) to H. Walpole, 15.7, 1768.

I read Chaucer still with as much pleasure as almost any of our poets. He is a master of manners, of description, and the first tale-teller in the true enlivened, natural way. . . . There is but little that is worth reading in Gower. . . . Sackville (afterwards the first Earl of Dorset of that name) was the best English poet, between Chaucer's and Spenser's time. His tragedy of Gorboduc is written in a much purer stile than Shakespeare's was in several of his first plays. Sackville imitates the manner of Seneca's tragedies very closely and writes without affectation or bombast, the two great sins of our oldest tragic writers. . . .

Webster, Marston, Goff, Kyd and Massinger . . . tolerable writers of tragedy in Ben Jonson's time. . . .

Carew (a bad Waller), Waller himself and Lord Lansdown, are all of one school; as Sir John Suckling, Sir John Mennis and Pryor are of another. Crashaw is a worse sort of Cowley . . . Herbert is lower than Crashaw, Sir John Beaumont higher, and Donne, a good deal so. . . .

There are three distinct *tours* in poetry; the design, the language and the versification . . . a fourth the expression; or manner of painting the humours, characters, and things. . . .

Dryden will be found to be softer and Waller sweeter . . . Virgil's Eclogues, in particular, are the sweetest poems in the world. . . . *Rotunditas versuum.* . . . Boileau the first poet of the French, in the same manner as Virgil of the Latin: Malherbe *longo intervallo* the second. Racine's character is justness and correctness; Corneille's passion and life: Corneille stumbles oftener and has greater excellencies. . . . Our best writers of comedy: Etherege, Vanbrugh, Wycherley, Congreve, Fletcher, Jonson and Shakespeare.

Pope in Spence.

J. Spence succeeded T. Warton (the elder) in Chair of Poetry, Oxford. He wrote *The Charliad*, an unpublished mock Epic with Pope; and see Index. There is no evidence that he ever lectured.

> The Thought romantic Memory detains
> In unknown cells, and in aerial chains;
> Imagination thence her flow'rs translates;
> And Fancy, emulous of God, creates.

. . . . . .

And Reason rises, the Newtonian Sun,
Moves all, guides all, and all sustains in one.
> W. Harte, *Essay on Reason* (Tutor to Chesterfield's natural son).

Look where Mœotis sleeps, and hardly flows
The freezing Tanais through a waste of snows.
> Pope, *The Dunciad* (a favourite couplet of his).

⚜ 1729, George II ⚜

MANNERS AND TASTES

Hail, mildly pleasing solitude,
Companion of the wise and good.
> J. Thomson, *Hymn on Solitude.*

Learning (at Oxford) is at so low an ebb at present, that hardly anything of the kind is sought after, except it be English, Scotch or Irish history.
> Hearne, Collections.

Poet . . . a character I detest unless I was able to maintain it as well as my Lady Winchelsea, 14.3.
Everybody is mad about japan work; I hope to be a dab at it.
> Mrs. Pendarves to Mrs. Ann Granville, 9.9.

Hutcheson, appointed to the Chair of Moral Philosophy at Glasgow, lectured in the Vernacular instead of in Latin. Perhaps the first in philosophy in a Scottish University.

Where's Troy, and where's the Maypole in the Strand?
Pease, Cabbages and turnips once grew where
Now stands New Bond Street and a newer Square;
Such piles of buildings now rise up and Down,
London itself seems going out of Town
Our Fathers crossed from Fulham in a Wherry,
Their sons enjoy a Bridge at Putney Ferry.

. . . . .

Think we that modern Words eternal are?
Toupet, and *Tompion*,[1] *Cosins*,[1] and *Colmar*[2]
Hereafter will be call'd by some plain Man
A *Wig*, a *Watch*, a *Pair of Stays*, a *Fan*.

     .   .   .

When *James* the *first*, at great Britannia's helm,
Rul'd this word-clipping and word-coining Realm,
No words to Royal favour made pretence,
But what agreed in sound and clashed in sense.

     .   .   .   .

What then? we now with just abhorence shun
The trifling Quibble, and the School-boys' pun.
J. Bramston, The Art of Politicks.

MUSIC

Yesterday I was at the rehearsal of the new opera composed
by Handel: I like it extremely but the taste of the town is so
depraved, that nothing will be approved of but the burlesque.
The Beggar's Opera entirely triumphs over the Italian one.
Mrs. Pendarves to Mrs. Ann Granville,
19.1.

POETRY

Of *Leinster*, fam'd for maidens fair,
    Bright *Lucy* was the grace;
Nor e'er did Liffy's limpid stream
    Reflect so sweet a face.
Tickell, Colin and Lucy (see 1748).

I have read *Cyder* (J. Philips) a Poem. I have it in very great
veneration.
Mrs. Pendarves to Mrs. Anne Granville,
19.1.

(Congreve) spoke of his Works as of trifles that were beneath
him; and hinted to me in our first conversation that I should
visit him upon no other Foot than that of a gentleman.
Voltaire, Letters on the English Nation
(1733).

---

[1] These are both the names of makers. Pope uses the word 'cosins'.
[2] A town in Alsatia which has also given its name to a pear.

1730 r. George II

MANNERS AND TASTES

I am always grieved to see the venerable Paternal Castle of a Gentleman of Ancient family dwindle down into an imperfect imitation of an Italian villa, and the good old profitable Orchard laid out into a waste of green, bounded by fruitless trees.

Gentleman's Mag.

PAINTING

The arts are greatly fallen among us of late, and there is nothing we excel in so much, at present, as the works in Mosaic. They are in greater perfection than they ever were, even among the antients. In their works of this kind . . . the design is often good, but the colouring indifferent or rather bad. They used nothing but stones with their natural colours and we use a paste or composition. . . . Fifteen thousand crowns for the copy of Dominichino's St. Jerome. . . .

Dominichino is in as high esteem now as almost any of the modern painters, at Rome. When you see any works of his and Guido's together, how much superior does he appear! Guido is often more showy; but Dominichino has more spirit, as well as more correctness. . . .

What they point out as the four most celebrated pictures (in Rome) are, Raphael's Transfiguration; Volterra's Descent from the Cross; Dominichino's St. Jerome and Andrea Sacchi's Romualdo.

Ficorini, Spence's Anecdotes.

POETRY

I have heard of the Wife of Bath, I think in Shakespeare.

(Cf. 1729) Swift to Gay

Taste is in a way to prevailing.

E. Wright, *Observations.*

> The whole air whitens with a boundless tide
> Of silver radiance, trembling round the world.

Thomson, *Seasons* (First complete edition, illustrated by Kent the landscape gardener).

(Sophonisba by James Thomson). The language is sublime and I think excels any play we have had a great while.

> Mrs. Pendarves to Mrs. Anne Granville,
> 9.9.

Considering the manner of writing then in fashion, the purity of Sir John Suckling's style is quite surprising. . . . For my part I prefer Corneille to Racine; he has more of Shakespeare in him. Indeed Racine's are the best crying plays. Molière is the only good large writer of comedies among the French. I am surprised that they pretend to set up Ariosto against Tasso in Italy. . . . Regnier is a very good poet . . . Boileau evidently the best of the French poets.

> Lockier, Spence's *Anecdotes*.

Colley Cibber succeeded Eusden as Laureate. He is the hero of Pope's *Dunciad*.

SCULPTURE

The superiority of the best antient sculptors over the moderns. We have no one, except Michael Angelo, that comes near them.

> Marquis Maffei in Spence.

The four most celebrated works of the modern sculptors in Rome are, Michael Angelo's Moses; Algardi's Story of Attila; Fiamingo's Susanna; and Bernini's Bibbiana.

> Ficorini, in Spence.

(In York Chapter House) are antick Postures, both of Men and Beasts. . . . Several Faces having different aspects, as one crying, another laughing, a third making wry Mouths, . . . Other chapiters represent the Leaves of several Trees, Fruits and Flowers; and the Pendants also with such wonderful and admirably Variety, that strike Wonder in the Beholders.

> T. Gent, *Ancient and Modern History of York*.

1731 r. George II

GARDENS

Something there is more needful than expense,
And something previous ev'n to taste—'tis sense

. . . . .

To build, to plant, whatever you intend,
To rear the column, or the arch to bend,
To swell the terras, or to sink the grot;
In all, let Nature never be forgot.
But treat the Goddess like a modest fair,
Nor over-dress, nor leave her wholly bare.
Let not each beauty ev'rywhere be spy'd,
Where half the skill is decently to hide.
He gains all points, who pleasingly confounds,
Surprizes, varies and conceals the bounds,
Consult the Genius of the place in all
That tells the waters or to rise or fall.

    .   .   .   .   .

Thro' his young Woods how pleas'd Sabinus stray'd
Or sat delighted in the thick'ning shade,
With annual joy the red'ning shoots to greet,
Or see the stretching branches long to meet!
His Son's fine Taste an op'ner Vista loves,
Foe to the Dryads of his Father's groves;
One boundless Green, or flourish'd Carpet views,
With all the mournful family of Yews;
The thriving plants, ignoble broomsticks made,
Now sweep those alleys they were born to shade.

    .   .   .   .   .

Lo, what huge heaps of littleness[1] around!
The whole a labour'd quarry above ground.
His Gardens next your admiration call,
On ev'ry side you look, behold the Wall!
No pleasing intricacies intervene,
No artful wildness to perplex the scene;
Grove nods at grove, each Alley has a brother,
And half the platform just reflects the other!
The suff'ring eye inverted Nature sees,
Trees cut to Statues, Statues thick as trees.

                     Pope, *Of Taste*, Moral Essay IV, To
                     Lord Burlington.

Mr. Langley who makes with the utmost exactness, beauty,
strength and duration all manner of sculptured or carved
ornaments for buildings and gardens, viz., bustos of gentlemen

[1] Cf. Walpole and Gray, 1739.

and ladies, living or dead at five guineas for each . . . All
manner of curious vases, urns, pineapples, pedestals for
sundials, balustrades, . . . columns and pilasters according to
the Tuscan, Doric, Ionic, Corinthian or Composite orders of
architecture.   Likewise all manner of rockwork, grottoes,
cascades, obelisks, porticos, and temples of view after the
grand manner of the old Romans. Together with great variety
of curious bustos and bas-reliefs of all the most eminent
emperors, kings, generals, admirals, ministers of state, philosophers, mathematicians . . . on trusses, pedestals or terms.

Daily Advertiser, 128.

MANNERS AND TASTES

For my part, I, who have no taste for an old musty stone,
look upon these countries (Italy, etc.) with an eye to poetry,
in regard that the sisters reflect light and images to one another.

Thomson to Dodington, 28.11.

MUSIC

In Days of Old, when *Englishmen* were—*Men*,
Their Musick like themselves was grave and plain;
The manly Trumpet and the simple Reed,
Alike with Citizen and Swain agreed.

> .   .   .   .   .

The *Gallick Horn*, whose winding Tube in vain,
Pretends to emulate the *Trumpet's* strain;
The *shrill-ton'd Fiddle*, and the warbling *Flute*,
The *grave Bassoon*, *deep Base*, and *tinkling Lute*,
The *jingling Spinnet*, and the *full-mouth'd Drum*,
A *Roman Capon*, and *Venetian Strum*.

J. Miller, *Harlequin Horace*.

On St. Cecilia's day in Dublin at St. Patrick's Cathedral
were performed Purcell's *Te Deum* and *Jubilate* and Corelli's
1st, 5th and 8th concertos.

Mrs. Pendarves to Mrs. Anne Granville,
25.11.

PAINTING

I am grown passionately fond of Hogarth's painting; there is more sense in it than any I have seen.

> Mrs. Pendarves to Mrs. Anne Granville, 30.6.

POETRY

Voltaire's *Brutus*; it is a fine tragedy, but I never saw one so affecting as George Barnwell. 13.7.
If you expect any sublimity in Barnwell you will be disappointed, the style is mean enough (by Lillo).

> Mrs. Pendarves to Mrs. Anne Granville, 5.8.

❦ 1732 r. George II ❦

ARCHITECTURE

Hampton Court Gateway on East of second quadrangle built.

Lord Burlington (altered Burlington House 1716) was so much for Palladio that he used to run down Michael Angelo. 'Tis true the latter did not follow the rules so much as the former, but then he had a more correct eye and is universally reckoned the best architect of the moderns, by the best judges, at Rome, as well as at Florence.

> Dr. Cocchi, in Spence.

MANNERS AND TASTES

The word "pittoresque" admitted by the French Academy.

Peck and booze.[1] Mrs. Pendarves' Letter, 30.12.

Shenstone at Oxford wore his own hair instead of a wig.

(White Kennett preaching at Court spoke of "a place which he thought it not decent to name in so polite an assembly.")

[1] "Peck" is thieves' cant, "bouse" is old English.

To rest the cushion and soft dean invite,
Who never mentions hell to ears polite.
>> Pope, *The Use of Riches* (Moral Essays III).

An equal mixture of good Humour
And sensible soft Melancholy.
>> Pope, *On a Certain Lady at Court* (Miscellanies III).

Life is a jest, and all things shew it:
I thought so once and now I know it.
>> Gay, *Epitaph for himself.*

MUSIC

Händel's *Haman & Mordecai* (later *Esther*, written 1720) banned at Haymarket by Gibson, Bishop of London.

NATURE

(The sea viewed from a cliff with a heavy swell breaking on rocks) raising a thousand great ideas.
>> Mrs. Pendarves to Mrs. Anne Granville, 4.7.

Haller, *Die Alpen* (in 45 years 30 editions, and translations into English, French, Italian and Latin).

(Chambéri) Ce que j'entends par un beau pays. Jamais pays de plaine, quelque beau qu'il fût, ne parut tel a mes yeux. Il me faut de torrents, des rochers, des sapins, des bois noirs, des montagnes, des chemins raboteux à monter et à descendre, des précipes à mes côtés qui me fassent bien peur...ce qu'il y a de plaisant dans mon gôut pour les lieux escarpés, est qu'ils me font tourner la tête; et j'aime beaucoup ce tournoiement, pourvu que je sois en sûreté.
>> Rousseau, J. J., *Confessions IV*, 2. (published 1782, translated 1783).

PAINTING

I must own that to my taste Corregio is the best of all our painters. His pieces are less pictures than those of Raphael himself.
>> Dr. Cocchi, in Spence.

Milton's

> They hand in hand with wandr'ing steps and slow
> Through Eden took their solitary way
>   altered to
> Then hand in hand with social steps their way
> Through Eden took, with Heav'nly comfort cheer'd,

and the Catalogues of cities, serpents and chivalry as well as Proserpine "gathering flowers" and "carried off by gloomy Dis", and "so stretch'd out huge in length the Arch-fiend lay" rejected as spurious by R. Bentley.

Dante wrote before we began to be at all refined; and of course his celebrated poem is a sort of Gothick work. He is very singular and very beautiful in his similies; and more like Homer than any of our poets since ... Dante, Galileo, and Machiavelli, are the three greatest geniuses that Florence has ever produced. Petrarca is the best of all our lyric poets; though there are several now who are very strenuous in preferring Chiabrera. ... The great Galileo used to compare (Ariosto's *Orlando*) to a melon-field: "You may meet with a very good thing here and there in it, (says he), but the whole of it is of very little value". ... The parts of (Ariosto's poem) are many of them more beautiful than those in Tasso's, but the whole in Tasso is, without comparison, more of a piece and better made. ... Your Spenser has taken much from him. ... If you look for a *right good* poet amongst us, 'tis what you must look for in vain. ... "That it would make an excellent poem if it were only put into rhyme" is just as if a Frenchman should say of a beauty, "Oh what a fine woman that would be, if she was but painted".

Dr. Cocchi, in Spence.

Malherbe was the first good poet among the French; and (J. B.) Rousseau is allowed by everybody to be their best now. ... Pope and Boileau are certainly the two best poets of all the moderns. ... Boileau writes more correctly and better than Pope; but Pope thinks more nobly, and has much more of the true spirit of poetry than Boileau.

Ramsay, in Spence.

Alc. "Appetite", saith that noble writer [Shaftesbury, advice to an Author] "which is elder brother to Reason, being the lad of stronger growth, is sure, on every contest, to take the advantage of drawing all to his own side. And Will, so highly boasted, is but at best a foot-ball or top between these youngsters, who prove very unfortunately matched; till the youngest, instead of now and then a kick or lash bestowed to little purpose, forsakes the ball or top itself, and begins to lay about his elder brother."

Cri. This beautiful parable for style and manner might equal those of a known English writer in low life, renowned for allegory [Bunyan?]

Berkeley, *Alciphron*, IV (cf. Swift, 1720).

1733 r. George II

ARCHITECTURE

(Kirkstall Abbey) its awful ruins; which, Good God! were enough to strike the most harden'd Heart, into the softest and most serious Reflexion.

T. Gent, *Ancient and Modern History of the Loyal Town of Ripon*.

GARDENS

My lord Bathurst (at Cirencester) has greatly improved the wood-house, which you may remember but a cottage, not a bit better than an Irish cabin. It is now a venerable castle, and has been taken by an antiquarian for one of King Arthur's.

Mrs. Pendarves to Dr. Swift, 24.10.

Mr. Kent was the sole beginner of the present National Taste in Gardening. Witness his works at Kensington Gardens below Bayswater. And at Lord Burlington's at Chiswick House: (the latter in 1733).

Spence, *Papers*.

MANNERS AND TASTES

Let then the fair one beautifully cry,
In Magdalene's loose hair and lifted eye,
Or drest in smiles of sweet Cecilia shine,
With simp'ring angels, palms, and harps divine.

. . . . .

If folly grow Romantic, I must paint it.

Pope, *Moral Essays II Ep.*

Queer country-puts extol Queen Bess's reign,
And of lost hospitality complain.
Say thou that do'st thy father's table praise,
Was there mahogena in former days?

J. Bramston, *Man of Taste.*

Nor can you ever *make me believe* you prefer the murmuring
of a purling stream, to a quaver of Cuzzoni. Your friend
the Reverend Dean would tell you this is all *"widowes' cant"*
and *"meer pruderie"*.

George Granville, Lord Lansdowne to
Mrs. Pendarves, 8.8.

POETRY

Great above rule and imitating none;
Rich without borrowing, nature was his own;
Yet is his sense debas'd by gross allay:
As gold in mines lies mix'd with dirt and clay.
Now, eagle wing'd, his heavenward flight he takes,
The big stage thunders, and the soul awakes;
Now, low on earth, a kindred reptile creeps;
Sad Hamlet quibbles and the hearer sleeps.

David Mallet, *Of Verbal Criticism.*

STYLE

Shaftesbury, *Characteristics*, sixth edition.

"All the best judges are agreed that we never had any work
in the English Language so beautiful, so delightful and so
instructive as these *Characteristics*."

❧ 1734 r. George II ❧

ARCHITECTURE

That true politeness we can only call,
Which looks like Jones's fabrick at Whitehall:
Where just proportion we with pleasure see,
Tho' built by rule, yet from all stiffness free.
Tho' grand, still plain, magnificent, not fine,
The ornaments adorning the design;
It fills the mind with rational delight,
And pleases on reflection, as at sight.
> J. Forrester, *The Polite Philosopher* (eight
> editions by 1776).

The silent streams, the gay, the wanton scene requires the
Corinthian order.
> R. Morris, *Lectures on Architecture.*

Model of Gothic Church for Worcester by T. White.

GARDENS

All gardening is landscape gardening. (This was spoken as
we were looking upon the round of the physic garden at
Oxford; And the view through it, that looks so much like a
picture hung up). [Presumably the view of Magdalen Tower].
> Pope in Spence.

MANNERS AND TASTES

Your situation (Cranham, near Painswick) is charming.
I love to be near the clouds, and a large extent of view gives
me the most exalted subjects for contemplation.
> Mrs. Pendarves to Mrs. Anne Granville,
> 2.4.

Dilettanti Society founded.

POETRY

H. Carey, *Chrononhotonthologos*, "the most tragical tragedy ever
yet tragedised".

Rymer is on the whole one of the best critics we ever had. . . .
Donne had no imagination, but as much wit, I think, as any

writer can possibly have ... Lord Dorset is the best of all those writers. ... Sir W. Davenant a better poet than Donne. ... Dr. Swift was a great reader and admirer of Rabelais; and used sometimes to scold me for not liking him enough. Lord Bolingbroke used to say that "he could never bear the Saffron Morning with her rosy fingers in prose".

Pope, in Spence (cf. Chesterfield 1739).

🌺 1735 r. George II 🌺

ARCHITECTURE

Maria. Oh, I Adore our new way of Building! so delicate, so quite *Novelle* and out of the Way.

Martin. Such noble Rusticks without, such elegant *Stuccho* within, and such a grove of Chimneys on top, ... a Lanthorn in the Hall as big as a Light-house.

J. Miller, The Man of Taste.

MANNERS AND TASTES

Delicious Regions, Plains, Woods, Waters, Shades,
Grotts, Arbours, Flow'rets, Downs and Rural Shades;
Arcadian Groves, sweet Tempe! Blest Retreats.

H. Brooke, Universal Beauty.

I have said it at home, I have said it abroad,
That the town is Man's world, but that this is of God.

I. H. Browne, A Pastoral Soliloquy.

A great castle (Audley End) belonging to the Counts of Suffolcia; it is a vast pile of building, but quite in the old taste.

H. Walpole to Gray, 10.10.

But Foster well this honest truth extends,
Where Mystery begins religion ends.

Savage, Progress of a Divine.

PAINTING

Hogarth's Academy founded.

POETRY

Collins (b. 1721) and J. Warton (b. 1722) at school at Winchester together.

Tread, with respectful awe,
Windsor's green glades, where Denham, tuneful bard,
Charm'd once the listn'ning Dryads with his song
Sublimely sweet.

Somerville, The Chace.

🎀 1736 r. George II 🎀

GARDENS

A charming Garden all Wilderness; much adapted to my
Romantick inclinations.

H. Walpole to C. Lyttleton, 27.7.

MANNERS AND TASTES

It is come, I know not how, to be taken for granted by many
persons that Christianity is not so much as a subject of inquiry,
but that it is now at length discoverd to be fictitious, . . . as if . . .
nothing remained but to set it up as a principal subject of mirth
and ridicule.

Butler, Analogy (cf. Hume, 1741).

White's Club opened. Perhaps the first.

In the afternoon there are billiards, looking over prints,
coffee, tea, cribbage.

Mrs. Pendarves. Letter.

At first (at Eton—1734) I was contented with tending a
visionary flock, and sighing some pastoral name to the echo
of the cascade under the bridge. How happy should I have
been to have had a kingdom only for the pleasure of being
driven from it and living disguised in an humble vale! As
I got further into Virgil and Clelia (Mme. de Scudéry) I found
myself transported from Arcadia to the garden of Italy and
saw Windsor Castle in no other view than the *Capitoli immobile
saxum.*

H. Walpole to Montague, 6.5.

POETRY

Gorboduc (Sackville, Earl of Dorset, 1561) reproduced by Spence at Pope's request.

W. Thompson in *The Nativity* imitated Spenser's metre and treatment of nature.

1737 r. George II

ANTIQUARIANISM

The Virtuoso, a Spenserian satire by Akenside in *Gentleman's Magazine.*

ARCHITECTURE

Radcliffe Camera begun by Gibbs at Oxford.

GARDENS

The lights and shades in gardening are managed by disposing the thick grove work, the thin, and the openings, in a proper manner: . . . You may distance things by darkening them, and by narrowing the plantations more and more towards the end, in the same manner as they do in painting.

Pope in Spence.

MANNERS AND TASTES

The time will come, when thou shalt lift thine eyes
To watch a long-drawn battle in the skies,
While aged peasants, too amazed for words,
Stare at the flying fleet of wondrous birds.
England, so long the mistress of the sea,
Where winds and waves confess her sovereignty,
Her ancient triumphs yet on high shall hear,
And reign, the sovereign of the conquer'd air.

Gray, *Luna Habitabilis.*

Two hundred pounds half-yearly paid,
Annuity securely made;

A farm some twenty miles from town,
Small, tight, salubrious, and my own,
Two maids, that never saw the town;
A serving-man not quite a clown:

. . . . .

May heav'n (it's all I wish for) send,
One genial room to treat a friend,
Where decent cupboard, little plate,
Display benevolence, not state.

. . . . .

And once in seven years I'm seen
At Bath or Tunbridge to careen.

> M. Green, *Cure for the Spleen* (cf. Pomfret,
> *Choice* 1700).

The Glasgow Presbytery prosecuted Hutcheson for teaching heresy: (*a*) that the standard of moral goodness was the promotion of the happiness of others, (*b*) that we could have a knowledge of good and evil without and prior to a knowledge of God (see 1725, 1729).

All Worldly's hens, nay partridge, sold to town,
His ven'son too, a guinea makes your own.

. . . . .

Heathcote himself, and such large acre'd men,
Lords of fat E'sham, or of Lincoln fen,
Buy every stick of wood that lends them heat,
Buy every pullet they afford to eat.

> Pope, *Epistle II, ii, of Horace Imitated.*

NATURE

A little Chaos of Mountains & Precipices; Mountains it is true, that don't ascend much above the Clouds, nor are the Declivities quite so amazing, as Dover-Cliff; but just such hills as people who love their Necks as well as I do, may venture to climb, & Crags, that give the eye as much pleasure, as if they were more dangerous: both Vale & Hill is cover'd over with most venerable Beeches, & other very reverend Vegetables, that, like most ancient People, are always dreaming out their old Stories to the Winds.

> Gray, to Horace Walpole, Aug., from
> Burnham (cf. Keats' *Hyperion*).

PAINTING

(Portrait of the Pope by Carlo Maratti).   The best portrait in the world.   I really do think him as good a painter as any of them.

Pope in Spence.

POETRY

If the Diction of *Leonidas* be softer and more harmonious than that of *Milton*, it may in fact be ascribed to Mr. *Pope*, as the great Polisher and Improver of our Verse, who had made the way much less difficult for Mr. Glover to ascend.

Common Sense, No. 10 for 9.4.

Brown fields their fallow sabbaths keep.

M. Green, *The Spleen.*

> Chaucer's worst ribaldry is learn'd by rote
> And beastly Skelton heads of houses quote:
> One likes no language but the "Faery Queen",
> A Scot will fight for "Christ's Kirk o' the Green".
>
> .   .   .   .   .
>
> (Shakespeare).
> For gain, not glory, wing'd his matchless flight,
> And grew immortal in his own despight.
>
> .   .   .   .   .
>
> Who now reads Cowley? If he pleases yet,
> His moral pleases, not his pointed wit;
> Forgot his epic, nay Pindaric art,
> But still I love the language of his heart.
>
> .   .   .   .   .
>
> But for the passions, Southern sure and Rowe,
>
> .   .   .   .   .
>
> Sons, sires and grandsires, all will wear the bays,
> Our wives read Milton and our daughters plays.
>
> .   .   .   .   .
>
> Loud as the wolves, on Orca's stormy steep
> Howl to the roarings of the Northern deep.
>
> .   .   .   .   .
>
> What shook the stage and made the people stare?
> Cato's long wig, flower'd gown and lacquer'd chair.
>
> .   .   .   .   .

But for the wits of either Charles's days,
The mob of gentlemen who wrote with ease.

. . . . . .

Ev'n copious Dryden wanted or forgot
The last and greatest Art, the Art to blot.[1]
                        Pope, *Epistle to Augustus* (Hor. Ep. II. i).

Sir John Denham's celebrated couplet on the Thames,

Though deep yet clear, though gentle yet not dull,
Strong without rage, without o'erflowing full,

owes a great part of its fineness to the frequency and variety
of the pauses. . . . I have nothing to say for rhyme, but that
I doubt whether a poem can support itself without it, in our
language; unless it be stiffened with such strange words, as
are likely to destroy our language itself. The high style, that
is affected so much in blank verse, would not have been borne,
even in Milton, had not his subject turned so much on strange
out-of-the-world things as it does. . . . The strongest contrast
of versification I am acquainted with is in Virgil's story of
Aristaeus,

Unde pater Tiberinus, et unde Anienta fluenta
Saxosusque sonans Hypanis, Mysusque Caicus

And the softest couplet that was ever written is in the same:—

Te, dulcis conjux, te solo in litore secum,
Te veniente die, te decedente canebat.

                (Virgil, Georgics iv, 370,466).   Pope in Spence.

J. Whitfield succeeded Spence in Chair of Poetry, Oxford;
apparently no published works.

❧ 1738 r. George II ❧

ANTIQUARIANISM

Excavations begun at Herculaneum (see 1709).

[1] Cf. Jonson, 1620.

MANNERS AND TASTES

If I had seen Stow on my way home (from Wales) I should have thrown out some very unmannerly reflections upon it; I should have smiled at the little niceties of art, and beheld with contempt an artificial ruin, after I had been agreeably terrified with something like the rubbish of a creation. . . . All these images together put me in mind of Poussin's drawings.

> T. Herring (Bishop of Bangor, later Archbishop of Canterbury) to W. Duncombe.

Probably the first iron railway, at Whitehaven.

POETRY

This mournful Truth is everywhere confest,
Slow rises Worth by Poverty deprest.

> Johnson, *London*.

STAGE

Comus staged at Drury Lane. Music by Arne.

✿ 1739 r. George II ✿

ARCHITECTURE

The great front of Versailles . . . a lumber of littlenesses.[1] . . . In short 'tis a garden for a great child.

> H. Walpole to West, 7.5.

The great front of Versailles. What a huge heap of littleness[1]. . . . Nothing can be vaster or more magnificent than the back front. . . . Everything you behold savours too much of art. . . . I am vastly delighted with Trianon.

> Gray to West, 22.5.

The palace (at Turin) is the very quintessence of gilding and looking-glass; inlaid floors, carved pannels, and painting wherever they could stick a brush.

> Gray to West, 16.11.

---

[1] Cf. Pope, *Moral Essays*, IV.109 (1731).

The churches (of Bologna) are more remarkable for their paintings than architecture, being mostly old structures of brick. . . . The country of Lombardy, hitherto, is one of the most beautiful imaginable; the roads broad and exactly straight, and on either hand vast plantations of trees, chiefly mulberries and olives.

Gray to his Mother, 9.12.

MANNERS AND TASTES

Most kinds of beauty are derived from sympathy. A man who shows us any house or building, takes particular care, among other things, to point out the convenience of the apartments, the advantages of their situation and the little room[1] lost in the stairs . . . and indeed it is evident the chief part of the beauty consists in these particulars . . . our interest is not in the least concerned . . . This observations extends to tables, chairs, etc. . . . Mr. Philips has chosen *Cider* for the subject of an excellent poem. Beer would not have been so proper, as being neither so agreeable to the taste nor eye. But he would certainly have preferred wine to either of them, could his native country have afforded him so agreeable a liquor. . . . It is evident that nothing renders a field more agreeable than its fertility, and that scarce any advantages of ornament or situation will be able to equal this beauty. . . . I know not but a plain overgrown with furze and broom, may be, in itself, as beautiful as a hill covered with vines or olive-trees, though it will never appear so to one who is acquainted with the value of each. . . . In painting . . . a figure which is not justly balanced is disgraceful . . . the principal part of personal beauty is an air of health[2] and vigour and such a construction of members as promises strength and activity. The mere view and contemplation of any greatness . . . enlarges the soul[3] and gives it a sensible delight and pleasure. A wide plain, the ocean, eternity, a succession of several ages; all these are entertaining objects, and excel everything, however beautiful, which accompanies not its beauty with a suitable greatness. . . . It is a quality very observable in human nature, that any opposition which does not entirely discourage and intimidate us, has

[1] i.e., small space.
[2] Cf. Burke, 1756.
[3] Cf. Kant, *Critique of Judgment.*

rather a contrary effect, and inspires us with a more than ordinary grandeur and magnanimity.[1] In collecting our force to overcome the opposition, we invigorate the soul, and give it an elevation, with which otherwise it would never have been acquainted. . . . To be convinced of this, we need only consider the influence of *heights* and *depths* on (the imagination). Any great elevation of place communicates a kind of pride or sublimity[1] of imagination. . . . We are not apt to imagine our posterity will excell or equal our ancestors.

Hume, Treatise II.

There was something respectable in those old hospitable Gothic halls, hung round with helmets, breast-plates, and swords of our ancestors; I entered them with a constitutional sort of reverence, and looked upon those arms with gratitude as the terror of former ministers and the check of kings . . . and when I see them thrown by to make way for some tawdry gilding and carving, I can't help considering such alterations as ominous even to our constitution. Our old Gothic constitution had a noble strength and simplicity in it, which was well enough represented by the bold arches and the solid pillars of the edifices.

Common Sense, 150.

MUSIC

(Paris opera) cracked voices, trilling division upon two notes and a half, accompanied by orchestra of humstrums, and a whole house more attentive than if Farinelli had sung.

12.4.

I never beheld anything more aimiable (than Genoa) . . . The rest of the day has been spent, much to our heart's content, in cursing French music and architecture, and in singing the praises of Italy.

Gray to West, 21.11.

NATURE

The convent of the Chartreux (near Paris). All the conveniences, or rather (if there was such a word) all the *adaptments* are assembled here, that melancholy, meditation, selfish

[1] Cf. Kant, *Critique of Judgment.*

devotion and despair would require. But yet 'tis pleasing. Soften the terms, and mellow the uncouth horror that reigns here, but a little and 'tis a charming solitude.

H. Walpole to West, 7.5.

The (Grande) Chartreuse ... on one hand is the rock, with woods of pine-trees hanging over head, on the other, a monstrous precipice almost perpendicular, at the bottom of which rolls a torrent, that sometimes tumbling among the fragments of stone that have fallen from on high, and sometimes precipitating itself down vast descents with a noise like thunder, which is still made greater by the echo from the mountains on each side, concurs to form one of the most solemn, the most romantic, and the most astonishing scenes I ever beheld.

Gray to his Mother, 13.10.

In our little journey up to the Grande Chartreuse, I do not remember to have gone ten paces without an exclamation, that there was no restraining. Not a precipice, not a torrent, not a cliff, but is pregnant with religion and poetry. There are certain scenes that would awe an atheist into belief without the help of other argument. One need not have a very fantastic imagination to see spirits there at noonday: you have Death perpetually before your eyes, only so far removed, as to compose the mind without frighting it. ... Mont Cenis, I confess, carries the permission mountains have of being frightful rather too far.

Gray to West, 11.11

You here meet with all the beauties so savage and horrid a place can present you with; Rocks of various and uncouth figures, cascades pouring down from an immense height out of hanging Groves of Pine Trees, and the solemn Sound of the Stream, that roars below, all concur to form one of the most poetical scenes imaginable.

Gray, *Journal in France*.

Precipices, mountains, torrents, wolves, rumblings, Salvator Rosa—the pomp of our park and the meekness of our palace.

But the road, West, the road! winding round a prodigious mountain, and surrounded with others, all shagged with hanging woods, obscured with pines or lost in clouds! Below a torrent breaking through cliffs, and tumbling through fragments of rocks! Sheets of cascades forcing their silver speed down channelled precipices, and hasting into the roughened river at the bottom. . . . This sounds too bombast and too romantic to one that has not seen it, too cold for one that has.

H. Walpole to R. West, 30.9.

Your description of the Alps makes me shudder, . . . There is a couple of verses . . .

> Others all shagg'd with hanging woods,
> Obscured with pines, or lost in clouds,

. . . are so good.

R. West to Walpole, 15.10 (see last entry).

The four last (days) in crossing the Alps. Such uncouth rocks, and such uncomely inhabitants! My dear West, I hope I shall never see them again.

Walpole to West, 11.11.

To prefer rocks and dirt to flowery meads and lovely Thames, and brimstones and fogs to roses and sunshine. When I arrive at these sensations, I may settle at Bath, of which I never dreamt.

Pope, *Letter to Richardson.*

PAINTING

(Le Sueur's St. Bruno at Paris Chartreux) I don't know what Raphael may be in Rome, but these pictures excel all I have seen in Paris and England.

H. Walpole to R. West, May.

POETRY

G. West, *On the Abuse of Travelling.*
(A Spenserian imitation in which the author explains such words as sooth, guise, elfin, prowess, wend, hight, dight, paramour, behest, caitiff).

In prose you would say "the beginning of the morning, or the break of day"; but that would not do in verse; and you must rather say "Aurora spread her rosy mantle". . . . This is what is called poetical diction.

> Lord Chesterfield to P. Stanhope, 8.7.
> (cf. Pope 1734).

STAGE

Molière's nights, whose pieces they are quite weary of.

> H. Walpole (from Paris) to West, 21.4.

I don't know what condition your Stage is in, but the French is in a very good one, at present. Among the rest they have a Madlle. Dumenil whose every look and gesture is violent Nature, she is Passion itself incarnate. I saw her the other night do the Phaedra of Racine.

> Gray to Ashton, 29.5.

❀ 1740 r. George II ❀

ANTIQUARIANISM

Stukely, *Stonehenge* (ascribes it and Avebury to Druids).

ARCHITECTURE

I have his Lordship's (Burlington) leave to say that (Lincoln) is by far the noblest Gothic structure in England . . . whoever had the conducting of it was well acquainted with the noblest buildings of old Rome and had united some of their greatest beauties in that one work.

> Simpson (q. by J. Essex, to Society of
> Antiquaries).

> (The Pantheon) Here, curious architect,
> If thou assay'st, ambitious, to surpass
> Palladius, Angelus, or British Jones;
> On these fair walls extend the certain scale,
> And turn th' instructive compass.
> > J. Dyer, *The Ruins of Rome.*

In three hours time we have seen all the good contents of (Siena): 'tis old, and very snug with few inhabitants. You must

not believe Mr. Addison about the wonderful Gothic nicety
of the dome: the materials are richer, but the workmanship
and taste not near so good as in several.

Walpole to West, 22.3.

(At Rome) you cannot pass along a street but you have views
of some palace, or square, or fountain, the most picturesque
and noble one can imagine. . . . St. Peter's I saw the day after
we arrived and was struck dumb with wonder.

Gray to his Mother, 2.4.

MANNERS AND TASTES

For realities, Windsor or Richmond Hill is infinitely preferable
to Albano or Frascati.

Gray to West, May.

The pilgrim oft
At dead of night, 'mid his oraison hears
Aghast the voice of Time, disparting towers,
Tumbling all precipitate, down-dash'd,
Rattling around, loud thundering to the Moon.

. . . . .

How sweet thy Diapason, Melancholy.

Dyer, Ruins of Rome (passage praised by
Johnson, 1779).

Those quiet and sentimental repasts.

Sterne to Eliz. Lumley. (first usage?)

A learned piece . . . a great admirer of Suckling; Milton she
has by heart, and Cowley is her bed-fellow . . . understands
architecture, and talks of the Corinthian, the Doric, Ionic
and Tuscan orders.

Sir J. Barnard, A Present for an Apprentice.

It is certain that an air of health, as well as of strength and
agility, makes a considerable part of beauty; and that a sickly
air in another is always disagreeable, upon account of that
idea of pain and uneasiness which it conveys to us.

Hume, Treatise of Human Nature III
(contrast Burke, 1756).

MUSIC

God save the King (H. Carey), music by Arne,[1] first performed; printed 1742, *Rule Britannia* (J. Thomson), music by Arne, first performed in *Alfred, a Masque* for Frederick, Prince of Wales.

PAINTING

(When our Author (Gray) was himself in Italy, he studied with much attention the different manners of the old masters. I find a paper written at the time in which he has set down several subjects proper for painting, which he had never seen executed, and has affixed the names of different masters to each piece, to shew which of their pencils he thought would have been most proper to treat it. As I doubt not that this paper will be an acceptable present to the Reynoldses and Wests of the age, I shall here insert it.—Mason 1775).

An Altar Piece—Guido

The top, a Heaven; in the middle, at a distance, the Padre-Eterno indistinctly seen, and lost, as it were, in glory. On either hand, Angels of all degrees in attitudes of adoration and wonder. A little lower, and next the eye, supported on the wings of Seraphs, Christ (the principal figure) with an air of calm and serene majesty, his hand extended, as commanding the elements to their several places: near him an Angel of superior rank bearing the golden compasses (that Milton describes); beneath, the Chaos, like a dark and turbulent ocean, only illumined by the Spirit, who is brooding over it.

A small Picture—Correggio

Eve newly created, admiring her own shadow in the lake.
(The famous Venus of this master, now in the possession of Sir William Hamilton, proves how judiciously Mr. Gray fixed upon his pencil for the execution of this charming subject.—Mason).

---

[1] Perhaps adapted from John Bull who in 1607 composed a setting of these four words and played it on the virginals at a feast of the Merchant Taylors' Company to King James. This is said to bear some resemblance to a musical script ascribed to him, which in turn bears some to Arne's anthem.

Another—Domenichino, or the Carracci

Electra, with the urn, in which she imagined were her Brother's ashes, lamenting over them; Orestes smothering his concern.

Another—Correggio

Ithuriel and Zephon entering the bower of Adam and Eve; they sleeping. The light to proceed from the angels.

Another—Nicholas Poussin

Alcestis dying; her children weeping, and hanging upon her robe; the youngest of them, a little boy, crying too, but appearing rather to do so, because the others are afflicted, than from any sense of the reason of their sorrow: her right arm should be round this, her left extended towards the rest, as recommending them to her lord's care; he fainting, and supported by the attendants.

Salvator Rosa

Hannibal passing the Alps; the mountaineers rolling down rocks upon his army; elephants tumbling down the precipices.

Another—Domenichino

Arria giving Claudius's order to Paetus, and stabbing herself at the same time.

N. Poussin, or Le Sueur

Virginius murdering his daughter; Appius at a distance, starting up from his tribunal; the people amazed, but few of them seeing the action itself.

Mason, *Life of Gray.*

Another—Domenichino

Medea in a pensive posture, with revenge and maternal affection striving in her visage; her two children at play, sporting with one another before her. On one side a bust of Jason, to which they bear some resemblance.

A Statue—Michael Angelo

Agave in the moment she returns to her senses; the head of her Son, fallen on the ground from her hand.

A Picture—Salvator Rosa

Æneas and the Sybil sacrificing to Pluto by torch light in the wood, the assistants in a fright. The Day beginning to break, so as dimly to shew the mouth of the cavern.

Sigismonda with the heart of Guiscardo before her. I have seen a small print on this subject, where the expression is admirable, said to be graven from a picture of Correggio. (Afterwards, when he had seen the original in the possession of the late Sir Luke Schaub, he always expressed the highest admiration of it; though we see, by his here giving it to Salvator Rosa, he thought the subject too horrid to be treated by Correggio; and indeed I believe it is agreed that the capital picture in question is not of his hand—Mason).

Another—Albano, or the Parmeggiano

Iphigenia asleep by the fountain side, her maids about her; Cymon gazing and laughing.

(This subject has been often treated; once indeed very curiously by Sir Peter Lely in the way of portrait, when his sacred Majesty Charles the Second represented Cymon, and the Dutchess of Cleveland and Mrs. Eleanor Gwin (in as indecent attitudes as his royal taste could prescribe) were Iphigenia and her attendants—Mason).

Mantegna was much the best painter in Europe, until Lionardo da Vinci so greatly advanced the art. It seems that the tawdry taste, brought into Italy by the Greeks (about the year 1013) continued quite down to the improvements of the latter.

Townley in Spence.

Certain it is that hitherto the manner (Ramsay) paints in is neither the valuable manner of Dahl, Kneller, Lilly (Lely?), Riley, Dobson, Vandyck, Rubens, or Titian—it is rather lickt than pencilled. . . . As to sculpture, that has of late years made greater advances than painting in many and rare works of several hands (Rysbrack, Schemak^r, Rubillac).

Vertue, MSS. (in B.M.).

STAGE

Garrick restored approximately Shakespeare's *Macbeth* from the version seen by Pepys, "excellent for divertissment and dances" (of witches). When he said "The devil damn thee black, thou cream-faced loon", he was hissed for gagging.

SUBLIMITY

The ideas of Eternity and immensity are to the Eye of the Soul, what an unbounded prospect is to that of the Body. They satisfy the insatiable thirst of Novelty, . . . I believe you will allow these lines the Character of sublime:—

> —who would lose
> Tho full of Pain, this intellectual being
> Those thoughts that wander thro' Eternity,
> To perish rather swallowed up and lost
> In the wide womb of uncreated Night
> Devoid of Sense and Motion—[1]

You say the sublime is a species of the Pathetic . . . The Pathetic, tis true, is one kind of Sublime, but there are many instances of the Sublime which have nothing to do with any Passion, but are direct appeals to the imagination, . . .

> How sweetly did they float upon the Wings
> Of Silence thro' the empty-vaulted Night,
> At every fall, smoothing the raven down
> Of Darkness, till it smil'd.[2]

Ashton to West, 13.8.

❧ 1741 r. George II ❧

MANNERS AND TASTES

If instead of saying that tastes are different, and that every man has his own peculiar one, you should let off a proverb and say That what is one man's meat is another man's poison . . . everybody would be persuaded that you had never kept company with anybody above footmen and housemaids.

Lord Chesterfield to P. Stanhope, 25.7.

[1] Milton, P.L. II. 146.
[2] Comus 249.

Garrett Wellesley, Earl of Mornington, played the violin in a public concert at Dublin.

Windham of Felbrigg and Hervey (afterwards Earl of Bristol) visited glaciers of Chamonix and acted Shakespeare at Geneva.

Marivaux, *La Vie de Marianne* translation finished, (psychological, thought to have influenced *Pamela*—"Marivaudage"). Crébillon says its "Characters not only say everything that they have done and everything that they have thought, but everything that they would have liked to think but did not."

There has been a sudden and sensible change in the opinions of men within these last fifty years, by the progress of learning and of liberty. Most people, in this island, have divested themselves of all superstitious reverence to names and authority. The clergy have entirely lost their credit: Their pretensions and doctrines have been ridiculed; and even religion can scarcely support itself in the world. The name of *king* commands little respect, and to talk of a king as God's vicegerent on earth, or to give him any of those magnificent titles which formerly dazzled mankind, would but excite laughter.

Hume, Essays, I, vii, cf. Butler, 1736.

(Duchess of Queensbury's Court dress)   Of white satin embroidered, the bottom of the petticoat as brown hills covered with all sorts of weeds, and every breadth had an old stump of a tree that ran up almost to the top of the petticoat, round which twined nasturtiums, ivy, honeysuckle, periwinkles, convolvuluses and all sorts of twinning flowers which spread and covered the petticoat; vines with the leaves variegated as you have seen them by the sun, all rather smaller than nature, which makes them look very light; the robings and facings were little green banks with all sorts of weeds, and the sleeves and the rest of the gown loose, twining branches of the same sort as those on the petticoat. Many of the leaves were finished with gold, and part of the stumps of the trees looked like the gilding of the sun.

Quoted by Richardson, Georgian England.

NATURE

O tu severi religio loci.

Gray, in Album at Grande Chartreuse.

POETRY

The Venetians . . . seem rather inferior to the other Italians in their genius for the arts. . . . With regard to the stage (The French) have excelled even the Greeks, who have far excelled the English. . . . The first polite prose we have was writ by a man who is still alive (Dr. Swift).

Of Civil Liberty.

How poor are those songs, where a happy flow of fancy has not furnished materials for art to embellish and refine!

The Epicurean.

As the eye in surveying a *Gothic* building is distracted by the multiplicity of ornaments, and loses the whole by its minute attention to the parts, so the mind, in *perusing* a work over-stockd with wit, is fatigued and disgusted, . . . even though that wit should in itself be just and agreeable.

. . . . . .

Beauty as well as virtue, always lies in a medium. . . . Corneille and Congreve, who carry their wit and refinement somewhat farther than Mr. Pope, . . . and Sophocles and Terence, who are more simple than Lucretius, seem to have gone out of that medium. . . . Virgil and Racine in my opinion lie nearest the centre.

Of Simplicity and Refinement, Hume *Essays.*

Paradisus Amissus Latine Redditus, Dr. Trapp, late Professor of Poetry, Oxford.

Lowth succeeded Whitfield in Chair of Poetry, Oxford (see 1753).

🌼 1742 r. George II 🌼

ANTIQUARIANISM

The great concourse of strangers . . . purposely to see (Glastonbury) Abbey . . . their greatest trade.

Defoe, *Tour* (3rd. ed.)

Ancient British (i.e., Welsh) Music, J. Parry ("the blind harper of Ruabon").

ARCHITECTURE

Gothic Architecture Improved (The Five Orders gothicised) Batty Langley.

MANNERS AND TASTES

Nothing else in fashion but cricket matches.

H. Walpole to Mann, 11.9.

They are statesmen. Do not you remember them dirty boys playing at cricket?

Gray to West, 27.5.

POETRY

> Darkness has more divinity for me;
> It strikes thought inward; it drives back the soul
> To settle in herself. . . . (senses)
> That half create the wondrous world they see.

E. Young, *Night Thoughts*, V. 126.

'Tis an age most unpoetical. 'Tis even a test of wit, to dislike poetry; though Pope has half a dozen old friends that he has preserved from the taste of last century. . . .

H. Walpole to West, 4.5.

The first part of Robinson Crusoe is very good. De Foe wrote a vast many things; and none bad, though none excellent, except this. . . . I always was particularly struck with that passage in Homer, where he makes Priam's grief for the loss of Hector break out into anger against his attendants and sons; and could never read it without weeping. (He read it then, and was interrupted by his tears. Spence).

Pope in Spence.

> O loved Simplicity! be thine the prize!
> Assiduous Art correct her page in vain!
> His be the palm who, guiltless of disguise,
> Contemns the pow'r, the dull resource, to feign.

Shenstone *To a Friend*.

Bear me, ye winds, indulgent to my pains
Near some sad ruin's ghastly shade to dwell!
There let me fondly eye the rude remains
And from the mouldering refuse build my cell!
Shenstone, To the Winds.

I read a page or two of the Faery Queen, and cared not to proceed. After that, Pope's *Alley* made me consider him ludicrously; and in that light, I think, one may read him with pleasure. I am ... from trifling and laughing at him, fairly in love with him. I think even the metre pretty, (though I shall never use it in earnest); and that the last Alexandrine has an extreme majesty. ... Those which afford the greatest scope for a ludicrous imitation [he does this in his *Schoolmistress*] are his simplicity and obsolete phrase and yet these are what give one a very singular pleasure in the perusal.
Shenstone.

The *Britanicus* of Mr. Racine I know was one of Mr. Gray's most favourite plays (cf. Gray's *Aggripina*).
Mason, Life of Gray (1775).

Sonnet on death of West, Gray (published after Gray's death, perhaps the first since Milton except one by Walsh). cf. 1692 and 1746.

STYLE

I will not decide what style is fit for our English stage; but I should rather choose one that bordered upon Cato [Addison's, produced 1713], than upon Shakespear. One may imitate (if one can) Shakespear's manner, his surprizing strokes of true nature, his expressive force in painting characters, and all his other beauties; preserving at the same time our own language. Were Shakespear alive now, he would write in a different style from what he did.
R. West to Gray, 4.4.

Joseph Andrews. The incidents are ill laid and without invention; but the characters have a great deal of nature, which always pleases even in her lowest shapes. Parson Adams is perfectly well; so is Mrs. Slipslop. ... However the exaltedness of some minds (or rather as I shrewdly suspect their insipidity and want of feeling or observation) may make them insensible to these light things (I mean such as characterize and paint nature) yet surely they are as weighty and much more useful than your grave discourses upon the mind, the passions and what not. Now as the paradisaical pleasures of the Mahometans consist in playing upon the flute and lying with Houris, be mine to read eternal new romances of Marivaux and Crébillon. . . . The language of the age is never the language of poetry; except among the French, whose verse . . . differs in nothing from prose. Our poetry . . . has a language peculiar to itself; to which almost everyone, that has written, has added something, by enriching it with foreign idioms and derivatives. Nay, sometimes words of their own composition or invention. Shakespeare and Milton have been great creators in this way; and no one more licentious than Pope or Dryden, who perpetually borrow expressions from the former. Let me give you some instances from Dryden, whom everyone reckons a great master of our poetical tongue.—Full of *museful mopings*—Unlike the *trim* of love—A pleasant *beverage*—A *roundelay* of love—Stood silent in his *mood*—With knots and *knares* deformed—His *ireful mood*—In proud *array*—His *boon* was granted—And *disarray* and shameful rout—*Wayward* but wise—*Furbished* for the field—*Foiled doddered* oaks—*Disherited*—*Smouldring* flames. *Retchless* of laws—*Crones* old and ugly—The *beldam* at his side—The *grandam* hag—*Villanize*[1] his father's fame—But they are infinite. And our language not being a settled thing (like the French) has an undoubted right to words of an hundred years old, provided antiquity have not rendered them unintelligible. In truth, Shakespeare's language is one of his principal beauties; and he has no less advantage over your Addisons and Rowes in this, than in those other great excellencies you mention. Every word in him is a picture. Pray put me the following lines into the tongue of our modern Dramatics:—

But I that am not shaped for sportive tricks",

. . . . .

to "Into this breathing world, scarce half made up."

(Richard III, I. i. 14-21.)

Gray to West, April.

---

[1] But cf. negro song (seventeenth century usage?) "scandalize my name," and "it will make me scandalized". *Two Gentleman of Verona* II, vii.

(Shakespeare's) old expressions have more energy in them than ours, and are even more adapted to poetry; certainly, when they are judiciously and sparingly inserted, they add a certain grace to the composition; in the same manner as Poussin gave a beauty to his pictures by his knowledge in the ancient proportions: But should he, or any other painter, carry the imitation too far, and neglect that best of models Nature,— I am afraid it would prove a very flat performance ... I have this further notion about old words revived ... I think them of excellent use in tales; they add a certain drollery to the comic, and a romantic gravity to the serious, which are both charming in their kind; and this way of charming Dryden understood very well. One need only read Milton to acknowledge the dignity they give the Epic. But now comes my opinion that they ought to be used in Tragedy more sparingly, than in most kinds of poetry. Tragedy is designed for public representation.

R. West to Gray, April.

🎕 1743 r. George II 🎕

GARDENS

(Euston) is one of the most admired seats in England, in my opinion because Kent has a most absolute disposition of it. Kent is now so fashionable that, like Addison's Liberty, he

Can make bleak rocks and barren mountains smile.

Kent's passion—clumps (of trees).

H. Walpole to H. Mann, 20.6.

MANNERS AND TASTES

English translation of a description of the Summer Palace at Pekin by Attiret, a French Jesuit missionary.

I think that season (Autumn) of the year the most pleasing, the most poetical ... The muses of the great simple country, not the little fine-lady muses of Richmond Hill.

James Thomson to Dr. Cranston, July.

PAINTING

Most capital pictures . . . (The Domenichino) beats all but the two Guidos.

To J. Chute, 20.8.

(Andrea del Sarto's colour) a mixture of mist and tawdry. . . . Domenichino whose communion of S. Jerome is allowed to be the second picture of the world. . . . In my opinion, all the qualities of a perfect painter never met but in Raphael, Guido and Annibal Caracci. The Florentine school—except Andrea del Sarto and the two Zucceros—their names are scarce known out of Tuscany. Dutch—drudging mimicks of Nature's most uncomely coarseness.

H. Walpole, Aedes Walpolianae (Pictures
at Houghton Hall). Printed 1747.

POETRY

I read the Faerie Queen, when I was about twelve with infinite delight; and I think it gave me as much when I read it over about a year or two ago.

Pope in Spence.

I have found out a gift for my fair,
I have found where the wood-pigeons breed;
But let me that plunder forbear,
She will say 'twas a barbarous deed.

Shenstone, Pastoral Ballad.

The Grave, R. Blair (begun 1731, blank verse rather Elizabethan than Miltonic).

STYLE

In most doubts whether a word is English or not or whether such a particular use of it is proper, one has nothing but authority for it. Is it in Sir William Temple, or Locke, or Tillotson?

Pope in Spence.

In talking over the design for a dictionary, that might be authoritative for our English writers; Mr. Pope rejected Sir Walter Raleigh twice, as too affected. The list of prose authors was quite settled. There were eighteen of them (Lord Bacon, Hooker, Hobbes, Lord Clarendon, Barrow, Tillotson, Dryden, Sir William Temple, Locke, Sprat, Atterbury, Addison, Swift, Lord Bolingbroke), but four of that number (Ben Jonson, L'Estrange, Congreve and Vanbrugh) were only named as authorities for familiar dialogues. . . . The list of writers that might serve as authorities for poetical language was begun upon twice, but left very imperfect. There were but nine mentioned (Spenser, Shakespeare, Fletcher, Waller, Butler, Milton, Dryden, Pryor, Swift) and two of those—Butler and Swift—only for the burlesque style. Fletcher too was only mentioned as an authority for familiar dialogue.

Spence.

🌼 1744 r. George II 🌼

MANNERS AND TASTES

                       Can Stow,
With all her Attic fanes, such raptures raise
As the thrush-haunted copse where lightly leaps
The fearful fawn the rustling leaves along?
     .   .   .   .
Rich in her weeping country's spoils, Versailles
May boast a thousand fountains, that can cast
The tortur'd waters to the distant heav'ns:
Yet let me choose some pine-topp'd precipice.
     .   .   .
            . . . Some black heath
Where straggling stands the mournful juniper
Or Yew-tree scath'd. . . .
Happy the first of men ere yet confin'd
To smoky cities
     .   .   .
What are the lays of Artful Addison,
Coldly correct, to Shakespear's warblings wild?

             J. Warton, *The Enthusiast.*

The first of August we went to Stowe, which is beyond description, it gives the best idea of Paradise that can be; even Milton's images and descriptions fall short of it, and indeed a Paradise

it must be to every mind in a state of innocence. . . . The buildings are indeed in themselves disagreeably crowded, but being
dedicated to Patriots, Heroes, Lawgivers and Poets, men of
ingenuity and invention, they receive a dignity from the
persons to whom they are consecrated. Others that are sacred
to imaginary powers, raise pleasing enthusiasm in the mind. . . .
The Temples that pleased me most for the design to which they
were consecrated were those to "Ancient Virtue", to "Friendship" and to "Liberty".

> Duchess of Portland, Letter (cf. Wesley
> 1779).

(The Archbishop of York's palace, Bishopsthorpe) was built
at a time of day when men paid more regard to convenience
than to uniformity. . . . It is a most agreeable house; and
pleases me more than if it had been designed by Lord Burlington or any other genius of the age.

> Anon. Letter (Nicholls *Illustrations* III,
> 454).

POETRY

The powers of Fancy, her delighted sons
To three illustrious orders have referr'd;
Three[1] sister graces, whom the painter's hand,
The poet's tongue confesses;—the sublime,[1]
The wonderful, the fair . . .

. . . . .

Mind[1]—*mind* alone; (bear witness, earth and Heaven!)
The living fountains in itself contains
Of Beauteous and Sublime; here hand in hand
Sit paramount the Graces; here enthroned
Celestial Venus, with divinest airs
Invites the soul to never-fading joy

> Akenside, *Pleasures of Imagination.*;
["The reputation of this exquisite passage" said he . . . "is
established by the consenting suffrage of all men of taste,

---

[1] He here paraphrases "Longinus" with *three* kinds. In 1757 (q.v.), after
Burke, he substituted *two*. For "mind" he then substituted "God". If, as has
been suggested, Burke's *Enquiry* was in fact not published till 1757, Akenside
may possibly have read it before then. The usual date is 1756. Or Burke may
have been influenced by Akenside.

though . . . you look as if you had a mind to attack it." "So far from it" said I "that I know nothing more splendid in the whole mass of our poetry."

> Hannah More (b. 1745), *Coelebs in Search of a Wife* 1809.]

(Akenside's *Pleasures of the Imagination*) seems to me above the middleing, & now & then (but for a little while) rises even to the best, particularly in Description. It is often obscure & even unintelligible, & too much infected with the Hutchinson-Jargon. [=Hutcheson *Inquiry* 1726].

> Gray to Wharton, 26.4.

> Thro' every nerve
> A sacred horrour thrills, a pleasing fear
> Glides o'er my frame. The forest deepens round.
> Armstrong, *The Art of Preserving Health.*

❧ 1745 r. George II ❧

MANNERS AND TASTES

Public gaming prohibited.

GARDENS

A Plan of Mr. Pope's Garden, as it was left at his Death, with a Plan and Perspective View of the Grotto. All taken by J. Serle his gardener. With an account of all the Gems, Minerals, Spars, and Ores of which it is composed and from whom and whence they were sent.

POETRY

I cannot bear modern poetry; these refiners of the purity of the stage and of the incorrectness of English verse are most wonderfully insipid. I had rather have written the most absurd lines in Lee than *Leonidas* (Glover) or *The Seasons*; as I had rather be put into the roundhouse for a wrongheaded quarrel than sup quietly at eight o'clock with my grandmother. There is another of these tame genius's, a Mr. Akinside [*sic*], who writes Odes; in one he has lately published he says "Light the tapers, urge the fire".

> H. Walpole to H. Mann, 29.3.

🌸 1746 r. George II 🌸

MANNERS AND TASTES

51 barbers of London fined £20 for hair-powder not made of starch.

Gentlemen's Magazine.

Cricket match Kent v. England at Finsbury. Kent, including Lord J. Sackville, captained by the Knole gardener, notched 111 to 110.

PAINTING

Canaletto in London painted *South-East Prospect of Westminster Bridge*, i.e., Lord Mayor's water-pageant, 29 Oct. (belonging to Duke of Buccleugh 1928).

POETRY

Feathered rover (=bird). Rolling sparkler (=eye).

Hervey, *Meditations among the Tombs.*

As (the author) is convinced that the fashion of moralizing in verse has been carried too far, and as he looks upon Invention and imagination to be the chief faculties of a poet, so he will be happy if the following Odes may be looked upon as an attempt to bring back Poetry into its right channel.

J. Warton, Preface to Odes.

> Where Maro and Musaeus sit
> Listening to Milton's loftier song. . . .
> Homer in rapture throws his trumpet down
> And to the Briton gives his amaranthine crown.

J. Warton, *Ode to Health.*

> εἴην εὑρησιεπής (motto)
> Tho' Taste, Tho' Genius bless,
> To some divine Excess,
> Faint's the cold Work till Thou inspire the whole;
> What each, what all supply,
> May court, may charm, our Eye,
> Thou, only thou, can'st raise the meeting Soul!

W. Collins, *Ode to Simplicity.*

	Critical Ordonnance	Pathetic Ordonnance	Dramatic Expression	Incidental Expression	Taste	Colouring	Versification	Moral	Final Estimate	Place
Ariosto	0	15	10	15	14	15	16	10	13	
Boileau	18	16	12	14	17	14	13	16	12	
Cervantes	17	17	15	17	12	16	—	16	14	=5
Corneille	15	16	16	16	16	14	12	16	14	=5
Dante	12	15	8	17	12	15	14	14	13	
Euripides	15	16	14	17	13	14	—	15	12	
Homer	18	17	18	15	16	16	18	17	18	=1
Horace	12	12	10	16	17	17	16	14	13	
Lucretius	14	5	—	17	17	14	16	0	10	=last
Milton	17	15	15	17	18	18	17	18	17	=3
Molière	15	17	17	17	15	16	—	16	14	=5
Pindar	10	10	—	17	17	16	—	17	13	
Pope	16	17	12	17	16	15	15	17	13	
Racine	17	16	15	15	17	13	12	15	13	
Shakespear	0	18	18	18	10	17	10	18	18	=1
Sophocles	18	16	15	15	16	14	—	16	13	
Spenser	8	15	10	16	17	17	17	17	14	=5
Tasso	17	14	14	13	12	13	16	.13	12	
Terence	18	12	10	12	17	14	—	16	10	=last
Virgil	17	16	10	17	18	17	17	17	16	=4

M. Akenside, *The Balance of Poets* (cf. 1758); only four are English

Two young Authors a Mr. Warton [Joseph] and a Mr. Collins, both Writers of Odes. It is odd enough, but each is the half of a considerable Man, and one the counterpart of the other. The first has but little Invention, very poetical choice of Expression, and a good Ear. The second, a fine fancy, model'd upon the Antique, a bad Ear, great Variety of Words, and Images with no Choice at all. They both deserve to last some years, but will not.

Gray to Wharton, 27.12.

> How low, how indigent the Proud,
> How little are the Great.

Afterwards altered to:—

> How low, how little are the Proud
> How indigent the Great

on account of the "point" of *little* and *great*.

Gray, Ode on the Spring (published 1747).

(Pope) the finest writer, one of them, we ever had.

Gray to Walpole, 2.2.

Pope and poetry are dead.

To H. Mann, 21.3.

Scotland is the last place on earth I should have thought of for turning anybody poet . . . There is a melancholy harmony in (the verses) that is delightful. . . . Now if one has a mind to be read one must write metaphysical poems in blank verse, which though I own to be still easier, have not half the imagination of romances and are dull without any agreeable absurdity. Only think of the gravity of this wise age, that have exploded Cleopatra and Pharamond (La Calprenède) and approve The Pleasures of the Imagination (Akenside), The Art of Preserving Health (Dr. J. Armstrong) and Leonidas (Glover). I beg the age's pardon; it has done approving these poems, and has forgot them. . . . I have lately read . . . Drummond's History of the five King Jameses (W. Drummond of Hawthornden, 1505-1649) and like it much.

H. Walpole to H. S. Conway, 24.10.

When I behold thee blameless Williamson.

> B. Stillingfleet, Sonnet (cf. Wordsworth
> sonnet "Spade with which Wilkinson!").

Stillingfleet was the first to be called a "bluestocking", by Admiral Boscawen.

❧ 1747 r. George II ❧

ARCHITECTURE

They are now whitewashing or rather dawbing the (Peterborough) cathedral, and new painting the roof in ridiculous filigree work, party coloured, that has no meaning in it; and above all they have, for greater ornament, painted the ceiling over the high altar in imitation of marble. They have made a new quire of paltry fir.

> Stukeley, *Family Memoirs*.

MANNERS AND TASTES

Cricket match on the Artillery Ground, London, between the ladies of Charlton and Singleton, Sussex, and the ladies of Westdean and Chilgrove.

The taste for busts and figures prevails much of late years and in some measure interferes with portrait-painting. The nobility now affect to have their busts done that way.

> *The London Tradesman.*

POETRY

What Cat's a foe to fish
altered to:
What Cat's averse to fish.

> Gray, *Death of a Favourite Cat*

Then Jonson came, instructed from the School,
To please in Method, and invent by Rule;
His studious Patience and laborious Art,
By regular Approach essay'd the Heart;
Cold Approbation gave the ling'ring Bays,
For those who durst not censure, scarce cou'd praise.

> S. Johnson, *Prologue for Garrick.*

241

As when a swain, belated on his way,
Sees, as he fancies, through the close of day,
A ghastly spectre—struck with pale affright
He measures back the ground in hasty flight;
Whilst his own shadow by reflection clear
Of silver Luna seen, augments his fear.
At ev'ry breeze, each rustling of the wind,
Startled he stops, yet dreads to look behind.
Still he believes the phantom at his heels
And his cold touch imaginary feels.

> G. Masters, *On Culloden* to the Duke of
> Cumberland (cf. Coleridge, *Ancient
> Mariner*).

I am not totally of your mind as to Mr. Lyttleton's Elegy,
though I love kids and fawns as little as you do. If it were all
like the fourth stanza I should be excessively pleased. Nature
and sorrow, and tenderness are the true genius of such things;
and something of these I find in several parts of it (not in
the orange-tree): poetical ornaments are foreign to the purpose;
for they only show a man is not sorry;—and devotion worse,
for it teaches him that he ought not to be sorry, which is all
the pleasure of the thing.

> Gray to Walpole, November (see next
> item).

IV

In vain I look around
O'er all the well-known ground
My Lucy's wonted foot-steps to descry;
Where oft we used to walk,
Where oft in tender talk
We saw the summer sun go down the sky;
Nor by yon fountains side,
Nor where its waters glide
Along the valley, can she now be found:
In all the wide-stretch'd prospects ample bound
No more my mournful eye
Can aught of her espy.
But the sad sacred earth where her dear ashes lie.

VI
Sweet babes, who like the little playful fawns

XIII
The verdant orange lifts its beauteous head.

XVIII
Yet, O my soul, thy rising murmurs stay,
Nor dare th' all-wise Disposer to arraign.

G. Lyttleton, *Monody.*

Beneath yon ruined Abbey's moss-grown piles
Oft let me sit, at twilight hour of Eve,
Where through some western window the pale moon
Pours her long-levell'd rule of streaming light;
While sullen sacred silence reigns around,
Save the lone screech-owl's note, who builds his bow'r
Amid the mouldering caverns dark and damp

. . . . .

'Mid hollow charnel let me watch the flame
Of taper dim, shedding a livid glare
O'er the wan heaps; while airy voices talk
Along the glimm'ring walls or ghostly shape
At distance seen, invites with beck'ning hand[1]
My lonesome steps, thro' the far winding vaults;
Nor undelightful is the solemn moon
Of night.
But let the sacred Genius of the Night
Such mystic visions send as Spenser saw,
. . . Or Milton knew.

. . . . .

The taper'd Choir, at the late hour of Pray'r,
Oft let me tread, while to th' according voice,
The many-sounding organ peals on high.

. . . . .

Thro' Pope's soft song tho' all the Graces breathe,

. . . . .

[1] Cf. Jonson, 1731, Pope, 1717.

Yet does my mind with sweeter transport glow,
As, at the root of many trunks reclin'd,
In magic *Spenser's* wildly-warbled song
I see deserted Una wander wide,

. . . . .

Weary, forlorn; than when the fated fair
Upon the bosom bright of silver Thames,
Launches in all the lustre of brocade;

. . . . .

The gay description palls upon the sense,
And coldly strikes the mind with feeble bliss.

T. Warton, *The Pleasures of Melancholy.*

SUBLIMITY

The Sublime in Writing is no more than a Description of the Sublime in Nature. . . . Notwithstanding *Longinus* intitles his Treatise a Treatise upon the *Sublime :* . . some part of his Treatise regards the *figurative Style*, some the *Pathetic*, and indeed some part regards what I think is properly called the sublime. However the Bulk of the Performance relates more to the *Perfection* of Writing in *general.*

J. Baillie, *On the Sublime.*

1748 r. George II

ANTIQUARIANISM

Pompeii discovered.

MANNERS AND TASTES

True wit or sense never yet made anybody laugh. . . . But it is low buffoonery, or silly accidents, that always excite laughter. . . . A man's going to sit down, in the supposition that he has a chair behind him, and falling down upon his breech for want of one, sets a whole company a-laughing; . . . a plain proof to my mind how low and unbecoming a thing laughter is: not to mention the disagreeable noise that it makes, and the shocking distortion of the face. . . . Many people, at first, from awkwardness or *mauvaise honte*, have got a very disagreeable and silly trick of laughing whenever they speak.

> Lord Chesterfield to P. Stanhope, 9.3.
> (cf. Hobbes 1650 and Congreve 1694).

Most of our young fellows here (London) display some Character or other by their dress; some affect the tremendous, and wear a great and fiercely cocked hat, an enormous sword, a short waistcoat and a black cravat, ... Others go in brown frocks, leather breeches, great oaken cudgels in their hands, their hats uncocked, and their hair unpowdered; and imitate grooms, stage-coachmen and country bumpkins.

> Lord Chesterfield to P. Stanhope. 30.12.

Mrs. Sinclair's cook-maid in Richardson's *Clarissa Harlowe* read Greene's *Dorastus and Fawnia* (=*Pandosto* 1588).

MUSIC

Germiniani "revolutionised" violin playing.

PAINTING

Carlo Maratti who died about thirty years ago and was the last eminent painter in Europe.

> Ld. Chesterfield to P. Stanhope, 18.11.

Whate'er Lorrain light-touched with softening Hue
Or savage Rosa dashed, or learned Poussin drew.

> Thomson, *Castle of Indolence.*

POETRY

("A versification" of Shakespeare, e.g., Hamlet's soliloquy):—
My anxious soul is torn with dreadful strife,
And hangs suspended between death and life;
Life! Death! dread objects of mankind's debate!
Whether superior to the shocks of fate,
To bear its fiercest ills with steadfast mind,
To Nature's order piously resign'd,
Or, with magnanimous and brave disdain,
Return her back th' injurious gift again.

> W. Hamilton of Bangour (author of
> *Braes o' Yarrow*), *Poems and Songs.*

Then let me rove some wild and heathy scene,
Or find some ruin midst its dreary dells,.
Whose walls more awful nod
By thy religious gleams.

[1746, now revised to:—]

Then lead, calm votaress, where some sheety lake
Cheers the lone heath, or some time-hallowed pile,
Or upland fallows grey
Reflect its last cool gleam.

Collins, *Ode to Evening*, Stanza VIII
(Dodsley).

T. Warton (senior, former Professor of Poetry, Oxford), *Poems* containing Spenserian and "Runic" poetry. Latter taken from W. Temple's quotation of Latin Version (in *Of Heroic Virtue*) of Regner Ladbrog's death-song (see 1690).

Addison, who had himself not above three or four notes in poetry, sweet enough, indeed, like those of a German flute, but such as soon tire and satiate the ear with their frequent return . . . Tickell . . . I forgive for the sake of his ballad [*Colin and Lucy*[1]] which I always thought the prettiest in the world. . . . *The Schoolmistress* [Shenstone] is excellent in its kind and masterly; and (I am sorry to differ from you, but) *London* [Johnson],[2] is to me one of those few imitations, that have all the ease and all the spirit of an original. The same man's verses at the opening of Garrick's theatre[3] are far from bad. Mr. Dyer (here you will despise me highly) has more of poetry in his imagination than almost any of our number; but rough and injudicious.

Gray to Walpole, n.d.

(Spenser has obsolete words and a simplicity of diction in some of the lines, which border on the ludicrous (Advertisement).

[1] See 1729.
[2] See 1738.
[3] See 1747.

As when a Shepherd of the *Hebrid-Isles*,[1]
Plac'd far amid the melancholy Main,
(Whether it be lone Fancy him beguiles;
Or that aerial beings sometimes deign
  To stand, embodied, to our Senses plain)
Sees in the naked Hill, or Valley low,
The whilst in Ocean *Phoebus* dips his Wain,
A vast Assembly moving to and fro:
Then all at once in Air dissolves the wondrous show.

J. Thomson, *Castle of Indolence*, XXX.

If Shakespeare's genius had been cultivated, those beauties which we so justly admire in him, would have been undisgraced by those extravagancies, and that nonsense, with which they are frequently accompanied.

Lord Chesterfield to P. Stanhope, 1.4.

The pedant, ... Plautus is his favourite author ... By this rule I might now write to you in the language of Spenser or Chaucer and assert that I wrote English ... but I should be a most affected puppy if I did so.

Lord Chesterfield to P. Stanhope, 17.9.

SCULPTURE

Monument to General Wade by Roubillac in Westminster Abbey. "The Goddess of Fame is preventing Time from destroying the General's trophies."

1749 r. George II

ARCHITECTURE

The Gothic stile of building could produce nothing nobler than Mr. Allworthy's house. There was an air of grandeur in it that struck you with awe and rivalled the beauties of the best Grecian architecture.

Fielding, *Tom Jones*.

[1] cf. Milton, *Lycidas*, Collins, *Superstitions* (see 1749) and Wordsworth.

MANNERS AND TASTES

Why the despotism of a government should cramp the genius of a mathematician, an astronomer, a poet, or an orator, I confess I never could discover. It may indeed deprive the poet or the orator of the liberty of treating certain subjects in the manner they would wish; but it leaves them subjects enough to exert genius upon, if they have it.

Lord Chesterfield to P. Stanhope, 7.2.

The solemn gloom which the moon casts on all objects is beyond expression beautiful, especially to an imagination which is desirous of cultivating melancholy ideas.

Fielding, *Tom Jones*.

In every Part It has Humanity for its Intention. In too many, it *seems* wantoner than It was meant to be: It has bold shocking Pictures; and (I fear) not unresembling ones, in high Life and in low. And (to conclude this two adventurous Guess-work from a Pair of forward Baggages) wou'd, every where, (we think,) *deserve* to please,—if stript of what the Author thought himself most sure to *please by*. And thus, Sir, we have told you our sincere opinion of *Tom Jones*.

Astraea and Minerva Hill to S. Richard-son (Dobson's *Fielding* in *English Men of Letters*).

You never saw so tranquil a scene, without the least air of melancholy; I should hate it if it was dashed with that.

H. Walpole to H. Mann, 4.6.

A vulgar man . . . has always some favourite word for the time being . . . such as *vastly* angry, *vastly* kind, *vastly* handsome, and *vastly* ugly. . . . He calls the earth *yearth*; he is *obleiged*, not obliged to you. He goes *to wards*, and not *towards*, such a place.

Ld. Chesterfield to P. Stanhope, 27.9.

MUSIC

If you love music, hear it; go to operas, concerts, and pay fiddlers to play to you; but I insist upon your neither piping nor fiddling yourself. It puts a gentleman in a very frivolous, contemptible light; brings him into a great deal of bad company.

Ld. Chesterfield to P. Stanhope, 19.4.

It was Mr. Western's custom every afternoon, as soon as he was drunk, to hear his daughter play upon the harpsichord; for he was a great lover of music, and perhaps, had he lived in town might have passed as a connoisseur, for he always excepted against the finest compositions of Mr. Handel.

Fielding, *Tom Jones*.

PAINTING

Sculpture and painting are very justly called liberal arts, ... which, in my opinion, is by no means the case of music. ... The Venetian school produced many great painters, such as Paul Veronese, Titian, Palma, etc. ... The only two Italian poets that deserve your acquaintance are Ariosto and Tasso.

Ld. Chesterfield to P. Stanhope, 22.6.

Call in too at Chardin's, who paints little pieces of common life.

D. Wray to Hon. Philip Yorke (in Paris).

POETRY

I was convinced ... Homer and Virgil could have no faults, because they were ancient; Milton and Tasso could have no merit, because they were modern. ... I dare assert too, in defiance of the favourers of the ancients, that Homer's hero, Achilles, was both a brute, and a scoundrel, and consequently an improper character for the hero of an epic poem.

Ld. Chesterfield to P. Stanhope, 7.2.

Such airy beings awe th' untutor'd swain;
Nor thou, though learn'd, his homelier thoughts neglect,
Let thy sweet muse the rural faith sustain:
These are the themes of simple, sure effect,
That add new conquests to her boundless reign,
And fill, with double force, her heart-commanding strain.

. . . . .

Unbounded is thy range; with varied style
Thy muse may, like those feath'ry tribes which spring
From their rude rocks, extend her skirting wing
Round the most marge of each cold Hebrid isle.

.   .   .   .

Then to my ear transmit some gentle song
Of those whose lives are yet sincere and plain,
Their bounded walks the rugged cliffs along,
And all their prospect but the wintry main.

.   .   .   .

Nor need'st thou blush that such false themes engage
Thy gentle mind, of fairer stores possest;
For not alone they touch the village breast,
But fill'd in elder time th' historic page;
There Shakespeare's self, with every garland crown'd
In musing hour his wayward sisters found.

> W. Collins, *Ode on the Popular Superstitions of the Highlands.* To Home, author of *Douglas* (published 1788).

There is a vast beauty, to me, in using a word of a particular nature in the eighth and ninth syllables of an English verse—I mean what is virtually a dactyl. For instance "And pikes, the tyrants of the watry plains". Let any person of an ear substitute "liquid" for "watry" and he will find the disadvantage.

> Shenstone, *Essays.*

The polite arts are scarce to be allowed except when consecrated to religious purposes. . . . Most kinds of music, painting and poetry have close connections with vice, particularly with the vices of intemperance and lewdness.

> D. Harley, *Observations on Man.*

PROSE

An Essay on the Power and Harmony of Prosaic Numbers by J. Mason (perhaps the earliest, cf. 1761, Hurd).

✤ 1750 r. George II ✤

ARCHITECTURE

New Designs for Chinese temples, triumphant arches, garden seats, palings, gazebos, &c.

W. and J. Halfpenny.

From the most profound Ignorance in Architecture, the most consumate Night of Knowledge, Inigo Jones started up, a Prodigy of Art, and vied even with his Master Palladio himself [see 1615] . . .
No sort of Pinnacle is worthy enough to appear in the Air, but a Statue. Pyramids are Gothic; Pots are modern French. Chimnies ought to be hid, if not, to be well adorned. No Roof can have Dignity enough to appear above a Cornice, but the Circular; in private Buildings it is excusable. The Ancients affected Flatness. . . .
Tracery induced too much mincing of the Stone into open Battlements and spindling Pinnacles, and little carvings without Proportion of Distance; so the essential Rules of good Perspective and Duration were forgotten. But about two hundred years ago . . . the architects also, ashamed of the modern Barbarity of Buildings, began to examine carefully the Ruins of *Old Rome.*

Wren, *Parentalia* (published 1750).

I am going to build a little Gothic castle at Strawberry Hill.
10.1.

The Grecian is only proper for magnificent and public buildings. Columns and all their beautiful ornaments look ridiculous when crowded into a closet or a cheese-cake-house. The variety is little and admits of no charming irregularities. I am almost as fond of the *Sharawaggi* or Chinese want of symmetry in buildings as in grounds or gardens. I am sure, whenever you come to England, you will be pleased with the liberty of taste into which we are struck.

25.2.

The dispersed buildings—I mean temples, bridges, etc.,—are generally Gothic or Chinese, and give a whimsical air of novelty that is very pleasing. . . . Two men who in my opinion have very little title to fame—Sir Harry Wotton and my Lord Chesterfield.

H. Walpole to H. Mann, 2.8.

Westminster Abbey: the moment I entered I felt a kind of awe pervade my mind which I cannot describe: the very silence seemed sacred. Henry VII's chapel is a very fine piece of Gothic architecture, particularly the roof; but I am told that it is exceeded by a chapel in the University of Cambridge. The finest poem in the English language, I mean Milton's *Il Penseroso*.

Burke to M. Smith.

Mrs. Montague remodeled her house in Hill Street. "Sick of Grecian elegance and symmetry, or Gothic grandeur and magnificence, we must all seek the barbarous gôut of the Chinese; and fat-headed pagods and shaking mandarins bear the prizes from the finest works of antiquity."

MANNERS AND TASTES

Johnson in the *Rambler* opposed the optimism of the deists and urged morality in literature (e.g., No. 4).

The British Senate, that temple of liberty and bulwark of Protestant Christianity, have this fortnight been pondering methods to make more effectual that horrid traffic of selling negroes. It has appeared to us that six and forty thousand of these wretches are sold every year to our plantations alone. It chills one's blood. I would not have to say that I voted for it, for the Continent of America.

H. Walpole to H. Mann.

Should the drinking of this Poison (gin) be continued in its present Height during the next twenty Years, there will, by that Time, be very few of the common People left to drink it.

Fielding, An Enquiry into the Causes of the late Increase of Robbers. (Hogarth's Gin Lane and the "Act for restricting the Sale of Spirituous Liquors" followed in the next year).

Annual consumption of tea, 2,325,000 lb. at 5/-. (Cf. 1706, 54,600 at nearly £1).

PAINTING

Hogarth's *Marriage à la Mode*, 6 pictures sold for 120 guineas framed.

Count Caylus founded a prize for "expression" at the Académie de Peinture et de Sculture.

POETRY

Though I formerly knew Italian extremely well, I could never understand (Dante); for which reason I had done with him. . . . The two poets worth your reading, and I was going to say, the only two, are Tasso and Ariosto. . . . Boileau very justly makes it the mark of a bad taste, to compare *le clinquant du Tasso à l'or de Virgile*. . . . Petrarca is, to my mind, a sing-song, love-sick poet.

Ld. Chesterfield to P. Stanhope, 8.2.

The taste of yr politest Countrymen in point of tragedy differs not much from the taste of a mob at a Bear Garden. 'Tis true we have too much of words, if you have too much of action.

Voltaire to Lord Lyttelton, 17.5.

PART IV
1751—1775

✻ 1751 r. George II ✻

ANTIQUARIANISM

Be yours the task, industrious, to recal
The lost inscription to the ruin'd wall;
Each *Celtic* character explain; or shew
How Britons ate a thousand years ago;
On laws of Jousts and Tournaments declame,
Or shine the rivals of the Herald's fame.

R. Cambridge, *The Scribleriad*.

Society of Antiquarians (London) incorporated.

Life is surely given us for other purposes than to foster what our ancestors have wisely thrown away and to learn what is of no value but because it has been forgotten.

Johnson, *Rambler* 121

ARCHITECTURE

Chinese taste—the principals are a good choice of chains and bells, and different colours of paint. As to the serpents, dragons, and monkeys, etc., they, like the rest of the beauties, may be cut in paper and pasted on anywhere, or in any manner. A few laths, nailed across each other, and made black, red, blue, yellow, or any other colour, or mixed with any sort of chequer work, or impropriety of ornament, completes the whole.

R. Morris, *Architectural Remembrancer*.

Dawkins and Wood visited and drew Palmyra and Baalbec.

All our ancient churches are called without distinction Gothic; but erroneously. They are of two sorts; the one built in Saxon [i.e., really in Norman style] times; the other during our Norman race of kings. Several *Cathedral* and *Collegiate* Churches of the first sort are yet remaining. . . . From (Palestine) our Saxon Churches took the whole of their ideas. . . . The architecture of the Holy Land was entirely Grecian.

... Norman [=Gothic] ... ideas much nobler. ... They in-
geniously projected (their edifices) to resemble Groves. ... It
would be no discredit to the warmest admirers of Jones and
Palladio to acknowledge that (Gothic) has merits.

> Warburton, edit. of Pope, Ep. IV. 29,
> note.

MANNERS AND TASTES

No passion when well represented can be entirely indifferent
to us; because there is none of which man has not, within him,
at least the seeds and principles. ...
The tear naturally starts to the eye at the apprehension of a
warm sentiment (of friendship). ...

Among the French the first questions with regard to a stranger
are, *Is he polite? Has he wit?* In our own country, the chief
praise bestowed is always that of a *good-natured, sensible fellow.*
... If a tragedy abounded in comic beauties, or a comedy in
tragic, the disproportions hurt the eye and convey a disagreeable sentiment to the spectator, the source of blame and
disapprobation.

> Hume, *Enquiry concerning the Principles of
> Morals.*

There is something extremely indelicate in professing a
Passion for a virtuous Woman before we have undergone a
sufficient Quarantine after the Contagion of an abandoned
one, and Man in such a Situation resembles a Centaur, half
human, half brute.

> Elizabeth ("Frances") to Richard
> Griffith ("Henry").

Her Air coquettish, but her Mind a Prude,
Her Body wanton, but her Soul not lewd.

> R. Griffith to Elizabeth (on their
> marriage).

R. and E. Griffith. *A Series of Genuine Letters between Henry
and Frances*, published 1757-70 and 1786 q.v., and see also
1768 (F. Burney).

He hears in one quarter of a cricket-match ... the white bear,
... a dancing dog ... a foot race in the adjacent village.

> Johnson, *Rambler*, 146.

Betty Thoughtless by Mrs. Hayward (Early domestic novel; perhaps influenced *Evelina*).

PAINTING

Two hundred pounds seems to be a very small sum for two undoubted Titian's of that size; but . . . large Italian pictures are now out of fashion at Paris.

22.4.

I love *la belle Nature*; Rembrandt paints caricatures.

Ld. Chesterfield to P. Stanhope, 10.5.

POETRY

Elegy Wrote in a Country Churchyard, Gray. Begun 1742.
4 editions in two months, 11 in two years.
        The Curfew tolls the knell of parting Day
"(squilla di lontana Che paia 'l giorno pianger, che si muore"
Dante, Purg. viii. Gray's note).

Alterations from the original:—
(*a*)   Some village Cato who with dauntless Breast
                        (2) Hampden
        The little tyrant of his Fields withstood
        Some mute inglorious Tully here may rest
                        (2) Milton
        Some Caesar guiltless of his Country's Blood.
        (2) Cromwell.

(*b*) The following stanzas of the MS. omitted:—

        Him have we seen the Greenwood side along,
        While o'er the Heath we hied, our Labour done,
        Oft as the Woodlark piped her farewell Song,
        With wistful Eyes pursue the setting Sun.

                .   .   .

        Hark! how the sacred Calm, that breaths around,
        Bids every fierce, tumultuous Passion cease;
        In still small accents whispering from the Ground
        A grateful Earnest of eternal Peace.

(c) The following stanza added in 3rd edition but dropped in 1753:—

> There scattered oft, the earliest of the Year,
> By Hands unseen, are Showers of Violets found;
> The Redbreast loves to build and warble there,
> And little Footsteps lightly print the Ground.

The first volume of Spenser is published with prints designed by Kent ... Our charming Mr. Bentley is doing Gray as much more honour as he deserves than Spenser.

H. Walpole, 13.6 to G. Montagu.

To imitate the fictions and sentiments of Spenser can incur no reproach, for allegory is perhaps one of the most pleasing Vehicles of instruction. But I am very far from extending the same respect to his diction or his stanza.

Johnson, Rambler, 121.

The mental disease of the present generation is ... a disposition to rely upon unassisted genius.

Johnson, Rambler, 154

In preface to poems of D. Triller the German editor complained of the impiety of calling poetical work *schöpferisch* (see Addison 1712).

> "Come, thick night!
> And pall thee in the dunnest smoke of hell,
> That my keen knife see not the wound it makes."

... The efficacy of this invocation is destroyed by the insertion of an epithet now seldom heard but in the stable, and dun night may come or go without any other notice than contempt. ... The sentiment is weakened by the name of an instrument used by butchers and cooks in the meanest employments; we do not immediately conceive that any crime of importance is to be committed with a knife.

Johnson, Rambler, 168.

W. Hawkins succeeded Lowth in chair of Poetry, Oxford. He published *Cymbeline, a Tragedy altered from Shakespeare* (1759), *The Thimble, an Heroi-Comical Poem* (1744) &c.

❦ 1752 r. George II ❦

ARCHITECTURE

A beautiful tomb, all in our trefoil taste, varied into a thousand little canopies and patterns (1405) ... Mereworth [Kent] which is so perfect in a Palladian taste, that I must own it has recovered me a little from Gothic ... A fine Rembrandt and a pretty La Hire [1606-56 painter to Louis XIV].

H. Walpole, to R. Bentley, 5.8.

MANNERS AND TASTES

Reynolds met Johnson (see Boswell) after returning from Rome.

Spence visited the Peak district.

(The *Cassandre* of de la Calprenède) was the occupation of thousands in the last century, and is still the private, though disavowed, amusement of young girls, and sentimental ladies.

Lord Chesterfield to P. Stanhope, 11.5.

Taste, A Comedy.

Foote.

Gentleman and Cabinet-Maker's Directory.

Chippendale.

The room represents a wood, and there is room left down the middle for thirty couple to dance; at one end is a portico on Doric pillars, lighted by baskets of flowers, the candles green wax, ... the trees are real trees with artificial leaves.

Mrs. Delany.

Old Style ended. Eleven days dropped in September. "Give us back our eleven days."

MUSIC

Essay on Musical Expression (anti-Händel).

Avison.

261

PAINTING

Ah Reynolds, this will never answer. You don't paint in the least degree in the manner of Kneller . . . Shakespeare in poetry and Kneller in painting, damme!

J. Ellys (King's Painter), in Northcote's *Life of Reynolds* (1813).

POETRY

The English ought to give up their notorious violation of all the unities; and all their massacres, sacks, dead bodies and mangled corpses. . . . The French should engage to have more action and less declamation; . . . more indulgence too should be shown to bright thoughts and to shining images. . . . Tragedy must be something bigger than life, or it would not affect us. . . . It is quite otherwise with Comedy. . . . As for Operas they are essentially too absurd and extravagant to mention.

23.1.

I admire (Homer's) beauties; but, to tell you the truth, when he slumbers, I sleep. Vergil, I confess, is all sense, and therefore I like him better than his model; but he is often languid, especially in his five or six last books, during which I am obliged to take a good deal of snuff. . . . I cannot possibly read our countryman Milton through! I acknowledge him to have some most sublime passages, some prodigious flashes of light; but then, you must acknowledge, that light is often followed by *darkness visible*. . . . Keep this secret for me; for if it should be known, I should be abused by every tasteless pedant, and every solid divine in England. . . . But the *Henriade* is all sense. . . . Was love ever painted with more truth and *morbidezza* than in the ninth book?

Lord Chesterfield to P. Stanhope, 4.10.

SCULPTURE

Monument to Admiral Sir Peter Warren by Roubillac in Westminster Abbey. "Hercules places the bust of the Admiral on a pedestal, while Navigation looks on with mournful admiration."

❧ 1753 r. George II ❧

ARCHITECTURE

The Grecian temple is glorious: this I openly worship: in the
heretical corner of my heart I adore the Gothic building.

H. Walpole to J. Chute, 4.8.

GARDENS

Our present artists in gardening far exceed the wildness of
nature; ... Their land, their water must be serpentine. The
old mansion immediately shot up into Gothic spires and was
plaistered over with stucco; the walls were notched with
battlements. ... The eye is saluted with a yellow serpentine
river, stagnating through a beautiful valley, which extends
nearly twenty yards in length. Over the river is thrown a
bridge, *partly in the Chinese manner*, and a little ship, with sails
spread and streamers flying, floats in the midst of it.

Coventrye, *The World*, XV.

MANNERS AND TASTES

With a view to fixing the fluctuating Ideas of Taste. ...
(1. Fitness, 2. Variety, 3. Regularity, "but only so much as
fitness requires", Serpentine line.) Have not many Gothic
buildings a great deal of consistent beauty? ... There is at
present such a thirst after variety that even paltry imitations
of Chinese buildings have a kind of vogue, chiefly on account
of their novelty. ... The full-bottom wig, like the lion's mane,
hath something noble in it, and adds not only dignity but
sagacity to the countenance. ... (St. Paul's is) the most
judicious application of every principle that has been spoken of.

Hogarth, *Analysis of Beauty*.

("The Serpentine made by Queen Caroline, 1727-37.)

Nothing, to use a vulgar expression, should come amiss.

Ld. Chesterfield to P. Stanhope, 27.5.

A few years ago everything was Gothic; our houses, our beds,
our book-cases, and our couches, were all copied from some

part or other of our old cathedrals. The Grecian architecture, where, as Dryden says,

> Firm Doric pillars found the lower base,
> The gay Corinthian holds the higher space
> And all below is strength and all above is grace,

that architecture, which was taught by nature and polished by the graces, was totally neglected. . . . According to the present prevailing whim, everything is Chinese.

Whitehead, The World, XII, 22.3.

I don't wonder Sir Charles Grandison should engage you so deeply; I long to have you read the fifth volume, which is extremely interesting and entertaining.

Mrs. Delany to Mrs. Dewes, 9.12.

The only preference that I shall pretend to give to the modern stage over Greece and Rome . . . the daily progress we make towards nature; . . . a cascade of real water. . . . The pantomime of the Genii narrowly escaped being damned, on my lady Maxim's observing very judiciously, *that the brick-kiln was horridly executed and did not smell at all like one*. . . . In gardening the same love of nature prevails. . . . There is not a citizen who does not take more pains to torture his acre and half into irregularities, than he formerly would have employed to make it as formal as his cravat. Kent, the friend of nature. . . .

H. Walpole, The World, VI, 8.2.

H. Walpole printed wall-paper in perspective to represent Gothic fret-work and also to imitate Dutch tiles.

Chinese switch-back bridge built over Thames at Hampton Court.

R. Adam went abroad till 1758 and visited Spalato.

(At Hagley, Sanderson Miller's) eligible ruin . . . has the true rust of the Barons' wars . . . cascade . . . Parnassus . . . hermitage. . . . Sir Christopher Wren, who built the tower of the great gate way at Christ Church has catched the graces of (true Gothic Taste).

H. Walpole to R. Bentley, September.

. . . Extravagant lovers and purchasers of China and Indian screens . . . while an exquisite painting of Guido passed unnoticed, and was set aside as unfashionable lumber. . . . A multiplicity of minute ornaments; a vast variety of angles and cavities; clusters of little columns, and a crowd of windows, are what distinguishes Meanness of manner in building from Greatness; that is the Gothic from the Grecian. . . . Whoever considers the latest importations of music and musicians from Italy, will be convinced that the modern masters of that country have lost that beautiful Simplicity. . . . Corelli among the modern-ancients and Handel in the present age . . . owe their excellence to simplicity.

J. Warton, *The World*, XXVI.

MUSIC

A l'égard des contres-fugues, doubles fugues, &c. ce sont évidemment des restes de barbarie et de mauvais goût, qui ne subsistent, commes les portails de nos églises gothiques, que pour la honte de ceux qui ont eu la patience de les faire.

Rousseau, J. J., *Letter on French Music* (or 1743?).

NATURE

Indeed, indeed, Jo, I should like the Alps very much if it was not for the hills, or as Desdemona lov'd Othello, I should adore 'em, if they would not frighten one so with all their beauty and fierceness . . . poor things, methought after all I was sorry to quit 'em.

E. Rolle to Spence, 12.7 (Spence's Anecdotes, App.).

Every part of the country (Scotland) presents the same dismal landscape. No grove, nor brook, lend their music.

Goldsmith to R. Bryanton, 26.9.

. . . the country (Holland). Nothing can equal its beauty; wherever I turn my eyes fine houses, elegant gardens, statues, grottos, vistas.

Goldsmith to Contarini (April or May).

One of the most beautiful vales here in England to walk in, with prospects that change every ten steps, and open something new wherever I turn me, all rude and romantic; in short, the sweetest spot to break your neck in or drown yourself in that ever was beheld.

> Gray to Mason (from Durham), 24.7.

POETRY

Shakespeare has carried the romantic, the wonderful, the wild, to the most pleasing extravagance.

> J. Warton, *The Adventurer*, No. 93.

Le Dante, Florentin, avait illustré la langue toscane par son poëme bizarre, mais brillant de beautés naturelles, intitulé *Comédie;* ouvrage dans lequel l'auteur s'éleva dans les détails au-dessus du mauvais goût de son siècle et de son sujet, et rempli de morceaux écrits aussi purement que s'ils étaient du temps de l'Arioste et du Tasse.

> Voltaire, *Essai sur les moeurs.*

R. Lowth, late prof. of Poetry at Oxford (afterwards Bishop of Oxford), *Praelectiones de Sacra Poesi Hebraeorum*, translated into English and German 1793.

Le noblesse de la style . . . ne nommer les choses que par les termes les plus généraux.

> Buffon, *Discours sur le style* (Inaugural to Académie).

A set of hereditary objects has been continued from one poet to another, which have been often made use of without any propriety either as to age or climate.

> J. Warton, *Dedicatory Epistle.*

The heros and heroines of the Age are cobblers and kitchen wenches . . . It has long been the endeavour of our English writers to represent people of quality as the vilest and silliest part of the nation.

> Lady M. W. Montagu, *Letters.*

SCULPTURE

(Of Roubillac's monument to Duke of Montagu at Warkton)
Charity under a female form, assisted by her children, was
fixing the medallion of the Duke on the temple of fame, and
the Duchess beholding it from below... Had the task of
commemorating her been attempted by a man of mean talents,
he would have placed the Duchess in her robes all alive
upon her own tombstone, looking at a poor snivelling boy
wiping his eyes with a white handkerchief, and weeping for
her death; or perhaps surrounded by a group of cherubims
and seraphims that continually do cry. Another of better
abilities would have placed The Graces in Affliction round her
tomb and bewailing her death, and herself alive at her own
funeral; and excepting this last thought the former part had
not been amiss, and yet it is vastly inferior to the present
design... in which the sculptor I am speaking of has conceived the happiest thought imaginable, he has made even the
fates themselves, under the figures of three beautiful women,
to convey this idea.

Spectator (revived), No. 16.

1754 r. George II

ARCHITECTURE

It has not escaped your notice how much of late we are
improved in architecture; not merely by the adoption of what
we call Chinese, nor by the restoration of what we call Gothic;
but by a happy mixture of both.

The World.

The Doge's Palace at Venice I have seen (which is in the
Arabesque manner) ... corruptions of the Greek architecture,
broke into little parts indeed, & cover'd with little ornaments,
but in a taste very distinguishable from that we call Gothic ...
who ever saw a Gothic Cupola? It is a thing plainly of Greek
original, I do not see anything but the slender Spires that serve
for steeples, which may perhaps be borrowed from the Saracen
Minarets in their Mosques.

. . . . .

I delight to hear you talk of giving your house *some Gothic
ornaments* already. If you project anything, I hope it will

267

be entirely within doors; & don't let me (when I come gaping into Coleman Street) be directed to the gentleman at the ten Pinnacles or with the Church-Porch at his door. . . . I am glad you enter into the Spirit of Strawberry-Castle, it has a purity & propriety of Gothicism in it (with very few exceptions) that I have not seen elsewhere. . . .

Lord Brooke . . . has sash'd the great Apartment (at Warwick Castle) and being since told that square sash-windows were not Gothic, he has put certain whim-whams within side the glass, which appearing through, are to look like fretwork. Then he has scooped out a little Burrough in the massy walls of the place for his little self and his children which is hung with chintzes in the exact manner of Berkeley Square or Argyle Buildings. What in short can a lord do nowadays that is lost in a great old solitary castle but skulk about and get into the first hole he finds, as a rat would do in like case?

Gray to Wharton, 18.9.

MANNERS AND TASTES

A picturesque picnic . . . Mr. Pitt . . . ordered a tent to be pitched, tea to be prepared and his French horn to breath Music like the Unseen Genius of the wood. . . . After tea we rambled about for an hour seeing several views, some wild as Salvator Rosa, others placid and with the setting sun, worthy of Claude Lorrain.

Mrs. E. Montagu, *Letters*.

What can be more adorned than Cicero's Philosophical Works? What more than Plato's? It is their eloquence only, that has preserved and transmitted them down to us, through so many centuries; for the philosophy of them is wretched, and the reasoning part miserable.

26.3.

You make use of two words which, though true and correct English, are however from long disuse become inelegant, and seem now to be stiff, formal and in some degree scriptural; the first is the word *namely*. . . . Instead of *namely*, I would always use *which is* or *that is*. . . . The other word is *mine own*. . . . *Namely* and *to wit* are very good words in themselves and

268

contribute to clearness, more than the relations which we now substitute. . . . If I may use that expression, *while* away your time.

Lord Chesterfield to P. Stanhope, 5.4.

She cultivated the arts without affectation.

H. Walpole, Epitaph on his Mother in Westminster Abbey.

The Apollo of the Belvedere Palace, the Medicean Venus, the fighting Gladiator, or the famous group of the Laocoon, may be disposed of in so many panels . . . or if Landscapes are more agreeable, for variety sake Prints done in this manner, taken from the works of *Salvator Rosa, Claude Lorrain, Gaspar Poussin, Berghem, Wouvermann* or any other great Master in the Way of Painting, may be introduced into Panels of the Paper and show the Taste of the Owner. . . . Persons who should prefer gaudy and unmeaning Papers . . . would prefer a Fan to a Picture of *Raphael, Carrace, Guido* or *Domenichino,* and those who chuse the *Chinese* manner ought to admire, in pursuit of that same Taste, the crooked, disproportioned and ugly, . . . *Tom d'Urfey to Shakespeare,* Sir *Richard Blackmore* to *Milton, Tate* to *Homer.* . . . There is a close analogy between the Love of Beauty in external Objects, and a Mind truly disposed to feeling all the softer and most amiable Sensations.

J. B. Jackson, *An Essay on Engraving and Printing in Chiaro Oscuro and the Application of it to Paper Hangings.*

(Vauxhall) where Mr. Tyers has had the ruins of Palmyra painted in the manner of the scenes so as to deceive the eye and appear buildings.

Mrs. Montagu, *Letter,* 9.7.

I remember the good time, when the price of a haunch of venison with a country friend was only half an hours walk upon a hot terrass; a descent to the two square fish-ponds overgrown with a frog-spawn; a peep into the hog-stye, or a visit to the pigeon house. How reasonable was this, when compared with the attention now expected from you to the number of temples, pagodas, pyramids, grottos, bridges, hermitages, caves, towers &c.

Cambridge, *The World,* LXXVI.

Savoy . . . one of the worst countries under heaven.

. . . . .

The house is very spacious. It is built in the form of an H; both fronts pretty much alike. The Hall, the dining parlour, two drawing-rooms, one adjoining to the study, the other to the dining parlour, are handsome and furnished in an elegant but not sumptuous taste; the hangings of some of them beautiful paper only. There is adjoining to the study, a room called the Music-parlour. . . . The dining-room is noble and well-proportioned: it goes over the hall and dining-parlour. It is hung with crimson damask, adorned with valuable pictures. The best bed-chamber adjoining is hung with fine tapestry. The bed is of crimson velvet, lined with white silk; chairs and curtains of the same.

> Richardson, *Letters of Sir C. Grandison*,
> VII.

PAINTING

Sale of Dr. Mead's pictures:—

> a Carlo Maratti £83
> a Holbein ⎫
>   Rubens ⎬ £100 each
>   Claude ⎭
> Watteau's *L'Amour Paisible* £42 and his
>   *Italian Comedians* £52.10.0. (see 1719).

Liotard exhibited in London.

Stubb's motive for going (to Italy) was to convince himself that nature was and is always superior to art whether Greek or Roman—and having received this conviction he immediately resolved upon returning.

> O. Humphry, *Memoir.*

POETRY

I stop, I gaze; in accents rude,
To thee serenest Solitude,
    Bursts forth th' unbidden lay:

. . . . .

> Enthusiast go, unstring thy lyre,
> In vain thou sings't if none admire,
> How sweet soe'er the strain.
> And is not thy o'erflowing mind
> Unless thou mixest with thy kind
> Benevolent in vain?
>
> W. Whitehead, *The Enthusiast*.

The Author, I thought, had corrupted his taste *by the Imitation of Shakespeare*, whom he ought only to have admired. But the same Author [John Home] has compos'd a new Tragedy on a Subject of Invention; and here he appears a true disciple of *Sophocles and Racine*. I hope in time he will vindicate the English Stage from the reproach of Barbarism.

> D. Hume in Spence, 15.10.

Though we are not satisfied as critics, yet we are transported as readers. . . . The pleasure which Spenser received in composing the *Faerie Queene* must necessarily be shared by its commentator. . . . In criticising upon Milton, Johnson, Spenser, and some other of our elder poets, not only a competent knowledge of all antient classical learning is requisite, but also an acquaintance with those books, which . . . were in repute about the time in which each author wrote, and which it is most likely he had read. . . . A romantic poet. . . . We who live in the days of writing by rule, are apt to try every composition by those laws which we have been taught to think the sole criteria of excellence . . . Spenser, and the same may be said of Ariosto, did not live in an age of planning . . . This admired but neglected poet. . . .

> .   .   .   .

> An hideous monster doth in darkness lie
> Whose dreadful shape was never seen of none

cf. A dreadful depth, how deep no man can tell. Omne ignotum pro magnifico. From a concealment of this kind arises the *sublime* in the following:—

> ghastly spectacle dismayed
> That secretlie he saw yet n'ote discourse.

> .   .   .   .

French poets are more fond of familiar manners than sublime fiction. "Les Français n'ont pas le [*sic*] tête epique" (Voltaire).

> T. Warton, *Observations on the Fairie Queene*.

🏵 1755 r. George II 🏵

ANTIQUARIANISM

We (moderns) can admit of nothing but what is accurate and perspicuous. (Primitives) required bold and astonishing images Europeans who have founded their taste. [or the French?]

> P. H. Mallet, *Introduction à l'Histoire de Dannemark. Monuments de la Mythologie et de la Poésie des Celtes.* (Cited by Gray to Mason, 13.1.58. Translated by Percy 1770.)

ARCHITECTURE

The Doric grave, where weight requires,
To give his manly strength aspires;
The light Corinthian, richly gay,
Does all embellishments display;
Between them see, with matron air,
Th' Ionic delicately fair!

> J. Dalton, *Thoughts on Building and Planting.*

The house has undergone Batty Langley [1698-1751] discipline: half the ornaments are of his bastard Gothic, and half of Hallet's mongrel Chinese. I want to write over the doors of most modern edifices "Repaired and beautified; Langley and Hallet, churchwardens". 5.7.

I every day see Greek, and Roman, and Italian, and Gothic architecture embroidered and inlaid in one another or called by each other's names. 4.8.

> H. Walpole to R. Bentley.

MANNERS AND TASTES

Our pious forefathers were content with exhibiting to us the usual emblems of death, the hour-glass, the skull, and the cross-marrow-bone; but these are not sufficient for our present more refined age. The Three Fatal Sisters mentioned in the Heathen Mythology must be introduced.

> B. Thornton, *The Connoisseur.*

In *Astonishment* and *Surprise* arising from *Terror* the *left leg* is drawn back to some distance from the other: under the same Affection of the Mind, but resulting from an *unhop'd for Meeting* with a beloved Object, the *right leg* is advanced to some distance before the left. *Impatience* and *Regret* at being detected in an iniquitous Design may be heightened by shuffling of the *Feet* without moving from the *Spot*.

A good Taste is that instantaneous Glow of Pleasure which thrills thro' our whole Frame and seizes upon the applause of the Heart, before the intellectual Power, Reason, can descend from the Throne of the Mind to ratify its Approbation.

J. Cooper, Letters Concerning Taste.

> O Solitude, romantic maid,
> Whether by nodding towers you tread,
> Or haunt the deserts' trackless gloom,
> Or hover o'er the yawning tomb.
>
> .   .   .   .   .
>
> You, Recluse, again I woo
> And again your steps pursue.

J. Grainger, Solitude.

NATURE

I shall delight to hear the ocean roar or see the stars twinkle in the company of men to whom Nature does not spread her volume or utter her voice in vain.

Johnson, letter to Langton, 6.5.

PAINTING

Hogarth promoted a picture exhibition for benefit of Foundling Hospital (see 1760).

R. Wilson returned from Italy.

POETRY

Shakespeare's Midsummer Night's Dream which is forty times more nonsensical than the worst translation of any Italian opera-books.

H. Walpole to R. Bentley, 8.2.

(A German has read the Elegy, which is) *jolie et Melancholique,
mais elle ne touche point la* [*sic*] *Coeur comme* Yonge's, *Night
Thoughts.*

Mason (from Hanover) to Gray, 27.6.

Metaphysic, e.g.

Call her the metaphysic of her sex
They say she tortures wit (Quoted from Cleveland, d. 1658).

Romance

A military fable of the Middle Ages—a tale of wild adventures,
of war and love.

Johnson, *Dictionary.*

'Tis by those
Milton's the model mainly chose
Who can't write verse and won't write prose.

R. Lloyd.

PROSE

This Richardson is a strange fellow. I heartily despise him,
and eagerly read him, nay, sob over his works in a scandalous
manner. The first 2 tomes of *Clarissa* touched me as being very
resembling to my maiden days; and I find in the pictures of
Sir Thomas Grandison and his lady, what I have heard of my
mother and seen of my father.

Lady Mary W. Montagu to Countess of
Bute, 22.9.

SCULPTURE

Roubillac's statue of Sir Isaac Newton in Trinity College
Chapel, Cambridge.

Nothing (at Rome) in the grand Greek style except the Niobe
group in the Villa Medici and the Pallas in the Villa Albani.

Winckelmann, *Geschichte der Kunst* (pubd.
1764).

❦ 1756 r. George II ❧

ARCHITECTURE

Is there a portal, colonnade, or dome,
The pride of Naples, or the boast of Rome?
We raise it here, in storms of wind and hail,
On the bleak bosom of a sunless vale;
Careless alike of climate, soil, and place,
The cast of Nature, and the smiles of Grace.
Hence all our stucco'd walls, Mosaic floors,
Palladian windows, and Venetian doors.

. . . . .

One might expect a sanctity of style
August and manly in an holy pile,
And think an architect extremely odd,
To build a playhouse for the Church of God;
Yet half our churches, such the mode that reigns,
Are Roman theatres or Grecian fanes;
Where broad-arch'd windows to the eye convey
The keen diffusion of too strong a day;
Where, in the luxury of wanton pride,
Corinthian columns languish side by side,
Clos'd by an altar exquisetely fine,
Loose and lascivious as a Cyprian shrine.

. . . . .

Form'd on his plans, our farms and seats begin
To match the boasted villas of Pekin
On every hill a spire-crown'd temple swells,
Hung round with serpents, and a fringe of bells;
Junks and balons along our waters sail,
With each a gilded cock-boat at his tail.

> J. Cawthorn (for recitation at Tunbridge
> School, where he was headmaster).

Antichità di Roma, Piranesi.

The style consists in crooked lines like Cs (which) . . . inverted,
turned and hooked together, take place of *Greek* and *Roman*
elegance. . . . Not because the possessor thinks there is or can

be elegance in such fond, weak, ill-jointed and unmeaning figures: it is usually because it is French.

. . . .

(Gothic cathedrals) have an air of majesty and grandeur which strikes and affect [*sic*] us, in spite of that profusion of ornaments which so immoderately disfigures them.

. . . .

We see many very beautiful pieces of workmanship in red brick; and to name one, the front of the green-house in Kensington-Gardens will be sure to attract every eye that has the least curiosity: but this should not tempt the judicious architect to admit them in the front walls of the building. In the first place, the colour is itself fiery and disagreeable to the eye; it is troublesome to look upon it: and, in summer, it has an appearance of heat that is very disagreeable: for this reason it is most improper in the country, though the oftenest used there, from the difficulty of getting grey. But a further consideration is, that in the fronts of most buildings of any expence there is more or less stonework: now ... there is something harsh in the transition from the red brick to stone; in the other the grey stocks come so near the colour of the stone that the change is less violent, and they sort better together.

. . . .

The common houses in London are all built in one way ... two rooms and a light closet on a floor, and if there be any little opening behind, to pave it. Some attempt to make flower gardens of these little spots but this is very idle ... and at the farther part to build the needful edifice, that cannot in London be removed farther off.

. . . .

For a noble hall nothing is so well as stucco; for a parlour wainscot seems properer; and for the apartment of a lady, hangings.

I. Ware, *Complete Body of Architecture.*

The simple and sublime have lost all influence, almost everywhere, all is Chinese or Gothic. Every chair in an apartment, the frames of glasses and tables must be Chinese: the walls covered with Chinese paper fill'd with figures which resemble nothing in God's creation, and which a prudent nation would prohibit for the sake of pregnant women. . . . Nay, so excessive is the love of Chinese architecture become, that at present foxhunters would be sorry to break a leg in pursuing their sport in leaping any gate that was not made in the eastern taste of little bits of wood standing in all directions.

The Gothic too has its advocates; you see a hundred houses built with porches in that taste, such as are belonging to many Chapels; not to mention that rooms are stuccoed in this taste, with all the minute, unmeaning carvings, which are found in the most Gothic Chapels of a thousand years standing.

J. Shebbeare, Letters on the English Nation.

GARDENS

(We) have made a garden . . . a sensible consideration, and adapted it to all states which are incident to human minds in general. The gay and airy temper finds the open and cheerful spots of light, which are acceptable to that disposition, and the melancholy mood finds the solitary and shady grove.

Shebbeare, Letters on the English Nation.

It is but a little way from the Palladian Portico to the Gothic tower; from the Lapland to the Chinese house; or from the Temple of Venus to the Hermitage.

No. 76.

Whatever may have been reported, whether truly or falsely, of the Chinese Gardens, it is certain that we are the first Europeans who have founded their taste. [or the French?]

R. Cambridge, The World, No. 118.

MANNERS AND TASTES

Most people must have observed the sort of sense they have had of being swiftly drawn in an easy coach on a smooth turf, with gradual ascents and declivities. This will give a better idea of the beautiful than almost anything else.

.   .   .   .   .

Whatever leads to raise man in his own opinion, produces a sort of swelling and triumph, that is extremely grateful to the human mind. And this swelling is never more perceived, nor operates with more force, than when without danger we are conversant with terrible objects,—the mind always claiming to itself some of the dignity and importance of the things which it contemplates. . . .

A clear idea is another name for a little idea. . . . No work of art can be great but as it deceives.
(Attributes of *Beauty*: Smallness, Smoothness, Gradual Variation, Delicacy of form and colour). Even a moderate appearance of ill-health. . . .
(Attributes of *Sublime*: Obscurity, Power, Privations, Vastness, Infinity) fill the mind with a sort of delightful horror. (Caused by (*a*) Succession, (*b*) Uniformity, e.g., the Rotund), Nothing is more prejudicial to the grandeur of buildings than to abound in angles.

> Burke, *Sublime and Beautiful* (Possibly not published till next year. Revised 1761. Contrast Hume 1740.)

Taste is at present the darling idol of the polite world, and the world of letters; and, indeed, seems to be considered as the quintessence of almost all the arts and sciences. The fine ladies and gentlemen dress with taste; the architects whether Gothic or Chinese, build with taste.

> *The Connoisseur*, No. 120, May 13.

The Rev. John Home deprived in 1757 of his presbyterian charge in Edinburgh for producing *Douglas* this year. It had been refused by Garrick.

MUSIC

Pergolesi, *Stabat Mater* first performed in England.

NATURE

The full perfection of Keswick consists of three circumstances beauty, horror, and immensity united; the second of which is alone found at Dovedale. . . . To give you a complete idea of these three perfections, as they are joined at Keswick would require the united powers of Claude, Salvator and Poussin. The first should throw his delicate sunshine over the cultivated vales, the scattered cots, the groves, the lake, and wooded islands. The second should dash out the horror of the rugged cliffs, the steeps, the hanging woods and foaming waterfalls; while the grand pencil of Poussin should crown the whole with the majesty of impending mountains. . . . Walk by still moonlight among these enchanting dales.

> Dr. J. Brown to Lord Lyttleton. (Printed 1767 Newcastle). He was vicar of Morland, near Penrith till 1756 when he removed to Essex.

(In Wales) the grandeur of the ocean, corresponding with that of the mountain, formed a majestical and solemn scene; ideas of immensity swelled and exalted our minds at the sight; all lesser objects appeared mean and trifling.

> George, Lord Lyttleton, *Letter*.

(Westmorland) ranges and groups of mountains horrible to behold.

> Amory, *Life of John Buncle*, vol. I.

> Yon stream that wanders down the dale,
> The spiral wood, the winding vale,
>
> . . . . .
>
> The structure of the Cyprian dame,
> And each fair female's beauteous frame,
> Shew, to the pupils of Design
> The triumphs of the *Waving Line*.
>
>> Anon. (Shenstone *Works*, See Hogarth 1753).

PAINTING

Auction at Prestage's; approximate prices:—

> Rubens landscape   £290
> Rubens and Snyders   280
> Teniers' "Gallery"   100
>> Mrs. Delany to Mr. Granville, 6.4.

POETRY

In that species of poetry wherein Pope excelled, he is superior to all mankind; and I only say, that this species of poetry is not the most excellent one of the art. . . . Donne and Swift were undoubtedly men of wit, and men of sense: but what traces have they left of *pure poetry?* . . . The most solid observations on human life, expressed with the utmost elegance and brevity are *morality*, and not *poetry.* . . . It is a creative and glowing *imagination.* . . . The sublime and the pathetic are the two chief sources of all glorious poesy. What is there transcendently sublime or pathetic in Pope? (Dedication).

It is somewhat strange, that in the pastorals of a young poet there should not be found a single rural image that is new. . . . (Milton's) mention of places remarkably romantic, the supposed habitation of Druids, bards and wizards, is far more pleasing to the imagination than (Pope's) obvious introduction of Cam and Isis as seats of the Muses. . . . I have dwelt chiefly on (Milton's *Nativity*) ode as much less celebrated than L'Allegro and Il Penseroso, which are now universally known; but which by a strange fatality, lay in a sort of obscurity, the private enjoyment of a few curious readers, till they were set to admirable music by Mr. Handel. . . .

Thomson was accustomed to wander away into the country for days and for weeks . . . while many a poet who has dwelt for years in the Strand, has attempted to describe fields and rivers. . . . Hence that disgusting impropriety of introducing what may be called a set of hereditary images. . . . Our poets write from and to the *Head* rather than the *Heart.*

. . . . . .

Perhaps the Inferno of Dante is the next composition to the Iliad, in point of originality and sublimity.

> J. Warton, *Essay on the Genius and Writing of Pope.* Vol. I, see 1782. (Quoted by Wordsworth in *Essay Supplementary.* Warton was school-fellow of White of Selborne, and teacher of Bowles, who edited Pope 1806.)

(Homer's hint of Helen's beauty) affects me much more than the minute description which Spenser has given of Belphoebe; though I own that there are parts in that description, as there are in all the descriptions of that excellent writer, extremely fine and poetical.

> Burke, *Sublime and Beautiful.*

There is this material difference between the former and present age of poetry; that the writers in the first thought poetically; in the last they only express themselves so. Modern poets seem to me more to study the manner how they shall write, than what is to be written.
R. Lloyd, The Connoisseur.

Total oblivion to which are now condemned (all plays of the Restoration). Dryden's plays, excepting a few scenes, are utterly disfigured by vice or folly.
Hume, Hist. of Great Britain.

The true lyric style, with all its flights of fancy, ornaments and heightening of expression, and harmony of sound, is in its nature superior to every other style.
Gray to Mason, 19.12.

> I've heard them lilting, at our ewe-milking,
> Lasses a' lilting, before dawn o' day;
> But now they are moaning, on ilka green loaning,—
> The Flowers of the Forest are a' wede away.
Jean Elliot, A Lament for Flodden.

1757 r. George II

ANTIQUARIANISM

Mr. Gray sends his compliments to Mr. Brocket. Shall be extremely obliged to him, if he would make inquiry (when he has occasion to go into Trin. Library) after the following Old English Books.

Paradise of dainty devices 1578 4to and 1585.
Englands Helicon.
W. Webbe's Discourse of Eng. Poetry 1585 4to.
Fr. Meres' Wit's Commonwealth: 1598 Lond: and 1634.
Sam. Daniel's Musa a Defence of Rhyme 1611 8vo.
Stephen Hawes' Pastime of Pleasure 1555 4to.
Gawen Douglas Palace of Honour 1533 London 1579 Edinb.
Earl of Surrey's Ecclesiastes 1567 4to.
    ,, ,, ,, 2nd and 4th Books of the Aeneid 1557. 12mo.
Gascoign's Works, 2v: 4to 1577 & 1587.

GARDENS

(The Chinese) artists distinguish three different species of
scenes, to which they give the appellations of pleasing, horrid
and *enchanted*. Their enchanted scenes answer in a great
measure to what we call *romantic*. . . . Sometimes they make a
rapid stream or torrent pass underground, the turbulent noise
of which strikes the ear of the newcomer, who is at a loss to
know whence it proceeds; at other times they dispose the rocks
and buildings . . . in such a manner that the wind passing
through the different interstices . . . causes strange and
uncommon sounds. . . . In their scenes of horror they introduce
impending rocks, dark *caverns* and impetuous cataracts . . . the
buildings are some in ruins. (Cf. Coleridge, *Kubla Khan*).
Cf. 1764 & 1772.

> Sir W. Chambers, *Designs of Chinese
> Buildings*.

(This account of Chinese gardens is reproduced by Dodsley
in his Description of Shenstone's Leasowes 1764. The words
italicised by the present editor, as well as an invisible but
audible river, recur in Coleridge.)

The gardens are charming, and as we drank tea in one of the
buildings, the family being very musical, the young ladies sang,
while the gentlemen accompanied on their German flutes. . . .
When in a little temple, on entering we laughed exceedingly
at the rural politeness of our beaux.

> Mrs. Lybbe Powys (Miss Girle).

MANNERS AND TASTES

The traveller with amazement sees
A temple, Gothic or Chinese,
With many a bell and tawdry rag on
And crested with a sprawling dragon;
A wooden arch is bent astride
A ditch of water four foot wide,
With angles, curves and zig-zag lines.

. . . . .

And now from Hyde Park corner come
The Gods of Athens and of Rome;
Here squabby Cupids take their places
With Venus and the clumsy Graces;
Apollo there, with aim so clever,
Stretches his leaden bow for ever.

R. Lloyd, *The Cit's Country Box.*

We have a sort of Jewish superstition and would not come to town on Saturday or Sunday though it were to defend the Holy of Holies. What Englishman does not sacrifice anything to go his Saturday out of town?

H. Walpole to G. Montague, 20.8.

Subscription library opened at Liverpool.

NATURE

I honour your Taste, for dropping Tears, at the Lake of Killarney ... I am persuaded that all the inhabitants of Wales must be romantic, there never was any place appeared so like enchanted ground.

Mrs. Griffith, *Letters between Henry and Frances*, see 1751.

Then say; were ever rising Landskips giv'n
Only to gaze on? No! for higher End—
To lead the intellectual Mind to trace,
Eye and admire, Perfection infinite—
Heav'ns matchless Skill, Benevolence, and Pow'r.

E. Barnard, *Virtue the Source of Pleasure.*

Tempestuous regions, Derwent's naked peaks,
Snowdon and blue Plynlymmon and the wide
Aerial sides of Cader-yddris huge.

J. Dyer, *The Fleece.*

POETRY

Even in his most frantic rhapsodies (Young's) there are innumerable fine things.

H. Walpole to Lord Stafford, 4.7.

K*

The Muse . . .
She deigns to hear the savage youth repeat,
In loose numbers wildly sweet,
Their feather-cinctured chiefs and dusky loves.

> Gray, *The Progress of Poetry* (written
> 1754).

Your Lordship's approbation is conclusive, and it stamps
a disgrace on the age, who have not given themselves the
trouble to see any beauties in these *Odes* of Mr. Gray. They
have cast their eyes over them, found them obscure, and looked
no farther, yet perhaps no composition ever had more sublime
beauties than are in each. I agree with your Lordship in
preferring the last (the Bard) upon the whole; the first three
stanzas and a half, down to *agonizing King*, are in my opinion
equal to anything in any language I undertsand. Yet the last
three of the first Ode (Progress) please me very near as much.
The description of Shakespeare is worthy Shakespeare: the
account of Milton's blindness, though perhaps not strictly
defensible, is very majestic: The character of Dryden's poetry
is as animated as what it paints, . . . As Greek as the expression
(*many-twinkling*) is, it struck Mrs. Garrick, and she says, on that
whole picture, that Mr. Gray is the only poet who ever understood dancing. I do not think that (his co-temporaries)
ever admired him, except in his Churchyard, though the Eton
Ode was far its superior, and is certainly not obscure. The
Eton Ode is perfect; those of more masterly execution have
defects, yet not to admire them is total want of taste. I have
an aversion to tame poetry; at best, perhaps, the art is the
sublimest of the *difficiles nugae;* to measure or rhyme prose is
trifling without being difficult.

To Lord Lyttleton, 25.8.

You are very particular, I can tell you, in liking Gray's *Odes*
—but you must remember that the age likes Akinside, and did
like Thomson. Can the same people like both?

H. Walpole to G. Montagu, 25.8.

Attentive Fancy, her delighted sons
In two illustrious orders comprehend.
. . . Still the form
Which Fancy worships, or sublime or fair
Her votaries proclaim. . . .

He, God most high, (bear witness Earth and Heaven)
The living fountains in himself contains
Of Beautious and Sublime.

Akenside *Pleasures of Imagination* (revised now or 1758. For
original see 1744, where he speaks of "mind" not "God",
and, before Burke (?), copies Longinus in naming *three* orders,
"the sublime, the wonderful, the fair").

I have got the old Scotch Ballad on which (Home's) Douglas
was founded; it is divine ... Aristotle's best rules are observed
in it, in a manner that shows the author had never read
Aristotle. It begins in the fifth act of the play: you may read
it two-thirds through without guessing what it is about; and
yet when you come to the end it is impossible not to understand
the whole story.

> Gil Maurice was an Earle's son,
> His fame it wexed wide.
> It was nae for his grete riches,
> Nae for his mickle pride; &c.

(cf. Percy, Reliques, III, p. 89).

Gray to Mason, June.

I am greatly struck with "The Tragedy of Douglas" [Home],
though it has infinite faults. The Author seems to me to have
revived the true Language of the stage which has been lost
for these hundred years; and there is one scene (between
Matilda and the old Peasant) so masterly that it strikes me
blind to all the defects in the world.

Gray, 10.8.

fell tube

> Whose iron entrails hide the sulphurous blast,
> Satanic engine.

Mason, *The English Garden* (published 1772).

T. Warton, Professor of Poetry, Oxford; succeeded Hawkins
in his father's old Chair (see Index of authors quoted).

On death of Cibber, laureateship refused by Gray and Akenside,
and given not to Thomson but to W. Whitehead (see Index).

Gray's *Bard* and *Progress of Poetry* printed at Strawberry Hill.

SCULPTURE

Monument to Admiral Watson by Scheemakers in Westminster Abbey. "The Admiral in a toga is sitting in the centre
holding a palm branch. On the right the town of Calcutta,
on her knees, presents a petition."

1758 r. George II

MANNERS AND TASTES

Say the word, if you have a compact neat box of red brick
with sash windows, or a grotto made of flints and shell-work,
or a walnut-tree with three mole-hills under it, stuck with
honey-suckles round a basin of gold-fishes. . . . I congratulate
you on your acquaintance with the *savage*, the *rude*, and the
tremendous.

To Palgrave, 6.9.

If you should lead me into a superb Gothic building with a
thousand clustered pillars, each of them half a mile high,
the walls all covered with fret-work, and the windows full
of red and blue saints, that had neither head nor tail, and I
should find the Venus of Medici in person perked up in a
long niche over the high altar, as naked as ever she was born,
do you think it would raise or damp my devotions?

Gray to Mason, 9.11.

About this date the rustic music-house at Vauxhall was rebuilt
in Gothic.

A line put into the post any time before 9 o'clock will find me
next morning at Strawberry Hill.

To Dr. Birch, 8.7.

Dipping my head in a pail of cold water every morning the
moment I am out of bed.

H. Walpole to Sir H. Mann, 11.1.

NATURE

Horrors like these at first alarm
But soon with savage grandeur charm,
And raise to noblest thoughts the mind:
Thus by thy falls, Lodore, reclined
The craggy cliffs, impending wood
Whose shadows mix o'er half the flood . . .
I view with wonder and delight,
A pleasing though an awful sight.

> Dr. Dalton (Queen's College, Oxford). *Descriptive Poem addressed to two Young Ladies at their Return from viewing the Mines near Whitehaven.*

PAINTING

His mouth was full of nothing but the grace of Raffaelle, the purity of Domenichino, the learning of Poussin, the air of Guido, the greatness of taste of the Caraches, and the sublimity and grand contours of Michael Angelo, with all the rest of the cant of criticism. . . . "Vandyke . . . had not the flowing line" . . . "What a pity it is that Raffaelle was not acquainted with the pyramidal principle . . . I have often lamented that so great a genius as Raffaelle had not lived in this enlightened age, since the art has been reduced to principles". These critics are continually lamenting that Raffaelle had not the colouring and harmony of Rubens, or the light and shadow of Rembrandt, without considering how much the gray harmony of the former, and the affectation of the latter would take from the dignity of Raffaelle, and yet Rubens had greater harmony and Rembrandt understood light and shadow: but what may be an excellence in a lower class of painting, becomes a blemish in a higher.

> J. Reynolds, *Idler*, No. 29. *The Art Connoisseur.*

I am glad you are master of a Pietà. . . . Palma (that is the *old* one) was a good colourist, like most of ye Venetians, but remarkable for bad drawing particularly of hands and arms.

> Gray to Wharton, 2.14.

The constant high price given for pictures: the other day at Mr. Furnese's Auction a very small Gaspar sold for 76 giuneas; and a Carlo Maratti, which too I am persuaded was a Giuseppe Chiari, Lord Egremont bought at the rate of 260 pounds. Mr. Spencer gave no less than 2,200 pounds for the Andrea Sacchi and the Guido from the same collection. The latter is of very dubious originality. My father, I think, preferred the Andrea Sacchi to his own Guido and once offered 700 pounds for it, but Furnese said "Damn him, it is for him; *he* shall pay 1000". There is a pewterer, at Cleeve, who some time ago gave 1000 pounds for four very small Dutch pictures.

9.2.

A copy of the King of France's Raphael went for 700 pounds. A Sigismunda, called by Corregio, but certainly by Furoni (*sic*) his scholar was bought in at upwards of 400 pounds.[1]

H. Walpole to H. Mann, 10.2.

Prices at Sir Luke Schaub's sale (approximate):—

	£	s	d
Guido's Boy and Lamb	£153	10	0
Claude Lorrain	105	0	0
Rembrandt Boy's Head	52	0	0
Rubens Landscape	76	0	0
Vandyke, Laughing Boy	126	0	0
Corregio (ascribed. Furini?) Sigismunda	200	0	0[2]
Raphael	703	10	0
View of Antwerp (Background City by Brill; Flemish foreground, Rubens; river L'Escaut, bridge and Buildings, Gillis; small figures, Velvet Breughel)	551	5	0

Mrs. Delany to B. Granville.

POETRY

E. Young (aet. 75) criticized Pope in *Advice to a young poet*.

With that great judge Corneille . . . I prefer Lucan to Virgil, . . . the poetic images, the versification and the language of the Aeneid are delightful, but take the story by itself and can anything be more silly and unaffecting?

H. Walpole to Zouch, 9.12.

[1] But see Delaney below.
[2] But see Walpole above.

	Place	Genius	Judgement	Learning	Versification	Total
Chaucer	(10)	16	12	10	14	=52
Spenser	(8)	18	12	14	18	=62
Shakespeare	(=5)	19	14	14	19	=66
Jonson	(9)	16	18	17	8	=59
Cowley	(=5)	17	17	15	17	=66
Waller	(11)	12	12	10	16	=50
Milton	(=2)	18	16	17	18	=69
Dryden	(=2)	18	16	17	18	=69
Addison	(4)	16	18	17	17	=68
Prior	(7)	16	16	15	17	=64
Pope	(1)	18	18	15	19	=70

Goldsmith's "Poetical Scale" in *Literary Magazine*, January. cf. 1746. All English here. cf. a Victorian scale given in Holman Hunt's *Pre-Raphaelite Brotherhood*.

🎴 1759 r. George II 🎴

MANNERS AND TASTES

All sorts of Rooms after the manner of the Arabian, Chinese, Persian, Gothic, Muscovite, Palladian, Vitruvian and Egyptian.
(Quoted) Lenygon, *English Furniture*.

Enough of Greece and Rome. The exhausted store
Of either nation now can charm no more;

. . . . .

On eagle wings the poet of tonight
Soars for fresh virtues to the source of light,
To China's eastern realms: and boldly bears
Confucius' morals to Britannia's ears.
W. Whitehead, Prologue to Murphy's
Chinese Orphan.

289

You shall see a grocer or a tallow-chandler sneak from behind the counter, clap on a laced coat and a bag, fly to the E.O. table, throw away fifty pieces with some sharping man of quality, while his industrious wife is selling a pennyworth of sugar, or a pound of candles to support her fashionable spouse in his extravagance.

Goldsmith, *The Bee.*
(*Of the Pride and Luxury of the Middling Class.*)

I doubt if any bargain of that kind is to be met with except at some old mansion-sale—in the country, where people will disdain tapestry, because they hear that Paper is all the fashion. . . .

Mr. W:(alpole) has lately made a new Bedchamber,[1] which as it is in the best taste of anything he has yet done, and in your own Gothic way, I must describe a little. You enter by a peaked door at one corner of the room (out of a narrow, winding passage, you may be sure) into an Alcove, in which the bed is to stand, formed by a screen of pierced work opening by one larger arch in the middle into the rest of the chamber which is lighted at the other end by a bow window of three bays, whose tops are of rich painted glass in mosaic. The cieling [*sic*] is coved and fretted in star and quatrefoil compartments, with roses at the inter-sections, all in papier-maché. The chimney on your left is the high-altar in the cathedral of Rouen (from whence the screen is also taken) consisting of a low sur-based Arch between two octagon Towers whose pinnacles almost reach the ceiling, all of nich-work. The Chairs and dressing-table are real carved ebony, pick'd up at auctions, the hangings uniform purple paper, hung all over with the court of Henry, ye 8th, copied after the Holbein's in the Queen's Closet at Kensington, in black and gold frames, the bed is to be either from Burleigh (for Ld Exeter is new furnishing it, and means to sell some of his original household-stuff) of the rich old tarnish'd embroidery; or if that is not to be had, and it must be new, it is to be a cut velvet with a dark purple pattern in a stone-colour satin ground, and deep mixt fringes and tassels.

Gray to Wharton, 18.9.

[1] Holbein Chamber, The Copies by Vertue in oil paper.

Saint Palaye, *Mémoires sur l'ancienne Chevalerie*, 1st vol. (3rd in 1781) perhaps influenced Hurd (1762); later edited *Aucassin et Nicolette*. The *Mémoires* translated into English 1784, by Mrs. Dobson.

NATURE

Heath in bloom would form a carpet agreeable enough to sight, if we could separate from its appearance the idea of the barrenness of the mountains and wilds which it covers.

> Gerard, *Essay on Taste* (Association theory).

PAINTING

(Mr. Ramsay) and Mr. Reynolds are our favourite painters and two of the very best we ever had. The former is bold and has a kind of tempestuous colouring, yet with dignity and grace; the latter is all delicacy. Mr. Reynolds seldom succeeds in women; Mr. Ramsay is formed to paint them.

> H. Walpole to Sir D. Dalrymple, 25.2.

I should grieve to see *Reynolds* transfer to Heroes and to Goddesses, to empty splendor and to airy fiction, that art which is now employed in diffusing friendship, in reviving tenderness, in quickening the affection of the absent, and continuing the presence of the dead.

> (Johnson?), *Idler*, 24.2.

POETRY

Perhaps I may return to my old Lydgate & Occleve.

> Gray to Mann, 6.10.

The last chorus, (of Mason's Caractacus) and the lines that introduce it, are to me one of the best things I ever read.

> Gray to J. Brown.

Imitations are of two kinds; one of Nature, one of Authors. The first we call *Originals*. . . . An *Original*, though but indifferent, yet has something to boast. . . . An *Original* may be said to be of a *vegetable* nature, it rises spontaneously from the vital root of Genius; it *grows*, it is not made: *Imitations* are often a sort of *Manufacture* wrought up by those *Mechanics, Art*, and *Labour*. . . . A *Genius* differs from a *good Understanding* as a Magician from a good Architect. . . . In the Fairyland of Fancy, Genius may wander wild; there it has creative power, and may reign arbitrarily over its own empire of Chimeras. . . . To the neglect of Learning, Genius sometimes owes its greater Glory. . . . Who knows if Shakespeare might not have thought less, if he had read more? . . . The less we copy the renowned Antients, we shall resemble them the more. . . . How much nobler if (Pope) had resisted the temptations of that Gothic demon (rhyme) which modern poetry, tasting, became mortal. . . . Rhyme, which in epic poetry is a sore disease, is in the tragic, absolute death. . . . Our lesser poetry stands in need of a toleration for it.

> E. Young, *Conjectures on Original Composition* to Richardson.

Shaftesbury has had more imitators in England than any other writer.

> Goldsmith, *The Bee, An Account of the Augustan Age in England.*

Dante . . . addressed a barbarous people in a method suited to their apprehensions, united Purgatory and the River Styx . . . and shows a strange mixture of good sense and absurdity. The truth is, he owes most of his reputation to the obscurity of the times in which he lived. . . . The revival of these pieces of forced humour, far-fetched conceit and unnatural hyperbole which have been attributed to Shakespeare, is rather gibbeting than raising a statue to his memory. . . . The tuneless flow of our blank verse, the pompous epithet.

> Goldsmith, *Enquiry into Present State of Polite Learning.*

All power of fancy over reason is a degree of insanity. . . . The business of the poet, said Imlac, is to examine not the individual, but the species—to remark general properties and large appearances. He does not number the streaks of the tulip, nor describe the different shades of the forest. He is to exhibit in his portraits of nature such permanent and striking features as recall the original to every mind, and must neglect those minute descriptions which one may have remarked and the other neglected, for those characteristics which are alike obvious to attention and neglect. . . . He must consider right and wrong in their abstracted and invariable state; he must disregard present laws and opinion, and rise to general and transcendental truths, which will always be the same.

Johnson, *Rasselas*.

❦ 1760 r. George II—George III ❦

ARCHITECTURE

Soon after (the reign of Henry VIII) the Grecian style was introduced, and no wonder when so many Italians were entertained in the King's service. They had seen that architecture revived in their own country in all its purity—but whether they were not perfectly masters of it, or that it was necessary to introduce the innovation by degrees, it certainly did not at first obtain full possession. It was plaistered upon Gothic, and made a barbarous mixture. Regular columns, with ornaments neither Grecian nor Gothic and half embroidered with foliage, were crammed over frontispieces, façades and chimnies, and lost all grace by wanting simplicity.

H. Walpole, *Anecdotes of Painting* (published 1762).

(On which, Gray:—)

By wanting simplicity. A Goth must not say this, and indeed the ugliness of this style is not owing to the profusion of ornaments: nor is it a *mixture*, nor plaistered upon Gothic for there is nothing Gothic left (except perhaps the ceilings), but it is all, as you say, neither Grecian nor Gothic; or else Grecian alone, divested of its proportions (its very essence), and with all its members mismatched. . . .
I beg leave to differ as to the era of Gothic perfection ["about the reign of Henry IV" H. Walpole *Anecdotes of Painting*] There is nothing finer than the nave of York Minister (in a great and simple style), or than the choir of the same church (in the rich & filigrane workmanship). But these are of Edward the Third's reign, the first in the beginning and the

latter in the end of it. The Lady Chapel [now Trinity Church] at Ely, and the lantern tower in the same Cathedral are noble works of the same time. . . . The Chapel of Bishop West who died in 1533 surpassed all other things of the kind.

Gray to H. Walpole, 2.9.

Walked out to see the different buildings of Palladio (in Vicenza) of which I am no admirer. His private houses are ill-adjusted. . . . the Villa Valmarana, which is painted in fresco by Tiepolo, with a good deal of spirit and whim.

J. Adam, Diary.

GARDENS

In the Queen's (Caroline, at Richmond) garden a labyrinth and Gothic building.

Dodsley, London and its Environs, (cf. Mason, 1773).

MANNERS AND TASTES

The *Managareth* or Chinese bedroom and dressing room in the attic storey, is excessively droll and pretty, furnish'd exactly as in China, the bed of an uncommon size, seven feet wide by six long. (At Eastbury, Worcs.).

Mrs. L. Powys (Girle), Diary.

Conveniences in every bedchamber; great mahogany projections . . . with holes with brass handles and cocks &c.

H. Walpole to G. Montagu, 27.3.

Colbert founded Franco-Chinese trading company.

Froissard is a favourite book of mine.

Gray to Wharton, 23.1.

We cannot live without destroying animals, but shall we torture them for our sport? . . . One of the bravest and best men I ever knew, Sir Charles Wager, I have often heard declare he would never kill a fly willingly. It is a comfortable reflection to me that all the victories of the last year have been gained since the suppression of the Bear Garden and prize-fighting.

H. Walpole to Sir D. Dalrymple, 20.6.

Another Louis Quatorze may make another Versailles, but the hand of the Deity only can make another Mucross (Muckross Gardens, Killarney).

Bishop Berkeley, *Letter*.

"How did *Garrick* speak?" . . . "Oh against all rule". . . . "Was the eye silent?" . . . "I look'd only at the stop watch." . . . "And what of this new book?" . . . "Oh out of all plumb . . . I had my rule and compasses etc. in my pocket; . . . and for the epick poem . . . upon an extract scale of *Bossu's* 'tis out. . . . The grand picture . . . there is nothing of the colouring of *Titian*, the expression of *Rubens*, the grace of *Raphael*, the purity of *Domenichino* the *corregiescity* of *Corregio*, the learning of *Poussin*, the airs of *Guido*, the taste of the *Carrachis*, or the grand contour of *Angelo*." Grant me patience, just Heaven! Of all the cants which are canted in this canting world . . . the cant of criticism is the most tormenting!

Sterne, *T. Shandy*, Bk. III, Ch. 12 (or 1761).

Polly Honeycombe (skit on contemporary fiction) Colman.

PAINTING

Exhibition of contemporary art held at Society of Arts. 6,582 catalogues sold in 2 weeks. Reynolds' exhibits highly praised in the *Imperial Magazine*. First regular exhibition of pictures in England? See 1755.

Sandby has made such a picture! such a bard! such a headlong flood! such giant oaks! such desert caves! If it is not the best picture that has been painted this century . . .

Mason to Lord Nuneham.

POETRY

Boileau: I see (*Spenser*) sometimes in company with Homer and Virgil, but oftener with Tasso, Ariosto, and Dante.

Pope: . . . There is a force and beauty in some of his *images* and *descriptions*, equal to any in those writers you have seen him converse with. But he had not the art of properly *shading* his pictures.

Lord Lyttleton, *Dialogues of the Dead*, XIV.

I do not like the monstrous irregularities of Shakespeare;
... I admire but some lively and masterly strokes in his
performances ... I know not whether you have preserved
the reputation your island enjoyed in point of literature when
Addison, Congreve, Pope, Swift were alive.

Voltaire, Letter in B.M.

> Had Shakespeare crept by modern rules,
> We'd lost his Witches, Fairies, Fools;
> Instead of all that wild creation,
> He'd formed a regular plantation.
>
> . . . . .
>
> When Shakespeare leads the mind a dance,
> From France to England, hence to France,
> Talk not to me of time and place;
> I own I'm happy in the chace.
> Whether the drama's here or there,
> 'Tis nature, Shakespeare, everywhere.
>
> . . . . .
>
> So Genius, of itself discerning,
> Without the mystic rules of learning,
> Can, from its present intuition,
> Strike at the truth of composition.
> Yet those who breathe the classic vein,
> Enlisted in the mimic train,
>
> . . . . .
>
> So mighty gentle all the while,
> In such a sweet descriptive style,
> While Chorus marks the servile mode
> With fine reflection, in an Ode,
> Present you with a perfect piece
> Form'd on the model of Old Greece.

R. Lloyd, *Shakespeare* (*Ep. to Garrick*).

Capell, *Prolusions or Select Pieces of Antient Poetry*, (Nut-brown
Maid, Edward III, etc.) "Compiled with great care from their
several Originals and offer'd to the Public as specimens of
the Integrity that should be found in the editions of worthy
Authors."

MacPherson's *Fragments of Ancient Poetry collected in the Highlands of Scotland and translated from the Gaelic or Erse Language* (1st instalment), highly praised by Hume in a letter, Aug. 16, 1760; completed in 1762, influenced Goethe, Chateaubriand and Byron. MacPherson, meeting Home, the author of *Douglas*, at Moffat, had been asked for Celtic poetry.

—My Old Scotch (or rather Irish) poetry. I am gone mad about them. They are said to be translations (literal and in prose) from the *Erse*-tongue, done by one Macpherson, a young Clergyman in the Highlands ... I was so struck, so *extasié* with their infinite beauty, that I writ into Scotland; This man is a very Demon of poetry, or he has lighted on a treasure hid for ages ... the whole external evidence would make one believe these fragments (for so he calls them tho' nothing can be more entire) counterfeit: but the internal is so strong on the other side, that I am resolved to believe them genuine.

To Wharton, June.

Another Scotch packet ... The idea that struck and surprised me most was the following:—

> "Ghosts ride on the tempest tonight;
> Sweet is their voice between the gusts of wind;
> *Their songs are of other worlds.*"

Did you never observe (*while rocking winds are piping loud*) that pause, as the gust is recollecting itself, and rising upon the ear in a shrill and plaintive note, like the swell of an Aeolian harp? I do assure you there is nothing in the world so like the voice of a spirit.

Gray to Stonehewer, 29.6.

Dyers' *Fleece*. I own I think it a very insipid poem. His *Ruins of Rome* had great picturesque spirit, and his *Grongar Hill* was beautiful ...
(*Ossian*) "they are poetry and resemble that of the East; that is they contain natural images and natural sentiment elevated, before rules were invented to make poetry difficult and dull. I like particularly the expression of calling Echo, "Son of the Rock", the Monody is much the best. 3.2.

Gray is "charmed with the two specimens of Erse poetry" ...
(Tristram Shandy) makes me smile 2 or 3 times at the beginning, but in recompense makes me yawn for 2 hours.

To Sir D. Dalrymple, 4.4.

Fingal is a brave collection of similies ... I cannot believe it genuine.   Cymbeline ... with a few pretty passages and a scene or two, is so absurd and tiresome.

H. Walpole to G. Montagu, 8.12.

PROSE

Tristram Shandy is still a greater object of admiration, the man as well as the book: one is invited to dinner, when he dines, a fortnight before.

Gray to Wharton, 22.4.

❧ 1761 r. George III ❧

MANNERS AND TASTES

It is mere pedantry in Gothicism to stick to nothing but altars and tombs, and there is no end of it, if we are to sit upon nothing but Coronation-chairs, nor drink out of nothing but chalices & flagons.

Gray to T. Wharton, 13.11.

... To do the folks [at Lynn] justice they are sensible and reasonable, and civilized; their very language is civilized since I lived among them.   I attribute this to their more frequent intercourse with the world and the capital, by the help of good roads and postchaises. 25.3.
My two passions, lilacs and nightingales.

H. Walpole to G. Montagu, 5.4.

> Thy shades, thy silence, now be mine,
> Thy charms my only theme:
> My haunt, the hollow cliff, whose pine
> Waves o'er the gloomy stream,
> Whence the scar'd owl, on pinions grey,
> Breaks from the rustling boughs,
> And down the lone vale sails away,
> To more profound repose.

J. Beattie, *Retirement*.

Addison. What can (the ruins of Kenilworth) call to mind but the memory of barbarous manners and a despotic government?...
Arbuthnot. The *Gothic* tilts and tournaments exceeded, both in use and elegance even, the *Graecian* gymnastics. ... I consider the legends of ancient chivalry in a very serious light.

Hurd, *Moral and Political Dialogues*, III.
On the Age of Elizabeth.

MUSIC
"Noblemen's and Gentlemen's Catch Club" founded.

PAINTING
"Hogarth is the best painter of life and manners in the universe, and I know that I gave £12 or £14 for his prints and would not take five hundred for them." "Lord, Hogarth! An absolute Bartholomew droll who ... pretends to laugh at the connoisseurs." "Wilson's Niobe? ... none of the colouring of Claude's glowing backgrounds."

St. James' Chronicle.

The majesty of Italian ideas almost sinks before the warm nature of Flemish colouring! Alas! don't I grow old? My young imagination was fired with Guido's ideas—must they be plump and prominent as Abishag to warm me now? Does great youth feel with poetic limbs as well as see with poetic eyes?

H. Walpole to G. Montagu, 25.3.

POETRY
My first acquantance with Mr. Gray was one afternoon drinking tea ... Mr. Gray turned quickly round to me and said, "Sir, do you read Dante?" ... He had a perfect knowledge of the Italian language and of the poets of Italy of the first class, to whom he certainly looked up as to his great progenitors and to Dante as the father of all; to whose genius, if I remember right, he thought it an advantage to have been produced in a rude age of strong and uncontrolled passions, when the muse was not checked by refinement and the fear of criticism. He preferred the *Gierusalemme Liberata* of Tasso *as a poem*, to Ariosto.

N. Nicholls, Rem. of Gray (published 1835).

The *Héloïse* cruelly disappointed me, but it has its Partisans among wch are Mason and Mr. Hurd. For me I admire nothing but *Fingal*.

> Gray to Wharton, Jan.

A servile race
Who, in mere want of fault, all merit place;
Who blind obedience pay to ancient schools,
Bigots to Greece, and slaves to musty rules[1]

. . . . .

Happy in tragic and in comic pow'rs
Have we not *Shakespeare*, is not *Johnson* ours?

> Churchill, *The Rosciad*.

(Pope)   But whilst each line with equal beauty flows
        E'en excellence, unvaried, tedious grows.

. . . . .

(Dryden) What if some dull lines in cold order creep,
        And with his theme the poet seems to sleep?
        Still, when his subject rises proud to view,
        With equal strength the poet rises too;
        With strong invention, noblest vigour fraught,
        Thought still springs up, and rises out of thought;
        Numbers enrolling numbers in their course,
        In varied sweetness flow, in varied force;
        The powers of Genius and of judgement join,
        And the whole Art of Poetry is thine.

> Churchill, *Apology*.

The second and third volumes of Tristram Shandy have universally met the contempt they deserve. . . . A new play of Voltaire's called *Tancred* . . . repairs the idea of his decaying parts, which I had conceived from his Peter the Great.

> Rev. H. Zouch, 7.3.

Voltaire's miserable imitation or second part or dregs of his Candide . . . his delightful ridicule of the Nouvelle Eloise called Prédiction.

> H. Walpole to H. Mann, 9.7.

---

[1] Cf. Keats. "Musty laws lined out with wretched rule". *Sleep and Poetry*.

"Ănd mānў ăn āmŏrŏus, mānў ā hūmŏroŭs lāy,
Whĭch mānў ā bārd hăd chāntĕd mānў ā dāy."

This, though it increases the number of the syllables, yet it
sweetens the flow of the verse, and renders the ear perfectly
reconciled to the irregularity of the metre.

J. Mason, *The Power of Numbers.*

Il nous a presque toujours manqué un degré de Chaleur;
nous avions tout le reste. L'origine de cette langueur, de
cette faiblesse monotone, venant en partie de ce petit esprit
de galanterie, si cher aux courtisans et aux femmes (Cites St.
Evremond).

Changements arrivés à l'art Tragique.

Les Anglais ont un terme pour signifier cette plaisanterie,
ce vrai comique, cette gaiété, ces failles, qui échappent à
un homme sans qu'il s'en doute—*humour.* (Cites Corneille,
Suite du Menteur "Cet homme a de l'humeur").

Voltaire *à l'Abbé d'Olivet*, 20.8.

Why will you not read Jeremy Taylor? Take my word for it,
he is the Shakespeare of divines.

Mason to Gray, 8.1.

    Sisera, . . .
He ask'd refreshment from the limpid wave:
The milky beverage to the chief she gave

F. Fawkes.

The more we attend to the composition of Milton's harmony,
the more we shall be sensible how he tried to vary his pauses,
his measures and his feet, which gives that enchanting air of
freedom and wildness to his versification, unconfined by any
rules but those which his own feeling and the nature of the
subject demands.

Gray, *Observations on English Metre.*

PROSE

The English tongue is naturally grave and majestic. The
rhythm corresponds to the genius of it; and runs, almost
whether we will or no, into iambics. But the continuity of this

solemn measure has an ill effect where the subject is not of
moment. Mr. Addison's delicate ear made him sensible of
this defect in the rhythm of our language, and suggested to
him the proper cure for it; which was to break the continued
iambic measures, especially at the end of a sentence ... by a
preposition or other short word ... whence a trochee.

R. Hurd. (On *Spec.* 94. Early criticism
of prose rhythm, cf. 1749, Mason).

STAGE

The Opera House is crowded this year like any ordinary
theatre. Elisi is finer than anything has been here in your
memory. ... We have heard nothing since I remember operas,
but eternal passages, divisions, and flights of execution; of
these he has absolutely none ... His point is expression.

Gray to Mason, 22.1.

Shakespeare's *Henry V* at Covent Garden: A great attraction
was the procession from the Abbey at the Coronation.

🎐 1762 r. George III 🎐

ARCHITECTURE

Judging by numbers, the Gothic taste of architecture must
be preferred before that of Greece, and the Chinese taste
probably before either.

Home, Lord Kames, *Elements of Criticism.*

James ("Athenian") Stuart and Nicholas Revett *Antiquities
of Athens.* Greek ornament tended to replace Palladian.

MANNERS AND TASTES

Two great ladies prevailed on (Kent) to make the designs
for their birthday gowns. The one he dressed in a petticoat
decorated with columns of the five orders; the other like a
bronze, in a copper-coloured satin with ornaments of gold.

H. Walpole. *Anecdotes of Painting.*

The journeymen carpenters, like the cabinetmakers, have entered into an association not to work unless their wages are raised; and how can one complain? The poor fellows, whose all the labour is, see their masters advance their prices every day, and think it reasonable to touch their share.

To H. Mann, 1.7.

For watch and Chain a hundred and thirty four guineas; the seals will cost sixteen more.

H. Walpole to H. Mann, 8.6.

G. Lavington, Bp. of Exeter and opponent of Wesley, author of *The Enthusiasm of Methodists and Papists Compared*, died. His epitaph on S. wall of Choir there says he was "A successful Exposer of Pretence and Enthusiasm." (Wesley himself said he was "content to bear the reproach of Christ but not that of Enthusiasm").

Longsword, Earl of Salisbury (historical novel in Scott's manner), T. Leland.

Chinese gimcracks; . . . nothing is truly elegant but what unites use with beauty.

Goldsmith, *Citizen of the World (Chinese Letters)*.

NATURE

The Peak, a countrey beyond comparison uglier than any other I have seen in England, black, tedious, barren, and not mountainous enough to please one with its horrors.

Gray to Wharton, 4.12.

PAINTING

Intrinsic beauty is discovered in a single object viewed apart without any relation to any other . . . *Relative* beauty founded on the relation of objects. . . .
Beauty of figure as arising from regularity, uniformity, proportion order and simplicity. . . .
Beauty in its very conception refers to a percipient. (An expressionist theory opposed to that of Hutcheson).

Home (Lord Kames), *Elements of Criticism*.
cf. Kant, *Critique of Judgement*.

As our poets warm their imaginations with sunny hills or sigh
after grottoes and cooling breezes, our painters draw rocks
and precipices and castellated mountains, because Virgil
gasped for breath at Naples, and Salvator wandered amidst
Alps and Appenines.

H. Walpole, *Anecdotes of Painting*.

POETRY

May there not be something in the Gothic Romance peculiarly
suited to the views of a genius, and to the ends of poetry? i.
The mummeries of the pagan priests were childish, but the
Gothic Enchanters shook and alarmed all nature ... you
would not compare the Canidia of Horace with the Witches
in Macbeth. And what are Virgil's myrtles, dropping blood,
to Tasso's enchanted forest? ... Shakespeare ... with a terrible
sublime ... gives us another idea of the *rough magic*, as he calls
it, of fairy enchantment:—

> ... Graves at my command
> Have open'd and let forth their sleepers.

The last circumstance you will say, is but the *animas imis
excire sepulcris*, of the Latin poet. But a very significant word
marks the difference. The fancies of our modern bards are
not only more gallant, but, on a change of the scene, more
sublime, more terrible, more alarming than those of the classic
fables. vi.
Even Shakespeare is greater when he uses Gothic manners
and machinery, than when he employs classical: which brings
us again to the same point, that the former have, by their nature
and genius, the advantage of the latter in producing the
sublime. vii.
The Gothic method of design in poetry may be, in some sort,
illustrated by what is called the Gothic method of design in
Gardening. A wood or grove cut out into many separate
avenues or glades was amongst the most favourite of the works
of art, which our fathers attempted in this species of cultivation.
... You and I, are, perhaps, agreed that this sort of gardening
is not of so true a taste as that which *Kent and Nature* have
brought us acquainted with; where the supreme art of the
designer consists in disposing his ground and objects into an
entire landscape. viii.

(Hurd contrasts poetry which addresses itself to the heart through the passions—which must be credible since we must believe before we can be affected—with the more sublime and creative poetry which addresses itself to the Imagination. The latter may be incredible.)

The fairy tales of Tasso do him more honour than what are called the more natural, that is the more classical parts of his poem. x.

Without *admiration*, which cannot be effected but by the marvellous of celestial intervention, I mean, the intervention of superior natures really existing, or by the illusion of the fancy taken to be so, no epic poem can be long lived. I am not afraid to instance in the Henriade itself, which, notwithstanding the elegance of the composition, will in a short time be no more read than the Gondibert of Sir W. Davenant, and for the same reason.

The *Faery Queene*, one of the noblest productions of modern poetry.

The classic manners arising out of the customary and usual situations of humanity.

Poor Spenser then

> . . . "in whose gentle spright
> The pure well-head of Poesie did dwell",

must, for aught I can see, be left to the admiration of a few lettered and curious men. xi.

Yet, tho' (Milton) dropped the tales, he still kept to the allegories of Spenser. And even this liberty was thought too much, as appears from the censure passed on his *Sin and the Devil* by the severer critics.

What we have gotten by this revolution, you will say, is a great deal of good sense. What we have lost, is a world of fine fabling; the illusion of which is so grateful to the *Charmed Spirit* . . . Earth-born critics, my friend, may blaspheme:

> But all the Gods are ravished with delight
> Of his celestial song, and music's wondrous might. xii.

Hurd, Letters on Chivalry and Romance,
cf. T. Warton, 1778.

If you publish these old pieces unimproved only, I consider them as not everyone's money, but as a prize merely for either virtuosoes, or else the manufacturers in this kind of ware; the Poets namely. (See 1765.)

Shenstone to Percy, February 3.

Every word in Shakespeare is a picture.

Gray to West.

Every article in his (Shakespeare's) description is particular. . . . His language, though barbarous, is concrete. . . . Perspicuity ought not to be sacrificed to any other beauty whatever.

Henry Home (Lord Kames), *Elements of Criticism.*

Dryden's tragedies are a compound of bombast and heroic obscenity, inclosed in the most beautiful numbers.

H. Walpole, *Anecdotes of Painting.*

There are certain words in every language particularly adapted to the poetical expression; some from the image or idea they carry to the imagination; and some from the effect they have upon the ear. . . . Homer mentions a person who played upon the lyre; the translator sets him before us warbling to the silver strings. If this be a deviation, it is at the same time an improvement.

Goldsmith, *On Poetry as distinguished from Other Writings.*

In my sixteenth year (b. 1747) I first read Ossian. If I did not dance for joy . . . I wept for joy.

Anna Seward (The Swan of Lichfield).

The sheet and weather-brace they now stand by
The lee, clue-garnet and the bunt-lines ply,
Jears, lifts, and brails a seaman each attends,
Along the mast the willing yard descends.

Falconer, *The Shipwreck.*

🌸 1763 r. George III 🌸

ARCHITECTURE

All the buildings of Henry the Second's time are of a clumsy and heavy proportion, with a few rude and awkward ornaments; and this style continues to the beginning of Henry the Third's reign, though with a little improvement as in the nave of Fountain's Abbey, etc. then all at once come in the tall piqued arches, the light clustered columns, the capital of curling foliage, the fretted tabernacles and vaultings and a profusion of statues, etc. that constitute the good Gothic style; together with decreasing and flying buttresses, and pinnacles on the outside.

> Gray to Mason, 8.2.

Alhambra, Pagoda, and Mosque built at Kew.

GARDENS

The only proof of our original talent in matter of pleasure; I mean our skill in gardening or rather laying out grounds. . . . It is not forty years, since the art was born among us; and it is sure, that there was nothing in Europe like it, and as sure, we then had no information on this head from China.

> Gray to Howe, 10.9.

[A park] romantic beyond the wantonness of imagination . . . An avenue of the tallest trees which lets in the prospect of a fruitful valley, bounded at a distance by a mountain, down the sides of which rushes a foaming cascade, which spreads with a thousand meandering streams in the vale below, . . . temples . . . in the most elegant style of simplicity . . . grotto . . . wildly lovely.

> Mrs. Brooke, *The History of Lady Julia Mandeville*.

MANNERS AND TASTES

A magnificent service of Chelsea China . . . £1200 . . . I cannot boast of our taste; the forms are neither new, beautiful nor various. Yet Sprimont the manufacturer is a Frenchman [really a Fleming]. It seems their taste will not bear transplanting! To Sir H. Mann, 4.3.
You have already gone beyond what I have ever seen in etching. To Lord Nuneham, 16.3.
Strawberry Hill . . . the ceiling is Harry the Seventh's Chapel *in propria persona*. To G. Montagu, 28.3.
One is a little tired of Carlo Maratti and Luca Jordano [*sic*].
. . . Peterborough; its front is admirable, but the inside has

no more beauty than consists in vastness! To G. Montagu, 25.7. (At Park Place) the bridge sublime, composed of loose rocks that will appear to have been tumbled there the very week of the deluge. One stone is of fourteen hundredweight. It will be worth an hundred of Palladio's bridges, that are only fit to be used in an opera. H. Walpole to G. Montagu, 3.10.

S. Johnson (in Greenwich Park). "Is not this very fine?" Boswell, "Yes, Sir, but not equal to Fleet St." J. "You are right, Sir." Boswell, *Life*, 30.7.

POETRY

The undaunted courage of Fingal . . . the shriek which he sends forth "as rolled into himself, he rose upon the wind", are so full of the most amazing and terrible majesty, that I know no passage more sublime in the writings of any inspired author.

H. Blair, *Dissertation on Ossian.*

Imagination dwelt many hundred years ago in all her pomp on the cold and barren mountains of Scotland. The truth (I believe) is that, without any respect of climates, she reigns in all nascent societies of man, where the necessities of life force every one to think and act much for himself.

Gray to Brown, 17.2.

Inquiry whether a Catalogue of the Armies sent into the Field is an essential part of an Epic Poem.

Gibbon, December 23.

> Strong is the lion—like a coal
> His eyeball—like a bastion's mole
> His chest against the foes;
> Strong the gier-eagle on his sail,
> Strong against tide th'enormous whale
> Emerges as he goes.
>
> Chris. Smart, *Song to David.*

Milton's P.L. in 46th edition and minor poems in 30th (See 1711).

Sir, I was once in company with (Adam) Smith, and we did not take to each other; but had I known that he loved rhyme as much as you tell me he does, I should have *hugged* him.

> Johnson in Boswell's *Life*, 9.7.

❦ 1764 r. George III ❦

GARDENS

Farther on we lose all sight of water, and only hear the noise, without having the appearance, a kind of effect which the Chinese are fond of producing.

> R. Dodsley, *A Description of the Leasowes,*
> cf. 1757 and 1772, and Coleridge's
> *Kubla Khan.*

MANNERS AND TASTES

Colbert founded Compagnie des Indes.

The most plain Directions for the Art of Drawing . . . Twenty-four new Country Dances.

> *The Ladies New and Polite Memorandum.*

(Walpole's *Castle of Otranto*) makes some of us cry a little, and all in general afraid to go to bed.

> Gray to Walpole, 30.12.

Richardson who wrote those deplorably tedious lamentations *Clarissa* and *Sir Charles Grandison*, which are pictures of high life as conceived by a bookseller, and romances as they would be spiritualized by a Methodist teacher. . . . I shall put your letter to Rheims into the foreign post with a proper penny.

> To G. Montagu, 20.12.

Swop situations with you.

> H. Walpole to H. Mann, 27.7.

Boswell visited Rousseau, who was drawing up laws for Corsica having just published *Émile* (see 1765 and 1769).

The highest beauty is in God. It is devoid of particular significance (Unbezeichnung) like pure water. Expression is an unfortunate necessity owing to the fact that human beings are always in some emotional state. Male figure is never pure beauty, but female can be beautiful. (summarized).

> Winckelmann, *Geschichte der Kunst des Alterthums*.

La bellezza é il caratteristico.

> Spalletti, *Saggio sopra la Bellezza*.

I first acknowledged, at the feet of the Venus of Medicis, that the chissel [*sic*] may dispute the pre-eminence with the pencil—a truth in the fine arts which cannot, on this side of the Alps be felt. (C.) . . . The passage of Mont Cenis, the regular streets of Turin, the Gothic cathedral of Milan, the scenery of the Boromean islands, the marble palaces of Genoa, the beauties of Florence, the wonders of Rome, the curiosities of Naples, the galleries of Bologna, the singular aspect of Venice, the Amphitheatre of Verona, and the Palladian architecture of Vicenza, are still present to my imagination. . . . The whole college of Cardinals was of less value in my eyes than the transfiguration of Raphael, the Apollo of the Vatican, or the massy greatness of the Coliseum. (E.)

> Gibbon, *Autobiography* (various versions).

The French . . . are as formal as we were in Queen Anne's days, and believe they make discoveries, when they adopt what we have had these 20 years. For instance, they begin to see beauties in the antique—everything must be *à la grecque*— accordingly the lace on their waistcoats is copied from a frieze.

> H. Walpole to Sir H. Mann, 9.4.

NATURE

A rural scene is never to me perfect without some kind of building . . . ruinated structure.

> Shenstone, *Unconnected Thoughts on Gardening*.

PAINTING

Two sweet children undoubtedly by Sir Peter Lely. This cost you £4-10s. . . . a fine Vandyck of the famous Lady Carlisle and her sister Leicester in one piece: it cost me 9 & 20 guineas.

H. Walpole to G. Montague, 10.5.

250 paintings belonging to Roger Hearne sold. None by an English Painter.

POETRY

One of the greatest geniuses that every existed, Shakespeare, undoubtedly wanted taste, . . . Inigo Jones seems to me to have had more taste than genius. Genius is original, invents, and taste selects, perhaps copies, with judgement.

H. Walpole to Chr. Wren, jnr. August 9.

(Shakespeare) uno di quei transcendenti poeti (whose genius soars beyond the reach of art).

G. Baretti, *Frusta Letteraria.*

(Johnson visiting Percy at Easton Maudit) chose for his regular reading the old Spanish romance of Felixmarte of Hircania, in folio, which he read quite through . . . I have heard him attribute to these extravagant fictions that unsettled turn of mind which prevented his ever fixing in any profession.

Percy.

Le théâtre anglais que Gilles Shakespeare a fait naître et a gâté.

Voltaire to Saurin, 28.2.

Simplicity . . . raised the venerable Dante, the father of modern poetry, above the succeeding poets of his country, who . . . have fallen under that just neglect, which time will ever decree to those who desert a just simplicity for the florid colourings of style, contrasted phrases, affected conceits, the mere trappings of composition and Gothic minutiae. It is this hath given to Boileau the most lasting wreath in France, and to Shakespeare and Milton in England.

Annual Register, Miscellaneous Essays, VII.

Some specimens of the Poetry of the Antient Welsh Bards.
Translated into English with Explanatory Notes. Evan Evans
(born in Cardiganshire, curate in Denbighshire; influenced
Gray's *Triumphs of Owen*, etc.).

Shenstone's Elegies published. May have influenced Gray
(Elegy 1751) as they were written 1743-6.

Mr. Pope's chief excellence lies in consolidating or condensing
sentences, yet preserving ease and perspicuity. In smoothness
of verse, perhaps he has been equalled: in regard to invention,
excelled.

Shenstone, *Allowing Merit in Others.*

✤ 1765 r. George III ✤

ARCHITECTURE

Saxon style . . . they had no tabernacles (or niches and
canopies), nor any statues to adorn their buildings on the
outside, which are the principal grace of what is called the
Gothic; . . . they used reliefs sometimes with profusion as
in the Saxon gateway of the Abbey at Bury. . . . Besides the
chevron work (or zig-zag moulding), there is also the *Billetted-
moulding* . . . the *Nail head*, . . . the *Nebule* (undulating line);
to adorn their vast massive columns there was the *spiral-grove*
and the *net* or *Lozenge-work* Possibly the pointed arch might
take its rise from those arcades we see in the early Norman
(or Saxon) buildings on walls, where the wide semi-circular
arches cross and intersect. . . . The wall south of the choir at
St. Cross of King Stephen's time . . . The rage of repairing,
beautifying, white-washing, painting, and gilding, and above
all, the mixture of Greek (or Roman) ornaments in Gothic
edifices. This well-meant fury has been, and will be little less
fatal to our ancient magnificent edifices, than the Reformation
and the Civil Wars.

Gray to Bentham (on History of Ely).

MANNERS AND TASTES

I had the happiness of passing the entire day of July 24 in
this romantic place, with the good fathers of the Grande
Chartreuse, and I reckon it among the most agreeable of my life.

John Wilkes.

I once more took a serious walk through the tombs in Westminster Abbey. What heaps of unmeaning stone and marble! But there was one tomb which showed common sense; that beautiful figure of Mr. Nightingale endeavouring to screen his lovely wife from death. Here indeed the marble seems to speak (by Roubillac).

C. Wesley, *Journal*.

Of all the towns in Italy I am least satisfied with Venice. . . . Old, and in general, ill-built houses, ruined pictures and stinking ditches dignified with the pompous denomination of canals, a fine bridge spoilt by two rows of houses upon it, and a large square, decorated with the worst architecture I ever saw.

Gibbon to his stepmother, 22.4.

Piranesi knighted by the Pope.

To blend the wonderful of old stories with the natural of modern novels, (and defends Shakespeare's tragi-comedy against Voltaire).

H. Walpole, *Castle of Otranto*, Pref. to 2nd Edition.

A novel (*The Castle of Otranto*) and such a novel, that no boarding-school Miss of thirteen could get through without yawning. It consists of ghosts and enchantments; pictures walk out of their frames, and are good company for half an hour together; helmets drop from the moon and cover half a family.

Gilly Williams to Selwyn, 19.3.

In this year the French King stated that 40,000 English had passed through Calais in the 2 years since the peace (of Paris).

H. Walpole to Lady Ossory, 8.11.1789 (and see 1785).

Boswell visited Corsica, and saw Paoli (see 1764 and 1769).

Peruke-makers petitioned the king against the growing habit of wearing natural hair.

As for *gentlemen*, says Sir Thomas Smith (*De Republica Anglorum* I.xx, d.1577), they be made good cheap in this kingdom: for whosoever . . . can live idly and without manual labour and will bear the port, charge and countenance of a gentleman, he shall be called master, and shall be taken for a gentleman.

Blackstone, *Commentaries* I, xii.

In their dress and equipages (the French) are grown very simple. We English are living upon their old gods and goddesses; I roll about in a chariot decorated with Cupids, and look like the grandfather of Adonis.

To H. Mann, 22.9.

I am as little pleased with (the French) taste in trifles. Crébillon is entirely out of fashion, and Marivaux a proverb; *Marivauder*, and *Marivaudage* are established terms for being prolix and tiresome.

To Gray, 19.11.

Another guess thing.

H. Walpole to H. Mann, 26.6.

(In Paris, which was raving over Richardson and Hume). Good people, they have no time to laugh. There is God and the King to be pulled down first.

H. Walpole to T. Brand, 19.10.

NATURE

The mountains are ecstatic, and ought to be visited in pilgrimage once a year. None but these monstrous creatures of God know how to join so much beauty with so much horror. A fig for your poets, painters, gardeners and clergymen that have not been among them; their imaginations can be made up of nothing but bowling-greens, flowering shrubs, horseponds, Fleet ditches, shell grottoes and Chinese rails.

Gray to Mason (from Highlands), Nov. (n.d.).

PAINTING

This saint (*Lady's Head in the character of a Saint* by Romney) is likely to have few votaries.

Public Advertiser.

(French) painters are bitter bad, and as much inferior to Reynolds and Ramsay as Hudson to Vandyck.

To Hon. H. S. Conway, 29.11.

I am almost tempted to prefer le Soeur [*sic*] to every painter I know.

H. Walpole to Gray, 19.11.

POETRY

(The *Reliques* are a) strange collection of trash (to Birch 2.2.). In a polished age like the present, I am sensible that many of these reliques of antiquity will require great allowances to be made for them. Percy, Preface to *Reliques*. (Polished and amplified unsparingly. 3 editions in 10 years).

Remember Dryden and be blind to all his faults.

Gray to Beattie, 2.10.

Spenser's . . . drawling stanzas.

H. Walpole to Cole, 9.3.

Wanting a buffoon, (Shakespeare) went into the senate-house for that which the senate house would certainly have afforded him. . . . His disposition led him to comedy. . . . Whenever he solicits his invention, or strains his faculties, the offspring of his throes is tumour, meanness, tediousness and obscurity. In narration he affects a disproportionate pomp of diction. . . . (Unities) The spectators are always in their senses and know, from the first act to the last, that the stage is only a stage. . . . If we thought murders and treason real, they would please no more. . . . Addison speaks the language of poets (in Cato) and Shakespeare of men. . . .
(Henry VIII. iv. 2). This scene is above any other part of Shakespeare's tragedies, and perhaps above any scene of any other poet, tender and pathetic, without gods, or furies, or poisons, or precipices, without the help of romantic circumstances and without improbable sallies of poetical lamentation, and without any throes of tumultuous misery.

Johnson, *Shakespeare*.

L*   315

The English have established a yearly festival in honour of the famous player-poet Shakespeare. We in France have not yet any festival in honour of Molière.

Voltaire.

✥ 1766 r. George III ✥

ARCHITECTURE

The Sainte Chapelle has answered my expectations.

To Cole, 18.1

Very beautiful; it is in the newest style (a ceiling design), and takes in some measure, as everything here [Paris] is now, from the oldest style, that is the antique.

To Miss A. Pitt, 1.3.

[Bristol] Cathedral is very neat and has pretty tombs . . . There is a new church besides of St. Nicholas, neat and truly Gothic; besides a charming old Church at the other end of the town. The cathedral or abbey at Bath is glaring and crowded with modern table monuments.

H. Walpole to G. Montagu, 22.10.

I was much disappointed at sight of the Pantheon, which, after all that has been said of it, looks like a huge cockpit open at top. (Depreciates also Coliseum and Venus dei Medici) . . . (The beauties of the Maison Carrée at Nîmes) are, indeed, so exquisite, that you may return to them every day with a fresh appetite for seven years together.

Smollett, Travels Through France and Italy. (Sterne's "Smelfungus").

At Nîmes . . . la maison quarrée, is, in my mind the finest piece of architecture that I ever saw; and the amphitheatre the clumsiest and the ugliest; if it were in England, everybody would swear it had been built by Sir John Vanbrugh.

Lord Chesterfield to P. Stanhope, 9.12.

University College (Oxford) hall. The oak rafters of roof concealed by a plaster ceiling of late gothic design; deal gothic panelling with crockets inserted, and a fireplace given by

Sir Roger Newdigate said to be a copy of a Gothic tomb at Ely. The plaster ceiling was perhaps modelled on the stone vaulting of the Convocation House (1634-7) or the plaster ceiling of B.N.C. chapel (1659). The ceiling was removed, the panelling replaced by oak and the fireplace concealed in 1906.

MANNERS AND TASTES

There is at least as much room for exercising the great arts of design and composition in laying out a garden as in executing a good painting.

T. Martyn, *The English Connoisseur.*

Ay, here's none of your strait lines here—but all taste—zig-zag —crinkum-crankum—in and out—right and left—so and again —twisting and turning like a worm.

Garrick and Colman, *The Clandestine Marriage.*

I have been at one opera, Mr. Wesley's. They have boys and girls with charming voices, that sing hymns, in parts, to Scotch ballad tunes. . . . The chapel is very neat, with true Gothic windows . . . Wesley spoke his sermon . . . there were parts and eloquence in it but . . . he acted very ugly enthusiasm.

H. Walpole to J. Chute, 10.10.

Men of little genius found them (Gay and Ovid) most easily imitated in their defects, and English poetry, like that in the latter empire of Rome, is nothing at present but a combination of luxuriant images, without plot or connection; a string of epithets that improve the sound without carrying on the sense. . . . Other fasionable topics, such as pictures, taste, Shakespeare, and the musical glasses. . . . We might as well prefer the tame correct paintings of the Flemish school, to the erroneous, but sublime animations of the Roman pencil. . . . My wife desired to be represented as Venus, and the painter was requested not to be too frugal of his diamonds in her stomacher and hair. Her two little ones were to be as Cupids by her side, while I, in my gown and band, was to present her with my books on the Whistonian controversy. Olivia would be drawn as an Amazon,[1] sitting upon a bank of flowers dressed

[1] Cf. Steel 1705.

in a green joseph, richly laced with gold, and a whip in her hand. Sophia was to be a Shepherdess with as many sheep as the painter could put in for nothing; and Moses was to be dressed out with an hat and white feather. Our taste so much pleased the squire, that he insisted on being put in as one of the family, in the character of Alexander the Great at Olivia's feet. . . . "Dryden and Rowe's manner, Sir, are quite out of fashion: our taste has gone back a whole century; Fletcher, Ben Johnson, and all the plays of Shakespeare, are the only things that go down"—"How!" cried I, "is it possible the present age can be pleased with that antiquated dialect, that obsolete humour, those over-charged characters, which abound in the works you mention?" . . . "The works of Congreve and Farquhar have too much wit in them for the present taste; our modern dialect is much more natural." . . . "My essays were buried among the essays upon liberty, eastern tales and cures for the bite of a mad dog; while Phalautus, Philalethes, Phileleutheros, and Philanthropos, all wrote better, because they wrote faster, than I." . . . Upon asking how he had been taught the art of a *connoscento* so very suddenly, he assured me that nothing was more easy. The whole secret consisted in a strict adherence to two rules; the one, always to observe, that the picture might have been better if the painter had taken more pains; and the other, to praise the works of Pietro Perugino. . . . There were not two men in his whole university (Louvain) who understood Greek.

O. Goldsmith, *Vicar of Wakefield*.

NATURE

A thinking soul cannot busy itself with low ideas on the shore of the broad sea; the immeasurable prospect widens the limits of the mind which at first appears to lose itself, but then returns to us greater than before.

Winckelmann, *Monumenti Antichi*. Geschichte d. Bildenden Kunst.

"The solemn mountains, the beautiful valleys, the falling streams, form one of the most charming countries (Westmorland) in the world in summer time, but in winter it is the most dreadful spot of earth to be sure."

Amory, *Life of John Buncle*, vol. II, cf. 1756.

Mountains are very good frames to a prospect, but here [Bath] they run against one's nose.

H. Walpole to G. Montagu, 18.10.

In the west part of [Kent] from every eminence the eye catches some long winding reach of the Thames or Medway, with all their navigation; in the east, the sea breaks in upon you, and mixes its white transient sails and glittering blue expanse with the deeper and brighter greens of the woods and corn. This last sentence is so fine, I am quite ashamed.

Gray to Nicholls, 26.8.

PAINTING

Reynolds . . . conceives extraordinary hopes of you.

Burke to J. Barry (n.d.).

[Raphael] had the serenity of Virgil, but wants the fire of Homer.

Smollett, *Travels Through France and Italy.*

In *Laocoon* Lessing depreciated colour and representation of action.

POETRY

Ed. Waller, the most celebrated Lyric Poet that England ever produced.

Biographia Britannica.

🙚 1767 r. George III 🙚

ARCHITECTURE

Mr. Adam . . . has made me cieling [*sic*] and Chimney-piece, and doors, which are pretty enough to make me a thousand enemies.

Eliz. Montagu to Lord Kames.

Grotesque Architecture, W. Wright.

319

GARDENS

At Blenheim, Croome and Caversham we trace
Salvator's wildness, Claude's enlivening grace,
Cascades and Lakes as fine as Risdale drew,
While Nature's varied in each charming view.
To paint his works wou'd Poussin's Powers require,
Milton's sublimity and Dryden's fire.

.   .   .   .

Born to grace Nature, and her works complete
With all that's beautiful, sublime and great!
For him each Muse enwreathes the Laurel Crown,
And consecrates to Fame immortal Brown. ("Capability")

Anon. *The Rise and Progress of the Present Taste in Planting.*

The Scots Magazine described the pleasure-grounds of Mr. Tyers, proprietor of Vauxhall, at Denbies, Dorking, including a Valley of the Shadow of Death.

A wild romantic dell.

W. J. Mickle, *The Concubine.*

MANNERS AND TASTES

I have seen his lordship of Cloyne [F. A. Harvey] often. He is very jolly and we devoured raspberry-puffs together in Cranbourn alley standing at a pastry-cook's shop in the street.

Gray to J. Brown, May.

MUSIC

At Covent Garden "a new instrument called a Piano Forte" (for accompaniment). Used for solos next year by J. C. Bach. But see 1709.

PAINTING

Besides Greuze and Loutherbourg, I can mention no living artist that I like in France; yet by the way we must allow Boucher and Pierre etc. to possess great mechanical merit, but the error is in the conception of things.

J. Barry to Sleigh, November.

320

POETRY

To Spenser much, to Milton much is due;
But in great Dryden we preserve the two.

Harte, *Vision of Death.*

Creative Imagination, the distinguishing characteristic of true Genius. . . . Wit and Humour are produced by the efforts of a *rambling* and *sportive* Fancy; [Genius] proceeds from the copious effusions of a plastic imagination.

W. Duff, *Essay on Original Genius* (cf. Coleridge).

B. Wheeler succeeded T. Warton (the younger) in Chair of Poetry at Oxford. Apparently no published works.

PART V
1768—1788

❈ 1768 r. George III ❈

MANNERS AND TASTES

Goldsmith's *Good Natur'd Man* nearly damned for vulgarly introducing a bailiff (But cf. Gray on Fielding 1742).

Carouselle at Royal Manege, Edinburgh (formal tournament or display of horsemanship). Duchess of Gordon gave prizes. (See *Scots Magazine* for year and Fergusson's *Life of Henry Erskine*, p. 285).

(*The Vicar of Wakefield*) I began it with distaste and disrelish having just read the elegant *Letters of Henry & Frances* (by E. and R. Griffith, anonymously, see 1751)... The style of the latter is so elegantly natural, so tenderly manly, so unassumingly rational!... Nevertheless before I am half thro' the first volume.... I was surprized into tears—and in the second volume I really sobb'd.... He advances many very bold and singular opinions,—for example he avers that murder is the sole crime for which death ought to be the punishment.... This doctrine might be contradicted from ... Scripture.... Upon the whole how far more was I pleased with the genuine productions of Mr. Griffith's pen.

F. Burney, *Early Diaries*, June.

The dearness of provisions incites, the hope of increased wages allures, and drink puts (mobs) in motion. The coal-heavers began ... and have stopped all coal coming to town. The sawyers rose too, and at last the sailors, who have committed great outrages on merchant ships, and prevented them from sailing.

H. Walpole to H. Mann, 12.5.

Lord Carlisle, at Rome, admired Coliseum by moonlight, Laocoon, Apollo of Belvedere, Niobe group.

(Letters to G. Selwyn.)

Captain Cook's first voyage.

The giving up of witchcraft is in effect giving up the Bible.

J. Wesley.

Preface to a translation from M. de la Condamine *An Account of a Savage Girl*.

Lord Monboddo.

Sterne has published two little volumes called *Sentimental Travels*. They are very pleasing, though too much dilated, and infinitely preferable to his tiresome *Tristram Shandy*, of which I could never get through three volumes.

H. Walpole to G. Montagu, 12.3.

Benevolence is unruffled, is benign. . . . It preserves a consistent decorum. . . . It throws a vail of candour over all things. . . . In fine, the virtues of superior eminence are these three, but the most illustrious of these is benevolence. I Cor. xiii.

E. Harwood, D.D. ("to clothe the vulgar version in the vest of modern elegance").

NATURE

(At Cobham) The river appears winding in a proper manner; that is, dark and gloomy, around a rough piece of grass, which has a consistent appearance, but what hurt me very much, was the contradiction of emotions raised by the scene behind; . . . elegant and agreeable; a smooth water, and sloping banks, closely shaven, with a little island in it, are all *agreeable* objects; and by no means affect the spectator in unison with the ruin of Grecian architecture, and the gloomy objects around. . . . Mr. *Dodsley* with his dingells and such expressive terms, might make amends for the want of a Claude Lorraine. . . . The general emotions which arise in viewing the rocks, the hanging woods, and deep precipices of *Persfield* are all those of the *sublime;* and when that is the case, the *beautiful* never appears in such bewitching colours, as those it receives from contrast.

A. Young, *Southern Tour*.

PAINTING

(In a landscape the figures should merely) create a little business for the eyes to be drawn from the trees in order to return to them with more glee.

Gainsborough to W. Jackson.

(Salvator) very great,—nobly expressive,—exquisite taste,—beautifully,—wonderfully pleasing. (Altered in 2nd edition, same year) to "often happy",—"expressive"—"good taste", —"well",—"pleasing".)

Gilpin, Essay on Prints.

H. Walpole, *The Mysterious Mother*, "sublimely" illustrated by Lady Di. Beauclerk.

Royal Academy of Arts in London founded. The Incorporated Society of Artists in Great Britain had received a Royal Charter in 1765.

POETRY

I think that Molière and even Regnard surpasses Aristophanes; —all the Greek tragedies seem to me the work of schoolboys in comparison with Corneille's sublime scenes and Racine's perfect tragedies. . . . Our constant connection with ladies' society has given us much more delicacy in our sentiments and propriety in our manners. I asked Pope why Milton, at a time when other poets in imitation of the Italians, wrote in rhyme, had not rhymed his Epic. His answer was: *Because he could not.*

Voltaire to Walpole, 15.7.

The fashion of pastoral plays is now so exploded throughout Italy.

Baretti, Account of Manners of Italy.

The excellence of our dramatic writers is by no means equal in number to the great men we have produced in other walks. Theatric genius lay dormant after Shakespeare; waked with some bold and glorious, but irregular and often ridiculous flights in Dryden; revived in Otway; maintained a placid pleasing kind of dignity in Rowe and even shone in his *Jane Shore*. It trod in sublime and classic fetters in *Cato*, but void of nature and the power of affecting the passions. In Southern it seemed a genuine ray of nature and Shakespear; but falling on an age still more Hottentot, was stifled in those gross and barbarous productions, tragicomedies. It turned to tuneful nonsense in the *Mourning Bride* (Congreve 1697), grew stark mad in Lee; whose cloak a little the worse for wear fell on Young; yet in both was still a poet's cloak. It recovered its senses in Hughes and Fenton, who were afraid it should relapse, and accordingly kept it down with a timid but aimiable hand —and then it languished. We have not mounted again above the two last.

H. Walpole, PS. to Mysterious Mother (cf.
Johnson on Congreve, 1779).

2,250 copies of Dodsley's reprint of Gray's poems sold, though Foulis' edition also sold well the same year.

Chatterton offered Rowley poems to Dodsley (begun 1764? when he was 12. One published this year in Farley's Bristol Journal).

❧ 1769 r. George III ❧

ARCHITECTURE

(Gothic) deceased in Henry the Eighth's reign, Archbp. Warham's tomb at Canterbury being, I believe, the last example of unbastardized Gothic . . . Holbein embroidered it with some morsels of true architecture; in Queen Elizabeth's reign there was scarce any architecture at all; I mean no pillars, or seldom; buildings then becoming quite plain. Under James a barbarous composition succeeded. A single plate of Inigo Jones, in his worst and heaviest style, should terminate the work, for he soon stepped into the true and perfect Grecian.

H. Walpole to Rev. W. Cole, 12.8.

GARDENS

And so you have a garden of your own, and you plant and transplant, and are dirty and amused! are not you ashamed of yourself? why, I have no such thing, you monster; nor ever shall be either dirty or amused as long as I live!

Gray to Nicholls, 24.6.

(Coade's Artificial Stone invented). A River God 9 feet high, with an Urn through which a stream of water may be carried (100 gns.), ... Psyche fitted up with spring-tubes for lights (5 gns.), ... busts of the Madonna (15/-), Queen Elizabeth (3 gns.), Homer, Marcus Aurelius, Cicero, Edward VI, Vandyck, Lord Chatham.

> Coade's Catalogue (1784).

Steam-engine invented by Watts and water-frame (for cotton) by Arkwright.

(Chitqua) a Chinese portrait modeller, lately arrived from Canton, one of those artists who make the Mandarin figures that are brought to England. ... He has ten guineas a piece for his little portraits.

> Bentley to J. Wedgwood, November.

Josiah Wedgwood opened "Etruria".

(Shakespeare Jubilee at Stratford). Of the most remarkable masks upon this occasions was James Boswell, Esqr., in the dress of an armed Corsican chief. He entered the amphitheatre about twelve o'clock. On the front of his cap was embroidered in gold letters *Viva la Libertà*—and on one side of it was a handsome blue feather and cockade, so that it had an elegant as well as a warlike appearance. He wore no mask, saying that it was not proper for a gallant Corsican. So soon as he came into the room he drew universal attention (see 1764, 1765).

> J. B., in *London Magazine* (with print).

To the left the jaws of *Borrodale*, with that turbulent Chaos of mountain behind mountain roll'd in confusion ... The shining purity of the *Lake*, just ruffled by the breeze enough to show it is alive, reflecting rocks, wood, fields & inverted tops of mountains. ... O doctor! [T. Wharton[I never wish'd more for you; & pray think, how the glass played its part in such a spot [A "Claude Glass", A planoconvex mirror about 4 inches in diameter in a black foil, "perhaps the best and most convenient substitute for a Camera Obscura" (Mason)]. . . . Saw the solemn colouring of night draw on, the last gleam of sunshine fading away on the hilltops, the deep serene of the waters, & the long shadows of the mountains thrown across them, till they nearly touched the hithermost shore. At distance heard the murmur of many waterfalls not audible in the daytime. Wished for the Moon, but she was *dark to me and silent, hid in her vacant interlunar cave.* 3.10.

Grasmere-water; its margin is hollowed into small bays with bold eminences: some of them rock, some soft turf that half conceal and vary the figure of the little lake they command. From the shore a low promontory pushes itself far into the water, and on it Stands a white village with the Parish Church rising in the midst of it, hanging enclosures, corn-fields, and meadows, green as an emerald, with their trees and hedges and cattle fill up the whole space from the edge of the water. Just opposite to you is a large farm-house at the bottom of a steep smooth lawn embosomed in old woods, which climb half way up the mountain's side, and discover above them a broken line of crags, that crown the scene. Not a single red tile, no flaming Gentleman's house, or garden walls break in upon the repose of this little unsuspected paradise, but all is peace, rusticity and happy poverty in its neatest most becoming attire. (8.10).

The gloomy uncomfortable day well suited the savage aspect of the place (Gordale Scar) and made it still more formidable: I stay'd there (not without shuddering) a quarter of an hour, and thought my trouble richly paid; for the impression will last for life. (13.11).

Gray, Journal.

I have a partiality to him [Bonstetten] because he was born among mountains, and talks of them with enthusiasm—of the forests of pines which grow darker and darker as you ascend, till the *nemorum nox* is completed and you are forced to grope your way; of the cries of eagles and other birds of prey adding to the horror.

Nicholls to Gray, 27.11.

There is a total extinction of all taste: our authors are vulgar, gross, illiberal. . . . Neatness and greenth are so essential in my opinion to the country, that in France, where I see nothing but chalk and dirty peasants, I seem in a terrestrial purgatory that is neither town nor country.

H. Walpole to G. Montagu, 16.10.

PAINTING

On the sight of the Capella Sistina, [Raffaelle] immediately from a dry, Gothic and even insipid manner, which attends to the minute accidental discriminations of particular and individual objects, assumed that grand style of painting which improves partial representation by the general and invariable ideas of nature. Reynolds, *Discourse I.* (On which Blake; "Minute discrimination is not accidental. All sublimity is founded on minute discrimination").

Style . . . a power over materials . . . by which conception or sentiments are conveyed. And in this, Ludovico Caracci (I mean in his best works) appears to me to approach the nearest to perfection.

Reynolds, *Discourse II.*

The Cappella Sistina is the production of the greatest genius that was ever employed in the arts.

Reynolds to J. Barry.

POETRY

Who would remember him (Milton) for his barbarous prose?

H. Walpole to H. S. Conway, 14.11.

Chatterton sent the Rowley poems to H. Walpole in March. (Gray detected them).

Voltaire talking to an Italian at Ferney named his favourite English poems:—Garth's *Dispensary*, Prior's *Henry and Emma* and Pope's *Prologue to Cato*, (Temple Bar, Jan. 1882).

✲ 1770 r. George III ✲

GARDENS

T. Whately, *Observations on Modern Gardening.* [Advises a broken bridge, leading nowhere, but with a plank to replace lost arch.

Also ruined temples with more modern cottages among them
to give reality.]

When a Frenchman reads of the Garden of Eden, I do not
doubt but he concludes it has something approaching to that
of Versailles, with clipped hedges, berceaux and trellis work
... In the gardens of Marshal de Biron at Paris there were
nine thousand pots of asters ... At Lady Oxford's, at
Piddletown, in Dorsetshire, there was, when my brother
married, a double enclosure of thirteen gardens, each, I
suppose not much above a hundred yards square, with an
enfilade of correspondent gates. Kent's ruling principle was
that Nature abhors a straight line [Kent had illustrated
Spenser's poems].

> H. Walpole, *On Modern Gardening*, pub-
> lished 1785.

MANNERS AND TASTES

Mr. Conway said ... he would do the business of the office
without accepting the salary. The King replied, "You are
a phenomenon!"

> 22.1.

Almacks has taken the *pas* of White's. .... Lord Stavordale, not
one and twenty, lost eleven thousand there last Tuesday, but
recovered it by one great hand at hazard: he swore a great
oath,—"Now, if I had been playing *deep*, I might have won
millions". His cousin, Charles Fox, shines equally there and
in the House of Commons. He was twenty-one yesterday
se'nnight; and already he is one of our best speakers. Yesterday
he was made a Lord of the Admiralty.

> H. Walpole to H. Mann, 2.2.

Slaughter's Coffee House

Mutton chop	3d.
Potatoes & butter	2d.
Bread	1d.
Porter, pint	2½d.

NATURE

I would at any time, with utmost pleasure, ride 40 miles to
view such another [landscape, near Rotherham] ... A large

ruin'd abbey [Rievaulx], in the midst, to appearance, of a small but beautiful valley, scattered trees appearing elegantly among the ruins, too elegantly picturesque to admit of description. It is a bird's eye landscape; a casual glance at a little paradise, which seems as it were in another region ... A most picturesque hill, intersected with green hedges,— one of the most truly pleasing objects in the world ... From hence [on Derwentwater] you coast a dreadful shore of fragments, which time has broken from the towering rocks, many of them of terrible size, through a path of desolation, sweeping rocks, trees, hillocks, everything, to the water; the very idea of a small shiver against the boat strikes with horror ...

[Near Haweswater] Three hills are in particular overlooked, cut into enclosures in a charming style, of themselves forming an elegant landscape, worthy the imitation of those who would give the embellishment of art to the simplicity of nature.

A. Young, *Northern Tour* (or 1771).

PAINTING

There are excellencies in the art of Painting beyond what is commonly called the imitation of Nature. ... The whole beauty and grandeur of the Art consists, in my opinion, in being able to get above all singular forms, local customs, particularities, and details of every kind; ... long laborious comparison ... by this means, he acquires a just idea of beautiful forms; he corrects Nature by herself, her imperfect state by her more perfect; ... it may be objected ... the beauty of the Hercules is one, of the Gladiator another, of the Apollo another ... but still none of them is the representation of an individual, but of a class ... yet the highest perfection of the human figure is not to be found in any one of them ... for perfect beauty in any species must combine all the characters which are beautiful in that species. ... There is a kind of symmetry or proportion which may be properly said to belong to deformity. ... Look only on those general habits which are everywhere and always the same. ... As the idea of beauty is of necessity but one, so there can be but one great mode of painting.

Reynolds, *Discourse III.*

The romantic imagination of Salvator Rosa was never inspired with a more tremendous idea, nor his extravagant pencil never produced a bolder precipice.

J. Craddock, *Letters from Snowdon.*

I can bear with Vittore Scapaccia [*sic*], the Bellinis etc. . . . whatever they have is right but they have not everything. But when art comes to pass maturity . . . manner and affectation get into play. . . . Titian is the only modern who fills up an idea of perfection in any one part of the art. There is no example of anything that goes beyond his colouring, whereas the parts of the art in which Michael Angelo and Raffael excelled are almost annihilated by the superiority of the antiques.

J. Barry to Burke, 8.9.

To copy nature is a task the most bungling workman is able to execute; to select such parts as contribute only to delight is reserved for those whom accident has blessed with uncommon talents, or such as have read the Ancients with indefatigable industry.

Goldsmith, *Life of T. Parnell.*

(The painter) is confined to a *span;* and lays down his little rules, which he calls the *principles of picturesque beauty,* merely to adapt such diminutive parts of nature's surface to his own eye as come within its scope. Hence, therefore, the painter who adheres strictly to the *composition* of nature will rarely make a good picture. . . . Arthur's Seat. . . . romantic but not picturesque . . . it is odd, misshapen and uncouth. . . . Four grand parts:—the *area* which is the river itself; the two *side-scenes,* which are the opposite banks and lend the perspective; and the *front-scene* which points out the windings of the river. . . . With three (cows) you are sure of a good group, except indeed they all stand in the same attitude and at equal distances.

Gilpin, *River Wye* (published 1782, cf. J. Austen, *Pride and Prejudice,* "You are charmingly grouped; the picturesque would be spoiled by a fourth." Written 1796-7, and cf. J. Austen, 1792, and Aikin, 1791).

Almost everything that is not immoveable is brought here from every country, as none pays so generously for real good pictures as the English; though I must confess I think it begins somewhat to fall off. . . . I have brought into England above fifteen hundred pictures.

J. Greenwood to Copley, April.

One West, who paints history in the taste of Poussin, gets three hundred pounds for a piece not too large to hang over a chimney. He has merit, but is hard and heavy, and far unworthy of such prices. The rage to see these exhibitions is so great that sometimes one cannot pass through the streets where they are.

H. Walpole to H. Mann, 6.5.

POETRY

He has considered the language of poetry as the language of life, and conveys the warmest thoughts in the simplest expression. . . . Misguided innovators . . . have indulged themselves in the most licentious transpositions and the harshest constructions, vainly imagining, that the more their writings are unlike prose, the more they resemble poetry. . . . It is, indeed, amazing, after what has been done by Dryden, Addison, and Pope, to improve and harmonize our native tongue, that their successors should have taken so much pains to involve it into pristine barbarity.

Goldsmith, Life of Parnell.

> The schoolboy wandering through the wood,
>   To pull the primrose gay,
> Starts, the new voice of spring to hear,
>   And imitates thy lay.

J. Logan, The Cuckoo.

As to description I have always thought that it made the most graceful ornament of poetry, but never ought to make the subject. Your ideas are new, and borrowed from a mountainous country, the only one that can furnish truly picturesque scenery.

Gray to Beattie, 2.7.

❧ 1771 r. George III ❧

ARCHITECTURE

James Bentham *History of Gothic and Saxon Architecture* (Preface to his History of Ely; (his ideal King's College Chapel).)

GARDENS

On ne peut sortir d'un jardin Anglais sans avoir l'âme aussi affecté qu'en sortant d'une tragédie.

Melchior Grimm.

MANNERS AND TASTES

What kind of taste and organs must those people have, who really prefer the adulterated enjoyments of the town to the genuine pleasures of a country retreat? . . . .

His huntsman every night entertains him with the adventures of the day's chase. . . . In the mean time, his broad brawn is scratched by one of his grooms. . . . He is also blessed with an only son, just returned from Italy, a complete fiddler and dilettante.

(At Scarborough) between the well and the harbour the bathing-machines are ranged along the beach.

Smollett, *Humphrey Clinker*.

(In Cavendish Sq.) A few frightened sheep within a wooden pailing [*sic*]. . . . To see the poor things starting at every coach and hurrying round and round their narrow bounds requires a warm imagination, indeed, to convert the scene into that of flocks ranging the fields, with all the concomitant ideas of innocence and pastoral life.

("Athenian") Stuart, *Critical Observations*.

Cricket: Nottingham v. Sheffield.

He was one of those figures which Salvator would have drawn; nor was the surrounding scenery unlike the wildness of that painter's backgrounds. The banks on each side were covered with fantastic shrubwood, and at a little distance, on the top of one of them stood a finger-post, to mark the direction of two roads . . . A rock, with some dangling wild flowers, jutted out above where the soldier lay, in which grew the stump of a large tree, white with age, and a single twisted branch shaded his face as he slept. "Father!" said Harley (who by this time found the romantic temper rising within him).

> H. Mackenzie, *Man of Feeling*, cf.
> Wordsworth, *Prelude IV*, 385.

The Birmingham Mercury advertised for sale a negro boy, healthy and of mild disposition.

NATURE

I have seen Lago di Gardi, Albano, De Vico, Bolsena and Geneva, and, upon my honor, I prefer Loch Lomond to them all . . . All is sublimity, silence and solitude. . . . Everything here is romantic. . . . The poems of Ossian are in every mouth.

> Smollett, *Humphrey Clinker* (his last novel,
> but first to use natural scenery).

PAINTING

All without is Grecian and all within Gothic.

. . . . .

If I am not mistaken this young gentleman of Bath [John Taylor] is the best landscape painter now living.

> Smollett, *Humphrey Clinker*.

The few works that remain of Parmegiano are not to be sure more valuable than the works of Raffael and Michael Angelo . . . Yet there is discernible in him powers imprisoned of a superior kind to what the others have shewn.

> 13.1.

In Turin I saw the royal collection of pictures, but, except a picture or two of Guido, which I did not like, all the rest are Flemish and Dutch, Rubens's, Vandyke's, Tenier's, Rembrandt, Scalken, &c. They are without the pales of my church, and though I will not condemn them, yet I must hold no intercourse with them.

> Barry to Burke (n.d., but clearly Paris
> 1771).

Greek and Roman fable ... familiar and interesting to all
Europe, without being degraded by the vulgarism of ordinary
life in any country. ... The great end of the Art is to strike
the Imagination. The Painter therefore is to make no ostentation of the means by which this is done. ... It is the inferior
style that marks the variety of stuffs. With him (the historical
Painter) the clothing is neither woolen nor linen nor silk or
velvet: it is drapery; it is nothing more. ... Next to these
(i.e., French—Poussin, Le Sueur, and Le Brun—who are imitators
of Bolognese, Romans and Florentines) but in a very different
style of excellence, we may rank the Venetian, together with
the Flemish and Dutch schools; ... many of the warmest
admirers of painting will think them unjustly degraded, ...
they accomplished perfectly the thing they attempted. But
mere elegance is their principal object, they seem more willing
to dazzle than to affect. ... His (P. Veronese) intention was
solely to produce an effect of light and shadow.

Reynolds, Discourse IV.

Masaccio's designs ... are nature itself and evidently the
precursors of Raphael [Copied by T. Patch]. He plainly
availed himself of their dignity, but scarce reached the infinite
truth of their expression. The action of the mouth in every
head almost surpasses any other master. ... Fra Bartolomeo,
another parent of Raphael, and whose ideas I thought if
possible greater; as there is such a scarcity of his works, and
as they have never that I know been engraved,—[The paintings
of Masaccio copied were burnt at S. Andrea's, Florence, about
this time]. To H. Mann, 20.1.
Two views of Verona by Canalleti, have been sold by auction
for 555 guineas; and, what is worse, it is come out that they
are copies by Marlow a disciple of Scott. Both master and
pupil are indeed better painters than the Venetian. ...
(Pantheon in Oxford St.), pillars of artificial *giallo antico*,
stucco grotesques, painted like Raphael's *loggia*, dome like
Pantheon glazed, £50,000. To H. Mann, 26.4.
(Le Sueur's life of S. Bruno at Chartreuse, Paris). If it is not
the first work in the world and must yield to the Vatican, yet
in simplicity and harmony it beats Raphael himself. ... There
is a vapour over all the pictures that makes them more natural
than any representations of objects,—I cannot conceive how

it is effected. You see them through the shine of a south east wind. . . . There is the purity of a Racine in them, but they give me more pleasure.

To J. Chute, 9.8.

Hamilton's Correggio . . . is divine and so is the price . . . £3000. It has all Correggio's grace and none of his grimaces, which, like Shakespeare, he is too apt to blend and confound.

H. Walpole to H. Mann, 18.11.

The Last Judgment: it is the greatest work of Michael Angelo, and perhaps of man . . . neither the Inferno of Dante nor the hell of Milton can furnish anything more terrible.

C. Burney, *Present State of Music in France* and *Italy*.

A man need go no further to study the Chinese than the China paper. . . . Some of the plants which are common to China and Java, as bamboo, are better figured there than in the best botanical authors that I have seen.

Sir J. Banks, *Journal*.

POETRY

I think we should wholly adopt the language of Spenser's time, or wholly renounce it. You say, you have done the latter; but, in effect, you retain *fared, forth, meed, wight, ween, gaude, shene, in sooth, aye, eschew etc.* . . .

> "Oh how cans't thou renounce the boundless store
> Of charms which Nature to her votary yields!
> The warbling woodland, the resounding shore,
> The pomp of groves, and garniture of fields."
> [*The Minstrel*, I. ix.]

This of all others is my favourite stanza. It is true poetry.

Gray to Beattie, 8.3.

(The Spenserian stanza) allows the sententiousness of the couplet, as well as the more complex modulation of blank verse.

J. Beattie, Preface to *The Minstrel* (influenced by Percy. Five editions of Book I by 1775).

In truth he was a strange and wayward wight,
Fond of each gentle and each dreadful scene:
In darkness, and in storm he found delight;
Nor less, than when on ocean wave serene
The southern sun diffus'd his dazzling shene.
Even sad vicissitude amused his soul:
And if a sigh would sometimes intervene,
And down his cheek a tear of pity roll,
A sigh, a tear, so sweet, he wish'd not to controul.

    .   .   .   .   .

There would he dream of graves and corses pale;
And ghosts, that to the charnel-dungeon throng,
And drag a length of clanking chain, and wail
Till silenc'd by the owl's terrific song
Or blast that shrieks by fits the shuddering isles along

    .   .   .   .   .

Ah what is mirth but turbulence unholy
When with the charm compar'd of heavenly melancholy?

Beattie, The Minstrel, I.

("resembles much what William was when I first knew him."
D. Wordsworth to J. Pollard, 1794, cf. 1787.)

Percy, *The Hermit of Warkworth* parodied by Johnson:—

I put my hat upon my head
And walked into the Strand
And there I met another man
Whose hat was in his hand.

Boswell. 20.3.

🌺 1772 r. George III 🌺

GARDENS

A large green field, scattered over with a few straggling trees,
and verged with a confused border of little shrubs and flowers.
. . . a little serpentine path turning in regular curves . . . Such
is the favourite plan of all our smaller gardens: and our larger
works are only a repetition of the small ones, more green
fields, more shrubberies, more serpentine walks and more
seats. . . . (Chinese) scenes of terror are composed of gloomy,

deep valleys, inaccessible to the sun, impending barren rocks, dark caverns and impetuous cataracts. The trees are ill-formed, forced out of their natural directions and seemingly torn to pieces by the violence of tempests. . . . Whatever else may serve to indicate the debility, the disappointments, and the desolation of humanity; which, by co-operating with the dreary aspect of autumnal nature, and the inclement tempera-ture of the air, fill the mind with melancholy, and incline it to serious reflections.

> Sir W. Chambers, *Dissertation on Oriental Gardening.* (Designer of Kew Pagoda. See 1757.)

(Mr. River's garden) laid out in a romantic taste, with a proper mixture of the allegro and the penseroso, the chearful and the gloomy; tufts of roses, jasmines, and the most fragrant flowering shrubs, with a serpentine walk of cypresses and laurels, here and there an urn, with a suitable inscription, and terminated by a rough arch of rock-work that covered a dripping fountain.

> R. Graves, *The Spiritual Quixote* (or 1773).

> that peculiar curve,
> Alike averse to crooked and to straight,
> Where sweet Simplicity resides; which Grace
> And beauty call their own; whose lambent flow
> Charms us at once with symmetry and ease.
>
> .   .   .   .   .
>
> More happy still, if one superior rock
> Bear on its brow the shiver'd fragment huge
> Of some old Norman fortress; happier far,
> Oh, then most happy, if thy vale below
> Wash, with the crystal coolness of its rills,
> Some mould'ring abbey's ivy-vested wall.

(Claude, Salvator and Ruysdael arbiters of the picturesque).
> Mason, *The English Garden.*

MANNERS AND TASTES

Sentimental! What is that? It is not English; he might as well say *Continental.* It is not sense. It conveys no determinate idea; yet one fool makes many. And this nonsensical word (who would believe it?) is become a fashionable one! However the book (Sterne's *Sentimental Journey*) agrees full well with the title, for one is as queer as the other.

J. Wesley, Journal, Feb. 11.

That a boy should take pleasure in darkness or a storm—in the noise of thunder or the glare of lightning; should be more gratified with listening to music at a distance than with mixing in the merriment occasioned by it; should like better to see every bird and beast happy and free, than to exert his ingenuity in destroying or ensnaring them—these and such like sentiments, which, I think, would be natural to persons of a certain cast, will, I know, be condemned as unnatural by others! ... The scenery of a mountainous country, the ocean, the sky, thoughtfulness and retirement, and sometimes melancholy objects and ideas, had charms in my eyes even when I was a schoolboy (born 1735).

> Beattie to Lady Forbes (on "The Minstrel" which he began to publish 1771; cf. Wordsworth, *Prelude*, and Beattie 1772, and Wordsworth, 1787).

In the case of Somersett a negro slave who had been brought to England, had escaped, been recaptured and put in chains to be returned to the West Indies, Lord Mansfield gave judgment that the institution was "so odious" that "nothing could be suffered to support it but positive law" and that consequently by setting foot in England Somersett became free. (Cf. Boswell 1777).

State Trials XI 339.

Down with everything noble and venerable and ancient amongst you; turn the Tower of London into a Pantheon, make a new Adelphi of the Savoy, and bid adieu to all ages but your own.

Cumberland, The Fashionable Lover.

(The Oxford Street Pantheon built this year by J. Wyatt, called by H. Walpole "the most beautiful edifice in England" —see 1773; and by Wordsworth "stately").

NATURE

O ye Northumbrian shades, which overlook
The rocky pavement and the mossy falls
Of solitary Wensbeck's limpid stream;
How gladly I recall your well-known seats
Belov'd of old, and that delightful time
When all alone, for many a summer's day,
I wandered through your calm recesses, led
In silence by some powerful hand unseen.
    Nor will I e'er forget you, nor shall e'er
The graver tasks of manhood, or the advice
Of vulgar wisdom, move me to disclaim
Those studies which possess'd me in the dawn
Of life, and fix'd the colour of my mind
For every future year.

> Akenside, *Pleasures of the Imagination*
> (final version); cf. Wordsworth, *Prelude*
> *VIII*, 468, the 1786 and final versions
> (ed. De Selincourt).

PAINTING

If you mean to preserve the most perfect beauty *in its most perfect state*, you cannot express the passions, all of which produce distortion and deformity, more or less, in the most beautiful faces. . . . Raffaelle had more Taste and Fancy; Michel Angelo, more genius and Imagination. The one excelled in beauty, the other in Energy.

> Reynolds, *Discourse V*.

POETRY

Vous appelez Cowley le Pindare anglais . . . c'était un poète sans harmonie . . . Le vrai Pindare est Dryden, auteur de cette belle ode intitulée *la Fête d'Alexandre, ou Alexandre et Timothée*. Cette ode . . . passe en Angleterre pour le Chef-d'oeuvre de la poésie la plus sublime et la plus variée; et je vous avoue que, comme je sais mieux l'anglais que le grec, j'aime cent fois mieux cette ode que tout Pindare.

> Voltaire, 9.3, to Chabanon.

I heard for the first time (in 1772) Shakespear's Plays quoted in the Pulpit; the Passage was from Hamlet:—

> That undiscover'd Country from whose Bourn
> No Traveller returns.

. . . I thought it very odd.

Mrs. Thrale, *Thraliana*, June, 1777, [cf. 1620].

SCULPTURE

The gates (of Baptistry at Florence) are fine. (Pisano and Ghiberti).

H. Walpole to Sir H. Mann, 20.9.

⁂ 1773 r. George III ⁂

ARCHITECTURE

(Sion House gateway) is all lace and embroidery, and as croquant as his (Adam's) frames for tables. From Kent's mahogany we are dwindled to Adam's filigree. He seems to tax Wyatt with stealing from him; but Wyatt has employed the antique with more judgement and the Pantheon is still the most beautiful edifice in England. What are the Adelphi buildings? warehouses laced down the seams, like a soldier's trull in a regimental old coat.

H. Walpole to Mason, 23.7.

MANNERS AND TASTES

George III told Beattie the English language was on the decline and named the Spectator as one of the best standards of the language.

(Sir W. Forbes' *Life and Writings of Beattie*, 1806.)

> O, let the Muse attend thy march sublime,
> And with thy prose, caparison her rhyme;
> Teach her, like thee, to gild her splendid song
> With scenes of Kuen-Ming and sayings of Li-Tsong;
> Like thee to scorn Dame Nature's simple fence,
> Leap each Ha Ha of truth and common sense.

. . . . .

344

To Richmond come, for see, untutor'd Brown[1]
Destroys those wonders which were once thy own.
Lo, from his melon-ground the peasant slave
Has rudely rush'd and levell'd Merlin's Cave;
Knock'd down the waxen Wizzard, seiz'd his wand,
Transform'd to lawn what late was Fairy land;
And marr'd, with impious hand, each sweet design
Of Stephen Duck,[2] and good Queen Caroline.

> W. Mason, *An Heroic Epistle to Sir W. Chambers.*

Dr. Goldsmith has written a comedy [*She Stoops*],—no it is the lowest of all farces. It is not the subject I condemn, though very vulgar, but the execution. The drift tends to no moral, no edification of any kind. The situations, however, are well imagined and make one laugh, in spite of the grossness.

> To Mason, 27.3.

Gray could not hear Voltaire's name with patience, though nobody admired his genius more; but he thought him so vile, that for the last years of his life he would read nothing he wrote. Well! but one must read him! Is there another author left in Europe who one wishes should write?

> H. Walpole to H. Mann, 9.9.

Johnson went to Scotland (not so much for scenery as for people and social problems). "Who can like the Highlands?"

> Boswell.

From the absurd bombast of Dr. Johnson down to the silly Dr. Goldsmith, though the latter changeling has had bright gleams of parts, and though the former had sense till he changed it for words. . . . I have seen Pope and lived with Gray.

> H. Walpole to W. Cole, 27.4.

The old Gothic Romance and Eastern Tale, however a refined critic may censure them as absurd and extravagant, will ever retain a most powerful influence on the mind.

> Mrs. Barbauld, *On the Pleasure Derived from Objects of Terror* (influenced young Wordsworth, see 1774).

---

[1] "Capability".
[2] Agricultural labourer and poet. Yeoman of Guard to Queen Caroline. Rector of Byfleet.

(At "Tingmouth") Today for the first time I bathed. . . . I was terribly frightened, and really thought I should never have recovered from the plunge, I had not breath to speak for a minute or two, the shock was beyond expression great; but after I got back to the machine, I presently felt myself in a glow that was delightful—it is the finest feeling in the world.

> F. Burney, *Early Diaries*, August.

Smoking has gone out [among the respectable fashionable, till the Crimean war].

> Dr. Johnson in Boswell's *Tour of the Hebrides*, 19.8.

PAINTING

Count Ugolino & his Children in the Dungeon as described by Dante.
> J. Reynolds in R. A.

£650 last week for a landscape of Niccolo Poussin; and Lord Chesterfield four hundred guineas for another; which somebody was so good as to paint a few months ago for Claude Lorrain.

> H. Walpole to H. Mann, 12.3.

The most capital picture in Mr. Strange's last sale. It is a landscape by Nicholas Poussins (*sic*) and was purchased by Sir Watkyn Wynn at the sum of six hundred and fifty pounds. . . . The prime cost was seven pounds odd shillings! and for that sum Poussins sold it.

> F. Burney, *Early Diaries*, March.

POETRY

Mr. Garrick has cut out the scene of the grave-diggers in Hamlet. I hope he will be rewarded with a place in the French Academy.

> H. Walpole to W. Mason, 9.1.

Mr. Rishton . . . is reading Spencer's Fairy Queen to us (his wife was Fanny's step-sister), in which he is extremely delicate, omitting whatever, to the poet's great disgrace, has crept in that is improper for a woman's ear.

> F. Burney, *Early Diaries*, August.

(It is not stated whether he told her this or she discovered it).

Foote's *Piety in Patterns* and Goldsmith's *She Stoops to Conquer* satirised sentimental comedy.

✤ 1774 r. George III ✤

MANNERS AND TASTES

Mrs. Delany began her artificial flower work ("Flower-music"), praised by H. Walpole.

Hoops at largest in ladies' dresses.

Anonymous Poem *Otaheite*. Idealization of the savage.

Captain Furneaux brought home "Omaiah" from Society Islands. Fêted, painted by Reynolds, &c.

The present *Lyon* of the times, according to the author of *The Placid Man's* term (anon. 1770), is Omy, the native of Otaheite; and next to him Mr. Bruce ... four years in Abyssinia.

Early Diaries, August.

Sentiments and *sensations* were the *last* fashions, ... They were laughed out of use just before laughing was abolished. The present *ton* is *refinement*; nothing *is to be* that *has been*, all things are to be *new polished* and *high finished*.

F. Burney, September.

NATURE

The extent of its (Hawkestone) prospects, the awfulness of its shades, the horrors of its precipices, the verdure of its hollows, and the loftiness of its rocks; the ideas which it forces upon the mind are, the sublime, the dreadful, and the vast. Above is inaccesible altitude, below is horrible profundity ... Hawkestone should be described by Milton.

Johnson, *Journey into N. Wales.*

PAINTING

One by Cuyp not large, and which he had bought dearly for 70 guineas sold for 290! . . . He sold one Guido for £2,000 . . . The "Doctors" at Houghton, the first picture in England, and equal to any in Italy but Raphael's, cost but a little above £600.

H. Walpole to H. Mann, 1.5.

We are very sure that the beauty of form, the expression of the passions, the art of composition, even the power of giving a general air of grandeur to a work, is at present very much under the dominion of rules . . . What we now call Genius, begins, not where rules, abstractedly taken, end, but where known vulgar and trite rules have no longer any place.

Reynolds, Discourse VI.

POETRY

Mr. Warton has contracted such an affection for his materials, that he seems almost to think that not only Pope but Dryden himself have added few beauties to Chaucer.

H. Walpole to W. Mason, 7.4. (T. Warton's History of English Poetry, Vol. I, this year.)

STAGE

Scenery designed by de Loutherbourg for *The Maid of the Oaks* (Burgoyne) at Drury Lane cost £1000.

1775 r. George III

ARCHITECTURE

(Gothic) reached its perfection in the reign of Henry VIII.

Mason, Life of Gray, cf. Gray and Walpole, 1760.

Now, even as it is, our faith in the influence of climates receives a great shock when we reflect upon the taste and character of the Egyptian genius, which is diametrically opposite to what it ought to be; it is massive, rude, and has more of geometry and heavy proportion, than it has of that light, elegant spirit and rich luxuriance of imagination, that, according to our philosophers, such a warm climate ought to have produced. On the other hand, modern Gothic building, which received its perfection in the north, is in the other extreme, of a flimsy lightness, and seems to be produced by the riot of an overheated, wild fancy, without the least degree of the supposed cool, heavy, northern judgement.

> J. Barry, *Inquiry into Obstructions to Arts in England.*

MANNERS AND TASTES

(At the Duke of Argyle's) A Chinese instrument called a gong made of copper.

> *A Peep into the Principal Seats and Gardens in and about Twickeneam,* by a Lady of Distinction.

The fashion now is to erect the toupée into a high detached tuft of hair like a cockatoo's crest.

> To Conway, October 6.

The Duchess of Northumberland has got very jollily through her task.

> H. Walpole, to Countess of Upper Ossory.

Port (first?) bought for Eton College at £45-15-9 per pipe.

Jane Austen, Lamb, Landor and Turner born.

An Heroic Epistle from Omaiah to the Queen of Otaheite, see 1774.

NATURE

> Now downward as I bend my eye
> What is that atom I espy,
> That speck in nature's plan?
> Great Heaven! is that a man?
>
> > Richard Cumberland, *Ode to the Sun* (on Gowder Crag).

349

An eye accumstomed to flowery pastures and waving harvests is astonished and repelled by this wide extent of hopeless sterility. . . . It will very readily occur that this uniformity of barrenness can afford very little amusement. . . .

I sat down on a bank such as a writer of Romance might have delighted to feign. I had indeed no trees to whisper over my head but a clear rivulet streamed at my feet. The day was calm, the air soft and all was rudeness silence and solitude. Before me and on either side were high hills which by hindering the eye from ranging forced the mind to find entertainment for itself. . . .

The imaginations excited by the view of an unknown and untravelled wilderness are not such as arise in the artificial solitude of parks and gardens. . . .

The phantoms which haunt a desert are want and misery and danger, the evils of dereliction rush upon the thoughts.

> Johnson, *Journey to Western Isles* (Record of 1773). See 1789.

PAINTING

We have received . . . the invaluable portrait of Sir Joshua Reynolds (by himself for the Uffizi) . . . it has quite eclipsed the portrait of Mengs who boasted of standing first.

> L. Sirès to Angelica Kauffman.

I do not find that we are got an inch nearer Raphael than we were. Sir Joshua has indeed produced the best portrait he ever painted, that of the Primate of Ireland (Richard Robinson afterwards Lord Rokeby).

> H. Walpole to Rev. W. Mason, 7.5.

Even the lowest people tell familiarly of Hannibal Scratchi, Paul Varnish, and Raphael Angelo.

> *Fugitive Miscellany.*

J. R. Cozens taken to Alps by Payne Knight.

David at Rome converted to classicism.

Louis Racine's discourse on *Paradise Lost* contrasted Milton favourably with Dante whose poem he compares to Michelangelo's *Last Judgement* which has pleasing details but misses the majesty of the subject.

Who but Shakespeare could render mirth pathetic? His exquisite scene of the grave-diggers . . . now so over-whelmed by the ignorance of French criticism that it is acted no more.
H. Walpole, *Thoughts on Tragedy*, Letter II to R. Jephson.

Of all great writers—I set Shakespeare first and alone.
Letter III.

(*Canterbury Tales*) a lump of mineral from which Dryden extracted all the gold, and converted into beautiful medals [*sic*].
H. Walpole to Rev. W. Mason, 14.4.

> Yet sure the force of Taste we feel
> In Addison—but not in Steele.
> R. Graves, *Of Taste and Elegance.*

Johnson's *Journey to the Western Isles*. . . . What a heap of words to express very little! And though it is the least cumbrous of any style he ever used, how far from easy and natural!
To Countess of Upper Ossory, 21.1.

Congreve . . . Our approbation is so occupied that our passions cannot be engaged. We do not believe that a company who seem only met to shew their wit, can have any other object in view. Their very vices seem affected.
H. Walpole, *Thoughts on Comedy* (cf. C. Lamb).

The sing-song and prettiness of Waller and Cowley . . . the sublimity of Milton and Homer.
S. Crisp to Fanny Burney.

Hawkesworth's version of Southerne's tragedy *Oroonoko* (noble negro) acted.

(Jephson's *Braganza*) nothing at all equal to it appearing [on the stage] in my time [say 50 years].

> H. Walpole to Countess of Upper Ossory, 1.2.

Mrs. Siddons' first London appearance (Portia).

Beggar's Opera revived with poetic justice for Macheath.

SCULPTURE

When Sculpture had made a most disagreeable appearance among us in the reigns of Queen Ann and King George I, Mr. Rysbrack (1693-1770) again presented her to us with all the charms of beauty and elegance.

> C. Rogers, *Purity in Imitation of Drawings*.

Sculpture in England has hitherto been almost wholly funerary; it has only recently been used for other purposes.

> J. B. Rouquet (or 1755, Friend of Hogarth).

✤ 1776 r. George III ✤

GARDENS

A place for holy meditation,
For solitude and contemplation;
Yet what himself will rarely use,
Unless to conn his weekly news;
Or with some jovial friends to sit in;
To take his glass, and smoke, and spit in.
> (The Hermitage) (cf. Beckford 1796).

To crown the whole, at length he'd made
Without water, a cascade.
Behind his artificial rock,
A cistern plac'd, he turn'd a cock,
And lo! the little Naiads spout
And splutter—till the tub ran out.
Not with more rapture Israel spied
The streams by Moses' rod supplied.
> R. Graves (The Cascade), *Euphrosyne*.

Mr. Hoare's gardens at Stourton (Stourhead see 1722) ...
I have seen the most celebrated gardens in England but these
far exceed them all. Others were delighted with the temples,
but I was not (1) because several of the statues about them
were mean; (2) because I cannot admire the images of devils—
and we know the gods of the heathen are but devils; (3)
because I defy all mankind to reconcile statues with nudities
either to common sense or common decency.

J. Wesley, *Journal.* 12.9.

MANNERS AND TASTES

Ladies this year wore goloshes, four distinct falls of lace from
the hat to the shoulders, and rolled curls on either side of the
neck; they continued to carry fans.

J. T. Smith, *A Book for a Rainy Day.*

Certainly the very best thing that can happen to a very young
man, is to fall desperately in love with a woman of fashion,
who is clever, and who likes him enough to teach him to
endeavour to please her, and yet keep him at his proper
distance.

Lady Pembroke to Rev. W. Coxe (her
son's tutor). 1.3.

(Lord G. Herbert's) drawing Master, as far as I can judge is a
good one, and will teach him in the *Grand style* and not in the
trifling taste of small finished landscapes.

Rev. W. Coxe to Lady Pembroke, 17.3.

NATURE

The Lake of Windermere differs very much from those of
Uls-water and Keswick. ... The paintings of *Pousin* describe
the nobleness of Uls-water; the works of *Salvator Rosa* express
the romantic and rocky scene of Keswick; and the tender
elegant touch of *Claude Loraine*, and *Smith* (George?), pencil
forth the rich variety of Windermere.

W. Hutchinson, *Excursion to the Lakes.*
(Cf. West, 1778.)

"Ulls-water Keswick and Windermere ... if they do not fairly
take the lead of all views of Europe, yet they are indisputably
such as no English traveller should leave behind."

R. Cumberland, *Ode to Romney.* Dedication.

W. Gilpin, *Observations in the Highlands of Scotland* published 1789 (People give name of picturesque to irregular beauties that are really romantic, e.g., Arthur's Seat. Praise of Scott's favourite view of Tweed. Burns' *Cotter's Saturday Night* quoted).

PAINTING

J. R. Cozens painted Alpine scenery (perhaps the first successfully). His "Hannibal crossing Alps" of this year was said by Turner to have taught him more than any other picture. Constable called him "all poetry" and "the greatest genius that ever touched landscape".

Il merito altissimo del divino vostro Michelangelo, sempre offrendolo non solo come principale, ma come unico modello a tutti coloro che coltivano l'arte del Disegno.
Reynolds to G. Pelli.

The terms beauty, or nature, which are general ideas, are but different modes of expressing the same thing. . . . In short, whatever pleases has in it what is analogous to the mind, and is, therefore, in the highest and best sense of the word, natural. The Roman and the Bolognian schools are reasonably preferred to the Venetian, Flemish or Dutch schools, as they address themselves to our best and noblest faculties. . . .
Reynolds, *Seventh Discourse.*

POETRY

We will allow a poet to express his meaning, when his meaning is not well known to himself, with a certain degree of obscurity, as it is one source of the sublime (on which Blake: "Obscurity is neither the source of the sublime nor of anything else".)
Reynolds, *Seventh Discourse.*

C'est moi qui le premier montrai aux François quelques perles que j'avais trouvées dans son énorme fumier.
Voltaire to d'Argental (Letter in dispraise of Shakespeare).

W. L. Bowles went to Winchester under J. Warton.

> Excess thou should'st indeed avoid
> Of plump or lean, nor would I choose th'adust
> And highly bilious . . .
> Angina, apthous sores, eruptions dire,
> Pertussis fierce and squalid atrophy.
>
> Downman, *Infancy III*.

J. Randolph succeeded Wheeler in Chair of Poetry, Oxford. He was also professor of Moral Philosophy, regius professor of Greek and divinity, Bishop of Oxford, Bangor and London, and catalogued the Aldines and incunabula in the Bodleian.

❧ 1777 r. George III ❧

GARDENS

(By Hagley gardens a villain would be) disarmed from executing his dark and bloody purposes; and every passion that corrodes the human breast, be lulled into a perfect calm.

> J. Heely, *Beauties of Hagley, Envil and the Leasowes*.

MANNERS AND TASTES

Clara Reeve, *The Champion of Virtue: A Gothic story*, reprinted 1778 as *The Old English Baron*, 13 editions, the last in 1883. The preface praises *The Castle of Otranto* but deprecates its extreme exaggerations. (Scott's biography of her in "Ballantyne's Novelists", defends Walpole's method).

Andrews the smuggler brought me this night about 11 a bagg of Hyson Tea 6 pound weight. He frightened us a little by whistling under the parlour window just as we were going to bed. I gave him some Geneva and paid him for the tea at 10/6 per pound.

> Parson Woodforde's *Diaries*, 29.3.

About this date Dr. Johnson "in company with some very grave men at Oxford" toasted "To the next insurrection of the negroes in the West Indies", in which, Boswell says he "discovered a zeal without knowledge" of "a status which in all ages God has sanctioned". This year he supported the successful application for freedom of Knight, a slave brought to Scotland. (Cf. Lord Mansfield 1772).

Jack (Wilkes) has a great variety of talk, Jack is a scholar, and Jack has the manners of a gentleman. . . . I would do Jack a kindness rather than not.

Johnson in Boswell, 12.9.

NATURE

The crater [on Etna, by night] could be discerned by a lurid red light which pierced the black clouds of smoke rolling from it. The scene was the most truly sublime that I have ever beheld.

Payne Knight, *Journal* (translated by Goethe in biography of Hackert).

PAINTING

The pieces of *Poussin* are not more uncommon, exotic and classical, the sketches of *Lorenese* more daring and sublime, or the descriptions of *Titian* more happy, natural, graceful, varied and charming, than (Thomson's *Seasons*) . . . frequently as wild and romantic as those of *Salvator Rosa*.

J. More, *Strictures Critical and Sentimental on Thomson's Seasons.*

John Wilkes moved in Parliament (Committee of Supply) for a National Gallery.

POETRY

My argument like the tales of our Novelists is a vehicle only; theirs as they profess, of Moral instruction. . . .
. . . Those characters in *Shakespeare*, which are seen only in part, are yet capable of being unfolded and understood in the whole. . . . He boldly makes a character act and speak from those parts of the composition which are *inferred* only and not

---

[1] Cf. A. Bradley, *Shakespearian Tragedy.*

distinctly shewn.[1] ... The *Apalachian* mountains, the banks of the Ohio shall resound with the accents of this Barbarism. ...

This (animation of characters) was not to be done from *without*, he must have *felt* every varied situation, and have spoken through the organ he had formed. ... Of Personifications ... those which are made out of abstract ideas are the creatures of the Understanding only, (e.g., beauty, virtue, etc. personified as Goddesses &c.) But as reason has its personifications so has passion ... Guilt beholds a devil ... envy hags and witches. ... True Poesy is *magic*, not nature: an effect from causes hidden and unknown. ... The very Players, who are, I think, the very worst judges of Shakespeare. ... Vice divested of disgust and terror is in its own nature ridiculous; ... the very same vices which spread horror and desolation thro' the Tragic scene, yet furnish the Comic with its highest laughter and delight.[1]

M. Morgan, Essay on Falstaff.

I have been reading Gray's *Works*, and think him the only poet since Shakespeare entitled to the character of sublime ... I once thought Swift's letters the best that could be written, but I like Gray's better.

Cowper to J. Hill, 20.4.

Deem not devoid of elegance ...
     themes unclassic falsely stil'd.

T. Warton. Sonnet on blank page of
Dugdale's Monasticon.

Whereso'er I turn my view,
All is strange, yet nothing new;
Endless labour all along,
Endless labour to be wrong;
Phrase that time has flung away;
Uncouth words in disarray,
Trick'd in antique ruff and bonnet,
Ode and elegy and sonnet.

Johnson on T. Warton's Poems (Croker).

[1] Cf. Plato, *Symposium* 223, "The same genius can write both tragedy and comedy", and Aristotle, *Poetics* V. I, "The Comic is a fault or defect neither fatal nor painful" and Plautus *Amphit.* Prologue.

1778 r. George III

ANTIQUARIANISM

Books printed in the black letter are sought for with the same avidity with which the English antiquary peruses a monumental inscription, or treasures up a Saxon piece of money . . . Verses which a few years past, were thought worthy the attention of children only, or of the lowest and rudest orders, are now admired for that artless simplicity which once obtained the name of coarseness and vulgarity.

Vicesimus Knox, *On the Prevailing Taste for the Old English Poets.*

ARCHITECTURE

(In stained glass) glaring colours, rendered still more glaring by transparency, seem to have constituted, in the idea of those who lived a century or two ago, the perfection of beauty . . . It is said to throw the mind into that serious temper, which is peculiarly adapted to the indulgence of devotion. Such an effect it may perhaps produce, in a great degree, on minds subject to superstition and fanaticism; . . . yet why light, one of the most glorious works of creation, should refrigerate the ardour of religion in the rational and dispassionate possessor of it, no good reason can be assigned.

V. Knox, *Essays* (cf. A. Wood, 1656, "Lovekin", 1661).

Sir John Vanbrugh's genius was of the first class, and in particular of movement, novelty and ingenuity, his works have not been exceeded by anything in modern times . . . crowded with barbarisms and absurdities . . . Movement is meant to express the rise and fall, the advance and recess with other diversity of form, so as to add greatly to the picturesque of the building . . . [These] have the same effect in architecture that hill and dale, foreground and distance, swelling and sinking, have in landscape; that is they serve to produce an agreeable and diversified contour that groups and contrasts like a picture.

J. and R. Adam, *Survey of the Arts in England.*

358

The massive entablature, the ponderous compartment ceiling, the tabernacle frame, almost the only species of ornament formerly known in this country, are now universally exploded, and, in their place, we have adopted a beautiful variety of light mouldings, gracefully formed, delicately enriched and arranged with propriety and skill. We have introduced a great diversity of ceilings, friezes and decorated pilasters, and have added grace and beauty to the whole by a mixture of grotesque stucco and painted ornaments, together with the painted rainceau with its fanciful figures.

R. and J. Adam, Architectural Works.

MANNERS AND TASTES

To say the truth, her speech was rather rough,
But as she promised him her heart,
Upon the whole he took it in good part,
And as he lov'd her, lik'd it well enough.

Sir John Henry Moore, The Duke of Benevento (Byronic style).

Harris is a prig and a bad prig.

Johnson in Boswell, 7.4.

Cute enough that, Miss Sukey.

F. Burney to S. Burney, 5.7.

The gnats in this part of the river (Delaware) are as large as sparrows; I have armed myself against them by wearing trousers.

Earl to Countess of Carlisle, 21.6–7.7.

There is a general levity in the age. We have physicians now in bag-wigs [i.e., not full bottomed].

Boswell.

A gentleman and lady with whom I travelled once; I suppose I must call them gentleman and lady, according to form, because they travelled in their own coach and horses. But at the first inn where we stopped, the lady called for—a pint of ale! and when it came, quarrelled with the waiter for not giving full measure.

Dr. Johnson in F. Burney, Diary, August.

Dolly Pentreath died at Mousehole; said to have been the last speaker of Cornish.

NATURE

Long has been the contention between the gentlemen of Derbyshire and Cumberland ... each claiming the superiority of natural beauties, and Dr. Brown has by many been thought to carry the dispute in favour of Keswick ... I should compare Dovedale to the soft and delicate maiden, and Keswick to the bold and sturdy Briton. ...
To *make the Tour* of the Lakes, to speak in fashionable terms, is the *ton* of the present hour.

Monthly Magazine.

From the delicate touches of *Claude*, verified on *Coniston* Lake, to the noble scenes of *Poussin*, exhibited on *Windermere*-water, and from there to the stupendous romantic ideas of *Salvator Rosa* realized in the Lake of *Derwent*.

T. West, *Guide to the Lakes*, 7 editions by
1799. (Cf. Hutchinson, 1776.)

PAINTING

Romney's ... pictures are hard, dry and tasteless, and such as you would not like in the least. And I am enough secure that he will never make a first rate painter.

J. Northcote to his brother, 26.12.

Homer revives in Milton's mighty line
And great Apelles lives again in thine.
In Courts let insects spread the gaudy wing;
For Kings let Reynolds paint and Whitehead sing.
Thee, Barry, thee no vulgar muse surveys
For thee her harp to string, her voice to raise.

General Advertiser (attributed to Barry!).

POETRY

(From the Renaissance we gained) much good sense, good taste, and good criticism. But in the meantime, we have lost a set of manners, and a system of machinery, more suitable to the purposes of poetry.

T. Warton, *History of English Poetry.*
Vol. II (Vol. I, 1774) (cf. Hurd, 1762).

Agostino Isola in *Pieces selected from the Italian Poets and translated into English* gives 26 of Metastasio, 5 of Ariosto, 3 of Petrarch, 2 of Tasso, 2 of Tassoni, 1 of Guarini and 1 anonymous. By "some Gentlemen of the University of Cambridge," perhaps by R. O. Cambridge, an Oxford man, nicknamed Cantabrigiensis.

Vous y verrez représenter les abominables pièces de Shakespeare traduites en notre langue, et toute l'auditoire se pâmer d'aise en entendant ces farces ridicules et dignes des sauvages de Canada . . . Mais vous voilà encore un Goetz de Berlichingen qui parait sur la scène, imitation détestable de ces mauvaises pièces Anglaises, et le parterre applaudit et demande avec enthousiasme la répétition de ces dégoûtantes platitudes.

> Frederick the Great, *De la Littérature Allemande.*

The last volume (of *Evelina*) almost distracted me, I have never been well since . . . It worked on me as much as the death of Desdemona.

> Miss Coussmaker to Susan Burney.

The two *wittiest* things in our Language in Verse & Prose are Dr. Young's "Conjectures on Original Composition", I think, and Dr. Swift's "Ballad on the South Sea".
The two Tragedies which go nearest one's Heart, I think,—in our Language I mean, are Southern's "Fatal Marriage" and Lillo's "Fatal Curiosity". The two best Comic Scenes in our Language according to my Taste are the scene between Squire Richard and Myrtilla in the "Provoked Husband" (Vanbrugh) and that between Sir Joseph Wittol, Nol Bluff and Sharper in the "Old Batchelor" (Congreve)—not the kicking scene but the friendly one. The two best *Declamatory* scenes where the Sentiments and Language are most perfect, seem to be the Scene between Juba and Syphax in Addison's "Cato" and that between the two Ladies in Johnson's "Irene".

> *Thraliana*, December.

Hayley's *Epistle on Painting* to Romney on his return from Italy. ("Hayley was the *work-basket* poet of that day,—His verses were upon every girl's sofa." Farrington, *Diary*, 15.4.1803.)

❦ 1779 r. George III ❦

GARDENS

(At Stowe) The buildings called Temples are most miserable, many of them both without and within. Sir John Vanbrugh's is an ugly clumsy lump, hardly fit for a gentleman's stable. The temples of Venus and Bacchus, though large, have nothing elegant in the structure, and the paintings in the former, representing a lewd story, are neither well designed nor executed . . . The statues are full as coarse as the paintings, especially those of Apollo and the Muses whom a person not otherwise informed might take to be nine milkmaids.

> J. Wesley, *Journal*, October 13 (cf. 1744, Duchess of Portland).

(Knowle Park) in regard to temples, obelisks, or any kind of buildings, will bear no comparison with (Hagley) since nothing is there of the sort. The house, which is very old, has the appearance of an antique chapel, or rather Cathedral . . . The windows are all of the small old casements; and the general air of the place is monastic and gloomy.

> F. Burney, *Diary*, August.

A fine piece of ruins built by the late Lord Holland, at a great expense, which, the day after I saw it, tumbled down for nothing; . . . much improved by this fortunate incident. It is hardly possible to put stones together with that air of wild and magnificent disorder which they are sure to acquire by falling of their own accord.

> Cowper to W. Unwin, July.

(Shenstone, 1745) began to point his prospects, to diversify his surface, to entangle his walks, and to wind his waters; . . . to place a bench at every turn where there is an object to catch the view; to make water run where it will be heard, or to stagnate where it will be seen. . . . Some praise must be allowed by the most supercilious observer to him, who does best what such multitudes are contending to do well.

> Johnson, *Lives of Poets*.

On the brow of one hill appear'd the Sibyl's temple, ruinated like that at Tivoli; a pediment, supported by Ionic columns, rose at the foot of another; the venerable Gothic tower of a parish church was discovered at a distance among the tufted trees; and the whole was terminated by some blue mountains in the horizon, and enlivened by a considerable stream, which ran winding down the valley; over which an old bridge of three arches makes a picturesque appearance. . . . "Aaron's well! you blockhead", says Columbella, "Arno's Vale, you mean." "Nay, nay", quoth Peter "I know as how the right name of it is Tadpole Bottom." . . . He had heard his honour wanted an hermit to live in his woods, and said that he should be very proud to serve him. . . .

Within this compass [an acre] however, they had continued to introduce every individual article of modern taste. Here was a large shrubbery, a small serpentine river over which was thrown a Chinese bridge of a considerable diameter; there was a Chinese pagoda, a Gothic temple, a grotto, a root house, a hermitage, a Cynic tub or two by the water-side.

> R. Graves, *Columella, or the Distress't Anchoret*. (Satire on Shenstone, with frontispiece to parody Claude).

MANNERS AND TASTES

Mrs. Thrale: "Do cry a little, Sophy" (Streatfield), in a wheedling voice, "pray do! Consider now, you are going today, and its very hard if you won't cry a little: indeed S.S. you ought to cry". While all the rest of us, in laughter, joined in the request, two crystal tears came into the soft eyes of the S.S. and rolled gently down her cheeks.

> F. Burney, *Diary*, 16.6.

NATURE

Our plan was to have seen the Lakes, where the whole World are running every summer.

> T. Bromley to Lord Herbert, 15.9.

The vetturino when on the mountain pulled a nightcap which he had on his head over his eyes, and I, following the example, did the same, concluding there must be some good reason for

so doing. By this means I saw nothing of the mountain except
that when I was on the summit of it the high wind blew my
hat off, and then I put up my cap to see what was become of it
... When my hat was brought to me I put it on my head, pulled
down my cap again and went on as before.

> J. Northcote, *Journal* (Crossing M. Cenis,
> on May 1).

PAINTING

Walpole (Lord Orford's) pictures from Houghton sold to
Empress Catherine of Russia for £40,555 as valued by B. West
and Cipriani.

(Claude and Reynolds) not very easy to distinguish from the
old.

> F. Burney, *Diary* I.

Sir Joshua's prices: fifty guineas for a head and two hundred
for a whole length.

> J. Northcote to brother, August 2.

At Bologna there are a thousand fine paintings. See the
leaning Tower if you can find it. At Florence ... remark the
Busts of Vespasian, Agrippa etc. Remember, if you pass
thro' Spoleto, not to omit seeing the sublime and extraordinary Bridge. At Perugia (if you ever pass) see the Paintings.

> Lord Pembroke to Lord Herbert.

Not so much struck with the Venus of Medicis as perhaps I
ought to have been. There are twenty things in Rome that
seemed to me superior ... The pictures in the Tribune, which
I liked best are Titian's naked Venus, Raphael's St. John, a
beautiful Sybyll by Guercino (the most pleasing).

> Lord Herbert, *Diary*, 8.11.

Lord Pembroke ... begs when you go to Paris ... you will sit
to Greuse in your Regimentals and Black Stock.

> T. Eyre to Lord Herbert, 15.12.

POETRY

If I were required to select from the whole mass of English poetry the most poetical paragraph, I know not what I could prefer to an exclaimation in the *Mourning Bride*. (CONGREVE 1697):—

> "How reverend is the face of this tall pile,
>   Whose ancient pillars rear their marble heads,
>   To bear aloft its arch'd and pond'rous roof,
>   By its own weight made steadfast and immovable,
>   Looking tranquillity! It strikes an awe
>   And terror on my aching sight. The tombs
>   And monumental caves of death look cold,
>   And shoot a chillness in my trembling heart."

. . . . .

Words too familiar, or too remote, defeat the purpose of a poet. From those sounds which we hear on small or on coarse occasions, we do not easily receive strong impressions or delightful images; and words to which we are nearly strangers, whenever they occur, draw that attention on themselves which they should transmit to things. . . .

> "In dreams they fearful precipices tread,
>   Or, shipwreck'd, labour to some distant shore:
>   Or, in dark Churches, walk among the dead;
>   They wake with horror, and dare sleep no more."
>
> (DRYDEN, *Annus Mirabilis*, 1667).
> One of the fairest flowers of English poetry.

. . . . .

Wit (ascribed to COWLEY, is) what is at once natural and new, that which though not obvious, is at its first production, acknowledged to be just, which he that never found it wonders how he missed; to wit of this kind the metaphysical[1] poets have seldom risen. But wit abstracted from its effects upon the hearer may be more rigorously . . . considered as . . . a combination of dissimilar images, or discovery of occult resemblances in things apparently unlike. Of wit, thus defined, they have more than enough; . . . the reader, though he sometimes admires is seldom pleased . . . Nor was the sublime more

---

[1] In J.'s Dictionary under "Metaphysic" (see 1755).

within their reach . . . for they never attempted that comprehension and expanse of thought . . . of which the first effect is sudden astonishment and the second rational admiration . . . If their conceits were far-fetched, they were often worth the carriage . . . Many noble lines such as the feeble care of WALLER could never produce. . . .

> "Call her the metaphysics of her sex
> And say she tortures wit."
>
> Cleveland.

Perhaps no composition in our language has been oftener perused than POMFRET'S *Choice* [First published separately 1700, 10th ed., 1736.

> Near some fair town I'd have a private seat,
> Built uniform, not little, nor too great;
> Better if on a rising ground it stood;
> On this side fields on that a neighbouring wood.
> It should within no other things contain
> But what are useful, necessary, plain;
> Methinks 'tis nauseous and I'd ne'er endure
> The needless pomp of gaudy furniture. &c.]

A system of life adapted to common notions, and equal to common expectations; such a state as affords plenty and tranquillity, without exclusion of intellectual pleasures. . . . He who pleases many must have some species of merit.

. . . . .

No more elegant funeral poem is to be found in the whole compass of English literature (than TICKELL'S Elegy on Addison, see 1721).

. . . . .

THOMSON thinks always as a man of genius, and looks round on Nature and on Life with the Eye which Nature bestows only on a Poet.

. . . . .

The attention naturally retires from a new tale of Venus, Diana and Minerva.

. . . . .

An epithet or metaphor drawn from Nature ennobles Art; an epithet or metaphor drawn from Art degrades Nature.[1] GRAY is too fond of words arbitrarily compounded. . . . That poetry and virtue go always together is an opinion so pleasing, that I can forgive him who resolves to think it true . . . The "Churchyard" (1751) abounds with images which find a mirror in every mind, and with sentiments to which every bosom returns an echo. The four stanzas beginning "Yet even these bones" are to me original . . . yet he that reads them here persuades himself that he has always felt them. Had Gray written often thus, it had been vain to blame, and useless to praise him. . . . His mind had a large grasp, his curiosity was unlimited and his judgment cultivated.

. . . . .

The English poems (of MILTON) though they make no promise of *Paradise Lost* have this evidence of genius, that they have a cast original and unborrowed. But their peculiarity is not excellence, . . . too often distinguished by repulsive harshness; the combinations of words are new but they are not pleasing; the rhymes and epithets seem to be laboriously sought and violently applied. . . .

(*Lycidas*) has no nature for there is nothing new. Its form is that of a pastoral, easy, vulgar and therefore disgusting. Poetry is the art of uniting pleasure with truth by calling imagination to the help of reason . . . It could only be by long prejudice and the bigotry of learning that Milton could prefer the ancient tragedies with their encumbrance of a chorus to the exhibition of the French and English stages . . . The innovators whom I oppose are turning off attention from life to nature. They seem to think that we are placed here to watch the growth of plants, or the motions of the stars. Socrates was rather of opinion that what we had to learn, was how to do good and avoid evil . . . We are perpetually moralists but we are geometicians only by chance. . . . Of the best of (the sonnets) it can only be said that they are not bad. . . .

(SHENSTONE'S *Pastoral Ballads*) An intelligent reader, acquainted with the scenes of real life, sickens at the mention of the *crook*, the *pipe*, the *sheep* and the *kids*.

Johnson, *Lives of Poets*.

[1] Cf. Bowles edit. Pope 1806: "Images . . . derived from Nature and Passion are always more sublime and pathetic than those drawn from Art and Manners."

(The other lives are; Denham, Butler, Rochester, Roscommon, Otway, Dorset, Stepney, J. Philips, Walsh, E. Smith, Duke, King, Sprat, Halifax, Parnell, Garth, Rowe, Addison, Hughes, Buckingham, Prior, Blackmore, Fenton, Lansdown. Yalden, Hammond, Somervile (*sic*), Savage, Swift, Broome, Pope, Pitt, Watts, A. Philips, West, Collins, Dyer, Young, Mallet, Akenside, Lyttleton. For the criticism of Blackmore see 1712).

Was there ever anything so delightful as the music of the Paradise Lost? It is like that of a fine organ; has the fullest and the deepest tones of majesty, with all the softness and elegance of the Dorian flute. Variety without end and never equalled, unless perhaps by Virgil. Yet the Doctor [Johnson] has little or nothing to say upon this copious theme . . . Oh! I could thresh his old jacket, till I made his pension jingle in his pocket.

> Cowper to W. Unwin, 31.10.

Possible to make one of (Johnson's) *Ramblers* into three other papers, that all should have exactly the same purport and meaning but in different phrases.

> H. Walpole to Countess of Upper Ossory, 1.2.

There are (said Dr. Johnson) three distinct kinds of judges upon all new authors or productions; the first are those who know no rules, but pronounce entirely from their natural taste and feelings; the second are those who know and judge by rules; and the third are those who know but are above the rules. These last are those you should wish to satisfy. Next to them rate the natural judges; but ever despise those opinions that are formed by rules.

> F Burney, *Diary* 20.10.

(Criticising the revival of ballad poetry—Percy, see 1771— on J. Warton).

> "Hermit hoar in solemn cell
> Wearing out life's evening gray;
> Smite thy bosom, sage, and tell,
> What is bliss, and which the way?"

Thus I spoke; and speaking sigh'd
Scarce repress'd the starting tear—
When the smiling sage reply'd—
"Come my lad and drink some beer".

Johnson in Boswell, 3.16.

Shakespeare's *Tempest* which for fancy, invention and originality is at the head of Beautiful improbabilities, is rendered by
the additions of Dryden a childish chaos of absurdity and
obscenity.

F. Burney, *Diary*, 20.10.

STAGE

The School for Scandal damped the new pieces.

Drury Lane, Treasurer's accounts.

🌺 1780 r. George III 🌺

MANNERS AND TASTES

(My windows) will command a very rich and gay prospect,
and will give me all the splendours of a Summer when I am
inclined to the allegro; when I am more inclined to the
penseroso, those windows may be shut against the garish day
and a large gothick window be thrown open.

Eliz. Montagu, Letter.

Their vast rambling mansions, spacious halls, and painted
casements, the gothic porch smothered with honeysuckles,
their little gardens and high walls, their box-edging, balls
of holly, and yew-tree statues, are become so entirely unfashionable now, that we can hardly believe it possible, that a
people who resembled us so little in our tastes, should resemble
us in anything else.

Cowper to Rev. W. Unwin, 6.8.

Sentiment was now exploded, and I therefore sought to diversify
(my books) with humours.

Sophia Lee, *A Chapter of Accidents*.

Nothing would she talk of but "dear Nature", and nothing abuse but "odious affectation".

F. Burney, *Diary*, I.

Lodgings at a Keeper's Lodge in Richmond Park; a Villa has always been my Hobby-Horse.

Lady Pembroke to Lord Herbert, April.

The Duke of Chartres carried me to his petite Maison at Moussow (near Paris), where we dined a pretty numerous, noisy company, there being some Females of the Party. After Dinner we amused ourselves in flinging one another into the water, at last by stripping naked and hunting the Hare through Wood, Water etc.

Lord Herbert, *Diary*, 19.5.

It was surely violence enough offered to that sentiment (of delicacy) in the female mind to have passed with tolerable composure the figure of the Apollo Belvedere in the Vestibule, without subjecting it to so formidable an ordeal as that in the antique room.

Open Letter to Sir J. Reynolds.

Wood, water, wilderness itself had an inexpressible charm for me; ... the pleasure of seeing romantic scenery, or what afforded me at least equal pleasure, the places which had been distinguished by remarkable historical events. The delight with which I regarded the former, of course, had general approbation, but I often found it difficult to procure sympathy with the interest I felt in the latter. Yet to me, the wandering over the field of Bannockburn was the source of more exquisite pleasure than gazing upon the celebrated landscape from the battlements of Stirling Castle ... I was unable with the eye of a painter to dissect the various parts of the scene, to comprehend how the one bore upon the other, to estimate the effect which various features of the view had in producing its leading and general effect ... But shew me an old castle or a field of battle, and I was at home at once, filled it with the combatants in their proper costume, and overwhelmed my hearers by the enthusiasm of my description ... If I have since been able in poetry to trace with some success the principles (of scenery), it has always been with reference to its general and leading features, or under some alliance with moral feeling.

> Sir W. Scott, *Autobiography* (1808, b, 1771), and see 1786.

PAINTING

The elements of a picture: Beauty (ancients); expression or significance (Raphael); the pleasant united with harmony (Coreggio); and colour (Titian).

> R. Mengs, *Opere*, published posthumously, I.

The Royal Academy at Somerset House (its first exhibition there) is opened. It is quite a Roman palace and finished in perfect taste as well as boundless expense . . . Gainsborough has fine landscapes there, of which one especially is worthy of any collection, and of any painter that ever existed.

> H. Walpole to Rev. W. Mason, May.

Annibal Caracci himself could not paint like our Raphael poet (Shakespeare).

> H. Walpole to Rev. W. Cole, 30.5.

Loutherbourg's *Eidophusikon* delighted Reynolds and Gainsborough. "Various Imitations of Natural Phenomena, represented by Moving Pictures". Perhaps sent Gainsborough to Lakes (1783).
(Described by A. Dobson, *At Prior Park*).

J. R. Cozens taken to Italy by Beckford.

Perugia pleased me greatly; to trace the works of old Peter[1] is an entertaining task. I took pleasure in persuading myself to think less of Raphael . . . A picture of Barocci at the Cathedral delighted me . . . I am not overfond of the works of that Master; tho' his pencil is always elegant, his line is too *enamely* . . . The whole Groupe of Marys rather excite sensuality than devotion.

> J. C. Hippisly to Lord Herbert, 1.1.

[1] Perugino.

POETRY

The Gothic productions of Dante . . . I hope you do not imagine
that I deny that Dante had an astonishing genius, and that
he had some passages of the highest sublime . . . His poem is
the worst that there is in any language . . . five or six beautiful
passages.

> M. Sherlock, *Letters from an English
> Traveller.*

1781 r. George III

ARCHITECTURE

Wentworth Castle . . . the perfectest specimen of architecture
I know (see 1785).

> H. Walpole to Earl of Stafford, 31.8.

The tower of [Gloucester] Cathedral is very handsome and
very light; which is more than can be said of the pillars of
the body of the church, which seem gouty and immoderately
swell'd. The choir is neat; and the great window over the altar,
as also that of the chapel beyond it, are much to be admir'd.

> 15.6.

[In Worcester Cathedral] there is a total want of stain'd
glass so necessary for church grandure to cast a dim religious
light. The chapel (which should appear grave) is deck'd out
in the Adamatic fashion.

> 2.7.

The new windows of this Chapel [New College, by Reynolds]
are at present the admiration of travellers, by being the
University boast . . . I must own I preferr'd the old high-
coloured paintings, and their strong, steady shade, to those
new and elegant-esteem'd compositions; and to speak my mind,
these twisting emblematical figures appear to me half-dress'd
languishing harlots; no doubt, but that men of skill have been
consulted, who determin'd them to be of the collegiate and
Gothic taste.

> 8.7.

Tintern Abbey. All description must fall short of its awful grandeur.

Torrington Diaries, 16.6.

NATURE

River Wye . . . infinitely surpassing all I had seen in Derbyshire, and rendering poor in my idea, the Totness River from Dartmouth.

Torrington Diaries, 15.6.

MANNERS AND TASTES

Mrs. Montagu's "Bas Bleu" club flourishing.

Last year a man at Turnham Green fixed up a board with this notice—*Ready made Temples sold here.*

To Rev. W. Mason, 27.1.

Converted Dicky Bateman from a Chinese to a Goth. Though he was the founder of the Sharawadgi taste in England, I preached so effectively that his every pagoda took the Veil.

H. Walpole to Earl of Strafford, 13.6.

I considered that the taste of the day was refined and delicate to excess, and that to disgust the delicacy of taste, by a slovenly inattention to it, would be to forfeit at once all hope of being useful.

To Rev. W. Unwin, 6.10.

In a few years, perhaps next year, the fine gentleman will shut up his umbrella and give it to his sister, filling his hand with a crab-tree cudgel instead . . . The love of change will have betrayed him into a propriety.

Cowper to Mrs. Newton, August.

> "Draw round yon knowl",
> Alcander cried, "in stately Norman mode,
> A wall embattled, and within its sward,
> Let every structure needful for a farm
> Arise in castle-semblance; the huge barn
> Shall with a mock portcullis arm the gate."

A glittering fane, where rare and alien plants
Might safely flourish . . .
High on Ionic shafts he had it tower,
A proud rotunda; to its sides conjoin'd
Two broad piazzas in theatric curve,
Ending in equal porticos sublime.
Glass roofed the whole, and sidelong to the south
'Twixt every fluted column, lightly reared
Its wall pellucid.

             Beauty scorns to dwell
Where Use is exiled . . .
As best befits the Genius of the scene.

> W. Mason, *The English Garden*, Bk. IV
> (first book in 1772).

Picturesque little mills . . . all exactly as a painter would have them . . . in most romantic and improbable situations, . . . the effect . . . that of painted landscapes of the most invented and poetic kind.

> Twining's Correspondence (*Recreations of a Country Parson in eighteenth century*, published 1882).

The *Chief attraction* was to meet the Bramin and the two Parsees.

> Hannah More to her sister.

PAINTING

Correggio, whose mouth is generally curled into a crescent, and in truth I think strains grace into almost a grimace.

> H. Walpole to Countess of Upper Ossory, 4.9.

POETRY

The Dean said "Stop a few minutes and you shall hear my girls sing a whimsical song" . . . "Papa, I can't indeed, I cannot sing such stuff" . . . and a very pretty little old song it was,

        "Drink to me only with thine eyes" etc.

but they stopped in the middle of the song. "Why don't you go?" cried Dr. Ogle, "Why the rest is nothing but about *stinks*."

> Charlotte Ann to Fanny Burney, 24.6 (or 1782).

The Library (Crabbe) I have read. There are some pretty lines and easy verses; but it is too long.

> To Countess of Upper Ossory, 4.9.

(It secured Burke's patronage).

Pope's rich English 5.2.

Aristotle's old hacked rules for the drama and the pedantry of a beginning middle and end.

> To Rev. W. Mason, 6.4.

I love Chaucer better in Dryden and Baskerville than in his own language and dress.

> H. Walpole, 13.11 to Rev. W. Mason, who offered him a black letter 1st edition for £1 1s.

> Oh come my fair one! I have thatch'd above
> And whiten'd all around my little cot,
> Shorn are the hedges leading to the grove,
> Nor is the seat and willow bower forgot.
> > Dr. H. Downman, *To Thespia*.

> With our Swords resistless Might
> We have thinned the Ranks of Fight
> (=Pugnavimus ensibus)
> Unmoved I quit the Realms of Light
> (=Non est lugenda mors)
> [or Non gemit vir fortis contra mortem].

A species of savage greatness, a fierce and wild kind of sublimity.

> Dr. H. Downman, *Death Song of Ragnor Lodbrach* (cf. Temple, 1690).

> The last dim wave, in boundless space
> Involved and lost.
> > Mickle, *Almada Hill*.

SUBLIME

The most magnificent object under heaven is the great deep . . .
One of Shakespeare's characters says "I am never merry when
I hear sweet music". The same effect that harmony seems to
have had upon him I have experienced from the sight and
sound of the ocean, which have often composed my thoughts
into a melancholy not unpleasing.

Cowper to W. Unwin, 26.9.

Longinus . . . who would have condemned to the flames that
"monstrum horrendum, informe, ingens" the Divina Comedia,
would have read some of its verses with transport. On perusing
the Canto of Count Ugolino, the sentimental soul of Longinus
would have exclaimed "Homer has nothing so sublime".

M. Sherlock, *Original Letters*.

1782 r. George III

ARCHITECTURE

The Colleges are mostly in the Gothic taste, and much over-
loaded with ornaments, and built with grey stone; which,
perhaps, while it is new, looks pretty well, but it has now the
most dingy, dirty and disgusting appearance . . . To me
Oxford seemed to have but a dull and gloomy look . . . *All
Soul's College*, a very elegant building . . . *Christ Church* and
Queen's College are the most modern, and I think, indisputably
the best built of all the Colleges.

Pastor Moritz, *Travels in England*, 25.6.
translated 1795.

Spires, those most graceful and picturesque of all elevations,
he proscribes as Gothic and barbarous, and thinks he has
exploded them forever by this Brobdingnagian puerility;
Ils assassinent les nuages. (He quotes from Girardin, *De la
composition des paysages*, who was a friend of Rousseau).

H. Walpole to Rev. W. Mason, 7.12.

It is not every man than can build a house who can execute a ruin. To give a stone its mouldering appearance—to make the widening chink run naturally through all the joints—to mutilate the ornaments—to peel the facing from the internal structure.

W. Gilpin, *Observations on Wye.*

MANNERS AND TASTES

For long, enamour'd of a barbarous age,
A faithless truant to the classic page;
Long have I lov'd to catch the simple chime
Of minstrel-harps and spell the fabling rime;
To view the festive rites, the knightly play,
That deck'd heroic Albion's elder day;
To mark the mouldering halls of Barons bold,
And the rough castle, cast in giant mould,
With Gothic manners Gothic arts explore,
And muse on the magnificence of yore.

  . . . . .

Such was a pensive bard's mistaken strain—
But, oh! of ravish'd pleasures why complain?
No more the matchless skill I call unkind
That strives to disenchant my cheated mind.
For when again I view thy chaste Design;
The just proportion, and the genuine line;
Those native portraitures of Attic art,
That from the lucid surface seem to start;
Those tints, that steal no glories from the day,
Nor ask the sun to lend his streaming ray;
The doubtful radiance of contending dyes,
That faintly mingle yet distinctly rise;
'Twixt light and shade the transitory strife;
The feature blooming with immortal life;
The stole in casual foldings taught to flow,
Not with ambitious ornament to glow;
The tread majestic and the beaming eye
That, lifted, speaks its commerce with the sky;
Heaven's golden emanation, gleaming mild
O'er the mean cradle of the virgin's child:
Sudden, the sombrous imagery is fled,
Which late my visionary rapture fed:

377

Thy powerful hand has broke the Gothic chain,
And brought my bosom back to truth again;
To truth by no peculiar taste confin'd,
Whose universal pattern strikes mankind;
To truth, whose bold and unresisted aim
Checks frail caprice and fashion's fickle claim;
To truth, whose Charms deception's magic quell,
And bind coy Fancy in a stronger spell.

    .   .   .   .   .

Reynolds! 'tis thine, from the broad window's height,
To add new lustre to religious light:
Not of its pomp to strip the ancient shrine,
But bid that pomp with purer radiance shine;
With arts unknown before, to reconcile
The willing Graces to the Gothic pile.

> T. Warton, *Verses on Reynolds'* (New College) *Window* (cf. Walpole, 1785).

On a very gloomy, dismal day, just such an one as it ought to be, I went to see Westminster Abbey.

> Pastor Moritz, *Travels in England*, 20.1.

A troop of Morrice dancers headed by the buffoon; but to me, their mummery appear'd tedious, and as little enjoy'd by the performers, as the spectators; the genius of the nation does not take this turn.

> *Torrington Diaries*, 28.6.

All arose at six o'clock in the morning, and "by the pale blink of the moon" we went to the sea-side where we had bespoke the bathing-woman to be ready for us, and into the ocean we plunged. It was cold, but pleasant. I have bathed so often as to lose my dread of the operation, which now gives me nothing but animation and vigour.

> F. Burney, *Diary*, 20.11.

Lady Di Beauclerk is painting a room ... It is nothing but a row of lilacs in festoons on green paper, but executed in as great a style as Michael Angelo would have done for a Pope's villa.

> To Rev. W. Mann, 4.8.

Your home-brewed rivers that people make with a drain, half a bridge, and a clump of evergreens and then overlay with a model of a ship.

H. Walpole to Earl Harcourt, 7.9.

Lamb and Coleridge went to Christ's Hospital

The letter in the 3rd Vol: of the Spectator 217[1] where the Man complains of his indelicate Mistress; ... even the Maid who was dressing my Hair, burst out o'laughing at the Idea of *a Lady* saying her Stomach ach'd, or that something stuck between her Teeth.

Thraliana, 4.11.

NATURE

The terrace at Richmond does assuredly afford one of the finest prospects in the world. Whatever is charming in nature, or pleasing in art, is here to be seen. Nothing I had ever seen, or ever can see elsewhere, is to be compared to it.

Pastor Moritz, *Travels in England*, 21.6.

Though the parts (of Tintern) are beautiful, the whole is ill-shaped ... (In 1771) a new object of pursuit: that of examining the face of a country by the rules of picturesque beauty. ... (Nature) is seldom so correct in composition as to produce a harmonious whole. Either the foreground or the background is disproportioned, or some awkward line runs through the piece; or a tree is ill-placed, or a bank is formal. ... The invented landscape was touched in fainter colours than the real ones. Yet it was more than *laid in*. It was almost finished.

W. Gilpin, *River Wye.*

Mr. Gilpin (his *Essay on Forest Trees* considered in a picturesque light. pubd. 1790). It is perfectly new, truly ingenious, full of good sense in an agreeable style, and void of all affectation.

H. Walpole to Rev. W. Mason, 10.1.

PAINTING

As the merits of the Venetian school consisted mostly in the mechanical conduct of the art, there has been proportionately less decay in its vigour than in the other schools of Italy.

First Academy Lecture.

[1] Budgell.

Painting is not, as has been said, a silent poem, and poetry a speaking picture; but much more truly painting is poetry realised; and full, complete, and perfect poetry is indeed nothing more than an animated account or relation of the mere conception of a picture. (Laokoon not mentioned).

Second Academy Lecture.

The object of art is not the imitation of mere nature, but the imitation of nature happily chosen and completed in all its circumstances so as to correspond with that possibility and perfection which the mind conceives, and with which only it can be satisfied. The completing this idea of art by uniting the several perfections of the several schools and great men, was the desideratum remaining. The Carraches set out with this noble object ... Tintoret is very unequal in his works, and has left behind him a greater number of bad, or (which is nearly the same thing) of middling works, than any other artist of reputation.

Barry, *Sixth Academy Lecture.*

POETRY

The *Seasons* of Thomson have been very instrumental in diffusing a general taste for the beauties of *nature* and *landscape*. It is only within a few years that the picturesque scenes of our own country, our Lakes, mountains, cascades, caverns and castles, have been visited and described ... The *largest* portion of (Pope's works) is of the *didactic, moral* and *satyric* kind; and, consequently, not of the most *poetic* species *of poetry* ... *Imagination* was not his predominant talent ... No man of true poetical spirit *is master of* himself while he reads (Homer and Milton) ... Where to place our admired *Pope?* Not, assuredly, in the same rank with *Spenser, Shakespeare* and *Milton* ... Next to *Milton* and just above Dryden ... Though *Dryden* be the greater genius, yet *Pope* is the better artist ... There are parts and passages in other modern authors, in *Young* and in *Thomson*, for instance, equal to any of *Pope;* and he has written nothing in a strain so truly sublime, as the *Bard* of *Gray*.

J. Warton, *Essay on Genius and Writings of Pope*, Vol. II, see 1756.

The amplification of a sentence, though it may add to its perspicuity, frequently diminishes its force.

No. 44.

The admirers of English Poetry are divided into two parties . . . On one side the lovers and imitators of Spenser and Milton and, on the other, those of Dryden, Boileau and Pope (Gray, the Wartons and Mason of the former, Johnson, Goldsmith and Hayley of the latter).

No. 129.

[Old Testament] the sublimest . . . book in the English Language.

V. Knox, *Essays Moral and Literary*, No. 167.

An epic poem (that most senseless of all the species of poetic composition, and which pedants call the *chef d'oeuvre* of the human mind) . . . a mixture of history without truth, and of romance without imagination. We are well off when from that *mésalliance* there spring some bastards called episodes, that are lucky enough to resemble their romantic mother more than their solemn father . . . Everybody failed in this but the inventor Homer . . . Virgil with every beauty of expression and harmony that can be conceived, has accomplished but an insipid imitation. His hero is a nullity, like Mellefont and the virtuous characters of every comedy, and some of his incidents, as the harpies and the ship turned to nymphs, as silly as Mother Goose's Tales. Milton, all imagination, and a thousand times more sublime and spirited, has produced a monster . . . Dante was extravagant, absurd, disgusting, in short a Methodist parson in Bedlam. Ariosto was a more agreeable Amadis of Gaul in a bawdy-house and Spenser, John Bunyan in rhyme . . . Voltaire who retained his good sense in heroics, lost his spirit and fire in them. In short epic poetry is like what it first celebrated, the heroes of a world that knew nothing better than courage and conquest. It is not suited to an improved and polished state of things. It has continued to degenerate from the founder of the family, and happily expired in the last bastard of the race, Ossian.

H. Walpole to Rev. W. Mason, 25.6.

The English national authors are in all hands. . . . My landlady,
who is only a taylor's widow, read her Milton; and tells me
that her late husband first fell in love with her, on this very
account; because she read her Milton with such proper empha-
sis . . . I myself bought Milton in duodecimo for two shillings,
neatly bound . . . The only translation from the German which
has been particularly successful in England, is Gesner's
"Death of Abel" (trnl. Mary Collyer, 1761). Klopstock's
"Messiah" as is well known has been but ill received . . .
The works of Mr. Jacob Boehmen, are all translated into
English.

Pastor Moritz, Travels in England, 9.6.

> (Pope) (his musical finesse was such,
> So nice his ear, so delicate his touch)
> Made poetry a mere mechanic art,
> And every warbler has the tune by heart.
>
> Cowper, Table Talk.

I could never agree with those who preferred (Pope) to Dryden;
nor with others (I have known such, and persons of taste and
discernment too), who could not allow him to be a poet at all . . .
So far, therefore, I have no quarrel with Johnson. But I
cannot subscribe to what he says of Prior . . . What shall we
say of his old fusty-rusty remarks upon *Henry and Emma?*
I agree with him that morally considered both the knight and
his lady are bad characters . . . There are few readers of poetry,
of either sex, in this country, who cannot remember how that
enchanting piece has bewitched them, who do not know that,
instead of finding it tedious, they have been so delighted with
the romantic turn of it, as to have overlooked all its defects. . . .
I wonder almost that as the Bacchanals served Orpheus, the
boys and girls do not tear this husky, dry commentator limb
from limb, in resentment of such an injury done to their darling
poet.

Cowper to W. Unwin, 5.1.

PROSE

Cecilia . . . immeasurably long, and written in Dr. Johnson's
unnatural phrase; I liked it far less than *Evelina* . . . The great
fault is that the authoress is so afraid of not making all her

dramatis personae set in character, that she never lets them say a syllable but what is to mark their character, which is very unnatural . . . But I am most offended at the want of poetical justice.

> H. Walpole to Countess of Upper Ossory, 1.10.

"Cecilia" sends us into peoples houses with our eyes swelled out of our heads with weeping. We take the book into the carriage and read and weep. . . . The children wept and sobbed aloud, my heart was bursting with agony.

> Lady Hales to Mrs. Phillips (Susan Burney), 27. 7.

❧ 1783 r. George III ❧

ARCHITECTURE

The Spire of St. Andrew's, Worcester, built

The façade of Peterborough is noble and in great taste.

> H. Walpole to Lady Ossory, 27.9.

GARDENS

The English were the inventors of the modern art of gardening. . . . Till within these few years, the French have been their chief opponents . . . All those who wish, in their gardens, to realize the conceptions of the great landscape painters, imitate the English.

> *Critical Review.*

MANNERS AND TASTES

I preached in the new preaching-house at Oxford . . . well filled with rich and poor scholars, as well as townsmen.

> J. Wesley, *Journal*, 14.7.

PAINTING

Sir Joshua . . . his last discourse to the Academy . . . is rather an apology for, or an avowal of, the object of his own style, that is effect, or impression on all sorts of spectators. This lesson will rather do hurt than good on his disciples, and make them neglect all kind of finishing. Nor is he judicious in quoting Vandyck, who at least specified silks, satins, velvets. Sir Joshua's draperies represent clothes, never their materials. Yet more: Vandyck and Sir Godfrey Kneller excelled all painters in hands; Sir Joshua's are seldom even tolerably drawn.

H. Walpole to Rev. W. Mason, 10.2.

POETRY

Simplicity is become a very rare quality in a writer . . . Swift and Addison were simple; Pope knew how to be so, but was frequently tinged with affectation; since their day I hardly know a celebrated writer who deserves that character.

Cowper to W. Unwin, 24.11.

To denote by an epithet that water is liquid or that snow is white, is no better than mere tautology.

H. Blair, Lectures on Rhetoric.

Mr. Crabbe is a more agreeable poet than your heroic friend Mr. Hayley, and writes lines that one can remember.

H. Walpole to Rev. W. Mason, 9.6.

Johnson read Crabbe's *The Village* "with great delight" but emended:—

> But, charm'd by him or smitten with his views,
> Shall modern poets court the Mantuan Muse?

to:—

> Must sleepy bards the flattering dream prolong,
> Mechanick echoes of the Mantuan song?

To Reynolds, 4.3.

For brutish Pan in vain might thee assay
With tinkling rhymes *and elegancies terse*, (v.l. *to dash thy nervous verse*)
Sound without sense.

Blake, Imitation of Spenser (date uncertain).

(Probably written some 10 years earlier).

> O thou with dewy locks, who lookest down
> Thro' the clear windows of the morning, turn
> Thy angel eyes upon our western isle,
> Which in full choir hails thy approach, O Spring!
>
> The hills tell each other, and the list'ning,
> Vallies hear; all our longing eyes are turned
> Up to thy bright pavillions: issue forth,
> And let thy holy feet visit our clime!
>
> Come o'er the eastern hills, and let our winds
> Kiss thy perfumèd garments; let us taste
> Thy morn and evening breath; scatter thy pearls
> Upon our love-sick land that mourns for thee,
>
> O deck her forth with thy fair fingers; pour
> Thy soft kisses on her bosom; and put
> Thy golden crown upon her languish'd head,
> Whose modest tresses were bound up for thee.
>> W. Blake, *To Spring*.

> Speak silence with thy glimmering eyes,
> And wash the dusk with silver.
>> W. Blake, *To Evening Star* (*Poetical Sketches*).

R. Holmes succeeded Randolph in Chair of Poetry, Oxford. He was the first Chancellor's prizeman for Latin Verse and published poems and a collation of the Septuagist.

SUBLIME

I was always an admirer of thunder-storms ... but especially an admirer of thunder rolling over the great waters.
>> Cowper to W. Bull, 3.8.

❧ 1784 r. George III ❧

MANNERS AND TASTES

Dryden's *Cock and Fox*, the standard of good sense, poetry, nature and ease ... The cast of the age (I mean in its compositions) is too sombre. The flimsy giantry of Ossian has introduced mountainous horrors. The exhibitions at Somerset House are crowded with Brobdingnag ghosts.

> H. Walpole to H. More, 13.11.

All the sounds that nature utters are delightful, at least in this country.

> 18.9.

We sent up a balloon from Emberton. . . .

I should as little have expected to hear that these (Friendly) islanders had such consummate skill in an art (dancing) that requires so much taste in the conduct of the person, as that they were good mathematicians and astronomers. (Cook's last voyage).

> To J. Newton, 16.8.

> I name thee not, lest so despised a name
> Should move a sneer at thy deserved fame
>> Cowper (to Bunyan), *Tirocinium* (published 1785).

"Very large white satin window curtains with pink satin ribbon binding and pink silk broad fringes with white buttons" supplied by Gillow to Lord Hardwicke, 18 New Cavendish St.

> MS. Soame Museum.

First Mail coach. Mail previously carried by post-boy at 5 miles an hour.

It was reported that at the Opera the Duchess of Rutland shouted "Damn Fox" and that Lady Maria Waldegrave retorted by shouting "Damn Pitt".

MUSIC

Händel Commemoration at Westminster Abbey, the *Messiah*. And Liverpool Musical Festival.

Notwithstanding the justness of the comparison by which you illustrate the folly and wickedness of a congregation assembled to pay divine honour to the memory of Handel, I could not help laughing at the picture you have drawn (in a sermon) of the musical convicts. A people so musically mad as to make not only their future trial the subject of a concert, but even the message of mercy from their King . . . [cf. *Task* vi:—

Content to hear
(O wonderful effect of music's power!)
Messiah's eulogy for Handel's sake.]

Cowper to J. Newton, 21.6 and 14.7.

PAINTING

The habit of contemplating and brooding over the ideas of great geniuses, till you find yourself warmed by the contact is the true method of forming an artist-like mind. . . .

Boucher . . . had often grace and beauty and good skill in composition; but, I think, all under the influence of a bad taste.

J. Reynolds, *Twelfth Discourse.*

POETRY

(The Bhagavad-gîtâ) a performance of great originality, of a sublimity of conception, reasoning and diction, almost unequalled.

W. Hastings (Letter from Benares), 4.10.

A poet of no great fame, of whom I did not know that he existed . . . His name was Collins.

To J. Newton, 19.3.

Beattie, the most agreeable and amiable writer I ever met . . . a poetical imagination.

Cowper to W. Unwin, 5.4.

If I could admire Dante, which asking Dr. Hayley's pardon I do not.

H. Walpole to Earl of Strafford, 7.9.

Miss Seward's poem call'd Louisa, which perfectly ryved my heart, and divested me of appetite, and wou'd ever "send the readers weeping to their beds".

Torrington Diaries, 19.7.

Unless we could imitate him (Pope) in the closeness and compactness of his expression, as well as in the smoothness of his numbers, we had better drop the imitation, which serves no other purpose than to emasculate and weaken all we write. Give me a manly rough line, with a deal of meaning in it, rather than a whole poem full of musical periods, that have nothing but their oily smoothness to recommend them!

Cowper, to bookseller Johnson, n.d.

❧ 1785 r. George III ❧

ARCHITECTURE

To be let and entered upon at midsummer. St. Catherine's Hermitage, most delightfully situated on the side of Lansdown Hill, about a thousand yards from the back of the Royal Crescent of Bath . . . serpentine walks in which is the Hermit's Hut, a comfortable room, a grotesque monument erected to the memory of Chatterton, a large cave, a small stable and thatched chaise-house.

St. James' Chronicle, 3788.

(Old St. Paul's) its vaults, shrines, iles, pillars and painted glass, rendered yet more awful by the accompaniment of the choral service. Does the present modern Church convey these feelings? Certainly not. We justly admire and approve Sir Christopher Wren's Grecian proportions. Truth and propriety gratify the judgment, but they do not affect the imagination.

T. Warton, Milton's Minor Poems.

We went to see the Prince's new palace in Pall Mall (Carlton House). It will be the most perfect in Europe. There is an august simplicity that astonished me. Every ornament is at a proper distance, and not one too large, but all delicate and new, with more freedom and variety than Greek ornaments . . . How sick one shall be, after this chaste palace, of Mr. Adam's gingerbread and sippets of embroidery!

H. Walpole to Lady Ossory, 17.9.

If a model is sought of the most perfect taste in architecture where grace softens dignity, and lightness attempers magnificence; where proportion removes every part from peculiar observation, and deliacy of execution recalls every part to notice; where the position is the most happy, and even the colour of the stone the most harmonious; the virtuoso should be directed to the new front of Wentworth Castle (Wentworth Woodhouse, refronted by William, 2nd earl, from his own design).

H. Walpole, *On Modern Gardening.*

MANNERS AND TASTES

A style may be excellent without grace: for instance Dr. Swift's . . . Addison himself was master of that grace, even in his pieces of humour, and which do not owe their merit to style; and from that combined secret he excels all men that ever lived, but Shakespeare, in humour, by never dropping into an approach towards burlesque and buffoonery, when even his humour descended to characters that in other hands would have been vulgarly low. Is it not clear that Will Wimble was a gentleman, though he always lived at a distance from good company? Fielding had as much humour, perhaps, as Addison; but, having no idea of grace, is perpetually disgusting. His innkeepers and parsons are the grossest of their profession; and his gentlemen are awkward when they should be at their ease. The Grecians had grace in everything . . . Milton . . . if his angels, his Satan and his Adam have as much dignity as the Apollo Belvedere, his Eve has all the delicacy and the graces of the Venus of Medicis; as his description of Eden has the colouring of Albano. Milton's tenderness imprints ideas as graceful as Guido's Madonnas: and the *Allegro, Penseroso* and *Comus* might be denominated from the three Graces.

H. Walpole to J. Pinkerton, 26.6.

(At Warwick) I was enwrapt in all the Chimeras of Chivalry, and romance; and I could have wished to see an armed knight issue from the castle, to lead us to a banquet.

Torrington Diaries, 7.7.

God made the country, man made the town, I.

Elegance . . .
Without it all is gothic as the scene
To which the insipid citizen resorts. III.

A soul in all things and that soul is God.
The beauties of the wilderness are his
That make so gay the solitary place
Where no eye sees them, and the fairer forms
That cultivation glories in are his. VI.

Cowper, Task.

The French excel us all in ornaments of taste—I mean, in such ornaments as do not rise to serious magnificence; but they must keep within doors: they may deck dress, furniture, china and snuff boxes; but buildings, cities, gardens, will not allow of spangles . . . Madame Piozzi's *Anecdotes of Dr. Johnson* . . . seem to have taken his brutal contradictions for *bons mots*. Some of his own works shew that he had at times strong excellent sense.

28.3.

La Piozza, from whom I have just seen a very clever letter to Mrs. Montague, to disavow a jackanapes who has lately made a noise here, one Boswell, by anecdotes of Dr. Johnson.

H. Walpole to Sir H. Mann, 16.3.

Gibbon was told that 40,000 English (including servants) were touring or resident on the continent.

(Cf. 1765.)

PAINTING

I don't wonder you was disappointed with Jarvis's windows (Reynolds' design) at New College; I had foretold their miscarriage. The old and new are as mismatched as an orange and a lemon; nor is there room enough to retire back and see half of the new; and Sir Joshua's washy Virtues make the "Nativity" a dark spot from the darkness of the shepherds, which happened, as I knew it would, from most of Jarvis's colours being transparent.

H. Walpole to Hon. H. S. Conway, 6.10
(cf. T. Warton, 1782).

Sir J. Reynolds at Brussels bought 5 Rubens, 3 Vandycks and a Snyders.

390

The best Masters whose most capital works we have here in Rome, particularly the Carracci, Domenichino, Poussin, Salvator Rosa &c.

Jacob More to Thomas Harvey (August).

Almost every man of taste is in some degree a collector of prints.

Strutt, *Dictionary of Engravers*.

POETRY

T. Warton, the younger, laureate in succession to Whitehead. He had also been professor of Poetry at Oxford, see index I.

Our versification contracted a new colouring, a new structure and phraseology; and the school of Milton rose in emulation of the School of Pope. (Preface). . . . Milton appears to have had a very bad ear . . . It is hard to say on what principle he modulated his lines (Bore a bright golden flowre but not in this soyl, *Comus* 633). . . .

. . . . .

> Towers and Battlements it sees
> Bosom'd high in tufted Trees.

(*l'Allegro*).

Where only a little is seen, more is left to the imagination. . . . Modern seats are seldom so deeply ambushed. . . . It is certainly a fault (in *Comus*), that the Brothers, although with some indications of anxiety, should enter with so much tranquillity, when their sister is lost, and at leisure pronounce philosophical panegyrics on the mysteries of Virginity. . . . Our Author is here only inferior to his own *Paradise Lost*. . . . My brother remembers to have heard my father say, that when he once, at Magdalene College Oxford, mentioned this volume [Milton's early poems] to Mr. Digby, the intimate friend of Pope, Mr. Digby expressed much surprise that he had never heard Pope speak of them, went home and immediately gave them an attentive reading, and asked Pope if he knew anything of this hidden treasure. Pope availed himself of the question: and accordingly we find him soon afterwards sprinkling his *Eloisa to Abelard* with epithets and phrases of a new form and sound, pilfered from the *Comus* and the *Penseroso*. It is a phenomenon in the history of English poetry, that Pope, a poet not of Milton's pedigree, should be their first copier.

T. Warton, *Milton's Minor Poems*.

For Chatterton, he was a gigantic genius, and might have soared I know not whither. In the poems avowed for his is a line that Rowley nor all the monks in Christendom could or would have written, and which would startle them all for its depth of thought and comprehensive expression from a lad of eighteen—"Reason, a thorn in Revelation's side". . . . I will read no more of Rousseau, his *Confessions* disgusted me beyond any book I ever opened . . . I revere genius; I have a dear friendship for common sense; I have a partiality for professed nonsense; but I abhor extravagance that is given for the quintessence of sense, and affectation that pretends to be philosophy.

4.7.

How little will Dr. Johnson be remembered, when confounded with the mass of authors of his own calibre? . . . The one nation worth studying was the Greek . . . I concentrate my admiration in the few centuries of Greece and for that marvellous period in the Roman history, when five excellent princes, though possessed of absolute power, succeeded to one another, Nerva, Trajan, Hadrian, and the two Antonines.

9.7.

Far was it ever from my thoughts to admire Dr. Akenside or to depreciate Boileau, or not to think Molière a genius of the first water. Who upon earth has written such perfect comedies? for *The Careless Husband* is but one—*The Nonjuror* [both by Colly Cibber] was built on *The Tartuffe;* and if *The Man of Mode* [Etherege] and Vanburgh are excellent, they are too indelicate—and Congreve, who beats all for wit, is not always natural; still less simple.

H. Walpole to C. of Upper Ossory, 29.8.

Ann Yearsley the milk-woman's poems published by H. More (see 1795).

Clara Reeve, *The Progress of Romance* (lent by Rose Aylmer to Landor 1797).

There is not, I believe, in all the world to be found an un-inspired poem so simple as those of Homer; nor in all the world a poem more bedizened with ornaments than Pope's translation of them. Accordingly the *sublime* of Homer in the hands of Pope becomes bloated and tumid and his description tawdry ... All his persons ... speak in an inflated and strutting phraseology ... No writer more pathetic than Homer because none more natural, and because none less natural than Pope in his version of Homer, therefore than he none less pathetic.

Cowper to J. Newton, 10.12.

Homer and *Virgil* have all the advantages of Nature and Art, they may easily allow to *Dante* that single one of appealing to Sentiments and Principles more general and more permanent.

H. Boyd, *Translation of the Inferno.*

(Denham) one should expect would have painted, as nearly as possible, the appearance of a fine river, amidst a beautiful region of hills, woods and vallies. Instead of this, we are presented with a tedious enumeration of supposed qualities (1640).

John Scott, *Critical Essays.*

The eagle is sublime, the lion majestic, the man graceful, the monkey pert, the bear ridiculously awkward ... The colouring of the swan is pure; his attributes are graceful; he never displeases you when sailing in his proper element. His feet may be ugly, his notes hissing, not musical, his walk not natural; he can soar, but it is with difficulty; still, the impression the swan leaves is that of grace. So does Racine. Boileau may be compared to the dog, whose sagacity is remarkable, as well as its fawning on its master and its snarling at those it dislikes. ... Aristophanes and Lucian, compared with moderns were, the one a blackguard, and the other a buffoon. In my eyes the *Lutrin* (Boileau), *The Dispensary* (Garth, 1699), and the *Rape of the Lock*, are standards of grace and eloquence not to be paralleled by antiquity; and eternal reproaches to Voltaire, whose indelicacy in the *Pucelle* degraded him as much when compared with these authors I have named, as his *Henriade* leaves Virgil, and even Lucan, whom he more resembles, by far his superior ... Apollo is graceful, Mercury elegant.

H. Walpole to J. Pinkerton, 26.6.

SUBLIME

Except the Bible, there never was in the world a book so remarkable for that species of the sublime that owes its very existence to simplicity, as the works of Homer. He is always nervous, plain, natural . . . In short, my dear, there is hardly anything in the world so unlike another, as Pope's version of Homer to the original.

Cowper to Lady Hesketh, 15.12.

1786 r. George III

ARCHITECTURE

All theories which attempt to direct or to control the Art, upon any principles falsely called rational, which we form to ourselves upon a supposition of what ought in reason to be the end or means of art, independent of the known first effect produced by objects on the imagination, must be false and delusive. For though it may appear bold to say it, the imagination is here the residence of truth . . . the effect itself being the test and the only test of the truth and efficacy of the means. (Approved by Hazlitt "On Genius and Common Sense", *Table Talk*). . . . The great end of all those arts is, to make an impression on the imagination and the feeling. The imitation of nature frequently does this. Sometimes it fails and something else succeeds. . . . As we have naturally a veneration for antiquity, whatever building brings to our remembrance ancient customs and manners, such as the castles of the Barons of Ancient Chivalry, is sure to give this delight . . . Gothic architecture . . . though not so ancient as the Grecian, is more so to our imagination, with which the artist is more concerned than with absolute truth. . . . As buildings depart from regularity (by additions etc.), they now and then acquire something of scenery by this accident, which I should think might not unsuccessfully be adopted by an architect in an original plan. Variety and intricacy are beauties and excellencies in every other of the arts which address the imagination: and why not in architecture ? . . . Vanbrugh understood light and shadow, and had great skill in composition. To support his principal object, he produced his second and third groups or masses;

394

he perfectly understood in his art what is the most difficult in ours, the conduct of the background . . . and no architect took greater care than he that his work should not appear crude and hard; that is, it did not abruptly start out of the ground, without expectation or preparation.

J. Reynolds, Thirteenth Discourse.

GARDENS

Upon it grew a hundred thickets of eglantine and other fragrant shrubs, a hundred arbors of roses, jessamines and honey-suckle, as many clumps of orange-trees, cedar, and citron whose branches interwoven with the palm, the pomegranate, and the vine, presented every luxury that could regale the eye or the taste. The ground was strewed with violets, hairbells, and pansies, in the midst of which sprang forth tufts of jonquils, hyacinths and carnations, with every other perfume that impregnates the air.

W. Beckford, Vathek (cf. Addison, 1712).

The new bridge at Henley—A Senator of Rome, while Rome survived, would have allowed it worthy of the Tiber; and it traverses a river a thousand times more beautiful; and some Verres, I suppose, some time or other, will strip it of Mrs. Damer's colossal masks.

H. Walpole to Lady Ossory, 30.8.

MANNERS AND TASTES

Good breeding is absolutely necessary to keep the most delicate affections alive.

R. and E. Griffith, Genuine Letters o,
Henry and Frances (Complete Edition, see
1751).

The whole Jemmy and Jenny Jessamy tribe I abhorred; and it required the art of Burney, or the feeling of Mackenzie, to fix my attention upon a domestic tale. But all that was adventurous and romantic I devoured without much discrimination, and I really believe I have devoured as much nonsense of this class as any man now living. Everything which touched on knight-errantry was particularly acceptable to me, and I soon attempted to imitate what I so greatly admired. My efforts, however, were in the manner of the tale-teller, not of the bard.

> Sir W. Scott, Autobiography (1808),
> b. 1771, and see 1780.

A well-educated British gentleman, it may be truly said, is of no country whatever, he unites in himself the characteristics of all foreign nations; he talks and dresses French, and sings Italian; he rivals the Spaniard in indolence, and the German in drinking, his house is Grecian, his offices Gothic, and his furniture Chinese.

> *The Lounger.*

NATURE

Background [Mountains and Lakes]; Off-skip [Valleys, Woods, Rivers]; Foreground [Rocks, Cascades, Broken ground, Ruins] . . . The pyramidical shape and easy flow of an irregular line will be found the truest source of beauty . . .
(Mountain colours) are rarely permanent; but seem to be a sort of floating, silky colours—always in motion—always in harmony—and playing with a thousand changeable varieties into each other. They are literally colours dipped in heaven . . .
Call for an ancient oak to give the foreground grandeur. . . .
(Between Dunmail Raise and Rydal) a view entirely of the horrid kind, not a tree appearing to add cheerfulness. With regard to the adorning such a scene with figures nothing could suit it better than a group of banditti. Of all scenes I ever saw, this was the most adapted to the perpetration of some dreadful deed. . . .
In a moral view the industrious mechanic is a more pleasing subject than the loitering peasant. But in a picturesque view it is otherwise. The lazy cowherd, resting on his pole, may be allowed in the grandest scene; while the laborious mechanic, with his instruments of labour, would be repulsed. The characters which are most suited to these scenes of grandeur, are such as impress us with some idea of greatness, wildness, or ferocity; all which touch on the sublime. Figures in long, flowing draperies; gypsies; banditti; and soldiers, not in modern regimentals, but as Virgil paints them "Longis adnixi hastis et scuta tenentes" . . . Salvator Rosa. . . . The actions of a

goat are still more pleasing than the shagginess of his coat. . . .
Cows are commonly the most picturesque in the months of
April and May, when the old hair is coming off. . . .
It is the aim of picturesque description to bring the images of
nature as forcibly and as closely to the eye as it can, by high
colouring. High colouring is not a string of rapturous epithets,
but an attempt to analyse the views of nature: to mark their
tints and varied lights and to express all this detail in terms
as appropriate and vivid as possible. . . .
The country at every step loses some of the wild strokes of
nature and degenerates, if I may so speak, into cultivation.

> W. Gilpin, *Observations on Lake District*
> (Lent to F. Burney by Mrs. Delany.
> Wordsworth asked for it in a letter,
> 21.3.1796, cf. Austen, 1796.)

M. Blanc first ascended (Paccard and Balmat).

PAINTING

(Velasquez' Leo X) one of the finest portraits in the world. . . .
(A Dürer portrait) a rare and curious thing.

> Sir J. Reynolds to Duke of Rutland.

Francesca & Paolo by H. Fuseli in R.A.

Bartolozzi, who is only fit to engrave for the *Pastor fido*, will
be to give a pretty enamelled fan-mount of Macbeth! Salvator
Rosa might, and Piranesi might dash out Duncan's castle;
but Lord help Alderman Boydell (an exhibitor) and the Royal
Academy!

> H. Walpole to Lady Ossory, 15.12.

POETRY

The is a barbarism . . . In the two best languages that ever
were spoken, the Greek and the Latin, there is no similar
encumbrance.

> Cowper to Lady Hesketh, 6.3.

397

❀ 1787 r. George III ❀

GARDENS

Carfax Conduit (1610) removed to Nunehan Park.

To suppose a place at first nobly grand—as nature gave it—it shou'd be all wood and water; and then taste shou'd cautiously scoop out the glades and thin the lawns: therefore no man can plant too much; let him cover his ground with trees, and he will then best see where to open views.

Torrington Diaries, 13.8.

MANNERS AND TASTES

Now did I love the dismal gloom
Of haunted castle's panelled room,

.   .   .   .   .

She brought me to a dungeon deep,
Then stopped, and thrice her hand she shook,
More pale and ghastly seemed her look.
The taper turned from green to red,
Flashed out, and with a shriek she fled.

Wordsworth, *The Vale of Esthwaite*
(Juvenilia, cf. 1771, Beattie).

I have read Savary's *Travels into Egypt:* [a favourite book with Kant] *Memoirs du Baron de Tott* (1784). Fenn's (Paston) *Original Letters;* the Letters of *Fredrick of Bohemia;* and am now reading *Memoirs d'Henri de Lorraine, Duc de Guise.* All these together with Madan's *Letters to Priestly.* . . . Mackenzie . . . has more of Addison's delicate humour than anybody.

Cowper to Lady Hesketh, 4.9 and 27.11.

M.C.C. founded.

Society for the suppression of the slave trade founded.

NATURE

De Saussure ascended M. Blanc (the second success, see Northcote 1779. Cf. Ruskin, Mod. Painters iv. 402. First ascent 1786).

The fashion of viewing the mountains and glaciers (has) opened us on all sides to the incursions of foreigners.

Gibbon, *Autobiography*, E.

PAINTING

The picture mania rages as strongly as the musical mania; no less than six places are now open for the exhibition of ancient and modern paintings.

Public Advertiser.

N. Poussin, *The Seven Sacraments* bought by Duke of Rutland (7 pictures) for £2000 and brought to London.

Reynolds, portrait of Lord Heathfield.

The great works of Rubens, (at Blenheim) which are, in my eyes, disgusting and indecent.

Torrington Diaries, 16.8.

POETRY

I have read Burns' poems twice; and though they be written in a language that is new to me, and many of them on subjects much inferior to the Author's ability, I think them on the whole a very extraordinary production. He is, I believe, the only poet these kingdoms have produced in the lower ranks of life since Shakespeare (I should rather say since Prior) who need not be indebted for any part of his praise to Charitable considerations of his origin and the disadvantages under which he has laboured. It will be a pity if he should not hereafter, divest himself of barbarism, and content himself with writing pure English, in which he appears perfectly qualified to excell. He who can command admiration dishonours himself if he aims no higher than to raise a laugh. . . . Barclay's Argenis (1621) . . . the most amusing romance that ever was written. . . . It is indeed the only one of an old date that I ever had the patience to go through with. I lent (Burns) to a very sensible neighbour of mine. But his uncouth dialect spoiled all; and, before he had half read him through he was quite *ram-feezled*.

Cowper to S. Rose, 24.7, 27.8.

1788 r. George III

MANNERS AND TASTES

Hepplewhite, *Cabinetmakers and Upholsterer's Guide*, introduced three feathers of his patron, the Prince Regent, inlay of satin wood, now first imported, and heart-shaped design.

NATURE

The banks of the Thames are scarcely more public than those of Windermere.

Wilberforce.

(The 'Lime Colonnade' at Weston) which our modern improvers . . . have displaced . . . because, forsooth, they are rectilinear. It is a wonder they do not quarrel with the sunbeams.

Cowper to Lady Hesbeth, 28.7.

It is difficult to prevent visionary ideas from improving a prospect. (Some "druidic" remains being erected at Park Place).

H. Walpole to Lord Stafford, 12.9.

(We) have been used to see the Muses labouring up . . . many hills since Cooper's and Grongar, and some gentle Bard reclining on almost every molehill.

Gentleman's Magazine.

MUSIC

(Farinelli's technique) "which excited such astonishment in 1734, would be hardly thought sufficiently brilliant in 1788 for a third rate singer at the opera." (d. 1782).

PAINTING

I take more interest in, and am more captivated with, the powerful impression of nature which Gainsborough exhibited in his portraits and in his landscapes, and the interesting simplicity and elegance of his little ordinary beggar-children, than with any of the works of the (Roman) School, since

(Sacchi and Maratti) ... the Ultimi Romanorum. ... We
have the sanction of all mankind in preferring genius in a
lower rank of art to feebleness and insipidity in the highest. ...
From the fields he brought into his painting room, stumps of
trees, weeds and animals of various kinds, and designed them.
... If Gainsborough did not look at nature with a poet's eye,
it must be acknowledged that he saw her with the eye of a
painter.

J. Reynolds, Fourteenth Discourse.

Value of prints exported from Britain to France exceeded that
of those imported thence.

POETRY

"He felt the chastity of silent woe", (Falconer, Shipwreck,
1762) a sweet line.

F. Burney, Diary, July.

Thompson was admirable in description: but it always seemed
to me that there was somewhat of affectation in his style,
and that his numbers are sometimes not well harmonized.
I could wish, too, with Dr. Johnson, that he had confined
himself to this country.

Cowper to Mrs. King, 19.6.

I can easily believe that any tongue (not excepting our old
barbarous Saxon, which, a bit of an antiquary as I am, I
abhor) is more harmonious than French. It was a curious
absurdity, therefore, to pitch on the most unpoetic language
in Europe, the most barren and the most clogged with dif-
ficulties. I have heard Russian and Polish song, and both
sounded musical; but to abandon one's own tongue, and not
adopt Italian, that is even sweeter, and softer, and more copious
than the Latin, was a want of taste that I should think could
not be applauded even by a Frenchman born in Provence.
But what a language is the French, which measures verses by
feet that never are to be pronounced; which is the case wherever
the mute *e* is found! What poverty of various sounds for rhyme,
when, lest similar cadences should too often occur, their
mechanic bards are obliged to marry masculine and feminine
terminations as alternately as the black and white squares of a
chess board! Nay, will you believe me, Madam,—yes, you will,

for you may convince your own eyes—that a scene of Zaïer (Voltaire) begins with three of the most nasal adverbs that ever snorted together in a breath? *Enfin, donc, désormais,* are the culprits in question. *Enfin donc,* need I tell your Ladyship that the author I alluded to at the beginning of this long tirade is the late King of Prussia? . . . But I only condemn it for verse and pieces of eloquence, of which I thought it alike incapable, till I read Rousseau of Geneva. It is a most sociable language and charming for narrative and epistles.

H. Walpole to Lady Craven, 11.12.

Scott in Edinburgh heard Mackenzie read a paper on romantic German literature.

PART VI
1789—1800

o

❧ 1789 r. George III ❧

ARCHITECTURE

(Clumber) chapel is in the modern, frippery, Adamatic style, and glazed with the modern stain'd glass, flurrying the sight and of no awful gloom.

Torrington Diaries, 9.6.

MUSIC

It may be asked, what entertainment is there for the mind in a *concerto*, *sonata* or *solo*? They are mere objects of gratification to the ear, in which, however, imagination may divert itself with the idea that a fine *adagio* is a tragical story; an *andante* or *grazioso* an elegant narrative of some tranquil event, and an *allegro*, a tale of merriment.

C. Burney, *History of Music IV*.

MANNERS AND TASTES

Mrs. Radcliffe (b. 1764, the date of *Castle of Otranto*). *The Castles of Athlin and Dumblayne*, a first novel. Scene in N.E. Scotland "the most romantic part of the Highlands".

How much the greatest event (the fall of the Bastille) is that has ever happened in the world, and how much the best!

C. J. Fox to Fitzpatrick, July.

Dr. R. Price preached on the fall of the Bastille.

Sherry bought for Eton College at £68 12s. 6d. per pipe.

There is something peculiarly sweet and amusing in the shapely figured aspect of chalk-hills in preference to those of stone, which are rugged, broken, abrupt and shapeless. . . . I never contemplate these mountains without thinking I perceive something analogous to growth in their gentle swellings and smooth fungus-like protuberances, their fluted sides and regular hollows.

White, *Natural History of Selborne*.

NATURE

An eye like Dr. Johnson's, which he himself acknowledged was accustomed only to see the beauties of landscape in "flowery pastures" and "waving harvests" cannot be attracted by the great and sublime in nature. As for a Scotch mountain being incapable of form, ("The appearance is that of matter, incapable of form or usefulness, dismissed by nature from her care and left in its original elemental state." Dr. Johnson) he can only mean that it cannot be formed into meadows. Its form as a mountain is grand and sublime in the highest degree.

W. Gilpin, *Observations on . . . The Highlands of Scotland* (see 1775).

PAINTING

Portraits by Sir Peter Lely, extremely soft and pleasing, and of subjects uncommonly beautiful.

F. Burney, *Diary*, 16.9.

POETRY

Read Sinbad's the Sailor's Voyages and you will be sick of Aeneas. . . . I never saw any other Oriental composition that was not bombast without genius and figurative without nature; like an Indian screen. . . . Criticism and comparison spoil many tastes. You should admire all bold and unique essays that resemble nothing else; *The Botanic Garden*, the *Arabian Nights* and *King's Chapel* are above all rules. . . . Your partiality to the pageantry of popery I do approve and I doubt whether the world would not be a loser (in its visionary enjoyments) by the extinction of that religion, as it was by the decay of Chivalry and the proscription of the heathen deities.

To Mary Berry, 30.6. (On *Arabian Nights*, cf. Wordsworth, *Prelude V* and VIII.)

[Erasmus Darwin's *Botanic Garden*]. If you are not a naturalist as well as a poetess, perhaps you will lament that so powerful a talent has been wasted to so little purpose. . . . The similies are beautiful, fine, and sometimes sublime; and thus the episodes will be better remembered than the mass of the poem itself, which one cannot call the subject. . . . Still . . . the author is a great poet, and could raise the passions, and possesses all the requisites of the art.

H. Walpole to Hannah More, 22.4.

(Also praised by Cowper, Hayley and Coleridge. Influenced young Wordsworth, partly by its theory of poetry, preferring concrete to abstract. On poetic "subject", cf. A. Bradley, *Poetry for Poetry's Sake*).

A line of his favourite Mason:—"Weave the light dance in festive freedom gay". Mr. Smelt is seriously of opinion Mrs. Carter's *Ode to Wisdom* is the best in our language. (Probably:—

> "The solitary bird of night
>   Through the thick shades now wings his flight,
>   And quits the time-shook tower;
>   Where sheltered from the blaze of day
>   In philosophic gloom he lay
>   Beneath his ivy bower", etc.

It was inserted by Richardson in Clarissa, Vol. II . . . (Mr. Farly thinks Pope's Eloisa) "but too beautiful, and that is its greatest fault" . . . (Young) What a nobleness of expression, when noble, has this poet! What exquisite feeling. What forcible ideas!

F. Burney, Diaries, 12.1, 18.2.

> Green sloping lawns construct the sidelong scene,
> And guide the sparkling rill that winds between.

E. Darwin, Botanic Garden.

Bowles, William L., published "XIV Sonnets on Picturesque Spots". Coleridge Sonnet on them.

As (Pope) was supposed to have improved upon his Master our poets seem ambitious of improving theirs. . . . He rejected every Thing that was not rich; they reject every Thing that is not brilliant. . . . He is everywhere clear and manly; they not infrequently torture into Obscurity, and refine into Imbecility. Tinsel Phrases and tinkling compound Epithets . . . to exclude any Mode of Expression from Poetry which is so unlucky as to find a Place in Prose.

J. Weston, Essay on the Superiority of
Dryden's Versification over that of Pope.

(The age of Pope) generally called the Augustan.

> Anna Seward, *Gentleman's Magazine*,
> April.

When thirst and hunger griev'd her most,
  If any food she took,
It was the berry from the thorn
  The water from the brook.

From every hedge a flower she pluck'd,
  And moss from every stone,
To make a garland for her Love,
  Yet left it still undone.

Still as she rambled was she wont
  To trill a plaintive song,
'Twas wild, and full of fancies vain,
  Yet suited well her wrong.

Oft too a smile, but not of joy,
  Play'd on her brow o'ercast;
It was the faint cold smile of Spring
  Ere Winter yet is past.

> T. Russell, *The Maniac* (cf. Wordsworth).

Deep in his breast he feels the deadly wound,
  And gnaws in bootless rage the unconscious ground.
The delineation, however, of these manners has been but a
secondary consideration. This performance is chiefly referred
to the tribunal of Fancy, and if there condemned, it makes no
further appeal.

> Rev. R. Hole. *Arthur or the Northern Enchant-
> ment. A Poetical Romance in Seven Books.*

PROGRESS

Flanges transferred from lines to wheels on railways. [Tennyson
appears to have been unaware of this when in *Locksley Hall*
(1877) he wrote:
"Let the great world spin for ever down the ringing grooves of
change"]

✿ 1790 r. George III ✿

ARCHITECTURE

Nothing can be more noble, more Gothic, or more elegantly carved than the front (now tottering) of Croyland Abbey; a beauty of the richest workmanship; my eyes gloried in beholding, whilst my heart sick'ned at the destruction.

Torrington Diaries, 2.7.

I wish William of Wickham were alive to employ and reward Mr. Wyatt.

H. Walpole to Hannah More, 25.7.

Gothic architecture is hastening out of fashion.

Gentleman's Magazine.

MANNERS AND TASTES

The age of chivalry is gone. That of sophisters, economists and calculators has succeeded; and the glory of Europe is extinguished for ever. Never more shall we behold that generous loyalty to rank and sex, that proud submission and dignified obedience, that subordination of the heart, which kept alive, even in servitude itself, the spirit of an exalted freedom.

Burke, *Reflections on F. Revolution*.

(Burke's *French Revolution*) came out this day sennight, and is far superior to what was expected, even by his warmest admirers. I have read it twice; and though of 350 pages, I wish I could repeat every page by heart. It is sublime, profound and gay. The wit and satire are equally brilliant; and the whole is wise, though in some points he goes too far: yet in general there is far less want of judgment than could be expected of *him* . . . 7,000 copies have been taken off by the booksellers already, and a new edition is preparing.

H. Walpole to Mary Berry, 8.11.

("Pure foppery" Francis. "Should be read by every gentleman" George III. "The noblest, deepest, most animated and exalted work I have ever read", Fanny Burney.)

The effect . . . produced by associations, in increasing the emotions of sublimity or beauty, is produced also, either in nature, or in description by what are generally termed Picturesque Objects. An old tower in the middle of a deep wood, a bridge flung across a chasm between rocks, a cottage on a precipice . . . suggest an additional train of conceptions. The Gothic Castle is still more sublime than all; because besides the desolation of Time, it seems also to have withstood the assaults of War. . . . Strong and Massy Furniture is everywhere vulgar and unpleasing.

Some years ago every article of [furniture] was made in what was called the *Chinese Taste*. . . . To this succeeded the *Gothic Taste*. . . . The Taste which now reigns is that of the *Antique*. Everything we now use, is made in imitation of those models which have been lately discovered in Italy.

Alison, Principles of Taste.

The Halls of Eblis (in *Vathek*) form an hell, solemn and striking as the fiery Deserts of Dante, or the Erebus of Milton.

Anna Seward to H. Repton.

The idea of dining without a napkin seems ridiculous to a Frenchman, but in England we dine at the tables of people of tolerable fortune without them.

A. Young, Travels.

NATURE

At the lake of Como, my mind ran through a thousand dreams of happiness, which might be enjoyed upon its banks, if heightened by conversation and the exercise of the social affections. Among the more awful scenes of the Alps, I had not a thought of man, or a single created being; my whole soul was turned to him who produced the terrible majesty before me.

Wordsworth to Dorothy, 6.9 (Walking
tour in Revolutionary France).

The contrast between this cultivated valley, and its savage boundaries, was so striking, that it seemed like Beauty reposing in the arms of Horror.

Helen Maria Williams, Julia (cf. Gilpin,
1792) ("A novel interspersed with poetical
pieces").

410

PAINTING

Luca Giordano and Carlo Dolce, no capital masters, and posterior to the excellent.

To Lord Hailes, 21.9.

Correggio never pleased me in proportion to his fame; his grace touches upon grimace; the mouth of the beautiful angels at Parma comes up almost into a half-moon. Still I prefer Correggio to the *lourd* want of grace in Guercino, who is to me a German edition of Guido.

28.11.

Pray worship the works of Masaccio . . . Raphael himself borrowed from him. Fra Bartolomeo, too, is one of my standards for great ideas; and Benvenuto Cellini's Perseus is a rival of the antique though Mrs. D(amer) will not allow it.

H. Walpole to Misses Berry, 29.11.

Lord Radnor paid £600 for the Portrait of the Spanish Admiral Pulido-Pareja and 500 for Vandyck's Gaston Duke of Orleans, (The Velasquaz is) "for vigorous and thoughtful painting unrivalled".

Gazetteer.

Turner first exhibited in R.A. Fuseli elected.

POETRY

Pye succeeded T. Warton as laureate. He was followed by Southey in 1813. Pye wrote *The Progress of Refinement* and other poems, *The Sportsman's Dictionary or Gentleman's Companion*, and other prose works.

Milton . . . is never quaint, never twangs through the nose, but is everywhere grand and elegant, without resorting to musty antiquity for his beauties. On the contrary, he took a long stride forward, left the language of his own day far behind him, and anticipated the expressions of a century yet to come.

Cowper to Lady Hesketh, 22.3

No two languages furnish *equipollent* words.

Lord Thurlow to Cowper.

❧ 1791 r. George III ❧

ARCHITECTURE

Greece where there is nothing left to be seen but that ugly
pigeon-house, the Temple of the Winds.

H. Walpole to M. Berry, 25.9.

(Lincoln) is the finest of our Cathedrals I ever saw; and why
not, when rebuilding in London, follow such a model? How
superior to a lumbering Grecian St. Pauls.

Torrington Diaries, 28.6.

MANNERS AND TASTES

More than four times the number of books are sold now
than were sold twenty years since. The poorer sort of farmers,
and even the poor country people in general, who before that
period spent their winter evenings in relating stories of witches,
ghosts, hobgoblins, etc., now shorten the winter nights by
hearing their sons and daughters read tales, romances, etc.,
and, on entering their houses, you may see *Tom Jones*, *Roderick
Random*, and other entertaining books stuck up on their bacon
racks. . . . Book clubs. . . . Sunday schools.

J. Lackington (bookseller), Memoirs.

Wilton—exquisite Vandykes . . . Milton Abbey Chapel, a
beautiful old building erected in the reign of Athelstan . . .
restoring by Wyatt . . . a really sweet structure, in the light
and most pleasing style of Gothic taste . . . (Road from
Bridport to Lyme), The most beautiful to which my wandering
destinies have yet sent me. It is diversified with all that can
compose luxuriant scenery, and with just as much of the
approach to sublime as is the province of unterrific beauty—
Chiddiock and Charmouth—two of the very prettiest villages
I have ever seen—(Powderham Castle) fitted up in Gallic
taste—as any celebrated cabinet makers'. (Glastonbury Abbey)
most elegant remains of monkish grandeur I ever chanced to
see—perfection of Gothic beauty. (Wells) old castle, now
Bishop's palace, dreary secluded and in bad old style.

F. Burney, Diary, August.

They now crop their hair short and wear no powder. Not being the etiquette yet, (London fops had to refuse an invitation to the Prince's birthday ball at Windsor).

H. Walpole to M. Berry, 8.8.

Sheraton *Cabinetmakers and Upholsterers Guide*. (The backs of chairs reversed to save coat-tails).

MUSIC

Haydn first came to London.

NATURE

One of the voyagers to the Northern seas in sailing up a river thus describes the scene:—
"The country", says he, "on each side was very romantic; but unvaried; the river running between mountains of the most craggy and barren aspect, where there was nothing to diversify the scene; but now and then the sight of a bear, or flights of wild fowl. So uninteresting a passage leaves me nothing farther to add."
It is hardly possible, in so few words, to present more picturesque ideas of the horrid and savage kind. We have a river running up a country broken on both sides with wild, romantic rocks, which, we know nature never constructs in a uniform manner. We naturally therefore conclude, they ran out, in some parts, into vast diagonal strata; on the ledges of which a group of bears might appear, howling at the boat. In other parts, the rocks would form lofty promontories, hanging over the river, and inhabited by numerous flights of screaming wild fowl. This is . . . copied with exactness from Captain King's sketch. And yet he has no conception that a scene so savage could present any other ideas than such as were disgusting. . . . The appearance of blue and purple trees, unless in remote distance, offends, and though the artist may have authority from nature for his practice, yet the spectator, not versed in such effects, may be displeased. Painting, like poetry, is intended to excite pleasure. . . . Of all undergrowth I know but one plant that is disagreeable; and that is the bramble. [The bramble was a favourite of the Pre-Raphaelites.]

W. Gilpin, *Remarks on Forest Scenery*.

413

A habit of looking at nature merely with reference to its affording objects for the pencil, has, at times, given a fastidiousness to (Gilpin's) feelings, and led him away from the perception of those beauties of a superior order which charm the simple lover of the country.

> J. Aikin, *Picturesque Fragment* (cf. Wordsworth *Prelude*, XII, 109:—
> "Unworthily, disliking here, and there
> Liking; by rules of mimic cut transferred
> To things above all art; . . . the moral power,
> The affections and the spirit of the place").

There is more nature in six lines of the Allegro and Penseroso, than in all the laboured imitations of Milton. What is there in Thompson of original?

> H. Walpole to Misses Berry, 18.9.

I would need the pen of Gessner to describe the lovely views which I saw today (Bolzano-Brixen), waterfalls tumbling from the tops of mountains, which are covered with vines and fields. These arid rocks are changed by the industrious peasants into fertile fields. . . .

Mama read the beginning of *Wateck* (Vathek) to us. I went to sleep.

> *Wynne Diaries*, 30.10.

PAINTING

The works of Michael Angelo, Raphael, etc., appear to me to have nothing of (the picturesque); whereas Reubens and the Venetian painters may almost be said to have nothing else. Perhaps *picturesque* is somewhat synonymous to the word *taste*, which we should think improperly applied to Homer and Milton but very well to Pope or Prior.

> J. Reynolds to W. Gilpin, 19.4.

Raeburn first exhibited in R.A.

Sir W. Hamilton, *Engravings from Ancient Vases.*

POETRY

Sound, sound the clarion, fill the fife,
Throughout the sensual world proclaim,
One crouded hour of glorious life
Is worth an age without a name.

> T. O. Mordaunt, *Verses During the War.*

You praise our sires, but, though they wrote with force,
Their rhymes were vicious and their diction coarse;
We want their *strength;* agreed. But we atone
For that, and more, by *sweetness* all our own.
(For instance)
"Hasten to the lawny vale,
Where yellow morning breathes her saffron gale
And bathes the landscape."

> (R. Merry, *Laurel of Libery* 1790).
> W. Gifford, *The Baviad.*

As when, around the clear bright moon, the stars
Shine in full splendour and the winds are hushed;
The groves, the mountain-tops, the headland heights
Stand all apparent, not a vapour streaks
The boundless blue, but ether opened wide,
All glitters, and the shepherd's heart is cheered.

> Cowper (*Iliad* VIII, 555, cf. 1611 and
> 1614 Chapman, 1674 Hobbes, 1720 and
> 1726 Pope).

1792 r. George III

ARCHITECTURE

Instead of following the modern style of building churches
and chapels, which are in general square chambers, with
small sash windows and fashionable decorations hardly to
be distinguished, when the altars and benches are removed,
from common assembly rooms, it was concluded upon to
imitate the models in this kind, which have been left to us by
our religious ancestors, who applied themselves to the cultivation and perfection of ecclesiastical architecture.

> J. Milner, *History of Winchester*, published
> 1798 (referring to the chapel he rebuilt
> this year at Winchester).

MANNERS AND TASTES

In this year were founded: (1) the London Corresponding Society by Thomas Hardy, a shoemaker; a political club for working men to promote parliamentary reform; subscription one penny weekly: (2) the Friends of the People by Lord Grey, "to restore Freedom of Election, and a more equal representation of the People in Parliament . . . to secure to the People a more frequent exercise of their Rights of Electing their Representatives", subscription 2½ guineas yearly.

Having a considerable taste for the Beauties of Nature, her curiosity to behold the delightful scenes it exhibited in that part of the World had been so much raised by Gilpin's Tour to the Highlands, that she had prevailed on her Father to undertake a Tour to Scotland. . . .

They said he was Sensible, well-informed, and Agreeable; we did not pretend to Judge of such trifles, but as we were convinced he had no soul, that he had never read the sorrows of Werter, and that his Hair bore not the least resemblance to auburn, we were certain that Janetta could feel no attraction for him.

> J. Austen, *Love and Freindship* (*sic*), written when "about 17", b. 1775. Her favourite poets Cowper and Crabbe.

A piece of Palladian architecture may be elegant in the last degree . . . But if we introduce it in a picture it immediately becomes a formal object and ceases to please. Should we wish to give it picturesque beauty, we must use the mallet . . . beat down one half of it, deface the other. Here is beauty indeed—Beauty lying in the lap of Horrour! . . .

> Heedless he, meanwhile,
> That what he deems the triumph of his taste,
> Is but a painted survey, a mere map;
> Which light and shade and perspective misplac'd,
> But serve to spoil.

> W. Gilpin, *Three Essays . . . to which is added a Poem in Landscape Painting* (cf. Williams, 1790).

POETRY

Dr. Darwin . . . *The Triumph of Flora* beginning at the fifty-ninth line, is most beautifully and enchantingly imagined: and the twelve verses that by miracle describe and comprehend the creation of the universe out of chaos, are in my opinion the most sublime passage in any author.

H. Walpole to T. Barrett, 14.4.

"Let there be light!" proclaimed the Almighty Lord,
Astonished Chaos heard the potent word;
Through all his realms the kindling ether runs,
And the mass starts into a million suns;
Earths round each sun with quick explosions burst,
And second planets issue from the first;
Bend, as they journey with projectile force,
In bright ellipses their reluctant course;
Orbs wheel in orbs, round centres centres roll,
And form, self-balanced, one reluctant whole;
Onward they move amid their bright abode,
Space without bound, the bosom of their God.

E. Darwin, *The Triumph of Flora.*

Soon shall thy arm, *Unconquer'd Steam!* afar
Drag the slow barge, or drive the rapid car;
Or on wide-waving wings expanded bear
The flying-chariot through the fields of air,
—Fair crews triumphant, leaning from above,
Shall wave their fluttering kerchiefs as they move;
Or warrior-bands alarm the gaping crowd,
And armies shrink beneath the shadowy cloud.

E. Darwin, *The Economy of Vegetation* (or 1791).

1793 r. George III (Louis XVI guillotined)

ARCHITECTURE

Florence . . . that beautiful tho' gloomy town. The Tuscan massy, grand style of architecture spreads a solemnity, 20.6.

Alfieri the great Sophocles of Italy.

Elizabeth Lady Holland, *Journal*, 22.6.

MANNERS AND TASTES

The man of taste and liberal accomplishments . . . The beauties of nature are all his own. He admires the overhanging cliff, the wide-extended prospect, the vast expanse of the ocean, the foliage of the woods, the sloping lawn and the waving grass. He knows the pleasures of solitude, when man holds commerce alone with the tranquil solemnity of nature . . . He enters with a true relish into the sublime and the pathetic. He partakes in all the grandeur and enthusiasm of poetry.

Godwin, *Political Justice*.

A serenity, a perfect complacency, a full satisfaction that wants nothing, looks forward to nothing, leaves no wish to be anything or anywhere but what I am and where I am then; all this mixed with more benevolence than I can find perhaps in any other situation. Set me in a romantic valley.

Twining's Correspondence. *Recreation of a Country Clergyman of the XVIII Century* (cf. Stevenson *Virginibus Puerisque*).

Queen Charlotte bought Frogmore and added Gothic temples, rural huts, ruins, hermitage, etc.

(See Ambulator for 1800 and Mme. D'Arblay, F. Burney, V.).

Comte de Lally-Tollendal writing to D'Arblay on his marriage asked in an elaborate P.S. to have his slippers and night-cap sent after him, "Où se cache-t-on quand on écrit de ces choses-là?"

F. Burney, *Diary*, V.

The first of ancient or modern Romances Tom Jones.

Gibbon, *Autobiography*, E.

> Once Man entirely free, alone and wild,
> Was bless'd as free—for he was Nature's child.
>
> .   .   .   .   .
>
> Confess'd no law but what his reason taught,
> Did all he wish'd and wish'd but what he ought.
>
> .   .   .   .   .

Ev'n so, by faithful Nature guarded, here
The traces of primaeval Man appear,
The simple dignity no forms debase,
The eye sublime, and surly lion-grace.
Wordsworth (The Swiss Peasant),
Descriptive Sketches.

Dorothy Wordsworth to J. Pollard on 10.7. compares William
to Beattie (see 1771).

PAINTING

Dutch and Flemish pictures from Orleans collection exhibited
in London and visited by 20,000 people at 1/- in last week.
Rembrandt's *Mill* fetched 500 gns.
Rubens' *Judgment of Paris*, 2000 gns.
„   *Continence of Scipio*, 800 gns.
„   *Thomyris*, 1200 gns.
„   *St. George*, 1000 gns.
Vandyck, *Family of Charles I*, 1000 gns.
Teniers several 3-500 gns.
Dow several 300 gns.

Beechey and Hoppner elected A.R.A.s, 13 & 12 votes
respectively.

The foreground of this Landscape (from St. George's Hill,
Walton-on-Thames) being barren and brown Heath it is only
for an extensive command of distance that it can be pleasing.

30.10.

Lawrence, R.A. . . . His price for portraits is 40 guineas for a
three-quarter, 80 guineas for a half-length, and 160 guineas
for a whole-length.

26.10.

Angelica Kauffman the paintress made about £14,000 while
she resided in England. Her application was very constant.
Zucchi made about £8,000 while he was in England.

6.11.

Beechey has 30 guineas for a three-quarter portrait. Romney
has the same. Beechey raised his price 10 guineas after the
last exhibition.

13.11.

Opie asked 100 guineas for picture of Ruth.

20.11.

Opie has bought a three-quarter length by Sir Joshua Reynolds, for which he gave . . . 60 guineas. The subject a girl resting on her arms. Opie thinks Sir Joshua was the greatest colourist that we have any knowledge of by their works, including the Italian and Flemish masters.

Hoppner dwelt much on the general bad taste which prevails in this country. That the silly poetry of the Della Cruscan (*sic*) and the works of Angelica in painting have captivated the public . . . He contemplates the works of Sir Joshua Reynolds with reverential respect.

Farrington, *Diaries*, 25.11.

Raphael and A. Caracci are the first masters at Rome.

4.6.

Pietro di Perugino, more known by the works of his disciples than from his own merits.

Eliz. Lady Holland, *Journal*, 17.6.

Flaxman's Designs from Dante published at Rome.

POETRY

I had Milton's example for it (inversion), not disapproved by Addison . . . I know that they give dignity and am sorry to part from this; but, to parody an old proverb, he who lives in the year ninety-three must do as in the year ninety-three is done by others.

Cowper to S. Rose, 17.2.

Hurdis succeeded Holmes in chair of poetry, Oxford. He published *The Village Curate, On the Prospect of the Marriage of the Prince of Wales* and other poems, and corresponded with Cowper.

Dr. Wolcot (Peter Pindar) . . . gave his opinion in favour of Dr. Young, author of the Night Thoughts, as next in poetical powers to Shakespeare.

Farrington, *Diaries*, 29.11.

SCULPTURE

The *Gladiator* is the finest statue in Rome. The *Laocoon* is *terribly* fine.

23.5.

A beautiful bronze statue of the *Boy picking out the thorn* in his foot.

Eliz. Lady Holland, *Journal*, 4.6.

STAGE

(Bannister in *The Children in the Wood*.) His transports of despair and joy are incomparable, and his various countenances would be adequate to the pencil of Salvator Rosa. He made me shed as many tears as I suppose the original ballad did when I was six years old.

H. Walpole to Miss M. Berry, 4.12.

❧ 1794 r. George III ❧

ARCHITECTURE

I wish you had seen Canterbury some years ago, before they whitewashed it.

H. Walpole to Mary Berry, 27.9.

(Barfreston Ch.) The Eastern Front is worthy of much observation, for where is more of Saxon antiquity, or an upper (rose) window of more Beauty?

Torrington, *Diaries*, 22.10.

GARDENS

T'adorn, arrange, to separate and select
With secret skill and counterfeit neglect
I sing—Do thou, O Price, the song attend.

· · · · ·

No leaf of fern, low weed or creeping thorn
But, near the eye, the landscape may adorn.

· · · · ·

Bless'd is the man, in whose sequestered glade
Some ancient abbey's walls diffuse their shade;
With mould'ring windows pierc'd, and turrets crown'd,
And pinnacles with clinging ivy bound.
Bless'd too is he, who 'midst his tufted trees,
Some ruin'd castle's lofty towers sees,
Imbosom'd high upon the mountain's brow,
Or nodding o'er the stream that glides below.
Nor yet unenvied, to whose humbler lot,
Falls the retired antiquated cot:—
Its roof with weeds and mosses cover'd o'er,
And honeysuckles climbing round the door;
While mantling vines along its walls are spread,
And clustering ivy decks the chimney's head.

．　　．　　．　　．　　．

No poor Baalbec dwindled to the eye
And Paestum's fanes with columns six feet high.

．　　．　　．　　．　　．

Hence, hence! thou haggard fiend, however called,
The meagre genius of the bare and bald.
Thy spade and mattock here at length lay down,
And follow to the tomb thy fav'rite Brown:
Thy fav'rite Brown, whose innovating hand
First dealt thy curses o'er this fertile land.

．　　．　　．　　．　　．

Keswick's favour'd pool,
Is made the theme of ev'ry wandering fool.

．　　．　　．　　．　　．

To make the landscape grateful to the sight,
Three points of distance always should unite;
And howsoe'er the view may be confin'd,
Three mark'd divisions we shall always find:
Not more.

> R. Payne Knight, *The Landscape.*

(To Uvedale Price, on Capability Brown; "imbosomed" and
"tufted trees" from Milton).

MANNERS AND TASTES

He sate down [with a flute, which "will have a romantic effect"]
amid the most awful part of the ruins [of Denbigh Castle];
the moon just began to make her rays predominant over the

lingering day-light; I pre-attuned my feelings to emotion; and the romantic youth instantly struck up the sadly pleasing tunes of *Miss Carey, The British Lion is my Sign* and *A roaring trade I drive.*

Coleridge to Southey, 15.7.

The whole formed a picture highly grotesque, the travellers plainly saw their danger. He sent forward a transforming eye into the distant obscurity . . . St. Aubert smiled and sighed at the romantic picture of felicity his fancy drew, and sighed again to think that Nature and simplicity were so little known to the world, as that true pleasures were thought romantic. Emily gazed with melancholy awe upon the castle, for though it was lighted up by the setting sun, the Gothic greatness of its features, and its mouldering walls of dark grey stone, rendered it a gloomy and sublime object.

Mrs. Radcliffe, Mysteries of Udolpho. (J.
Warton sat up all night reading it. She
visited the Rhine this year).

It is not here that a sunset is improved by a Claude Lorrain's glass (Smyrna), 29.9.

Morritt of Rokeby, Letters.

(Continually quotes Gilpin on scenery. "Arch-master" of the Dilettanti Society. Founder of Travellers Club).

Lord Rokeby, a very singular man who allows his beard to grow, eats only raw meat.

Farrington, Diaries, 29.11.

Cataracts and mountains are good occasional society, but they will not do for constant companions.

W. Wordsworth to M. Mathews, 7.11.

PAINTING

Turner praised by *St. James Chronicle* (13.5) for outline, colour and subject, and by *Morning Post* as among best exhibitors at the Academy, where he now appeared for first time.

Alb. Dürer, Holbein, etc., which are very ugly; but striking
as they shew the progress of the art.

Morritt of Rokeby, *Letters*, 24.6.

The study of pictures can only produce any real advantage
if we use it as a school in which we may learn to enlarge,
correct and refine our view of Nature and by that route become
good judges of scenery . . . (Guido Reni) that pleasing languor
which the union of all that is beautiful impresses on the soul . . .
Corelli's famous pastorale . . . Salvator has a savage grandeur,
often in the highest degree sublime . . . a Handel chorus . . .
vastness and obscurity. But Mola's scenes and figures are, for
the most part, neither sublime nor beautiful; they are the
most perfect examples of the higher style of the picturesque . . .
Roughness and sudden variation joined to irregularity . . . A
capricious movement of Scarlatti or Haydn . . . Salvator Rosa
is one of the most remarkable among painters for his picturesque
effects. . . There are so few perfect compositions in nature.

Uvedale Price, *Essay on the Picturesque*
(cf. Gilpin, 1782).

Stothard, Lawrence and Westall were elected Royal
Academicians on Feb. 10. Hoppner is much mortified at losing
the election. Mr. West gave a casting vote in favour of Westall.
The general opinion is that Lawrence this year is inferior to
Hoppner.

30.4.

This day I recd. a letter from Sir George Beaumont at Chelten-
ham desiring me to purchase a picture by Wilson belonging
to Ld. Thanet, now in sale at Vandergucht who demanded
100 guineas for the picture . . . Vandergucht told me that the
pictures of Wilson are getting into great request . . . the
pictures of Gainsborough are decreasing in value . . . He sold
a Claude for 1500 guineas.

15.7.

(The gift of Sir G. Beaumont's pictures and the purchase of the
Angerstein collection were the foundation of the National
Gallery in 1824. See 1797 and 1799).

(Charles James Fox) entertains the highest opinion of Sir Joshua Reynolds—and thinks very favourably of Northcote and Opie—Of West he spoke with contempt, and thinks slightly of the works of Fuseli.

Farrington, Diaries, 18.9.

T. Girtin, aged 19, exhibited at R.A.

POETRY

A poet of whom I had heard but little, Cowper: he is excellent, and hugely repaid the labour of reading many hundred lines in blank verse, many of which are inharmonious.

Elizabeth Lady Holland, Journal, 10.6.

Ainsi, à observer depuis Homère jusqu'à nos jours, les progrès de la littérature, qu'on peut regarder comme l'expression de la société, on la voit passer graduellement du genre familier et naïf et en quelque sort domestique, au genre d'un naturel plus noble, et qu'on peut appeler public.

De Bonald, Théorie du pouvoir politique et religieux. Du style et de la littérature.

1795 r. George III

ANTIQUARIANISM

Chair of Anglo-Saxon founded at Oxford.

ARCHITECTURE

I never saw the Ionic order more beautiful, and begin really to think the ancient Grecians were inspired by some genius of elegance and taste that has since given over business.

(Erectheum).
Morritt of Rokeby, Letters, 18.21.1.

Carter, the Gothic draughtsman, has been at Durham lately, and is much dissatisfied with alterations making by Wyatt in the Cathedral; who instead of restoring, which is all that Carter thinks ought to be done, is introducing parts quite out of character.

Farrington, Diaries, 25.11.

[Vanbrugh's] first point seems to have been massiness, as the foundation of grandeur. Then to prevent that mass from being a lump, he has made various bold projections of various heights which from different points serve as the foregrounds to the main building. And, lastly, having probably been struck with the variety of outline against the sky in many Gothic buildings, he raised on the top a number of decorations. . . . There is no pure Gothic. . . . If the owner of such a spot, instead of making a regular front and sides, were to insist on having many of the windows turned towards the points where the objects were most happily arranged, the architect would be forced into the invention of a number of picturesque forms and combinations which otherwise might never have occurred to him; and would be obliged to do what so seldom has been done—accommodate his building to the scenery, not make that give way to his building.

Uvedale Price, Essay on Architecture.

GARDENS

The eye of taste or experience hates compulsion and turns away in disgust from every artificial means of attracting it; for this reason an avenue is most pleasing, which, like that at Langley Park, climbs up a hill and, passing over the summit, leaves the fancy to conceive its termination.

H. Repton, Sketches and Hints of Landscape Gardening.

Il ne pouvait plus s'arracher au spectacle mélancolique et doux de la nuit éclairée par la lune. . . . Il voyait avec un plaisir inconnu jusque-là le spectacle des variétés de la nature, la naissance et la fin du jour, le chant des oiseaux, le murmure des eaux, les nattes des prairies. . . . Il passait des heures entières méditant au fond des bois, et le soir il y restait jusqu'à minuit à la lueur de l'astre argenté des amours.

Napoléon Buonaparte, Clisson et Eugénie
(Revue des deux Mondes, Nov., 1939.)

MANNERS AND TASTES

My ingenious contemporaries have so fully possessed themselves of every bastion and buttress, of every gallery and gateway, together with all their furniture of ivy mantles and mossy battlements, tapestry and old pictures, owls, bats and ravens, that I . . . have hardly a watch-tower, a Gothic arch, a cedar parlour, an illuminated window left to help myself.

Charlotte Smith, The Banished Man (2nd ed.).

To trace the possible effects of the principal abuses of the social system on a Youth more accustomed to feel than to reason; who is doomed, when his sentiments have been roused to a high-toned enthusiasm, by contemplating the wildest features of nature through the magnifying medium of sensibility, to view not only the effects of the selfish principle in others, but to feel himself its unfortunate victim.

Ch. Lloyd, Oswald.

Lewis, *The Monk*. (Sale prohibited till expurgated next year). "*Alonzo the Brave and the Fair Imogene*." He influenced Scott and procured the publication of his translation of Götz von Berlichingen.

Tax of a guinea on use of hair-powder.

NATURE

Beholding constantly the Best possible we at last become ourselves the best possible. In the country, all around us smile Good and Beauty. Thompson, in that most lovely Poem, The Castle of Indolence, says You cannot shut the Windows of the Sky . . . Alas! Alas! she *can* deny us all this and can force us to *wish* and *wish* away the bitter Little of life, in the felon-crowded Dungeon of a great City.

To Dyer, Jan.

Dovedale, a place beyond expression tremendously sublime.

Coleridge to Poole, Aug.

PAINTING

Calonne sale. Best prices:—

Claude, *Enchanted Castle*, 520 gns.
N. Poussin, *Triumph of David*, 600 gns.
D. Teniers, *Village Feast*, 700 gns.
N. Poussin, *Bacchanalian Dance*, 870 gns. (Nat. Gallery).
Murillo, *Gipsy Girl*, 640 gns.
Sal. Rosa, *Seaport*, 500 gns.

Picture of Parmigiano bought by the Marquiss of Abercorn for 1500 gns.

9.12.

Fuseli spoke lightly of the Last Supper at Milan by Leonardo da Vinci. Among the Apostles some of the characters are expressive, but not elevated.

Farrington, 23.12.

"St. Peter Weeping" by *Guido* reckoned the first of his works and the most faultless picture in Italy. *Agostino Caracci* is nowhere so great as in his mellow picture representing the "Woman taken in Adultery".

22.11.

"St. Agnes" [lately in the Pinacoteca, Turin] Ld. Holland read me a passage out of a letter from Charles Fox, from which it appears that he reckons this picture almost the best in Italy, and the masterpiece of Domenichino.

Eliz. Lady Holland, *Journal*, 25.11.

POETRY

The sonnet; a form of composition I do not love, and which is almost intolerable in any language but Italian, which furnishes such a profusion of rhymes. To our tongue the sonnet is mortal, and the parent of insipidity. The imitation in some degree of it was noxious to a true poet, our Spenser; and he was the more injudicious by lengthening his stanza in a language so barren of rhymes as ours; The consequence is that many lines . . . are unmeaning or silly.

H. Walpole to W. Roscoe, 4.4.

All the critics—J. Warton, Twining, Nares and Dr. Charles— say that Metastasio's *Estratto dell' Arte Poetica d'Aristotele,* which I am now translating, is the best dramatic criticism that has ever been written. "Bless my heart!" says Warton, "I, that have been all my life defending the three unities, am overset."

Dr. Burney in F. Burney, *Diary*, 7.5.

Wordsworth met Coleridge. Wrote *Borderers* under Godwin's influence.

Southey and Coleridge lectured at Bristol.

Surely solitude is the soul's home! She has no other; even when her finest energies go forth in love and friendship, and by placing her happiness in the power of others, she robs herself; yet she pursues that happiness by the strength of imagination; and loves the shadow never to be overtaken; till finding her folly too late, she returns to solitude and reflection.

> The rising sun is thine, the sultry noon,
> Grey-footed morning, and the evening star;
> The midnight shadow, when the silent moon
> Half-horn'd, on ending space is seen afar.

Ann Yearsley (The Bristol Milkwoman) *The Royal Captives.*

Sir W. Scott translated Goethe *Erl-König* (1782).

1796 r. George III

ARCHITECTURE

(Fonthill to be) an ornamental building which should have the appearance of a convent, be partly in ruins, and yet contain some weatherproof apartments.

Beckford to architect Wyatt.

(The tower, 278 feet high, fell in 1825.)

St. Peter's . . . The circular colonnade before it has the most chaste and noble effect, and no church equals it in approach. I prefer, in point of architecture, the principal façade of St. Paul's to that of St. Peter's exclusive of this, and I wonder such a front could be built with the Pantheon before their eyes. The dome is a glorious thing, and the building altogether is a study for a man's life . . . I own, however, though I think it the most magnificent building in the world, St. Peter's fails in impressing the mind with the religious, gloomy awe one feels so naturally in the long aisles of a Gothic building, for which there is no accounting; but it is impossible to walk in York Minster without a sensation which its namesake here does not produce, though more admirable in every way perhaps.

29.3.

A still more favourite sight of mine here has been the Coliseum by moonlight . . . The shadows were so varied by the trembling light that shot through the arches, and the gradation from the circular form of the building, that scarce any object was ever so calculated for an effect of this sort; I have seen nothing in Rome which has struck me so much, and I have seen most of the admired buildings in it. The Pantheon is the most entire and the most beautiful model of ancient architecture here. The portico is admirable, and the large, low dome is, I think, of a more pleasing shape than the higher proportions of that at St. Peter's . . . What possible language can convey an idea of Raphael's paintings, or do justice to the Apollo of Belvedere? The Laocoon is, I think, at the head . . . the most difficult subject, and, being equally fine, has greater merit. It is really horribly natural.

Morritt of Rokeby, Letters, 1.4.

MANNERS AND TASTES

Round this cave no gaudy flowers were ever permitted to bloom; this spot was sacred to pale lilies and violets . . . Here he formed schemes of delusive joys, stifled the rising sigh, stopped the flowing tear, and in social converse with his dear friend Henry Lambert would oftentimes smoke a comfortable pipe, when the soft radiance of the moon played upon the pearly bosom of the adjacent waters.

Beckford, Modern Novel Writing (cf. R. Graves, 1776).

(Marianne) Nay, mamma, if he is not to be animated by Cowper! (also Shakespeare, Thomson, Scott's Marmion and "every book that tells how to admire an old twisted tree") . . . And you, ye well-known trees! but you will continue the same. No leaf will decay because we are removed! . . . I consider a cottage as the only form of building in which happiness is attainable . . . Admiration of landscape scenery has become a mere jargon . . . (Edward) I shall call hills steep, which ought to be bold; surfaces strange and uncouth, which ought to be irregular and rugged; and distant objects out of sight, which ought only to be indistinct through the soft medium of a hazy atmosphere. . . . A fine country . . . unites beauty with utility . . . a troop of tidy, happy villagers please me better than the finest banditti in the world.

> J. Austen, *Elinor and Marianne*. (Published as *Sense and Sensibility*, 1811, cf. Gilpin, 1786. It excellently reproduces contemporary discussions about taste.)

The proud Keep of Windsor, rising in the majesty of proportion and girt with the double belt of its kindred and coeval towers.

> Burke, *Letter to a Noble Lord.*

De Saussure *Voyages dans les Alpes* (Vol. i. 1779 ii-iv. 1796. Read by Kant).

How I like Camilla? I do not care to say how little . . . This author knew the world and penetrated characters before she had stepped over the threshold; and now she has seen so much of it she has little or no insight at all.

> H. Walpole to Hannah More. 29.8.

Miss Burney for her new novel of Camilla had 1100 guineas subscription, and sold the copy of the work afterwards for 1000 guineas. The novel is so indifferent, it renders the genuineness of her former works suspected.

> Farrington, *Diaries*, 2.9.

PAINTING

Palace Pitti . . . There is vast number of beautiful pictures, some beautiful ones of Rubens, Titian, Guido, but what I liked best was the Vergin della Seggia of Raphael.

> 14.5.

Was again in admiration and extacy in seeing the Venus and Groop of Niobe and the Mercury of jean de Bologna.

> Betsy Wynne, *Diary*, 21.5.

Rembrandt's *Susannah and the Elders* [perhaps now in Louvre] offered for 160 guineas and his *Daniel's Vision* [recently in Berlin] for 210, or both for 350. Sir Joshua valued them at 950.

> 27.1.

West, Cosway and Humphrey spoke warmly in favour of the designs of Blake the Engraver, as works of extraordinary genius and imagination. Smirke differed in opinion from what he had seen, so do I.

19.2.

Lord Berwick has bought the Cuyp with the large horses from Bryant. West some years since gave 900 guineas for it: Lord Berwick pays Bryant 800 guineas.

9.5.

Fuseli . . . mentioned Blake the engraver, whose genius and invention have been much spoke of; Fuseli has known him several years and thinks He has a great deal of invention, but that "fancy is the end and not a means in his designs". He does not employ it to give novelty and decoration to regular conceptions, but the whole of his aim is to produce singular shapes and odd combinations.

24.6.

Buttal's sale I went to. Gainsborough's picture of a Boy in a Blue Vandyke dress sold for 35 guineas. Several of His drawings were sold in pairs, some went so high as 8 guineas and half the pair.

Farrington, *Diaries*, 16.12.

POETRY

(Southey's Joan of Arc, contributions to Bk. II by Coleridge) is alone sufficient to redeem the character of the age we live in from the imputation of degenerating in Poetry, were there no such beings extant as Burns and Bowles, Cowper and—fill up the blank how you please, I say, nothing . . . Your simile of the Laplander "by Niemis" lake, or Balda Zhiok, or the mossy stone of Solfar Kapper will bear comparison with any in Milton for fullness of circumstance and lofty-pacedness of Versification.

10.6.

Burns was the god of my idolatry, as Bowles of yours . . . but you conciliate matters when you talk of the "divine Chit-chat" (of Cowper).

Lamb to Coleridge, 10.12.

Gifford spoke highly of (Burns') powers, saying He thought Burns had more of the true spirit of poetry than any man of his time.

28.7.

In the works of Shakespeare Fox gave the preference to Lear, as being the strongest proof of his extraordinary powers . . . [R. Payn] Knight thought Macbeth superior to Lear in its machinery and poetical excellence.

Farrington, *Diaries*, 5.5.

Translations from German:—

Haller, *The Alps* (1732).
Bürger, *Lenore* (1773), *William and Helen* and *The Chase* (1786) (W. Scott).
Gesner, *Laura or the Influence of a Kiss*.
Wieland, *Silent Fairy Tales*, *Peregrinus Proteus* (1791).
Schiller, *Cabal and Love* (1784), *Fiesco* (1783).

❀ 1797 r. George III ❀

ARCHITECTURE

Wyatt and Lysons much regretted taking away the beautiful Gothick Window at the West end of Windsor Chapel—to make room for the painted glass picture by West, who has persuaded the King to do it. . . .

6.11.

Wyatt thinks St. Peter's, at Rome, bad architecture. It is divided into little parts. It is the size which makes it striking. There is no good modern architecture in Rome—the best specimens are by Raphael. That of Michael Angelo, is very bad. . . . He thinks St. Paul's, in London, very deffective. Window over window, where there is only one story, divides the architecture into little parts, and exhibits a false Idea, as they signify different stories while there is only one. The three *Porticos* are the best parts of the architecture, but should have been only one range of Pillars, instead of Pillars over Pillars.

The best effect of these pillars is from inside of the building when they come into comparison with the Houses. The Portico of St. Martin's in the Fields is good, and excepting the windows, the body of the Church is well designed. The Spire bad.

Farrington, Diaries, 7.11.

MANNERS AND TASTES

"Perhaps" said Mrs. Gardiner, "to the Lakes". "My dear, dear Aunt", (Elizabeth) rapturously cried, "what delight! what felicity! You give me fresh life and vigour. Adieu to disappointment and spleen! What are men to rocks and mountains?"

J. Austen, *First Impressions* (published as *Pride and Prejudice* 1813).

Why is it so sublime to stand at the foot of a dark tower, and look up its height to the sky and the stars?

Ann Radcliffe, Journals.

PAINTING

Opie thinks Lawrence is in a better way to have the opinion of posterity in his favour than Hoppner, who being entirely raised on the works of another (Sir Joshua) and much inferior, cannot lastingly secure the public of his own time, or posterity. Opie thinks Hoppner will be held at the rate of Sir Peter Lely ... he remarked that Lawrence's pictures have a tortoiseshell appearance.

4.1.

Sir George [Beaumont] saw Laborde's collection of the Orleans pictures this afternoon with the "Raising of Lazarus" by Sebastian del Piombo from a design by Michael Angelo, [now stored in the National Gallery]. He is in raptures. It is as large as the transfiguration of Raphael, as a rival to which picture it was painted, and Sir George entirely gives it the preference.

11.3.

Sawrey Gilpin elected R.A. over Beechey. Baker ... said Beechey is the *second* if not the *first* artist in this country ...

434

Marchant defended the Academy by the opinion of Romney [never R.A.] who said the election had done credit to the Society.

12.3.

Mitford [historian] said He thought the characteristic of Claude's pictures is *grandeur*. Sir George [Beaumont] differed from him—thinking Beauty is the prevailing excellence. I agreed with him and asked Mitford. If grandeur is the characteristic of Claude, what is the distinguishing excellence of N. Poussin?; in my opinion all the claims of Claude to Grandeur arose simply from the nature of the scenery which his pictures represent.

20.3.

Fluxman elected A.R.A.

6.11.

Blake's eccentric designs were mentioned. Stothard supported his claims to genius, but allowed He had been misled to extravagances in his art, and He knew by whom. Hoppner ridiculed the absurdity of his designs, and said "Nothing would be more easy than to produce such. They were like the conceits of a drunken fellow, or madman. Represent a fellow sitting in the moon and drowning the sun out . . . that would be a whim of as much merit" . . . Flaxman was mentioned, who Hoppner spoke of with contempt as a draughtsman. "I cannot draw, but I can draw better than Flaxman can, and his thoughts are all borrowed and purloined from a variety of things which he has seen. He has nothing original about him." Stothard defended Flaxman's claims but thought him over-rated.

11.12.

Northcote said "Opie is the first painter of his time; thinks . . . Fuseli . . . a butterfly . . . ingenious and fanciful and amusing, but has no strength of mind, timid, capricious, vain and affected."

Farrington, *Diaries*, 12.12.

Trumbull Sale. Best prices:—

Pordenone, *Dejanira*, 588 gns.
Berghem, *Landscape*, 945 gns.
Raphael, *Madonna du Corset Rouge*, 890 gns.

(Turner's *Fishermen coming Ashore at Sunset*). "We never beheld a piece of the kind possessing more imagination or exciting more awe and sympathy in the spectators."

The Times.

(At the last Academy, the public) went to see Mrs. Taylor by Hoppner; Lady Young by Beechey; some gentlemen by Lawrence and the drawings of Westall.

The Oracle.

POETRY

I prefer the graceful rambling of his (Cowley's) essays even to the courtly elegance and ease of Addison—abstracting from this the latter's exquisite humour.

10.1.

Southey certainly has no pretensions to vie with you in the sublime of poetry; but he tells a plain tale better . . . I think (*Religious Musings*) the noblest poem in the language next after the Paradise Lost.

Lamb to Coleridge, 5.2.

Wordsworth has written a tragedy himself . . . There are in the piece those *profound* touches of the human heart which I find three or four times in *The Robbers* of Schiller, and often in Shakespeare, but in Wordsworth there are no *inequalities*.

June.

Wordsworth complains, with justice, that Southey writes *too much at his ease.* He certainly will make literature more *profitable to him* from the fluency with which he writes, and the facility with which he pleases himself; his exquisite beauties will lose half their effect from the bad company they keep. Besides I am fearful that he will begin to rely too much on *story* and *event* in his poems, to the neglect of those lofty *imaginings*, that are peculiar to and definitive of the poet.

Coleridge to J. Cottle.

(Contemporary) English style the best.

Godwin, *The Enquirer.*

Finished Dante's Purgatorio.

H. F. Cary, Jan., 1-22.

Nothing can exceed the exquisite taste with which the diction of *The Botanic Garden* (E. Darwin) is selected ... A playfulness of fancy, an unbounded variety of fiction, an imagination wild and terrific as that of Dante or Shakespeare.

> N. Drake, *Literary Hours* (or 1798).

"Wild to the blast flew the sculls and the bones" is as grand as any of Dante's terrifics.

> Anna Seward to Miss Ponsonby.

✿ 1798 r. George III ✿

ARCHITECTURE

(York Cathedral) is certainly both grand and spacious, but inferior to any Gothic buildings I have seen. It is scarcely as fine as Salisbury, and certainly not equal to that of Amiens. ... Bleak and dreary moors, which may have charms to a sportsman's eye, but can afford nothing but wearisome disgust to the traveller. (See 1799).

> Eliz. Lady Holland, *Journal*.

To combine irregularity into the picturesque is the excellence of cottage construction. (picturesque=Rysdael; Grand=Claude and Poussin; savage=Salvator Rosa).

> J. Malton, *Essays on British Cottage Architecture*.

GARDENS

To Crookham. Walked about the squire's grounds. Quaint waterfalls about, about which Nature was very successfully striving to make beautiful what art had deformed—ruins, hermitages, etc., etc. In spite of all these things, the dell romantic and beautiful though everywhere planted with unnaturalized trees.

> D. Wordsworth, *Journal* (Alfoxden).

MANNERS AND TASTES

Fountains Abbey ... nothing that I have seen in England bears any comparison to the pleasure I received in seeing it ...

Such is the superstitious awe inspired by monastic gloom, that I almost wished it were possible to indulge in a serious mood.

Journal of Eliz. Lady Holland, 17.7.

The opinion of Lord Orford's letters is that they will raise his reputation as an author: that though sometimes on trifling subjects yet never dull.

Farrington, *Diaries*, 13.12.

(Catherine reads Pope, Gray, Thomson. Mr. Thorpe reads Fielding and Lewis. Novels discreditable but the Spectator respectable) Cecilia and Camilla are works where the highest powers of the human mind are displayed . . .

(Henry Tilney) talked of foregrounds, distances and second distances; side screens and perspectives; lights and shades; and Catherine was so hopeful a scholar, that when they gained the top of Beechen Cliff, she voluntarily rejected the whole city of Bath, as unworthy to make part of a landscape.

J. Austen, *Northanger Abbey*.

(begun this year, finished 1803, published 1818. Satire on Mrs. Radcliffe).

The name of a cottage had interested her (Lady Templeton) and to know people who inhabited one appeared to give her a romantic pleasure.

F. Burney, *Diary*, June-July.

It was a wonder to the lower orders throughout all parts of England to see the avenues to the churches filled with carriages. This novel appearance prompted the simple country people to enquire what was the matter.

Annual Register.

PAINTING

Bryan's Exhibition of Orleans collection opened at the Lyceum and in Pall Mall on Wednesday. Augustine has the picture by Sebastian del Piombo [Lazarus, in National Gallery] for 3500 guineas. Smirke . . . thinks it a very foolish picture. No colouring, no character, so said Bourgeois.

Farrington, *Diaries*, 28-29.12.

Sale of Orleans Italian pictures: Prices fetched:—

Ascription		gns.
Leonardo,	*La Colombine*	250
Raphael	*Holy Family*	700
,,	*La Belle Vierge*	3,000
,,	*St. John in Wilderness*	1,500
,,	*Vierge au Palmier*	1,200
,,	*Vision of Ezekial*	800
Seb. del Piombo,	*Raising of Lazarus*	3,500
Correggio,	*Madonna*	1,200
,,	*Duke of Valentino*	500
An. Caracci,	*Jupiter and Danae*	500
,,	*Landscape* (Le Batelier)	600
,,	*St. Roch*	500
,,	*Vision of St. Francis*	500
,,	*La Chasse au Vol*	600
,,	*Descent from Cross*	4,000
,,	*Toilet of Venus*	800
,,	*Bath of Diana*	1,200
,,	*Repose in Egypt*	700
Lud. Carraci,	*Vision of St. Catherine*	600
Ag. Carraci,	*Christ & Magdalene*	500
Albano,	*Baptism*	700
Domenichino,	*Christ and Cross*	800
,,	*Landscape*	500
,,	*St. John Evangelist*	600
Guercino,	*Presentation*	600
,,	*David and Abigail*	800
Titian,	*Rape of Europa*	700
,,	*Diana and Actaeon*	2,500
,,	*Diana and Callista*	2,500
,,	*Phillip II & Mistress*	1,000
,,	*Vénus à la Coquille*	800
Tintoretto,	*Descent from Cross*	600
Velasquez,	*Lot and Daughters*	500
N. Poussin,	*VII Sacraments*	700
,,	*Birth of Bacchus*	500
,,	*Exposure of Moses*	800

Also		£	s.	d.
Rubens,	*Ceres and Pomona*	514	10	0
,,	*Diana and Nymphs*	1,050	0	0
P. Potter,	*Death of Adonis*	1,407	10	0
,,	*Cattle in Landscape*	1,110	10	0
Rembrandt,	*The Centurion*	1,522	10	0

POETRY

The rage for German plays still continues.

Journal of Eliz. Lady Holland, 20.11.

Translations from German:—

Schiller, *Don Carlos* (1787) also in 1795.
Goethe, *Clavigo* (1774).

"Aesthetic" first used in English (O.E.D.).

> The dragon's wing,
> The magic ring,
>   I shall not covet for my dower.

Wordsworth, *Peter Bell*, Lyrical Ballads.

Coleridge's ballad "The Ancient Mariner" is, I think, the clumsiest attempt at German sublimity I ever saw.

Southey to Taylor, 5.9.

(Coleridge) lamented that Wordsworth was not prone enough to believe in the traditional superstitions of the place, and that there was something corporeal, a matter-of-factness, a clinging to the palpable, or often to the petty in his poetry.

. . . . .

(Wordsworth) had been to see *The Castle Spectre* by Monk Lewis, while at Bristol, and described it very well. He said "it fitted the taste of the audience like a glove".

Hazlitt, *First Acquaintance with Poets* (1823)

STAGE

(Close of Act II) Enter the Rajah on the elephant, returning from hunting the tiger, preceded by his hircarrahs or military messengers and his state palanquin. The Vizier on another elephant. The Princess in a gaurie, drawn by buffaloes. The Rajah is attended by his Fakeer or soothsayer, his officer of state, and by an ambassador from Tippoo Sultaun in a palanquin; also by Nairs or soldiers from the South of India— Poligars, or inhabitants of the hilly districts, with their hunting dogs—other Indians carrying a dead tiger, and young tigers in a cage—a number of sepoys—musicians on camels and on foot—dancing girls, etc. etc.

Cobb, *Ramah Droog.*

("performed with universal applause at the Theatre Royal, Covent Garden").

🎕 1799 r. George III 🎕

ARCHITECTURE

Not that I am an enthusiastic admirer of Grecian architecture in any way but in a temple . . . The circular arch, as in the Pont du Gard . . . is very grand; otherwise in vast works I like the Gothic architecture, which, to use an affected phrase, is more *impressive* in lofty structure.

Eliz. Lady Holland, *Journal*, 17.8.

(The King) said Robt. Smirke's architectural drawing was very neat, and creditable to Him, but said He, I am a little of an architect and think that the Old School (that of Lord Burlington's period which had more of magnificence) is not enough attended to, that the Adam's [*sic*] have introduced too much of neatness and prettiness, and even, added His Majesty, Wyatt inclines rather too much that way.

Farrington, *Diaries*, 16.1.

MANNERS AND TASTES

(C. J. Fox) professed liking fairy tales, romances, novels etc. The only sort he admitted were dull are the old French ones of Mlle. Scudéry Le Grand Cyrus &c.—tho' he made a few exceptions, especially for ye Princesse de Cleves [Madame de la Fayette], as well he might, for that is very pretty.

10.3.

A milliner who is just arrived from Paris . . . says that Paris never was yet at such a pitch of luxury and *recherche* in dress as at present.

Eliz. Lady Holland, *Journal*, 13.10.

Mrs. Sarah Fletcher, aged 29, sunk and died a Martyr to Excessive Sensibility. Her Nerves were too delicately spun.

Epitaph, Dorchester (Oxon.).

PAINTING

Gainsborough was a universal admirer of fine pictures, and not exclusively devoted to any one in particular. With Rubens, Vandyke, Morellio (*sic*) and Velasquez.

6.1.

In the pictures of Turner and the drawings of Girtin, there is evidently genius and feeling, from which much may be expected.

21.1.

(Gainsborough) was passionately fond of the pictures of Berghem and Cuyp.

28.1.

Set up Girtin against Turner, who they say effects his purpose by industry—the former more genius—Turner finishes too much.

9.2.

(Beckford) Gave 7,000 guineas for the 2 Claudes and the small pictures, one of which, the Nativity by L. Carracci, West says is a very beautiful picture . . . Mr. Angerstein offered £4,000 for the Claude which has the Sacrifice in it. West observed that Claude had so continued his lights that the eye always settled upon the distance and the center of the picture —as the eye naturally does in viewing the scenes of nature. He remarked how carefully Claude had avoided sharp and decided forms in the distance, gradually *defining* the parts as he came nearer to the foreground. He thinks Claude began his pictures by laying in simple gradations of flat colours from the horizon to the top of the sky—and from the horizon to the foreground, with putting clouds into the sky or specific forms into the landscape till He had fully settled these gradations. When He had satisfied himself in this respect, He painted in his forms, by that means securing a due gradation—from the Horizontal lines to the top of his Sky—and from the horizontal line to the foreground. Smirke remarked how entirely all positive colour was avoided, even to the draperies of the figures. Turner said He was both pleased and unhappy while he viewed it, it seemed to be beyond the power of imitation.

8.5.

Turner called—I told him there would be no doubt of his being elected an Associate if He put His name down. He expressed himself anxious to be a member of the Academy. Mr. Angerstein is to give him 40 guineas for his drawing of Carnarvon Castle. The price was fixed by Mr. A. and was much greater than Turner would have asked.

27.5.

(The purchase of the Angerstein collection for £57,000 in 1829 was, with Sir G. Beaumont's gift, the foundation of the National Gallery, see 1794).

(Turner) thinks of charging Mr. Beckford 40 guineas each for the drawings of Fonthill Abbey. They are 7.

10.7.

Turner told me has no systematic process for making drawings —He avoids any particular mode that He may not fall into manner. By working and occasionally rubbing out, He at last expresses in some degree the idea in his mind.

21.7.

Turner reprobated the mechanically systematic process of drawing. He thinks it can produce nothing but manner and sameness. Turner has no settled process but drives the colours about till He has expressed the Idea in his mind.

Farrington, *Diaries*, 16.11.

W. Beckford bought the two Altieri Claudes and four small Old Masters for 7000 gns. Two Gainsborough portraits sold for 1 guinea at Christies. Turner elected an Associate of R.A.

An altar piece (at Goslar) by the celebrated Lucas Cranack in which the faces of the Apostles are marvellously ugly but lively and natural. It is an admirable painting.

Coleridge to T. Poole, 19.5.

P*

POETRY

It is singular that in the continued contemplation of such a subject, as the place of eternal punishment for so great a part of the human race, he (Dante) should not once be elevated into grandeur of description or sublimity of sentiment...
fleas, . . . ordure.

G. T., *Monthly Magazine*, July.

Beautiful as the *Griselda* is in ye Italian (Boccaccio), I am almost disposed to prefer our Chaucer's English Version.

Journal of Eliz. Lady Holland, 25.9.

Wordsworth settled in Lakes.

"You have made me hunger and thirst after German poetry."

Southey to W. Taylor of Norwich (early translator of it. He began in 1796).

Translations from German:—

Goethe, *Goetz of Berlichingen*, 1773 (by W. Scott).
Lessing, *The School for Honour or the Chance of War*.
Kotzebue. To this date 70 editions or versions of various works published in England.

> Why to yon mountain turns the musing eye,
> Whose sunbright summit mingles with the sky?
> Why do those cliffs of shadowy tint appear
> More sweet than all the landscape smiling near?
> 'Tis distance lends enchantment to the view,
> And robes the mountain in its azure hue.

T. Campbell, *The Pleasures of Hope*, cf. 1645 (Suckling) and 1687 (Norris).

✺ 1800 r. George III ✺

ARCHITECTURE

I was curious to ascertain whether the Gothic architecture of Henry VII (*sic*) Chapel [at Cambridge] would please me now as it did many years ago, long before I saw the wonders of Italy. I found time and comparison had not in the least diminished my admiration of it.

Eliz. Lady Holland, *Journal*, 12.1.

MANNERS AND TASTES

Old English Castles are objects only of a sort of poetical interest.
. . . Our imagination instantly takes flight to the distant Ages
of Chivalry which are blended in our Minds with Romance.
And the Pleasure we feel at seeing an antique relique of
Desolation resembles the Impressions of Tragedy. But a *new*
Ruin the walls sometimes black with Smoak (Königstein,
blown up by French 1792) . . . awakens feelings of real and
actual Misery.

H. Crabb Robinson, 17.12.

The usual trash of Johnsons, Gibbons, Robertsons etc. . . . I
know of no mountain in the North equal to Snowdon but then
we have (at Keswick) an encampment of huge mountains, in
no harmony perhaps to the eye of the mere painter but always
interesting, various and as it were nutritive . . . Wordsworth
"the latchet of whose shoes I am unworthy to unloose".

Coleridge to Godwin, Sept.

MUSIC

About this date Beethoven wrote accompaniment to some
Scottish and other poems collected by G. Thomson. He was
merely given the traditional melodies.

PAINTING

The Landscape (from Llangollen to Corwen) though pleasing
is not such as much to interest a painter, as it does not afford
such assemblege of objects as he would wish to imitate.

2.9.

(Melchair) remarked on the insufficiency of persons who drew
passing hastily through picturesque countrys, making a number
of black lead pencil outlines and leaving them to be finished
and effects given at home, saying that it required that time
should be allowed to observe nature, and to mark the changes
in the appearance of objects at different times of the day.

Farrington, *Diaries*, 19.8.

Dear Sculptor of Eternity,
    You, O dear Flaxman, are a sublime archangel.

W. Blake, 21.9.

Flaxman Elected R.A.

At Udney sale Col. Murry bought L. Caracci's *Repose* for 1100 guineas.

POETRY

Gray, the first lyric bard the world has produced . . . The present Dean of Christchurch's (Cyril Jackson) assertion that of all, in every age and nation, who have aspred to the name of poet, only four deserve it: Homer, Dante, Ariosto and Shakespeare.

Anna Seward to Rev. R. Fellowes.

Schillar (*sic*) in his *Cabal and Love* which I saw last night and think to be one of the noblest productions of the age.

H. Crabb Robinson to T. R. (Frankfort),
21.6.

Coleridge joined at Grasmere Wordsworth and his sister who settled there the year before.

The gaudiness and inane phraseology of many modern writers . . . To choose incidents and situations from common life, and to relate or describe them, throughout, as far as was possible in a selection of language really used by men, and, at the same time, to throw over them a certain colouring of imagination, whereby ordinary things should be presented to the mind in an unusual aspect . . . Humble and rustic life was generally chosen; the essential passions of the heart . . . speak a plainer and more emphatic language; . . . such men hourly communicate with the best objects, from which the best part of language is originally derived . . . All good poetry is the spontaneous overflow of powerful feelings . . . The invaluable works of our early writers . . . are driven into neglect by frantic novels, sickly and stupid German tragedies, and deluges of idle and extravagant stories in verse . . . Personifications of abstract ideas rarely occur in these volumes . . . I have wished to keep the reader in the company of flesh and blood . . . There neither is nor can be any *essential* difference between the language of prose and metrical composition . . . Poetry is the . . . impassioned expression which is in the countenance of all Science . . . it takes its origin from emotion recollected in tranquillity.

Wordsworth, *Preface to Lyrical Ballads.*

446

Pref. to Lyrical Ballads (replacing original Advertisement, 1798). In 1802 was added the appendix on Poetic Diction, and with the text of the Preface was incorporated about 18 pages on the character of the poet. In the 1815 Poems the Preface to L. B. was reprinted as the appendix and a new preface was given with an Essay Supplementary. It is this new preface which contains the distinction between Imagination and Fancy, later elaborated by Coleridge.

PROSE

(Bishop Burnet's *History of his own Time*). None of the Damned philosophical Humeian indifference, so cold, and unnatural, and inhuman! None of the damned Gibbonian fine writing . . . None of Mr. Robertson's periods with three members.

Lamb to Manning, 1.3.

We must allow, Lamb, that Hume is *easy, sweet, clear* etc. Gibbon *pointed, terse, brilliant* etc.; and Robertson *judicious, vigorous*, etc. (N.B. I have read about 17 pages of Hume's History, 153 of Gibbon's, and 19 of Robertson's).

Manning to Lamb, 9.3.

INDICES

I. Authors Quoted or Cited (including the titles of anonymous works).

II. Authors and Artists Criticised or Mentioned (including
the titles of anonymous works).

III. Subjects and Places.

All references are to years, not pages.
Nos. 0-99 refer to XVII century years, 1600-1699.
Nos. 100-200 refer to XVIII century years, 1700-1800.

I

449

II

III

Q*

475